AUSTRALIA
2019

19th Edition

By Lee Mylne

FROMMER'S STAR RATINGS SYSTEM

Every hotel, restaurant, and attraction listed in this guide has been ranked for quality and value. Here's what the stars mean:

★ Recommended
★★ Highly Recommended
★★★ A must! Don't miss!

AN IMPORTANT NOTE

The world is a dynamic place. Hotels change ownership, restaurants hike their prices, museums alter their opening hours, and buses and trains change their routings. And all of this can occur in the several months after our authors have visited, inspected, and written about these hotels, restaurants, museums, and transportation services. Though we have made valiant efforts to keep all our information fresh and up-to-date, some few changes can inevitably occur in the periods before a revised edition of this guidebook is published. So please bear with us if a tiny number of the details in this book have changed. Please also note that we have no responsibility or liability for any inaccuracy or errors or omissions, or for inconvenience, loss, damage, or expenses suffered by anyone as a result of assertions in this guide.

CONTENTS

1 WHAT'S GREAT ABOUT AUSTRALIA 1

2 AUSTRALIA IN CONTEXT 12

3 SUGGESTED ITINERARIES 34
Australia in 1 Week 34
Australia in 2 Weeks 40
Australia for Families 43

4 SYDNEY 48
Essentials 48
Neighborhoods in Brief 52
Fast Facts 58
Where to Stay 59
Where to Eat 70
Exploring Sydney 78
Organized Tours 91
Especially for Kids 93
Outdoor Activities 93
Shopping 99
A Day Trip to the Blue Mountains 100

5 MELBOURNE 105
Essentials 105
Neighborhoods in Brief 109
Fast Facts 112
Where to Stay 113
Where to Eat 118
Exploring Melbourne 126
Shopping 140
Day Trips from Melbourne 141

6 BRISBANE 154
Essentials 154
Neighborhoods in Brief 160
Fast Facts 162
Where to Stay 163
Where to Eat 165
Exploring Brisbane 168
Organized Tours 173
A Day Trip to the Great Barrier Reef 176

7 CAIRNS & THE GREAT BARRIER REEF 178
Essentials 178
Cairns 184
Port Douglas 205
Townsville & Magnetic Island 212
The Whitsundays 219
Southern Great Barrier Reef Region 228

8 THE NORTHERN TERRITORY 236
Essentials 237
Darwin 240
Kakadu National Park 255
Alice Springs 264
Uluru–Kata Tjuta National Park 280

9 TASMANIA 291
Essentials 292
Hobart 294
Day Trips from Hobart 307
Launceston 310

10 PLANNING YOUR TRIP TO AUSTRALIA 319

INDEX 337

MAP LIST 345

ABOUT THE AUTHOR 351

The Sydney skyline and harbor at night.

A LOOK AT AUSTRALIA

From the rugged Outback with Uluru, the otherworldly monolith sacred to the Aboriginal peoples; to the Great Barrier Reef (the only living structure on earth that can be seen from space); to beaches that extend as far as the eye can see, Australia is custom-made for adventure seekers. But it's also for lovers of innovative cuisine, fine wine, and sophisticated performing arts in Sydney, Melbourne, Brisbane, and beyond. From cuddling koala bears to climbing the Harbour Bridge, educating yourself on the country's fascinating Aboriginal culture, and exploring dynamic, modern cities, our EasyGuide presents the best of a nation of superlatives. So g'day, and good journey!

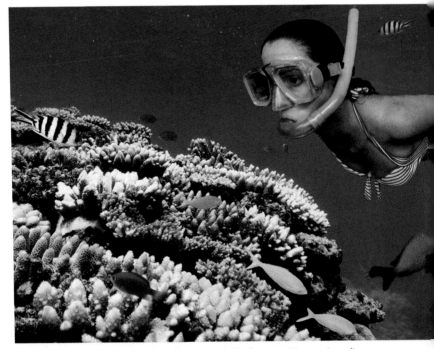

Snorkeling or diving the Great Barrier Reef is tops on the list for many visitors to Australia.

THE BEST OF SYDNEY & MELBOURNE

Completed in 1973, the instantly recognizable Sydney Opera House (p. 85) dominates the harborfront and houses several theaters and concert halls.

Most surf beaches north and south of Sydney Harbour offer shops with board rentals, and group and individual surfing lessons are available. See p. 95.

The monorail glides through downtown, with Sydney Tower, the city's tallest structure, overhead. The tower has a viewing platform, plus a revolving bar and restaurant. See p. 90.

Fresh pasta at Otto Ristorante, Sydney (p. 76).

Paddy's Markets in Sydney (p. 100) features hundreds of stalls selling everything from cheap clothes to produce to imported gifts.

The Rocks, Sydney's waterfront historic area, is characterized by colonial-era buildings, with boutiques, pubs, restaurants, and exclusive hotels. See p. 79.

On the banks of the Yarra River, Melbourne's Southbank area is known for its restaurants, bars, and public spaces.

Melbourne's tram network, founded in 1885, is the world's oldest, and still operates many vintage tramcars, like this beauty outside of Flinders Street Station.

Melbourne's elaborate, constantly changing graffiti is found on several streets in the city center. Here, an artist tags a wall on Hosier Lane. See p. 129.

Scary and atmospheric Old Melbourne Gaol (p. 132), where the notorious bushranger Ned Kelly was hanged.

Wineries, windswept beaches, gardens, and wildlife make the Mornington Peninsula a popular day trip from Melbourne. See p. 144.

Phillip Island (p. 141), an easy 2-hour drive from Melbourne, offers visitors a wealth of wildlife encounters, from parading penguins to this plump koala, getting ready for his close-up.

QUEENSLAND & THE GREAT BARRIER REEF

Much of Brisbane's remaining colonial architecture is centered around Queen Street Mall (p. 169), a shopping and entertainment area known for name-brand and local retailers, plus stylish dining and hotels.

An artificial beach and lagoon, plus shops, cafes, and weekend markets, make South Bank Parklands (p. 172) a colorful retreat in Brisbane's city center.

On top of Mount Coot-tha just outside Brisbane, Summit Restaurant focuses on local produce and wines, all served with sweeping views of the city. See p. 166.

A saltwater swimming lagoon, a wide sandy beach, and surrounding parklands make the Esplanade a highlight of a visit to Cairns.

The Tjapukai Culture Park in Kuranda (p. 196) offers a range of immersive aboriginal experiences, all in a rainforest setting. The Night Fire program features a join-in *corroboree,* or Aboriginal nighttime dance.

The waters off Lady Elliot Island offer snorkeling, diving, and reef walking, as well as the chance to see green and loggerhead turtles, which nest on the beach from November to March. See p. 234.

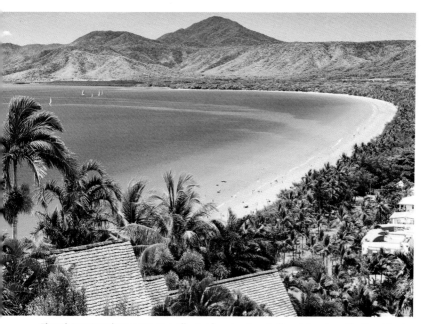

Though Port Douglas is a stepping-off point for adventures in the rainforest and the Great Barrier Reef, its famous Four Mile Beach (p. 209) tempts visitors to do nothing at all.

During the Australian winter, which runs from June to September, humpback whales pass through the waters of the Great Barrier Reef.

The Whitsundays are a group of more than 70 islands replete with bays, beaches, dazzling coral reefs, fishing spots, and rainforest. Pictured here, Whitehaven Beach (p. 226).

Cinnamon clownfish nest in a section of ribbon reef in the waters north of Cairns.

THE NORTHERN TERRITORY

The tropical Top End city of Darwin (p. 240) has a frontier vibe—casual, outdoorsy, and diverse, with significant Aboriginal and Asian populations. Note how high this footbridge is, to allow for Wet season flooding in the creek below.

Kakadu National Park, a 3-hour drive east of Darwin, offers not only stunning natural beauty but also ancient Aboriginal rock art, like these paintings at Nourlangie Rock (p. 260).

The Alice Springs Telegraph Station Historical Reserve (p. 272) marks the site of the first European settlement in Alice Springs.

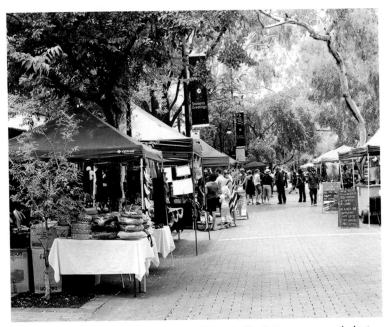

The weekly Sunday market, as well as galleries and shops in Alice Springs, are among the best places to buy authentic Aboriginal paintings, sculpture, and crafts. See p. 275.

Kangaroo sightings are common in the Outback. The large marsupials are most active at night, early morning, and late afternoon.

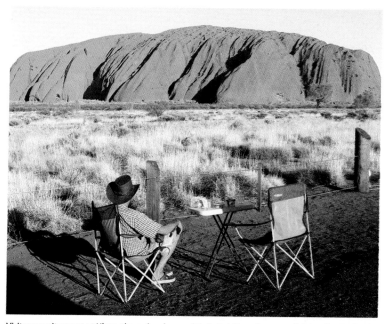

Visitors await sunset at Uluru, the red rock monolith that defines the rugged Australian Outback. Climbing the rock, which is sacred to Aborigines, is strongly discouraged and will be banned completely after September 2019 (p. 288).

TASMANIA

Hobart's picturesque harbor is the focal point of the Tasmanian capital.

Surrounded by ferns, rainforest, and gum trees, Russell Falls is a gem of Mount Field National Park (p. 309).

The Port Arthur Historic Site (p. 307) explores the dark history of the former penal colony, and is the most-visited sight on Tasmania.

WHAT'S GREAT ABOUT AUSTRALIA

Australia is like nowhere else you've been. It has truly unique wildlife, some of the world's best natural scenery, the most brilliant scuba diving and snorkeling, the best beaches, the oldest rainforest (110 million years and counting), the oldest human civilization (some archaeologists say 40,000 years, some say 120,000), the best wines, the best weather, and the most innovative East-meets-West-meets-someplace-else cuisine—all bathed in sunlight that brings everything up in Technicolor. Prepare yourself for a lifetime of memories.

Scarcely a visitor lands on these shores without having the **Great Barrier Reef** at the top of their to-do list. And so they should. While parts of the reef are in dire straits from coral bleaching caused by rising water temperatures, those that aren't affected show what a glorious natural masterpiece it is—don't leave it too late to see it! Also high on most lists is **Uluru,** a sacred monolith that (rightly) attracts hundreds of thousands of tourists (including celebrities and royalty, such as Britain's Prince William and his wife Catherine, the Duchess of Cambridge). And it's not just "The Rock" you should see; the vast Australian desert all around it is equally unmissable. The third attraction on most visitors' lists is **Sydney,** Australia's glittering harborside city.

Of course, there is much more to Australia than just these highlights. For those who have more time, the Australian Capital Territory, South Australia, Western Australia, vast tracts of inland Queensland, and many Outback areas have much to offer, too. But I know you can't do everything or go everywhere, so in this book, I'll introduce you to those three iconic attractions as well as the places that are their gateways—Brisbane, Cairns, the Reef-adjacent coastal cities of Queensland, and Darwin and Alice Springs in the Northern Territory—as well as Australia's other major city, Melbourne, in Victoria, and the smaller cities on the island state of Tasmania, Hobart and Launceston.

THE NORTHERN TERRITORY
See Chapter 8

Timor Sea

Bathurst Island   Melville Island

Darwin   KAKADU NATIONAL PARK

Bonaparte Archipelago

Katherine

Buccaneer Archipelago

INDIAN OCEAN

Victoria Hwy.

Kununurra   KATHERINE GORGE NATIONAL PARK

Lake Argyle

KIMBERLEY   Ord River

Derby

PURNULULU NATIONAL PARK

Broome   NORTHERN

TANAMI DESERT

Great Northern Hwy.

Port Hedland   GREAT SANDY DESERT

Coastal Hwy.

Ningaloo Reef Marine Park

WEST MACDONNELL NATIONAL PARK

GIBSON DESERT

WATARRKA NATIONAL PARK (KINGS CANYON)

HAMERSLEY RANGE   Tropic of Capricorn

Exmouth

Coral Bay   North West Hwy.

ULURU-KATA TJUTA NATIONAL PARK

Mt. Olga   Uluru (Ayers Rock)

WESTERN AUSTRALIA

Shark Bay   Monkey Mia

Great Northern Hwy.

Denham

GREAT VICTORIA DESERT

Geraldton

Brand Hwy.

NULLARBOR PLAIN   NULLARBOR NATIONAL PARK

Kalgoorlie

Great Eastern Hwy.

Eyre Hwy.

Rottnest Island   Perth   Esperance Hwy.

Great Australian Bight

Fremantle

Esperance

South Coast Hwy.   Tasmania

Margaret River   Bass Strait

Albany   Devonport   Launceston

INDIAN OCEAN

Hobart

0   500 mi
0   500 km

TASMANIA
See Chapter 9

Thursday
Island

*Coral
Sea*

ARNHEM
LAND

*Gulf
of
Carpentaria*

CAPE
YORK
PENINSULA

*SOUTH
PACIFIC
OCEAN*

Cooktown

DAINTREE
NATIONAL
PARK

Port Douglas

Cairns

TERRITORY

Mission
Beach

QUEENSLAND
See Chapter 7

Townsville

*Whitsunday
Islands
National
Park*

Tennant
Creek

Barkly Hwy.

Mt. Isa

Flinders Hwy.

Proserpine

Stuart Hwy.

Landsborough Hwy.

Mackay

MACDONNELL RANGES

Alice Springs

Longreach

Capricorn Hwy.

Rockhampton

Gladstone

SIMPSON DESERT

QUEENSLAND

Bundaberg

Bruce Hwy.

Mitchell Hwy.

Fraser
Island

See Chapter 6

SOUTH
AUSTRALIA

Coober Pedy

Brisbane

Sunshine
Coast

LAMINGTON
NATL. PK.

Gold
Coast

Lightning
Ridge

Darling River

FLINDERS RANGES
NATIONAL PARK

Coffs
Harbour

Stuart Hwy.

Barrier Hwy.

Broken Hill

Dubbo

Oxley

Tamworth

New England Hwy.

Port
Macquarie

NEW
SOUTH WALES

BLUE MTNS.
NATL. PK.

Pacific Hwy.

Port Pirie

Mildura

Newell Hwy.

Newcastle

Adelaide

Murray River

Sydney

Hume Hwy.

See Chapter 4

Kangaroo
Island

Dukes Hwy.

Wodonga

Princes Hwy.

CANBERRA

VICTORIA

Albury

Mt. Koscluszko

A.C.T.

Princes Hwy.

SNOWY
MOUNTAINS

Tasman Sea

Mt. Gambier

Ballarat

Melbourne

Geelong

See Chapter 5

Apollo Bay

To Tasmania (see inset)

Great Barrier Reef Marine Park

GREAT DIVIDING RANGE

AUSTRALIA'S best AUTHENTIC EXPERIENCES

o **Seeing the Great Barrier Reef (QLD):** It's a 2,000km-long (1,240-mile) natural wonder of coral, vibrant colors, and bizarre fish life—and it comes complete with warm water and year-round sunshine. When you're not snorkeling over coral and giant clams, scuba diving, calling at tropical towns, or lying on deserted island beaches, you'll be trying out the sun lounges or enjoying the first-rate food. See p. 180.

o **Experiencing Sydney (NSW):** Sydney is more than just the magnificent Harbour Bridge and Opera House. No other city has beaches in such abundance, and few have such a magnificently scenic harbor. Our advice: Try to spend a week here, because you're going to need it. See p. 48.

o **Exploring the Wet Tropics Rainforest (QLD):** Folks who come from skyscraper cities such as New York City and London can't get over the moisture-dripping ferns, the neon-blue butterflies, and the primeval peace of this World Heritage rainforest stretching north, south, and west from Cairns.

A scuba diver viewing large orange-colored common gorgonian during a dive at the Great Barrier Reef.

Hike it, four-wheel-drive it, or glide over the treetops in the Skyrail gondola. See p. 184.

The Skyrail Rainforest Cableway near Cairns glides above the canopy of the Wet Tropics Rainforest.

- **Bareboat Sailing (QLD):** "Bareboat" means unskippered—that's right, even if you think port is an after-dinner drink, you can charter a yacht, pay for a day's instruction from a skipper, and then take over the helm yourself and explore the 74 island gems of the Whitsundays. It's easy. Anchor in deserted bays, snorkel over dazzling reefs, fish for coral trout, and feel the wind in your sails. See p. 227.

- **Exploring Kata Tjuta (the Olgas) & Uluru (NT):** This sacred, mysterious, and utterly unforgettable landscape may well be the highlight of your time in Australia. Uluru and Kata Tjuta demand at least 3 days to see everything there is to offer. See p. 280.

- **Taking an Aboriginal Culture Tour:** Seeing the landscape through the eyes of Australia's indigenous people, hearing the creation stories of their ancestors, and learning more about Aboriginal culture will give you a different perspective on Australia, no matter which part of it you are in. See p. 260.

THE best OF THE OUTDOORS

- **Blue Mountains (NSW):** Many bushwalks in the Blue Mountains National Park offer awesome views of valleys, waterfalls, cliffs, and forest. All are easy to reach from Sydney. See p. 100.

- **Four Mile Beach (QLD):** The sea is turquoise, the sun is warm, the palms sway—and even the low-rise hotels lining this country beach in Port Douglas can't spoil the feeling that it is a million miles from anywhere. But isn't there always a serpent in paradise? In this case, the "serpents" are north Queensland's seasonal and potentially deadly marine stingers. Come from June through September to avoid them; confine your swimming to the stinger-net enclosures the rest of the year. See p. 209.

- **Larapinta Trail (NT):** Starting from Alice Springs in the Red Centre, this 250km (155-mile) semi-desert trail winds through the stark crimson McDonnell Ranges. You don't have to walk the entire length—plenty of day-length and multi-day sections are possible. This one's for the cooler months only (Apr–Oct). See p. 277.

Taking in the sights at Blue Mountains National Park.

o **The MacDonnell Ranges (NT):** Aboriginal people say these red rocky hills were formed by the "Caterpillar Dreaming" that wriggled from the earth here. To the east and west of Alice Springs are dramatic gorges, idyllic (and icy cold) water holes, cute wallabies, and ancient Aboriginal rock carvings. See p. 276.

o **Surfing:** No visit to Oz could really be considered complete without checking out one of the iconic Aussie activities—surfing. It's not just the rush of the waves that pulls people in, it's the ethos and everything that goes with surfing. Every state has its special spots where the surf can be especially challenging—and in Sydney, those spots are right in the suburbs! See p. 95.

o **Uluru–Kata Tjuta National Park (NT):** Don't go home until you've felt the powerful heartbeat of the desert. Uluru will enthrall you with its eerie beauty. Nearby Kata Tjuta is equally interesting, so make the time to wander through the Valley of the Winds. Hike or cycle around Uluru's base, burn around it on a Harley-Davidson, or saunter up to it on a camel. See p. 280.

o **Whitehaven Beach (QLD):** It's not a surf beach, but this 6km (3¾-mile) stretch of white silica sand on uninhabited Whitsunday Island is pristine and peaceful. Bring a book, curl up under the rainforest lining its edge, and fantasize that the cruise ship is going to leave without you. See p. 226.

AUSTRALIA'S best RESTAURANTS

- **Bennelong** (Sydney, NSW): With an unbeatable location inside the Sydney Opera House, with views of the Sydney Harbour Bridge, this is one of Australia's best restaurants. And it's just perfect for a pre- or post-theater supper. See p. 74.

- **Donovans** (Melbourne, VIC): What better way to end the day than with a glass in hand, watching the sun go down over St Kilda Beach, while you're perched on the veranda at this beachy restaurant in a former 1920s bathing pavilion? See p. 125.

- **e'cco bistro** (Brisbane, QLD): Simple food elegantly prepared and accompanied by an extensive wine list has won this stylish bistro a stack of awards. Booking ahead is essential. See p. 165.

- **Flower Drum** (Melbourne, VIC): Praise pours in for this upscale eatery serving exquisite Cantonese food. Service is impeccable. See p. 121.

- **Hanuman** (Darwin, NT): A fusion of Chinese and Malaysian cuisine amply demonstrates Darwin's connection to Asia, in a stylish setting with excellent service. See p. 247. There's also a branch in Alice Springs (p. 270).

- **Icebergs Dining Room & Bar** (Sydney, NSW): Come here for exquisite food and one of the best ocean views in the Southern Hemisphere. Not surprisingly, seafood features highly on the menu. It's our top pick for lunch in Sydney. See p. 77.

- **MoVida** (Melbourne, VIC): Like a little corner of Spain, this spot is relaxed and fun, with seriously good food and good wine. Melburnians flock here for the tapas and *raciones*. If it's full, try one of the two sister restaurants, **MoVida Next Door** and **MoVida Aqui**. See p. 122.

The entire continent of Australia is ringed with legendary surfing spots.

The veranda at Donovans offers the perfect view of sunset over St Kilda Beach in Melbourne.

- **Salsa Bar & Grill** (Port Douglas, QLD): The animated atmosphere and attractive surroundings set the scene for an excellent dining experience. Appetizers and main courses run the gamut from simple fare to sophisticated tropical creations; desserts are fantastic. Book as far ahead as possible. See p. 208.
- **Tetsuya's** (Sydney, NSW): Chef Tetsuya Wakuda is arguably Sydney's most famous chef, and his imaginative nouveau Japanese creations guarantee that this hip eatery is not only a constant number one in Australia, but also ranks among the top restaurants in the world. See p. 74.

AUSTRALIA'S best HOTELS

- **Sir Stamford at Circular Quay** (Sydney, NSW): Plush and luxurious, with a clubby feel that's relaxed rather than stuffy, Sir Stamford is also perfectly located, a short walk from Circular Quay and the Opera House, and just across the road from the Royal Botanic Gardens. See p. 62.
- **Sofitel Sydney Darling Harbour** (Sydney, NSW): Exceptional views of Darling Harbour, spacious rooms, and touches of French style combine to make this one of Sydney's most beautiful hotels, all just a short walk from the city center. See p. 67.
- **The Reef House** (Palm Cove, QLD): Airy rooms look onto tropical gardens, waterfalls cascade into pools, mosquito nets drape over the beds, and you could swear pith-helmeted colonial officers will be back any minute to finish their gin-and-tonics in the Brigadier Bar. Idyllic Palm Cove Beach is just across the road. See p. 188.

- **qualia** (Hamilton Island, Whitsundays, QLD): This is one of Australia's most glamorous island resorts, an exclusive adults-only enclave away from the hurly-burly of the main island accommodations. Each private pavilion has its own plunge pool, and there's a decadent day spa. See p. 224.
- **Longitude 131°** (Uluru, Red Centre, NT): The luxury option at the Ayers Rock resort scene, Longitude 131° is an African-style safari camp set in the dunes, with great views of Uluru. It's very exclusive and very expensive, but you'll experience the Outback in style. See p. 284.
- **The Russell** (The Rocks, Sydney, NSW): This B&B, wonderfully positioned in the city's old quarter, is the coziest place to stay in Sydney. It has creaky floorboards, a ramshackle feel, brightly painted corridors, and rooms with immense character. See p. 64.
- **Marae** (near Port Douglas, QLD): Lush bushland full of butterflies and birds is the setting for this gorgeous B&B in a contemporary timber Queenslander house. Owners John and Pam Burden promise a warm welcome and a fine tropical breakfast. See p. 207.
- **The MONA Pavilions** (Hobart, TAS): Eight luxury state-of-the-art pavilions dedicated to Australia's most famous artists and architects are set on the banks of the Derwent River, as part of the Museum of Old and New Art (MONA) complex. See p. 297.
- **The Olsen** (Melbourne, VIC): With a giant mural by one of Australia's greatest living artists, John Olsen, and a stunning suspended swimming pool, this flagship of the Art Series Hotels is worth the splurge. Or try one of its sister hotels in Melbourne: **The Cullen, The Blackman,** or **The Larwill Studio.** See p. 116.

Cocktails on the Dunes at Longitude 131°, a luxury safari camp in the Outback.

THE best PLACES TO VIEW WILDLIFE

o **Lone Pine Koala Sanctuary (QLD):** Cuddle a koala (and have your photo taken doing it) at this park in Brisbane, the world's first and largest koala sanctuary. Apart from some 130 koalas, lots of other Aussie wildlife—including wombats, Tasmanian devils, 'roos (which you can hand-feed), and colorful parakeets—are on show. See p. 169.

o **Hartley's Crocodile Adventures (QLD):** Cruise a beautiful lagoon surrounded by paperbark trees to spot crocodiles in their natural setting, and then watch the daily "croc attack" show. There are also snakes, koalas, cassowaries, and other animals to see at this family-run wildlife park just north of Cairns. See p. 196.

o **Australian Butterfly Sanctuary (QLD):** Walk through the biggest butterfly "aviary" in Australia, in Kuranda, near Cairns, and you'll spot some of the most gorgeous butterflies on the continent, including the electric-blue Ulysses. See many species of butterfly feed, lay eggs, and mate; and inspect caterpillars and pupae. Wearing pink, red, or white encourages the butterflies to land on you. See p. 203.

o **Heron Island (QLD):** Any time of year, you'll spot wonderful wildlife on this "jewel in the reef" off Gladstone, but the best time to visit is November to March, when the life cycle of giant green loggerhead and hawksbill turtles is in full swing. From November to January, the turtles come ashore to lay their eggs. From late January to March, the hatchlings emerge and head for the water. You can see it all by strolling down to the beach, or join a university researcher to get the full story. See p. 229. **Mon Repos Regional Park,** near Bundaberg in Queensland (p. 233), is another good turtle-watching site.

o **Moonlit Sanctuary (VIC):** For the chance to see many of Australia's nocturnal animals, including some that are now extinct in the wild (the eastern quoll, the red-bellied pademelon, the southern bettong), take a guided night tour at this sanctuary on the Mornington Peninsula. See p. 145.

Get up close with colorful residents of the Australian Butterfly Sanctuary in Kuranda.

Whitehaven Beach on uninhabited Whitsunday Island.

THE best DIVING & SNORKELING

- **Port Douglas (QLD):** Among the fabulous dive sites off Port Douglas, north of Cairns, are Split-Bommie, with its delicate fan corals and schools of fusiliers; Barracuda Pass, with its coral gardens and giant clams; and the swim-through coral spires of the Cathedrals. Snorkelers can glide over the coral and reef fish life of Agincourt Reef. See p. 210.
- **Cairns (QLD):** Moore, Norman, Hardy, Saxon, and Arlington reefs and Michaelmas and Upolu cays—all about 90 minutes off Cairns—offer great snorkeling and endless dive sites. Explore on a day trip from Cairns, or join a live-aboard adventure. See p. 197.
- **The Whitsunday Islands (QLD):** These 74 breathtaking islands offer countless dive sites both among the islands and on the Outer Great Barrier Reef, 90 minutes away. Bait Reef on the Outer Reef is popular for its drop-offs. Snorkelers can explore not just the Outer Reef but also patch reefs among the islands and rarely visited fringing reefs around many islands. See p. 225.
- **Heron Island (QLD):** Easily the number-one snorkel and dive site in Australia—if you stayed in the water for a week, you couldn't snorkel all the acres of coral stretching from shore. Take your pick of 22 dive sites: the Coral Cascades, with football trout and anemones; the Blue Pools, favored by octopus, turtles, and sharks; Heron Bommie, with its rays, eels, and Spanish dancers; and more. Absolute magic. See p. 229.
- **Lady Elliot Island (QLD):** Gorgeous coral lagoons, perfect for snorkeling, line this coral cay island off the town of Bundaberg. Boats take you farther out to snorkel above manta rays, plate coral, and big fish. Divers can swim through the blowhole, 16m (52 ft.) down, and see gorgonian fans, soft and hard corals, sharks, barracudas, and reef fish. See p. 234.

AUSTRALIA IN CONTEXT

2

When most people think of Australia, they conjure up images of bounding kangaroos, dusty red deserts, and golden sandy beaches. The Sydney Opera House is right up there, too. They imagine drawling accents and slouch hats, suntanned lifeguards, and men who wrestle crocodiles for the fun of it. Well, it's all that—and more (apart from the crocodile wrestling)! This huge continent is truly remarkable, offering everything from rolling green hills, dense ancient rainforests, and historic towns, to vast areas of sparsely inhabited ochre-red Outback, to giant coral reefs and deserted beaches, unique animals and plants, cosmopolitan modern cities, and intriguing Aboriginal culture.

Most people visiting Australia for the first time head to Sydney or Melbourne. They explore the Red Centre and the giant rock Uluru; or they take to the warm waters of the Great Barrier Reef to dive or snorkel. But it's also often the places that come to visitors by chance, or through deeper research, that remain locked in their memories forever. Who could forget holding a koala in your arms, or feeding a kangaroo from the palm of your hand? Or traveling ochre-red dirt tracks and seeing emus running alongside their 4WD? This book concentrates on the areas that are the most traveled (and on every visitor's wish list) but it also takes you to some of the lesser-known treasures of each city and some of our personal favorite places and experiences. Of course, no travel experience is complete without a little background information, which is where this chapter comes in.

AUSTRALIA TODAY

Perhaps it's to do with the weather, or the wide-open spaces, or the quality of the light, but Australians are generally an optimistic, positive lot—and to me, that's a big part of the country's appeal. Phrases like "It's a lucky country, mate," and "she'll be right" (meaning everything will be okay) may have become clichés, but they sum up the attitude held by most Australians. The food is good and there's plenty of it; the education system is mostly good (and mostly free, unless you choose to pay for a private school or you happen to be saddled with student loans to cover university fees); gun ownership is heavily restricted; the public healthcare system is universal and largely free or inexpensive; and the government (whichever persuasion it is) is generally stable. It's a great place to live—even though it can sometimes feel a long, long way from everywhere else.

Of course, nothing is totally clear-cut. The country has plenty of socially disadvantaged areas, and many of Australia's indigenous people in particular are struggling on the fringes of mainstream society.

As a nation, Australia is also facing tough challenges in balancing the benefits of industry with caring for the environment. Australia makes a massive amount of revenue from mining, supplying China with a significant proportion of its iron and other metals, as well as supplying the rest of the world with everything from uranium and coal to natural gas. This inevitably means the ruin of some once-pristine landscapes. Australia also has one of the world's highest per capita levels of greenhouse gas emissions (nearly twice the OECD average and more than four times the world average) and suffers from severe droughts and dramatic weather events that most experts believe are the result of human-induced climate change.

Australia is also one of the world's fastest-growing industrialized nations. In 2017, the population hit the 24.7-million mark, a figure driven in recent years by immigration, with around 250,000 people settling here in the year to September 2017.

One thing Australia realized early on was the importance of tourism to its economy. Around 8.9 million people visited in 2017. You'll find Australians helpful and friendly, and services, tours, and food and drink to rival any in the world. Factor in the landscape, the indigenous culture, the sunshine, the unique wildlife, and some of the world's best cities, and, all in all, you've got a fascinating, accessible destination of amazing diversity and variety.

LOOKING BACK AT AUSTRALIA
The Beginning

In the beginning, there was the Dreamtime. Australia's indigenous people have lived on this land for 60,000 years or more. Their "Dreamtime" stories explain how they see the creation story and what followed. In scientific terms, a supercontinent split into two, and over millions of years continental drift carried the great landmasses apart. Australia was part of what we call Gondwanaland, which also divided into South America, Africa, India, Papua New Guinea, and Antarctica. Giant marsupials evolved to roam the continent of Australia. The last of these creatures are believed to have died out around 20,000 years ago, possibly helped toward extinction by drought, or by Aboriginal hunters, who lived alongside them for thousands of years.

THE ancient art OF AUSTRALIA

A history of the Aboriginal people lies partly in the **rock paintings** they have left behind all over Australia. In the tropical north, for example, a wide-ranging body of prehistoric art decorates sandstone gorges near the tiny township of Laura on the rugged Cape York Peninsula. Depictions on rock-shelter sites range from spirit figures of men and women to eels, fish, wide-winged brolga birds, crocodiles, kangaroos, snakes, and stenciled hands. One wall, the "Magnificent Gallery," stretches more than 40m (131 ft.) and is adorned with hundreds of Quinkan figures—Quinkans being the Aboriginal spirits associated with this region.

Much Aboriginal rock art is preserved in national parks. Some of the best are Nourlangie Rock and Ubirr Rock in the Northern Territory's Kakadu National Park (p. 255). Nourlangie features "X-ray"-style paintings of animals and from there you can also walk to see more paintings at Nanguluwur. There are also ancient paintings near Uluru in the Red Centre (p. 279). Other rock art sites readily accessible on day trips from major Australian cities include Ku-Ring-Gai Chase National Park, and the Royal National Park near Sydney; the Grampians National Park west of Melbourne; and the fabulous hand stencils at Mutawintji National Park near Broken Hill in New South Wales. In Queensland, Carnarvon National Park (about 400km/249 miles west of Brisbane) offers a breathtaking display of early indigenous paintings.

Early European Explorers

The existence of a great southern land had been on the minds of Europeans since the Greek astronomer Ptolemy drew a map of the world in A.D. 150 showing a large landmass in the south, which he believed existed to balance out the land in the Northern Hemisphere. He called it Terra Australia Incognita—the "Unknown Southland."

Portuguese ships reached Australia as early as 1536 and charted part of its coastline. In 1606, William Jansz was sent by the Dutch East India Company to open up a new route to the Spice Islands and to find New Guinea. He landed on the north coast of Queensland instead and fought with local Aborigines. Between 1616 and 1640, many more Dutch ships made contact with Australia as they hugged the west coast of what they called "New Holland," after sailing with the westerly winds from the Cape of Good Hope.

In 1642, the Dutch East India Company, through the governor general of the Indies, Anthony Van Diemen, sent Abel Tasman to search for and map the great Southland. During two voyages, Tasman charted the northern Australian coastline and discovered Tasmania, which he named Van Diemen's Land.

The Arrival of the British

In 1766, the Royal Society hired James Cook to travel to the Pacific Ocean to observe and record the transit of Venus across the sun. In 1770, Cook charted the east coast of Australia in his ship the HMS *Endeavour*. He claimed the land for Britain and named it New South Wales. On April 29, Captain Cook landed at Botany Bay, which he named after the discovery of scores of plants hitherto unknown to science. Turning northward, he passed an entrance to a possible harbor that appeared to offer safe anchorage and named it Port Jackson, after the secretary of the admiralty, George Jackson. Back in Britain, King George III viewed Australia as a potential colony and repository of Britain's overflowing prison population, which could no longer be transported to the United States of America following the War of Independence.

The First Fleet left England in May 1787, made up of 11 store and transport ships (none of them bigger than the passenger ferries that ply modern-day Sydney Harbour from Circular Quay to Manly) led by Arthur Phillip. Aboard were 1,480 people, including 759 convicts. Phillip's flagship, the *Supply,* reached Botany Bay in January 1788, but Phillip decided the soil was poor and the surroundings too swampy. On January 26, now celebrated as Australia Day, he settled for Port Jackson (Sydney Harbour) instead.

The convicts were immediately put to work clearing land, planting crops, and constructing buildings. Phillip decided to give some convicts pardons for good behavior and service, and even granted small land parcels to those who were especially industrious.

When gold was discovered in Victoria in 1852 and in Western Australia 12 years later, hundreds of thousands of immigrants from Europe, America, and China flooded the country in search of fortune. By 1860, more than a million non-Aboriginal people were living in Australia.

The final 10,000 convicts were transported to Western Australia between 1850 and 1868, bringing the total shipped to Australia to 168,000. Some early colonial architecture, built and designed by those convicts, still remains in

Aboriginal rock art at Nourlangie, Kakadu National Park, Northern Territory, Australia.

THE ABORIGINAL "stolen generations"

When Captain James Cook landed at Botany Bay in 1770 determined to claim the land for the British Empire, at least 300,000 **Aborigines** were living on the continent. Despite varying estimates of how long Aboriginal people have inhabited Australia (some believe it to be since the beginning of time), there is scientific evidence that people were walking the continent at least 60,000 years ago.

At the time of the arrival of Europeans, there were at least 600 different tribal communities, each linked to their ancestral land by **"sacred sites"** (certain features of the land, such as hills or rock formations). They were hunter-gatherers, spending about 20 hours a week harvesting the resources of the land, the rivers, and the ocean. The rest of their time was taken up by complex social and belief systems, as well as by life's practicalities such as making utensils and weapons.

The basis of Aboriginal spirituality rests in the **Dreamtime** stories, which recount how ancient spirits created the universe—earth, stars, moon, sun, water, animals, and humans. Much Aboriginal art is related to their land and the sacred sites that are home to the Dreamtime spirits. Some Aboriginal groups believe these spirits came in giant human form, while others believe they were animals or huge snakes. According to Aboriginal custom, individuals can draw on the power of the Dreamtime spirits by reenacting various stories and practicing certain ceremonies.

When the British came, bringing their unfamiliar diseases along with them, entire coastal communities were virtually wiped out by the onset of smallpox. Even as late as the 1950s, large numbers of Aborigines in remote regions of South Australia and the Northern Territory succumbed to deadly outbreaks of influenza and measles.

Although relationships between the settlers and Aborigines were initially peaceful, conflicts over land and food led to skirmishes in which Aborigines were massacred and settlers and convicts attacked. Within a few years, some 10,000 Aborigines and 1,000 Europeans had been killed in Queensland alone, while in Tasmania, a campaign to rid the island entirely of local Aborigines was

Sydney, Tasmania, and to a lesser extent in Brisbane. Be on the lookout for buildings designed by the colonial architect Francis Greenway. Between 1816 and 1818, while still a prisoner, Greenway was responsible for the Macquarie Lighthouse on South Head, at the entrance to Sydney Harbour, and also Hyde Park Barracks and St. James Church in the city center.

Federation & the Great Wars

On January 1, 1901, the six states that made up Australia proclaimed themselves to be part of one nation, and the Commonwealth of Australia was formed. In the same ceremony, the first governor-general was sworn in as the representative of the Queen, who remained head of state.

In 1914, Australia joined Britain in World War I. In April of 1915, the Australian and New Zealand Army Corps (ANZAC) formed a beachhead on the peninsula of Gallipoli in Turkey. The Turkish troops had been warned, and 8 months of fighting ended with 8,587 Australian dead and more than 19,000 wounded. That day, April 25, is commemorated each year as Anzac Day.

ultimately successful, with the last full-blooded Tasmanian Aborigine dying in 1876. By the start of the 20th century, the Aboriginal people were considered a dying race. Most of those who remained lived in government-owned reserves or church-controlled missions.

Massacres of Aborigines continued to go largely or wholly unpunished into the 1920s, by which time it was official government policy to remove light-skinned Aboriginal children from their families. Many children of these "stolen generations" were brought up in white foster homes or church mission stations and never reunited with their biological families. Many children with living parents were told that their parents were dead. This continued into the 1970s.

Today, there are some 649,000 people living in Australia who claim Aboriginal and Torres Strait Islander descent—2.8 percent of the population. About 60 percent of indigenous people live in New South Wales and Queensland, but the Northern Territory has the greatest proportion of Aboriginal residents, at around 30 percent. In general, a great divide still exists between them and the rest of the population. Aboriginal life expectancy is 10 to 12 years lower than that of other Australians, with overall death rates around two times higher. Aborigines make up the highest percentage of the country's prison population, and reports continue to emerge about Aborigines dying while incarcerated.

It was not until 1962 that Aboriginal people were given the right to hold citizenship or vote in Australia, and only in 1992 did the High Court of Australia expunge the concept of *terra nullius* and acknowledge the pre-existing rights of indigenous Australians. Aboriginal people are still not recognized in the Australian Constitution.

In 2007, then-Prime Minister Kevin Rudd made an official apology on behalf of his Labor Government to the "stolen generations." National Sorry Day is held on May 26 each year, when Australians of all backgrounds march in parades and hold other events around the country to honor the Stolen Generations. It is followed by National Reconciliation Week (May 27–June 3).

Australians fought in World War II in North Africa, Greece, and the Middle East. In March 1942, Japanese aircraft bombed Broome in Western Australia and Darwin in the Northern Territory. In May 1942, Japanese midget submarines entered Sydney Harbour and torpedoed a ferry before ultimately being destroyed. Later that year, Australian volunteers fought an incredibly brave retreat through the jungles of Papua New Guinea on the Kokoda Track against superior Japanese forces.

Recent Times

In 1986, an act of both British and Australian Parliament once and for all severed any remaining ties to the United Kingdom. Australia had begun the march to complete independence. Today, Australia is a member of the British Commonwealth and Queen Elizabeth II is the head of state, but a democratically elected Parliament is headed by a Prime Minister who is leader of the majority or coalition ruling party. As well as the Commonwealth (federal) Government, each state also has its own "local" government.

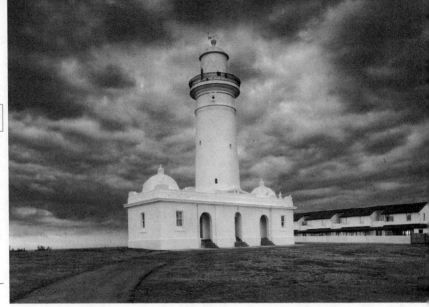

The Macquarie Lighthouse on South Head, Sydney Harbour.

Waves of immigration have brought in millions of people since the end of World War II. It was not until 1974 that the left-of-Center Whitlam Labor government put an end to the White Australia policy, which had largely restricted black and Asian immigration from 1901 on. ("White" Australia—a term always used to distinguish the Anglo-Saxon population from that of the indigenous people of Australia—widened its scope in the 1850s due to conflict between European settlers and Chinese immigrants in the gold fields.) Government statistics show that in 2013, almost 28 percent of the population was born overseas. Of those, 6 percent were born in the U.K., 3 percent from New Zealand, with others from Europe and Asia. New waves of immigration have recently come from countries such as Iraq, Sudan, and Somalia. So what's the typical Australian like? Well, he's hardly Crocodile Dundee.

AUSTRALIA IN POPULAR CULTURE

Movies

Australia has produced its fair share of movies, good and bad. Some of the better ones are listed here.

o *Walkabout* **(1971):** Hauntingly beautiful and disturbing, this movie set in the Australian desert stars Jenny Agutter and the Aboriginal actor David Gulpilul. A white girl and her brother get hopelessly lost and survive with help from a doomed Aboriginal hero.

o *Picnic at Hanging Rock* **(1974):** This mesmerizing Peter Weir movie is about a group of schoolgirls and a teacher who go missing at an eerie rock

A Moment in Time

In 1964, a group of 20 nomadic women and children became the last Aboriginal people to make "first contact" with Europeans. They were living in the Great Sandy Desert, south of Broome, in Western Australia. When they first saw two officers from the Weapons Research Establishment, who were checking land destined for a series of rocket tests, the Aborigines presumed the white-skinned creatures were ghosts.

formation north of Melbourne. It's set at the beginning of the 20th century, when bonnets and teapots were the norm.

o **Mad Max (1979):** Mel Gibson fights to the death in the Outback, which presents the ideal setting for a post-apocalyptic world. The movie was so popular that it spawned three sequels: *The Road Warrior* (1981), *Mad Max: Beyond Thunderdome* (1985), and *Mad Max: Fury Road* (2015).

o **Gallipoli (1981):** Peter Weir brilliantly captures the World War I military disaster that saw Australian and New Zealand troops fighting against overwhelming odds on the Turkish coastline.

o **The Man from Snowy River (1982):** Kirk Douglas, Tom Burlinson, and Sigrid Thornton star in this startling Australian movie that showcases the mountainous wilderness of Australia, where wild horses roam.

o **Crocodile Dundee (1986):** Paul Hogan shot to worldwide fame as a "typical" crocodile-wrestling Outback hero. He wears the same hat and a few more wrinkles in *Crocodile Dundee II* (1988) and *Crocodile Dundee in L.A.* (2001).

o **Shine (1991):** This portrayal of the real-life classical pianist David Helfgott, who rose to international prominence in the 1950s and '60s before having a nervous breakdown, is remarkable. Oscar-winner Geoffrey Rush gives a powerful performance as Helfgott; Sir John Gielgud plays Helfgott's teacher.

o **Strictly Ballroom (1992):** A boy, played by Paul Mercurio, becomes a champion ballroom dancer in this whimsical, playful movie.

o **Muriel's Wedding (1994):** This classic Australian comedy tells the tale of Muriel Heslop (Toni Collette), a young woman who dreams of getting married and moving far away from her boring life in Porpoise Spit. Fabulous characters, great catchphrases, and Abba music abound.

o **The Adventures of Priscilla, Queen of the Desert (1994):** A trans woman takes to traveling through the desert in a big pink bus with two drag queens. They sing Abba classics and dress the part, kind of. Where else but Australia . . .?

o **The Dish (2000):** This comedy about Australia's role in the Apollo 11 mission in 1969 was set around a group of characters operating the Parkes/Canberra radio telescope.

o **Rabbit Proof Fence (2002):** This fictionalized tale addresses the real-life experience of Aboriginal children plucked from their homes in order to put them in white foster families, or—as is the case in this true story of three girls—to train them to work as domestic servants.

o **Australia (2008):** An English aristocrat in the 1930s, played by Nicole Kidman, arrives in northern Australia. After an epic journey across the country with a rough-hewn cattle drover played by Hugh Jackman, she is caught in the bombing of Darwin during World War II. Mixed reviews for this one—make up your own mind, if you're inclined!

o **Samson and Delilah (2009):** This challenging movie depicts two indigenous Australian 14-year-olds living in a remote Aboriginal community who steal a car and escape their difficult lives by heading off to Alice Springs.

o **Animal Kingdom (2010):** Jacki Weaver's role as a crime family matriarch in this gripping drama set in Melbourne won her multiple awards, and an Oscar nomination for Best Supporting Actress.

o **Red Dog (2011):** A tearjerker family flick about a kelpie looking for his master in a Western Australian Outback mining town, this film was adapted from the novel by Louis de Bernières and based on a true story. A prequel, *Red Dog: True Blue*, was released in 2016.

o **Last Cab to Darwin (2014):** A taxi driver from outback Broken Hill discovers he has terminal cancer and decides to drive to Darwin to take advantage of new euthanasia laws. The film is uplifting rather than morbid, with a great performance by Michael Caton in the lead role.

o **Lion (2016):** Based on the true story of Saroo Brierley (played by Dev Patel), an Indian orphan adopted by an Australian couple (played by Nicole Kidman and David Wenham), Lion traces Saroo's search for his birth family. Shot in Tasmania and India, it garnered a slew of awards including six Oscar nominations (including one for Best Picture).

o **Breath (2018):** The film adaptation of Tim Winton's bestselling novel of the same name (p. 22) is worth seeing if only for its spectacular Western Australia scenery and surf scenes. Then there's the star and director, Simon Baker, of *The Mentalist*.

Music

Aboriginal music has been around for tens of thousands of years. Best known is the sound of the **didgeridoo,** made from a hollowed-out tree limb. Listen carefully and you might hear animal sounds, including the flapping of wings and the thumping of feet on the ground. You might hear the sounds of wind, or of thunder, or trees creaking, or water running. It just goes to show how connected the Aboriginal people were, and still are in many cases, to the landscape they lived in. For contemporary fusions of indigenous and Western music, look for music by Yothu Yindi, Christine Anu, and the late Geoffrey Gurrumul Yunupingu (who sings only in his own language).

As far as Australian rock 'n' roll goes, you might know a few of the following names. The big star in the 1950s was Johnny O'Keefe, but he soon gave way to the likes of the Easybeats. Running into the 1970s, you find the Bee Gees, AC/DC, Sherbet, John-Paul Young, and the Little River Band. Others who made a name for themselves included the solo stars Helen Reddy, Olivia Newton-John, and Peter Allen. The 1980s saw Men at Work, Crowded House, The Go-Betweens, Hunters and Collectors, Kylie Minogue, and Midnight Oil. INXS, Silverchair, and Savage Garden took us into the 1990s, which Kylie managed to stitch up, too. Jet and the Vines were both Australian rock groups that saw considerable international success in the 21st century, along with, you guessed it, Kylie Minogue. For songs with a contemporary Australian voice, go no further than Paul Kelly. In recent years, the best-known Australian singer in the U.S. has probably been Gotye, who won three Grammy awards in 2013.

The haunting tones of the musical instrument known as the didgeridoo include animal sounds and flapping of wings.

Australia's Literature

Australian literature has come a long way since the days when the bush poets A. B. "Banjo" Paterson and Henry Lawson penned their odes to a way of life now largely lost. The best known of these is Paterson's epic *The Man from Snowy River,* which first hit the bestseller list in 1895 and was made into a film. But the literary scene has always been lively, and Australia has a wealth of classics, many of them with the Outback at their heart.

Miles Franklin wrote *My Brilliant Career,* the story of a young woman faced with the dilemma of choosing between marriage and a career, in 1901 (made into a film starring Judy Davis in 1979). *We of the Never Never* (1902), by Mrs. Aeneas Gunn, tells the story of a young woman who leaves the comfort of her Melbourne home to live on a cattle station in the Northern Territory. *Walkabout* (1959), by James V. Marshall, explores the relationship between an Aborigine and two lost children in the bush (made into a powerful film by Peter Weir in 1971). Colleen McCullough's *The Thorn Birds* (1977) is a romantic epic about forbidden love between a Catholic priest and a young woman (made into a television miniseries in 1983).

A good historical account of Australia's early days is Geoffrey Blainey's *The Tyranny of Distance,* first published in 1966. Robert Hughes's *The Fatal*

Shore: The Epic of Australia's Founding (1987) is a best-selling nonfiction study of the country's European history.

For a contemporary, if somewhat dark, take on the settlement and development of Sydney, delve into John Birmingham's *Leviathan* (1999). From an Aboriginal perspective, *Follow the Rabbit-Proof Fence* (1997), by Doris Pilkington, tells the true story of three young girls from the "stolen generation" who ran away from a mission school to return to their families. (A movie version was released in 2002; see p. 19.)

Modern novelists include David Malouf, Elizabeth Jolley, Helen Garner, Sue Woolfe, and Peter Carey, whose *True History of the Kelly Gang* (2001), a fictionalized autobiography of the outlaw Ned Kelly, won the Booker Prize in 2001. West Australian Tim Winton evokes his part of the continent in stunning prose; his 2008 novel *Breath* was turned into a movie in 2018 (p. 20). Matthew Condon's *The Trout Opera* (2007) remains one of my all-time favorite Australian novels, covering a century through one man's life. The multi-award-winning *The Light Between Oceans,* by Australian novelist M. L. Stedman, is set in a Western Australian lighthouse. And don't pass up Richard Flanagan's masterpiece *The Narrow Road to the Deep North,* which won the Booker Prize in 2014.

Outsiders who have tackled Australia include Jan Morris and Bill Bryson. Morris's *Sydney* was published in 1992, and Bryson's *In a Sunburned Country* (2001), while not always a favorite with Australians, may appeal to American readers.

EATING & DRINKING IN AUSTRALIA

For a long time, the typical Aussie home-cooked meal consisted of the English-style "meat and three veg" and a Sunday roast. Spaghetti was something foreigners ate, and zucchini and eggplant (aubergine) were considered exotic. Then came mass immigration and all sorts of food that people once only read about in *National Geographic.*

The first big wave of Italian immigrants in the 1950s caused a national scandal. The great Aussie dream was to have a quarter-acre block of land with a hills hoist (a circular revolving clothesline) in the backyard. When Italians started hanging freshly made pasta out to dry on this Aussie icon, it caused an uproar, and some clamored for the new arrivals to be shipped back. As Australia matured, southern European cuisine became increasingly popular, until olive oil was sizzling in frying pans the way only lard had previously done.

In the 1980s (following the repeal of the White Australia policy in 1973), waves of Asian immigrants hit Australia's shores. Suddenly, everyone was cooking with woks. These days, a fusion of spices from the East and ingredients and styles from the Mediterranean make up what's become known as Modern Australian cuisine.

Still, some of the old ways remain. Everyone knows that Aussies like a barbecue, usually referred to as a "barbie." Most Aussies aren't really that

"Bush tucker," hunter-gatherer foods indigenous to Australia, and increasingly popular on restaurant menus.

adventurous when it comes to throwing things on the hot plate and are usually content with some cheap sausages and a steak washed down by a few beers. While you might see kangaroo, crocodile, and emu on the menu at some restaurants, Australians tend not to indulge in their local wildlife that much, preferring to stick to introduced species instead.

Seafood is popular, as you would expect, and a typical Christmas Day meal usually includes prawns and/or fish.

In the big cities, you'll find every kind of cuisine, including Thai, Vietnamese, Italian, Spanish, Middle Eastern, and Indian. Even the smallest town usually has a Chinese restaurant (of varying quality). Melbourne is proud of its coffee culture, but American readers should note that the bottomless cup of coffee is rare.

Note: Many Australian restaurants are flexible on hours, generally staying open until the last diners leave. In the listings in this book, a restaurant is often said to be open until "late." In practice, midnight would probably be the latest for a restaurant to stay open—if the diners were still spending!

Another note: Many restaurants allow you to bring your own wine (referred to simply as BYO) but some may charge a corkage fee of a few dollars, even when there's a screw-cap and no cork.

Beer & Wine

If you order a beer in a pub or bar, you should be aware that the standard glass size differs from state to state. Thus, in Sydney you can order a schooner or a smaller midi. In trendy places, you might be offered an English pint or a half-pint. In Melbourne and Brisbane, a midi is called a pot, while in Darwin it's called a handle, and in Hobart a ten. It can be confusing! You can get smaller glasses, too, though thankfully they're becoming rare. These could either be called a pony, a seven, a butcher, a six, or a bobbie, depending on which city you're in. If in doubt, just mime a big one or a small one, and you'll get your meaning across.

As far as wine goes, Australia has come a long way since the first grape vines arrived on the First Fleet in 1788. Today, more than 550 major companies and small winemakers produce wine commercially in Australia. There are dozens of recognized wine-growing regions, but the most well-known include the Hunter Valley in New South Wales; the Barossa Valley, McClaren Vale, Coonawarra, Adelaide Hills, and the Clare Valley in South Australia; the Yarra Valley in Victoria; and Margaret River in Western Australia.

Aboriginal Foods

In the past couple of decades, many Australian chefs have woken to the variety and tastes of "bush tucker," as native Aussie food is tagged. Now it's all the rage in the most fashionable restaurants, where wattleseed, lemon myrtle, and other native tastes have a place in one or two dishes on the menu. Below is a list of some of those foods you may encounter.

o **Bunya nut:** Crunchy nut of the bunya pine, about the size of a macadamia.

o **Bush tomato:** Dry, small, darkish fruit; more like a raisin in look and taste.

o **Native cranberry:** Small berry that tastes a bit like an apple.

o **Illawarra plum:** Dark berry with a strong, rich, tangy taste.

o **Kangaroo:** A strong meat with a gamey flavor. Tender when correctly prepared, tough when not. Excellent smoked.

o **Lemon aspen:** Citrusy, light-yellow fruit with a sharp, tangy flavor.

o **Lemon myrtle:** Gum leaves with a fresh lemon tang; often used to flavor white meat.

o **Lillipilli:** Delicious juicy, sweet pink berry.

o **Quandong:** A tart, tangy native peach.

o **Wattleseed:** Roasted ground acacia seeds that taste a little like bitter coffee. Sometimes used in cakes.

One ingredient you will not see on menus is **witchetty grubs;** most people are too squeamish to eat these fat, juicy, slimy white creatures. They live in the soil or in dead tree trunks and are a common source of protein for some Aborigines. You eat them alive, not cooked. If you are offered one in the Outback, you can either freak out (as most locals would do)—or enjoy its pleasantly nutty taste as a reward for your bravery.

THE LAY OF THE LAND

People who have never visited Australia wonder why such a huge country has a population of just 24.5 million. The truth is, much of Australia is uninhabitable, and about 90 percent of the population lives on only 2.6 percent of the continent, mainly clustered around the coast, where the only relatively decent rainfall occurs. Compounding that is the fact that Australia falls victim to long droughts. Most of Australia is harsh Outback, characterized by saltbush plains, arid brown crags, shifting sand deserts, and salt-lake country. People survive where they can in this arid land because of one thing—the Great Artesian Basin. This saucer-shaped geological formation comprises about a fifth of Australia's landmass, stretching over much of inland New South Wales, Queensland, South Australia, and the Northern Territory. Beneath it are massive underground water supplies stored during Jurassic and Cretaceous times (some 66–208 million years ago), when the area was much like the Amazon basin is today. Bore holes bring water to the surface and allow sheep, cattle, and humans a respite from the dryness.

As for the climate, as you might expect with a continent the size of Australia, it can differ immensely. The average rainfall in central Australia ranges between just 200 to 250mm (8–10 in.) a year. Summer daytime temperatures range from 90° to 104°F (32°–40°C). In winter, temperatures range from around 64° to 75°F (18°–24°C). Summer in the Southern Hemisphere roughly stretches from early November to the end of February, though it can be hot for a couple of months on either side of these dates, depending where you are.

Parts of the Northern Territory and far northern Queensland are classified as tropical, and as such suffer from very wet summers—often referred to simply as "the Wet." Flooding can be a real fact of life up here. The rest of the year is called "the Dry," for obvious reasons.

Most of Queensland and northern New South Wales are subtropical. This means warm summers and cool winters. Sydney falls into the "temperate" zone, with generally moderate temperatures and no prolonged periods of extreme hot or cold conditions. Parts of central Victoria can get snow in winter, while the Australian Alps, which run through southern central NSW and northeastern Victoria, have good snow cover in winter.

The Queensland coast is blessed with one of the greatest natural attractions in the world. The **Great Barrier Reef** (see chapter 7) stretches 2,000km (1,240 miles) from off Gladstone in Queensland to the Gulf of Papua, near Papua New Guinea. It's relatively new, not more than 8,000 years old, although many fear that rising seawater, caused by global warming, will cause its demise. As it is, significant damage has already been caused by the invasive crown-of-thorns starfish and a bleaching process believed to be the result of excessive nutrients flowing into the sea from Australia's farming land.

Australia's other great natural formation is, of course, **Uluru**—which is sometimes (but not commonly) still called by the name Europeans gave it, Ayers Rock (p. 280).

Australia's Wildlife

Australia's isolation from the rest of the world over millions of years has led to the evolution of forms of life found nowhere else. Probably the strangest of all is the **platypus.** This monotreme, or egg-laying marsupial, has webbed feet, a ducklike bill, and a tail like a beaver's. It lays eggs, and the young suckle from their mother. When a specimen was first brought back to Europe, skeptical scientists insisted it was a fake—a concoction of several different animals sewn together. It is unlikely you will see this shy, nocturnal creature in the wild, but several wildlife parks have them.

Australia is also famous for **kangaroos** and **koalas.** There are 45 kinds of kangaroos and **wallabies,** ranging in scale from small rat-size kangaroos to the man-size red kangaroos. The koala is a fluffy marsupial (not a bear!) that eats gum (eucalyptus) leaves and sleeps about 20 hours a day. There's just one koala species, although those found in Victoria are much larger than those in more northern climes.

The animal you're most likely to come across in your trip is the **possum,** named by Captain James Cook after the North American opossum, which he thought they resembled. (In fact, they are from entirely different families of the animal kingdom.) The brush-tailed possum is commonly found in suburban gardens, including those in Sydney.

Then there's the **wombat.** There are four species of this bulky burrower in Australia, but the common wombat is, well, most common.

The **dingo** is a wild dog, varying in color from yellow to a russet red, mainly seen in the Outback. Because dingoes can breed with escaped "pet" dogs, full-blooded dingoes are becoming increasingly rare.

Commonly seen birds in Australia include the fairy penguin or **Little Penguin** along the coast, **black swans, parrots, cockatoos,** and **honeyeaters.**

DANGEROUS NATIVES

Snakes are common in Australia, but you will rarely see one. The most dangerous land snake is the taipan, which hides in the grasslands in northern

Hand-feeding kangaroos at Brisbane's Lone Pine Koala Sanctuary.

Australia—one bite contains enough venom to kill up to 200 sheep. If by the remotest chance you are bitten, immediately demobilize the limb, wrapping it tightly (but not tight enough to restrict the blood flow) with a cloth or bandage, and call ✆ **000** for an ambulance. Antivenin should be available at the nearest hospital.

One creature that scares the living daylights out of anyone who visits coastal Australia is the **shark,** particularly the Great White (though these marauders of the sea are mostly only found in colder waters, such as those off South Australia). Unprovoked shark attacks are relatively rare, particularly when you consider how many people go swimming. The Australian Shark Attack File kept at Sydney's Taronga Zoo recorded 17 unprovoked attacks in 2016, and two deaths. To put this in perspective, 53 unprovoked attacks (and no fatalities) occurred in U.S. waters (including 10 in Hawaii) that year—the most worldwide—according to the International Shark Attack File maintained by the Florida Museum of Natural History. (More than 60 percent of these occurred off the coast of Florida.) You are more likely to get hit by a car on your way to the beach than to get taken by a shark. Certainly, more people drown in Australian waters than are victims of shark attack.

There are two types of **crocodile** in Australia: the relatively harmless freshwater croc, which grows to 3 meters (10 ft.) long, and the dangerous estuarine (or saltwater) crocodile, which reaches 5 to 7 meters (16–23 ft.). Freshwater crocs eat fish; estuarine crocs aren't so picky. Never swim in or stand on the bank of any river, swamp, or beach in northern Australia unless you know with certainty that it's croc-free.

Spiders are common all over Australia, with the funnel web spider and the red-back spider being the most aggressive. Funnel webs live in holes in the ground (they spin their webs around a hole's entrance) and stand on their back legs when they're about to attack. Red-backs have a habit of resting under toilet seats and in car trunks, generally outside the main cities. Caution is a good policy.

If you go bushwalking, check your body carefully. **Ticks** are common, especially in eastern Australia, and can cause severe itching and fever. If you find one on you, pull it out with tweezers, taking care not to leave the head behind.

Fish to avoid are **stingrays** (Australian television star Steve Irwin was killed by a stingray barb through the heart), as well as **porcupine fish, stonefish,** and **lionfish.** Never touch a **cone shell,** or an **octopus** if it has blue rings on it, and be wary of the painful and sometimes deadly tentacles of the **box jellyfish** along the northern Queensland coast in summer. This jellyfish is responsible for more deaths in Australia than snakes, sharks, and saltwater crocodiles. Closely related to the box jellyfish is the **Irukandji,** which also inhabits northern Australian waters. This deadly jellyfish is only 2.5 centimeters (1 in.) in diameter, which makes it very hard to spot in the water. If you brush past a jellyfish, or think you have, pour vinegar over the affected site immediately—authorities leave bottles of vinegar on beaches for this purpose. Vinegar deactivates the stinging cells that haven't already affected you, but doesn't affect the venom that has already been injected. If you are in the tropics and you believe you may have been stung by a box jellyfish or an Irukandji, seek medical attention immediately.

In Sydney and north Queensland, you might come across **"stingers,"** also called "blue bottles." These long-tentacled blue jellyfish can inflict a nasty stinging burn that can last for hours. Sometimes you'll see warning signs on patrolled beaches. The best remedy if you are severely stung is to wash the affected area with fresh water and have a very hot bath or shower (preferably with someone else, just for the sympathy).

Threats to the Landscape

Australia is suffering from climate change, water shortages, and serious threats to wildlife and ecosystems. The country is one of the highest per capita polluters in the world, thanks largely to its reliance on mining and coal-fired power generation.

Meanwhile, the Great Barrier Reef is being damaged by coral bleaching, which occurs when water temperatures rise. Corals can recover, but if the heat persists, or if bleaching happens too frequently, they can die. Nutrient-rich sediment washed out to sea from farmland doesn't help matters much, as nutrient-loving algae colonize the already hard-hit corals. The runoff can also contain pesticides and herbicides, which damage the reef further and make it more vulnerable to the introduced crown-of-thorns starfish, which likes snacking on coral.

As for Australia's native animals and birds—well, history hasn't been too kind to them. At least 22 species of birds, 4 frog species, and 27 mammal species have become extinct since European settlement in Australia. Habitat destruction and introduced species have been the main causes of extinctions. Classified as "critically endangered" or "endangered" today are 24 species of fish, 19 species of frogs, 28 species of reptiles, 65 species of birds, 44 species of mammals, 49 other animals, and 683 species of plants. Many more are classified as vulnerable.

RESPONSIBLE TRAVEL

Sustainable travel—and its close cousin, responsible travel—are important issues in Australia, and you'll find plenty of places that claim to be eco-friendly. So how do you find the places that will truly help you make as little impact as possible on our fragile environment? When planning your trip, look for Australian tourism operators who are accredited under **Ecotourism Australia's** Eco Certification Program (www.ecotourism.org.au). The **Eco Certification** logo is carried by tours, attractions, cruises, or accommodations that have been recognized as environmentally, socially, and economically sustainable. Ecotourism Australia's online **Green Travel Guide** carries a list of its accredited businesses.

Australians are increasingly aware of their environmental responsibilities. Recycling is common, with local government areas providing bins for general household refuse, paper, and glass. Most states of Australia—except New

RESOURCES FOR responsible TRAVEL

In addition to the resources for Australia listed above and below, the following websites provide valuable wide-ranging information on sustainable travel.

o Sustainable Travel International (www.sustainabletravel.org) promotes ethical tourism practices.

o Carbonfund (www.carbonfund.org) and **Cool Climate Network** (www.coolclimate.berkeley.edu) provide info on "carbon offsetting," or offsetting the greenhouse gas emitted during flights. For general info on volunteer travel, visit www.goabroad.com/volunteer-abroad and www.idealist.org.

South Wales—have now banned single-use plastic bags; take a reusable bag to carry your shopping in. There is also a growing national campaign to ban plastic straws because of their impact on marine life; at least 30 tour operators on the Great Barrier Reef have agreed to ban them.

Because of frequent and prolonged droughts, Australians have become more aware of where their water supply is coming from. You might be surprised at how water-conscious the average Australian is these days. That said, what we gain on one hand we often lose on the other. Gas-guzzling four-wheel-drives are popular, four-wheelers zip around the Outback and on some beaches, and air travel within Australia is generally necessary. If you are keen to offset the large carbon footprint created by your flight to Australia, use public transport where you can, turn electronic gadgets off at the wall when you aren't using them, and recycle batteries if possible. Don't throw cigarette butts on the ground—you risk a possible hefty fine, and your butt might end up polluting Australia's waterways.

Choose a **hotel** designed to reduce its environmental impact with its use of non-toxic cleaners and renewable energy sources. The hotels may be reducing their emissions further by utilizing local food, energy-efficient lighting, and eco-friendly forms of transport. Most hotels now offer you the choice of using the same towels for more than one night—and of course, you should, because laundry makes up around 40 percent of an average hotel's energy use. Some accommodations offer the same option regarding bed linens if you're staying more than one night.

Choose **tours** that are eco-friendly, environmentally sustainable, and preferably employ local guides. Opt for a sailing boat rather than a giant motor cruiser to discover the Barrier Reef or the Whitsunday Islands in Queensland, for example, or an Aboriginal guided walking tour over a large coach excursion.

If you are looking for a way of "giving something back" on your holiday, several organizations offer the opportunity to do some **volunteer work** in Australia, such as helping to save endangered wildlife. Often there is a fee involved to cover transportation, accommodations, meals, and so on. **Conservation Volunteers Australia** (www.conservationvolunteers.com.au; ℗ 1800/032 501 in Australia, or 03/5330 0200) offers a range of projects across Australia, including tree planting, wildlife surveys, heritage restoration, and more. **Real Gap Experience** (www.realgap.com.au) offers several volunteer options in Australia, including in a wildlife sanctuary on Kangaroo Island in South Australia. **Willing Workers on Organic Farms** (WWOOF) offers the chance for volunteers to do 4 to 6 hours of work a day in exchange for meals and accommodations, usually in the farmers' family home. WWOOFers (as they are known) have the pick of more than 1,500 host farms around the country. Check out the website (www.wwoof.com.au) or call ☎ **03/5155 0218.** The state tourism website for **Victoria** (www.visitvictoria.com/information/volunteer) also recommends volunteering opportunities in that state. Another useful resource is the government website, **www.volunteer.vic.gov.au.**

WHEN TO GO

When it is winter in the Northern Hemisphere, Australia is basking in the Southern Hemisphere's summer, and vice versa. Midwinter in Australia is July and August, and the hottest months are November through March. Remember, unlike in the Northern Hemisphere, the farther south you go in Australia, the colder it gets.

The Travel Seasons

Airfares to Australia are lowest from mid-April to late August—the best time to visit the Red Centre and the Great Barrier Reef.

HIGH SEASON   The peak travel season in the most popular parts of Australia is the Aussie winter. In much of the country—particularly the northern half—the most pleasant time to travel is April through September, when daytime temperatures are 66° to 88°F (19°–31°C) and it rarely rains. June, July, and August are the busiest months in these parts; you'll need to book hotels and tours well in advance, and you will pay higher rates then, too.

On the other hand, Australia's summer is a nice time to visit the southern states, and even in winter temperatures rarely dip below freezing.

Generally, the best months to visit Australia are September and October, when it's often still warm enough to hit the beach in the southern states, it's cool enough to tour Uluru, and the humidity and rains have not come to Cairns (although it will be very hot by October).

LOW SEASON   October through March (summer) is just too hot, too humid, or too wet—or all three—to tour the Red Centre. North Queensland, including Cairns, suffers an intensely hot, humid wet season from November or December through March or April. This is known as "the Wet" and affects most of northern Australia ("the Dry" is from May to October). So if you decide to travel at this time—and lots of people do—be prepared to take the heat, the inconvenience of potential flooding, and the slight chance of encountering cyclones.

Steer Clear of the Vacation Rush

Try to avoid Australia from Boxing Day (December 26) to the end of January, when Aussies take their summer vacations. In popular seaside holiday spots, hotel rooms and airline seats get as scarce as hen's teeth, and it's a rare airline or hotel that will discount full rates by even a dollar.

Australian National Public Holidays

On national public holidays, services such as banking, postal needs, and purchase of alcohol might be limited or unavailable. There may also be additional holidays as declared by individual states and territories, such as Melbourne Cup Day (1st Tuesday in November), based on the country's most famous thoroughbred horse race—"the race that stops the nation."

o **New Year's Day,** January 1. Expect the usual fireworks and festivities to begin the night of December 31 to ring in the New Year.

o **Australia Day,** January 26. This national day recognizes the First Fleet's arrival in 1788, when 11 ships made their way from England to establish a colony in Australia.

o **Good Friday,** the Friday before Easter, observed the first Friday after the full moon (on or after March 21).

o **Easter Monday,** day after Easter Sunday.

o **Anzac Day,** April 25. ANZAC (Australian and New Zealand Army Corps) Day recognizes those who have served the nation in times of war.

o **Christmas Day,** December 25. *Note:* If Christmas is on a weekend day, the next Monday is termed a public holiday.

o **Boxing Day,** December 26. Originally a British tradition involving gift-giving, Boxing Day is now an Australian holiday, and some sports kick off their seasons on this date. If Boxing Day falls on a Saturday, the next Monday is deemed a public holiday. If it falls on a Sunday, the next Tuesday is the holiday.

Australia Calendar of Events

For an exhaustive list of events beyond those listed here, check www.frommers.com, where you'll find a searchable, up-to-the-minute roster of what's happening in cities all over the world.

JANUARY

Sydney Festival. Highlights of Sydney's visual and performing-arts festival include 75 free events at indoor and outdoor venues—including the Sydney Opera House, Royal Botanic Garden, and Barangaroo Reserve—across the city. The festival involves about 154 events featuring 1,330 artists. Call (C) **02/8248 6500** or go to www.sydneyfestival.org.au. 3 weeks from early January.

The Australian Open. The Asia/Pacific Grand Slam is played every year at the Melbourne Park National Tennis Centre. Tickets go on sale in October via Ticketek (www.ticketek.com.au; (C) **1300/888 104** in Australia, or 03/9039 9407). For more info check out www.ausopen.com. Last 2 weeks of January.

Australia Day. This national public holiday marks the landing of the First Fleet of

New Year's fireworks over Sydney Harbour Bridge.

convicts at Sydney Cove in 1788. Every town puts on some kind of celebration; in Sydney, there are ferry races and tall ships on the harbor, food and wine stalls in Hyde Park, open days at museums, and evening fireworks. www.australiaday.com.au. January 26.

FEBRUARY

Sydney Gay & Lesbian Mardi Gras. Two weeks of events, culminating in a spectacular parade of costumed dancers and decorated floats, watched by several hundred thousand onlookers. Contact Sydney Gay & Lesbian Mardi Gras (www.mardigras.org.au; ☎ **02/9383 0900**). Late February/early March.

MARCH

Formula 1 Australian Grand Prix, Melbourne. The first Grand Prix of the year, on the international FIA Formula 1 World Championship circuit, is battled out on one of its fastest circuits. For tickets, call ☎ **1800/100 030** in Australia, or order online at www.grandprix.com.au. 4 days in 2nd week of March.

Melbourne International Comedy Festival. Venues all over the city participate in this festival of laughs, which attracts top Australian and international talent. For

tickets, contact Ticketmaster (www.comedy festival.com.au; ☎ **136 100,** or 132 849). Late March/mid-April.

APRIL

Anzac Day, nationwide. Australia's national day of mourning for servicemen and -women who have died in wars and conflicts. Commemorative services are held even in the smallest towns; major cities hold street parades for returned servicemen and -women. Visit www.anzacportal.dva.gov.au for details of services throughout Australia. April 25.

MAY

Vivid. Sydney's spectacular light festival illuminates some of the city's best locations, including the Sydney Opera House, Sydney Harbour Bridge, Darling Harbour, and Sydney Town Hall, along with other venues around the city. And it's all free. Contact Vivid Sydney (www.vividsydney.com; ☎ **02/9931 1111**). 3 weeks in late May to mid-June.

JUNE

Sydney Film Festival. Premieres of Aussie and international movies take place in the State Theatre and other venues. Contact the Sydney Film Festival (www.sff.org.au; ☎ **1300/733 733** in Australia, or 02/8220 6600). 2 weeks in June.

AUGUST

Henley-on-Todd Regatta, Alice Springs. Sounds sophisticated, doesn't it? It's actually a harum-scarum race down the dry bed of the Todd River in homemade "boats," made from anything you care to name—an old 4WD chassis, say, or beer cans lashed together. The only rule is the vessel has to look *vaguely* like a boat. Contact the organizers at ✆ **0417/864 085** (mobile phone) or visit www.henleyontodd.com.au. 3rd Saturday in August.

Melbourne International Film Festival. About 350 films—new releases, shorts, and avant-garde movies—from 50 countries play at venues around the city (www.miff.com.au; ✆ **03/8660 4888**). 3 weeks in August.

SEPTEMBER

Melbourne Fringe. The city's streets, pubs, theaters, and restaurants play host to everyone from jugglers and fire-eaters to musicians and indie productions covering all art forms (www.melbournefringe.com.au; ✆ **03/9660 9600**). 3 weeks in September.

Brisbane Festival. A highlight of this arts festival is Riverfire, a spectacular pyrotechnics display best seen from the riverbank. The festival program includes music, theatre, dance, comedy, opera, circus, and more. For info and tickets, check www.brisbanefestival.com.au. 3 weeks in September.

NOVEMBER

Melbourne Cup, Flemington. They say the entire nation stops to watch this A$3.5-million horse race. If you're not actually at the track, you're glued to the TV—or, well, you're probably not an Australian. It's a public holiday in Melbourne, but all over the country women wear race-day hats to the office and work is abandoned for a late chicken and champagne lunch while the race is run at 3pm. For tickets, contact Ticketek (www.ticketek.com.au; ✆ **132 849** in Australia); for information, visit www.flemington.com.au. 1st Tuesday in November.

DECEMBER

Sydney Hobart Yacht Race. Find a cliff-top spot near the Heads to watch the glorious show of spinnakers, as 100 or so yachts leave Sydney Harbour for this grueling world-class race to Hobart, Tasmania. The organizer is the Sydney-based Cruising Yacht Club of Australia (www.cyca.com.au; ✆ **02/8292 7800**). Starts December 26.

New Year's Eve, Sydney. Watching the Sydney Harbour Bridge light up with fireworks is a treat. The main show is at 9pm, not midnight, so young kids don't miss out. Pack a picnic and snag a harborside spot by 4pm, or even earlier at the best vantage point—Mrs. Macquarie's Chair in the Royal Botanic Garden. December 31.

The Sydney Hobart Yacht Race is a world-class sailing event.

SUGGESTED ITINERARIES

Australia's size and its distance from Northern Hemisphere destinations are the two most daunting things about planning a visit here. A week or two is just enough time to scrape the surface of this vast, complex, and fascinating place. It's a long way to come for just a week, but if that's all you can spare, you still want to see as much as possible. While my inclination is to immerse myself in one spot, I know that not everyone can do that. Seeing as much as possible is often a priority, so here are some ideas on how to do just that.

If you're a first-time visitor, with just 1 or 2 weeks, consider **"Australia in 1 Week"** or **"Australia in 2 Weeks."** These itineraries can be adapted to suit your needs; for example, you could replace the Cairns section of "Australia in 1 Week" with the Uluru/Red Centre suggestions in "Australia in 2 Weeks," flying from Sydney to Uluru.

If you're traveling as a family, the **"Australia for Families"** itinerary is designed to give you some ideas on keeping the young ones occupied (while still being interesting for parents!).

Getting around this continent, where major attractions are thousands of miles apart, can be challenging and time-consuming. Flying is the only way to cover long distances efficiently, but it can also be expensive. Remember to build flying time into your itineraries, and don't try to pack in too much on the days you fly—even domestic flights can be draining, some clocking in at around 3 hours. See "Getting There" and "Getting Around," in chapter 10, for information on air passes and getting the best rates on Australia's domestic carriers.

My best advice: If the pace gets too hectic, just chill out and re-order your sightseeing priorities. Take time to meet the locals and ask their advice on what you should see as well.

AUSTRALIA IN 1 WEEK

Australia is so vast that in 1 week you'll only be able to get to a small corner of it—perhaps one city or a few of its natural wonders. It will be memorable, nevertheless, and careful planning will maximize your time and allow you to see some of the major sights.

Use the following itinerary to make the most of a week in Australia, but make sure you don't exhaust yourself trying to cram everything in. Australians are a laid-back lot, generally, and in some places the pace is relaxed. And that's just the way to enjoy it. One week provides barely enough time to see the best of Sydney, which for most people is the entry point to Australia.

If you have one week and want to head farther afield, there are two main choices, depending on your interests. The **Great Barrier Reef** is a must for divers, but you have to allow time on either side of your reef trip for flying. There are no such problems with Australia's other icon, **Uluru,** in the heart of the **Red Centre.** This triangle of highlights is something of a cliché, but it still gives you a complete Australian experience. Realistically, you will have to choose between the Reef and the Rock, or forego scuba diving while you are in Queensland.

Day 1: Arrive in Sydney ★★★

Check into your hotel and spend whatever time you have upon arrival recovering from the almost-guaranteed jet lag. If you arrive in the morning and have a full day ahead of you, try to stay up. Hit the nearest cafe for a shot of caffeine to keep you going. Head to **Circular Quay,** and from there get a fantastic view of **Sydney Harbour Bridge ★★★** (p. 83) before strolling to the **Sydney Opera House ★★★** (p. 85) and soaking up some history at **The Rocks ★★★**. If you have time, take the ferry from Circular Quay to Manly Beach and round off a fairly easy day with fish and chips. Then head to bed for some much-needed sleep.

Sydney's Circular Quay.

Australia in 1 or 2 Weeks

ARNHEM LAND

Gulf of Carpentaria

CAPE YORK PENINSULA

Thursday Island

Coral Sea

Great Barrier Reef Area

Coral Sea

Daintree

DAINTREE NATIONAL PARK

Port Douglas

Yorkeys Knob

Kuranda

Cairns

3

Cooktown

DAINTREE NATIONAL PARK

Port Douglas

6

5

4

Cairns

Mission Beach

SOUTH PACIFIC OCEAN

TERRITORY

Tennant Creek

Barkly Hwy.

Mt. Isa

Landsborough Hwy.

Flinders Hwy.

Townsville

Whitsunday Islands National Park

Proserpine

Mackay

MACDONNELL RANGES

Alice Springs

10-11

Capricorn Hwy.

Longreach

Rockhampton

Gladstone

SIMPSON DESERT

BACK TO SYDNEY

Bundaberg

Fraser Island

G R E A T

SOUTH AUSTRALIA

Coober Pedy

QUEENSLAND

Mitchell Hwy.

7

D I V I D I N G

Brisbane

R A N G E

Sunshine Coast

Gold Coast

LAMINGTON NATL. PK.

Stuart Hwy.

FLINDERS RANGES NATIONAL PARK

Darling River

Lightning Ridge

New England Hwy.

Coffs Harbour

Barrier Hwy.

Broken Hill

Oxley Hwy.

Tamworth

Pacific Hwy.

Port Macquarie

Port Pirie

Dubbo

BLUE MTNS. NATL. PK.

Newcastle

NEW SOUTH WALES

Mildura

Hwy.

3

Sydney

1-2

Adelaide

Kangaroo Island

Murray River

Newell Hwy.

12-14

Hume Hwy.

Wodonga

Princes Hwy.

★ **CANBERRA**

Dukes Hwy.

Princes Hwy.

VICTORIA

Albury

Mt. Kosciuszko

SNOWY MOUNTAINS

A.C.T.

Mt. Gambier

Ballarat Geelong

Melbourne

Apollo Bay

To Tasmania (see inset)

Tasman Sea

Day 2: Explore Sydney

Start with a ride to the top of the **Sydney Tower** ★ to experience Sydney's highest open-air attraction, **Skywalk** (p. 90), a breathtaking 260m (853 ft.) above Sydney. Harnessed onto a moving, glass-floored viewing platform that extends out over the edge of the tower, you can view all of Sydney's landmarks, including the Sydney Harbour Bridge, the Sydney Opera House, Sydney Harbour, and even the Blue Mountains beyond. Don't worry, it's not as scary as it sounds. For an introduction to Australia's wildlife, head to **Taronga Zoo** ★★★ (p. 91) or the **Sydney Aquarium** ★ (p. 87). If you have time to spare, another great choice is **Featherdale Wildlife Park** ★★★ (p. 90), but keep in mind it's about an hour and a half from the city center. If you enjoy museums, put the **Australian Museum** ★★ (p. 88), the **Australian National Maritime Museum** ★★ (p. 86) at Darling Harbour, and the interactive **Powerhouse Museum** ★★★ (p. 87) on your list for the day. For insight into Sydney's beginnings as a convict settlement, visit the **Hyde Park Barracks Museum** ★★ (p. 88), a convict-built prison. Finish off your day with a twilight (or later on weekends) **BridgeClimb** ★★★ (p. 83) up the Sydney Harbour Bridge.

Day 3: The Blue Mountains ★★★

Take the train from Central Station to **Katoomba** (p. 101) for a day, exploring the beauty of the Blue Mountains—only 2 hours from Sydney. Once there, jump on the **Blue Mountains Explorer** bus (p. 102), which allows you to hop on and off wherever you please. There are also many

Wombat cuddling at Featherdale Wildlife Park.

Night Fire by Tjapukai offers enchanting Aboriginal experiences.

day-tour operators running to the Blue Mountains from Sydney. Which-ever mode of transport you use, don't miss the spectacular **Three Sisters** (p. 103) rock formation, best viewed from Echo Point Road at Katoomba. Make sure you also spend some time at **Scenic World ★** (p. 103), where you can ride the world's steepest railway into a valley full of ancient rainforest, and come back up on a cable car—among other adventures that kids especially will enjoy. At the end of the day, head back to Sydney and have dinner somewhere with a view of the harbor, such as **Sydney Cove Oyster Bar** (p. 74) or **Bennelong** (p. 74), or one of the new band of restaurants at Barangaroo, such as **Love.fish** (p. 75).

Day 4: Cairns, Gateway to the Great Barrier Reef

Take the earliest flight you can from Sydney to Cairns—flight time is 3 hours—and check into a hotel in the city, which on such a tight schedule will make getting to the major attractions quicker and easier than staying out of town on the northern beaches. Explore the city a little and see some wildlife—including a massive saltwater crocodile—in the bizarre setting of the **Cairns ZOOM and Wildlife Dome ★★** (p. 194), atop the Hotel Sofitel Reef Casino. You will have the rest of the day to head out to visit **Tjapukai ★★** (p. 196), an Aboriginal cultural park. If you are not going to the Red Centre, this is a great place to learn about Aboriginal culture and life, albeit in a theme-park kind of way. You could spend several hours here, or save the visit for the evening, when **Night Fire by Tjapu-kai** offers a different look at traditional ceremonies, including dinner and a fire-and-water show.

Day 5: A Day Trip to the Reef ★★★

Day trips to the Great Barrier Reef leave from the **Reef Fleet Terminal.** The trip to the outer reef takes about 2 hours, and once there you will spend your day on a pontoon with about 300 people. Experienced divers may prefer to take a day trip with one of several dive charter companies that take smaller groups and visit two or three reefs. The pontoons of the big operators also offer the chance to take a scenic flight—a truly spectacular experience. Divers must spend another 24 hours in Cairns before flying. If you are content to snorkel, ride the glass-bottom boats, and soak up the sun, you will be able to fly the next day. After returning to Cairns, take a stroll along the **Esplanade** and eat at one of the busy cafes and restaurants that line the strip.

Day 6: Kuranda, a Rainforest Village ★★

Waiting out the day after diving (you can't fly for 24 hours after you've been on a dive) gives you a chance to discover another aspect of Australia—its rainforests. Take a trip to the mountain village of **Kuranda** aboard the steam train along the **Kuranda Scenic Railway ★★★** (p. 202), past waterfalls and gorges. In Kuranda, explore the markets and the nature parks and maybe take a **Kuranda Riverboat Tour ★★** (p. 204), which runs about 45 minutes. Return on the **Skyrail ★★★** cableway (p. 194), which carries you over the rainforest (you can get to ground level at a couple of stations on the way) to the edge of Cairns. The views are sensational. This is a big day out!

Day 7: Cairns to Sydney

In the morning, head to the airport for your flight to Sydney. Unless you are lucky enough to have an international flight directly out of Cairns, you will spend most of your last day in Australia returning to Sydney. With the time you have left in Sydney, treat yourself to dinner at a restaurant overlooking the harbor, with its bridge and the Opera House illuminated. It's a sight you'll carry home with you.

AUSTRALIA IN 2 WEEKS

With 2 weeks, your visit to Australia will be much more relaxed and you'll get a greater sense of the diversity of Australia's landscape, wildlife, and people. You will be able to explore the country's trio of icons—Sydney, the Great Barrier Reef, and Uluru—in more depth, and maybe even have time to go outside those areas, especially if you limit your icons to two instead of three.

Days 1–6: Sydney to Cairns

Follow the itinerary as outlined in "Australia in 1 Week," above.

3

SUGGESTED ITINERARIES | Australia in 2 Weeks

Day 7: Cairns to Uluru

Leave Cairns as early as you can. Your flight to Ayers Rock Airport will take around 3 hours. Make sure you book a direct flight, not one that goes via Sydney! Try to get a window seat for the spectacular views as you fly over the Outback. If you take the early flight, you can be in **Uluru** by around 10am, which gives you the entire day to take in the enormity of this fabulous monolith. Take the shuttle from **Ayers Rock Resort** (the only place to stay, albeit one with many accommodation choices; p. 283) to the Rock. Spend some time in the impressive and interesting **Uluru–Kata Tjuta Cultural Centre** (p. 282), near the base of Uluru, and explore the area on one of the many walking trails or tours. End the day by watching the sun set over Uluru—an unforgettable sight. After doing all that in a day, you'll be ready for a quiet dinner at whatever hotel you've chosen.

Day 8: Exploring Uluru ★★★

Sunrise is one of those magical times at Uluru, so make the effort to get up early. This is also a great time to do the 10.6km (6½-mile) **Base Walk** circumnavigating Uluru (p. 287), which takes 2 to 3 hours. There are many ways to experience Uluru, including camel rides, Harley-Davidson tours, and helicopter joy flights, but walking up close to the Rock beats them all.

You will also have time today to head to **Kata Tjuta** (also called "The Olgas"; p. 289), where you'll see there's much more to the Red Centre than just one rock. Kata Tjuta is about 48km (30 miles) west of Uluru, but plenty of tour operators go there if you don't have your own wheels.

Exploring Uluru–Kata Tjuta National Park on foot.

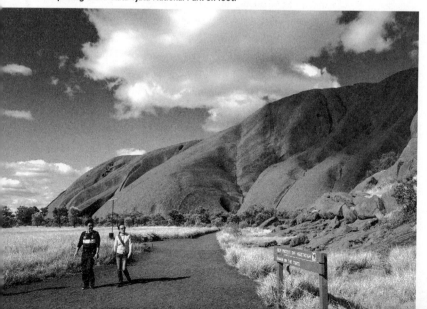

End your day in the desert with the **Sounds of Silence** dinner or the slightly more upmarket, more intimate **Tali Wiru** ★★★ dinner (p. 285), run by Ayers Rock Resort. Sip champagne as the sun sets over Uluru to the eerie music of the didgeridoo, and then tuck into kangaroo, barramundi, and other native foods. But it's not the food you're here for—it's the silence and the stars. Package it with a visit to the incredible **Field of Light,** to walk through an amazing art installation of 50,000 stems of light.

Day 9: Uluru to Kings Canyon

Hire a four-wheel-drive vehicle and tackle the long Outback drive from Uluru to Alice Springs, stopping for a night at **Kings Canyon Resort** (www.kingscanyonresort.com.au). It is 306km (190 miles) from Uluru to Kings Canyon (also known as **Watarrka National Park**), which offers another unbeatable look at Outback Australia. You can spend the afternoon walking up the side of the canyon and around the rim. Parts of it are very steep, and the whole hike will take you around 4 hours, but the trip is well worth the effort. A gentler walk is the short and shady canyon floor walk.

Day 10: Kings Canyon to Alice Springs

Get an early start for Alice Springs, and take the unpaved but interesting **Mereenie Loop Road,** which threads through the **Glen Helen Gorge** or the historic **Hermannsburg** mission settlement (p. 278). Whichever road you take, the scenery is like nowhere else. You will probably spend most of the day driving to Alice, making a few stops along the way.

On arrival, check into a hotel and head out to one of the local restaurants, several of which offer sophisticated versions of "bush tucker," including kangaroo, emu, and crocodile dishes.

Hiking Kings Canyon/Watarrka National Park.

Day 11: Alice Springs

If you can stand another early start, take a **dawn balloon flight** over the desert (p. 274), usually followed by a champagne breakfast. If you don't head back to bed immediately for a few hours of catch-up sleep, there are plenty of attractions to discover, including the **Alice Springs Desert Park** ★★★ (p. 271) for a look at some unusual Australian creatures; the **School of the Air** ★★ (p. 273); and the **Royal Flying Doctor**

Service ★★ base (p. 273). In the afternoon, drop into the **Mbantua Fine Art Gallery and Cultural Museum** (p. 275) to see some of the best Aboriginal art from the outlying communities in the desert region called Utopia, famed for its paintings. Alternatively, visit the **Alice Springs Telegraph Station Historical Reserve** ★★ (p. 272), set in an oasis just outside town, for a look at early settler life. Finish the day with a **sunset camel ride** (p. 274) down the dry Todd River bed and have dinner at the camel farm.

Day 12: Alice Springs to Sydney

Direct flights from Alice Springs to Sydney leave in the early afternoon, so you'll have all morning to explore more of the town and perhaps buy some Aboriginal art. (This is one of the best places to get it.)

On arrival in Sydney, after an almost 3-hour flight, check into your hotel and spend the evening discovering the city's nightlife.

Day 13: A Day at Bondi Beach

For sands of a different hue from those you've experienced in recent days, take the bus to Sydney's most famous beach, **Bondi** (p. 93), and spend the day lazing on the sand or—in summer, at least—taking a dip in the surf. Take a public bus or the Bondi Explorer from Circular Quay, which gives you a choice of harborside bays and coastal beaches. The scenic cliff-top walk to **Bronte Beach** is recommended, or you can continue farther to **Coogee.**

Day 14: Sydney

Your final day in Australia can be spent on last-minute shopping and seeing those Sydney sights that you haven't yet had time for. Cap it all off with a seafood dinner somewhere with a fantastic view of the Harbour Bridge.

AUSTRALIA FOR FAMILIES

Australia is a wonderful destination for kids—and not just because of the kangaroos and koalas. Our suggestion is to explore Sydney for 2 days with family in tow, then head up to the beautiful Blue Mountains on a day trip to ride the cable car and the world's steepest railway. The climax comes with a few days of exploring the Barrier Reef and the rainforest around Port Douglas.

Days 1 & 2: Sydney

First off, head to Circular Quay to see the **Sydney Opera House** ★★★. A tour inside might be a bit much for younger kids, but you can walk around a fair bit of it and take the obligatory photos of Australia's most famous landmark. To stretch your legs, head from here into the **Royal Botanic Garden** (p. 96) to spot long-beaked ibises wandering around the grass and hundreds of fruit bats squabbling among the treetops. Walk back past the Opera House and the ferries to **The Rocks,** where you can take a quick stroll through the historic streets, stopping for a look at some of the trendy shops or the market on Saturdays.

There are plenty of places to eat lunch at Circular Quay, where you can sit outside and watch the world go by. After lunch, take a ferry to **Taronga Zoo ★★★**, where a cable car zips you up the hill to the main entrance. All the kids' favorite animals are here, from kangaroos and koalas to platypuses, located in a nocturnal house. A farmyard section edges onto a playground, with lots of water features to give your kids a sprinkle on a hot day.

On **Day 2,** head to the city center for an elevator ride up to the top of **Sydney Tower ★** (p. 90), where you can look right across Sydney as far as the Blue Mountains in the distance. Entry includes admission to the 4D Cinema Experience. It's a short walk from here to Darling Harbour, where you can cap off the morning with a visit to **SEA LIFE Sydney Aquarium ★**. The sharks that swim right above your head are huge, but the penguins are hard to beat for cuteness.

Eat lunch at one of the many cheap eateries at Darling Harbour before taking the ferry from near the Aquarium back to Circular Quay.

If it's a hot day, or you simply want to hit the beach, you have two choices: From Circular Quay, you can take a half-hour ferry ride or a 15-minute high-speed JetCat trip to **Manly** (p. 94). Here you can laze the afternoon away and even rent a surfboard or bodyboard. Or hop a bus to **Bondi Beach** (p. 93), where you can reward your efforts with gelato or a late-afternoon pizza from **Pompei's** (p. 78).

Sharks at SEA LIFE Sydney Aquarium.

The Scenic World Railway descends through the ancient tree fern forest.

Day 3: The Blue Mountains

You could easily spend a couple more days with the kids having fun in Sydney, but you shouldn't miss a trip to the mountains. If you go, prepare for a long day; pack plenty of snacks and a few favorite toys. Several companies run tour buses to the area, stopping off at an animal park along the way. The best one to visit is **Featherdale Wildlife Park** ★★★ (p. 90), where you can get up close to more kangaroos, koalas, and Tasmanian devils. The tour also stops at **Scenic World** ★ (p. 103), where you can take the short ride on the Scenic Railway. It's very steep, so hold on tight. At the bottom, you'll find yourselves among an ancient tree fern forest—it's truly remarkable. A short walk takes you to the **Skyway,** a cable car that travels 300m (984 ft.) above the Jamison Valley.

Elsewhere in the mountains, there are fabulous views across craggy bluffs and deep bowls of gum trees. See chapter 4 for details.

Days 4, 5 & 6: The Reef & the Rainforest

Now it's time to head north to the Tropics. You'll need to fly, of course; otherwise it would take you several days to drive up the coast. The flight from Sydney to Cairns takes 3 hours. As a family, you might prefer to base yourselves in **Port Douglas** (p. 205) rather than Cairns—the Port Douglas beach is huge and uncrowded, and some of the best Barrier Reef trips originate from here. "Port," as the locals call it, is about an hour's drive from Cairns, so your first day will be largely taken with getting there.

After all that traveling, take the rest of the day to relax on beautiful **Four Mile Beach,** but remember to swim inside the nets off the sand; the "stingers" (box jellyfish) around here can cause life-threatening stings, especially where kids are concerned.

On **Day 5,** it's time to visit the **Reef.** Thankfully, the dangerous jellyfish are very uncommon on the Reef itself. Cruise boats take around 90 minutes to get from Port Douglas to the outer reef; but once there, you are in for some amazing snorkeling. Expect to see numerous species of corals and fish, and even an occasional turtle. A good seafood lunch is generally served on board, so you won't go hungry!

Sydney's kid-friendly Luna Park amusement park.

Day 6 will be another nature experience, this time meeting some of the giants of the north. In the morning, head out to **Mossman Gorge** ★★★ (p. 210), a 15- to 20-minute drive from Port Douglas, for some Aboriginal culture in the rainforest with **Ngadiku Dreamtime Walks,** guided by a member of the local Kuku-Yalanji tribe. On your way back to Cairns, stop off at **Hartley's Crocodile Adventures** ★★★ (p. 196) to see crocs in their natural habitat. After the 3pm "croc attack" show, you'll have

Swimming hole in Mossman Gorge.

time for a leisurely drive back to Cairns to get ready for your departure. See chapter 7 for detailed information on these attractions.

Day 7: Fly Back to Sydney

If you have time to kill before you leave Sydney, take the kids by ferry to **Luna Park** ★, just across from Circular Quay, or walk there across the Harbour Bridge. Although this fun park is small, with few rides suitable for younger kids, it does boast a magnificent view across to the Harbour Bridge and Opera House, which look glorious after the sun's gone down.

The iconic Sydney Opera House.

the suburbs, it gets very crowded during rush hours (around 7–9am and 4–6:30pm). If you have lots of luggage, it's probably best to take a taxi. The train takes 10 minutes to reach the Central Railway Station. Trains leave every 10 minutes and cost A$18 one-way for adults and A$14 for children from the international terminal. Round-trip tickets are available only if you want to return to the airport on the same day.

BY TRAIN

Central Station (© **131 500** for Sydney Trains, or 132 232 for NSW Train-Link interstate trains) is the main city and interstate train station. It's at the top of George Street in downtown Sydney. All interstate trains arrive here, and it's a major Sydney Trains hub. Many city buses leave from neighboring Railway Square for such places as Town Hall and Circular Quay.

BY BUS

Greyhound coaches (© **02/9212 9505**) operate from the Central Station Coach Terminal at the Western Forecourt of the station (Bays 5 and 6, up the escalators from Eddy Ave.).

BY CRUISE SHIP

Ships dock at the **Overseas Passenger Terminal** in The Rocks, opposite the Sydney Opera House, or the White Bay Cruise Terminal in the suburb of Rozelle, about 5km (3 miles) from the city center.

BY CAR

Drivers enter Sydney from the north on the Pacific Highway, from the south on the M5 and Princes Highway, and from the west on the Great Western Highway.

SYDNEY

Warm-natured, sun-kissed, and naturally good-looking, Sydney is rather like its lucky residents. Situated on one of the world's most striking harbors, where the twin icons of the Sydney Opera House and Harbour Bridge steal the limelight, relaxed Sydney is surprisingly close to nature. Within minutes you can be riding the waves on Bondi Beach, bushwalking in Manly, or gazing out across Botany Bay, where the first salt-encrusted Europeans arrived in the 18th century. You can understand why they never wanted to leave.

For that "I'm in Sydney!" feeling, nothing beats the first glimpse of the white-sailed Opera House and the iconic Harbour Bridge, which you can climb for a bird's-eye view of the sparkling harbor. Move on to the Royal Botanical Garden's tropical greenery and the Museum of Contemporary Art's cutting-edge exhibitions. With 70 beaches close by—from the fizzing surf of famous Bondi Beach to Manly's coastal walks and pine-flanked bays—it's no wonder Sydneysiders look so bronzed and relaxed.

Don't let the knockout views of Sydney Harbour distract you from your shopping in The Rocks' specialty shops and galleries, or under the soaring glass arches of the Queen Victoria Building. You can also dine on a different cuisine every night in multicultural Sydney—whether late-night noodles in Chinatown, tasty tapas in the Spanish Quarter, or authentic Thai curries on bohemian King Street. BYO restaurants and sensible prices make eating out affordable in all but the very top places—French-Japanese Tetsuya's, for instance. Head to Circular Quay's sleek waterfront restaurants for the Opera House view and Australia's distinctive modern cuisine—a fusion of Australian, Mediterranean, and spicy Asian flavors.

There's so much to do in Sydney that you could easily spend a week here and still not see it all.

ESSENTIALS

Arriving
BY PLANE
Sydney International Airport (www.sydneyairport.com.au) is Australia's largest and busiest airport, used by more than 40 international airlines. Shuttle buses and the Airport Link train link the

---

Taxi Savvy

Taxi queues can be long, and drivers may try to cash in by insisting you share a cab with other passengers in line at the airport. Here's the scam: After dropping off the other passengers, the cabdriver will attempt to charge you the full price of the journey, despite the fact that the other passengers paid for their sections. You certainly won't save any money sharing a cab if this happens, and your journey will be a long one. If you are first in line in the taxi stand, the law states that you can refuse to share the cab. Taxi drivers appreciate a tip, but there is no compulsion to do so. If you've had good service, a 10 percent tip is enough.

A taxi from the airport to the city center costs about A$55. An expressway, the Eastern Distributor, is the fastest way to reach the city from the airport. There's a A$5 toll (the taxi driver pays the toll and adds the cost to your fare), but there is no toll on the road heading back to the airport. A 10 percent credit-card charge applies, and the Sydney airport charges a A$4.25 fee to catch a taxi from there. An **Uber** ride is a better deal, costing around A$30 from the international terminal to the city center.

international and domestic terminals. Single tickets on both cost A$6. The bus journey takes up to 10 minutes, the train 2 minutes. Buses run every 30 minutes from 6am to 9pm (more often in the morning peak period); the train is more frequent, and runs from 5am to midnight. Bus stops are on arrivals levels, at T1 Bus Bay 1 (near the McDonald's) and at T2 on the first roadway in the center of the terminal. **Qantas** and **Virgin Australia** offer seamless transfer services.

KST Airporter coaches (www.kst.com.au; © 02/8339 0155) travel to the city center from bus stops outside the terminals every 15 minutes. This service will drop you off (and pick you up) at hotels in the city, Kings Cross, and Darling Harbour. Pickups from hotels require at least 3 hours' advance notice; you can book online. One-way tickets cost A$17 adults and A$12 children 4–10; round-trip tickets cost A$32 adults and A$20 children.

In both terminals, you'll find luggage carts, wheelchairs, a post office (daily 7am–8pm), mailboxes, currency exchange, duty-free shops, restaurants, bars, stores, showers, luggage lockers, a baggage-hold service for larger items, ATMs, and tourist-information desks. You can rent mobile phones in the international terminal. **Smarte Carte** (at the southern end of the arrivals level) has luggage storage for A$13 a day for a small bag and A$16 for a suitcase or backpack. Luggage trolleys are free to use in the international arrival terminal but cost A$4 outside departure terminals (you'll need coins).

Between the Airport and the City Center
The airport is 8km (5 miles) from the city center. **Airport Link** (www.airportlink.com.au) trains connect both terminals to the city stations of Central, Museum, St. James, Circular Quay, Wynyard, and Town Hall. You'll need to change trains for other Sydney stations. Unfortunately, the line has no dedicated luggage areas, and because it's also a commuter train to the city from

Visitor Information

The Sydney Visitor Centre, corner of Argyle and Playfair streets, The Rocks (www.bestof.com.au; ℂ **02/8273 0000**), is a good place to pick up maps, brochures, Youth Hostel Association (YHA) cards, and general tourist information. It is open from 9:30am to 5:30pm daily (closed Good Friday and Christmas Day). In Manly, find the **Hello Manly Booking and Information Centre** (www.hellomanly.com.au; ℂ **02/9976 1430**) at Manly Wharf (where the ferries come in). It's open Monday to Friday from 9am to 5pm; on weekends and public holidays, it's open 10am to 4pm. It's closed Christmas Day.

City of Sydney information kiosks at Circular Quay (corner of Pitt and Alfred sts.) and at Kings Cross (corner of Dixon and Goulbourn sts.) provide maps, brochures, and advice and are open daily (except Christmas Day) from 9am to 5pm.

A good website for events, entertainment, dining, and shopping is **www.sydney.com**.

City Layout

Sydney is one of the largest cities in the world, covering more than 1,730 sq. km (675 sq. miles) from the sea to the foothills of the Blue Mountains. Thankfully, the city center, or Central Business District (CBD), is compact. The jewel in Sydney's crown is its magnificent harbor, which empties into the South Pacific Ocean through headlands known as North Head and South Head. On the southern side of the harbor are the high-rises of the city center; the Sydney Opera House; a string of beaches, including Bondi; and the inner suburbs. Next to Circular Quay and across Sydney Cove from the Opera House is The Rocks, a cluster of small streets that was once part of a historic slum; it's now a tourist attraction. The Sydney Harbour Bridge and a tunnel connect the city center to the high-rises of the North Sydney business district and the affluent suburbs and beaches beyond.

Sydney Tower is the city's tallest structure and an easy-to-spot landmark.

MAIN ARTERIES & STREETS

The city's main thoroughfare, George Street, runs up from **Circular Quay,** past Wynyard train station and Town Hall, to Central Station. From Circular Quay to The Rocks, it's a 5- to 10-minute stroll; to Wynyard a

10-minute walk; and to Town Hall a 20-minute stroll. At the time of this writing, George Street was still a mass of construction work as a new light rail system, due to be completed in 2019, is being built. Other main streets running parallel to George include Pitt, Elizabeth, and Macquarie streets. **Macquarie Street** runs up from the Sydney Opera House, past the Royal Botanic Garden and Hyde Park. **Martin Place** is a pedestrian thoroughfare between Macquarie and George streets, about halfway between Circular Quay and Town Hall—in the heart of the city center. The easy-to-spot Sydney Tower, facing onto pedestrian-only **Pitt Street Mall** on Pitt Street, is the main city-center landmark. Roads meet at **Town Hall** from Kings Cross to the east and Darling Harbour to the west. From Town Hall to the near side of Darling Harbour it's about a 10-minute walk.

Sydney Neighborhoods in Brief

SOUTH OF SYDNEY HARBOUR

Circular Quay Tucked between the Harbour Bridge and the Sydney Opera House, this transport hub for ferries, buses, and trains is a good spot for a stroll, with outdoor restaurants and street performers. The Rocks, the Royal Botanic Garden, the Contemporary Art Museum, and the main shopping area (centered on Pitt and George sts.) are a short walk from here.

The Rocks This small historic area, a short stroll west of Circular Quay, is packed with colonial stone buildings, intriguing back streets, boutiques, pubs, tourist stores, restaurants, and hotels. It's the most exclusive place to stay in the city, with shops geared toward Sydney's yuppies and wealthy tourists. On weekends, a portion of George Street becomes The Rocks Market, selling souvenirs and crafts. There's a food market on Fridays. Check out www.therocks.com for event info.

Town Hall In the heart of the city, this area is home to the main department stores and two Sydney landmarks, the Town Hall and the Queen Victoria Building (QVB) shopping arcade. Nearby are Sydney Tower and the stores of Pitt Street Mall. Farther up George Street you'll find Sydney's Spanish district (enter at Liverpool St.) and Chinatown.

Darling Harbour Designed as a tourist precinct, Darling Harbour features Sydney's main convention, exhibition, and entertainment centers; a waterfront promenade; the Sydney Aquarium; an IMAX theater; the Australian Maritime Museum; the Powerhouse

Museum; The Star casino; a food court; and plenty of shops. Nearby are the restaurants of Cockle Bay and King Street Wharf. To reach Darling Harbour, take a ferry from Circular Quay (Wharf 5) or the light rail from Central Station. Check out www.darling harbour.com.

Kings Cross & the Suburbs Beyond "The Cross" is the city's red-light district—and also home to some of Sydney's best-known nightclubs and restaurants, along with backpacker hostels and some upscale hotels. The colorful main drag, Darlinghurst Road, is crammed with strip joints, prostitutes, and drunks—there's a heavy police presence and usually plenty of "ordinary" people around, but do take care. Beyond the Cross lie the waterfront neighborhoods of Elizabeth Bay, Double Bay, and Rose Bay (take train to the Edgecliff stop).

Paddington/Oxford Street This central-city neighborhood, centered on trendy Oxford Street, is known for its terrace houses, off-the-wall boutiques and bookshops, and restaurants, pubs, and nightclubs. It's also the heart of Sydney's large gay community and has lots of gay bars and dance spots. Take bus nos. 333, 380, or 397 from Circular Quay; no. 440 from Central Station; or nos. 333, 378, or 380 from Bondi Junction; or the train to Museum Station.

Darlinghurst Between grungy Kings Cross and upscale Oxford Street, this grimy, terraced area is home to some of Sydney's best cafes—though it's probably not wise to wander time for a leisurely drive back to Cairns to get ready for your departure. See chapter 7 for detailed information on these attractions.

Day 7: Fly Back to Sydney

If you have time to kill before you leave Sydney, take the kids by ferry to **Luna Park** ★, just across from Circular Quay, or walk there across the Harbour Bridge. Although this fun park is small, with few rides suitable for younger kids, it does boast a magnificent view across to the Harbour Bridge and Opera House, which look glorious after the sun's gone down.

SYDNEY

Warm-natured, sun-kissed, and naturally good-look-ing, Sydney is rather like its lucky residents. Situ-ated on one of the world's most striking harbors, where the twin icons of the Sydney Opera House and Har-bour Bridge steal the limelight, relaxed Sydney is surprisingly close to nature. Within minutes you can be riding the waves on Bondi Beach, bushwalking in Manly, or gazing out across Botany Bay, where the first salt-encrusted Europeans arrived in the 18th century. You can understand why they never wanted to leave.

For that "I'm in Sydney!" feeling, nothing beats the first glimpse of the white-sailed Opera House and the iconic Harbour Bridge, which you can climb for a bird's-eye view of the sparkling harbor. Move on to the Royal Botanical Garden's tropical greenery and the Museum of Contemporary Art's cutting-edge exhibitions. With 70 beaches close by—from the fizzing surf of famous Bondi Beach to Manly's coastal walks and pine-flanked bays—it's no wonder Syd-neysiders look so bronzed and relaxed.

Don't let the knockout views of Sydney Harbour distract you from your shopping in The Rocks' specialty shops and galleries, or under the soaring glass arches of the Queen Victoria Building. You can also dine on a different cuisine every night in multicultural Sydney—whether late-night noodles in Chinatown, tasty tapas in the Spanish Quarter, or authentic Thai curries on bohemian King Street. BYO restaurants and sensible prices make eating out afford-able in all but the very top places—French-Japanese Tetsuya's, for instance. Head to Circular Quay's sleek waterfront restaurants for the Opera House view and Australia's distinctive modern cuisine—a fusion of Australian, Mediterranean, and spicy Asian flavors.

There's so much to do in Sydney that you could easily spend a week here and still not see it all.

ESSENTIALS

Arriving
BY PLANE
Sydney International Airport (www.sydneyairport.com.au) is Australia's largest and busiest airport, used by more than 40 inter-national airlines. Shuttle buses and the Airport Link train link the

Taxi Savvy

Taxi queues can be long, and drivers may try to cash in by insisting you share a cab with other passengers in line at the airport. Here's the scam: After dropping off the other passengers, the cabdriver will attempt to charge you the full price of the journey, despite the fact that the other passengers paid for their sections. You certainly won't save any money sharing a cab if this happens, and your journey will be a long one. If you are first in line in the taxi stand, the law states that you can refuse to share the cab. Taxi drivers appreciate a tip, but there is no compulsion to do so. If you've had good service, a 10 percent tip is enough.

A taxi from the airport to the city center costs about A$55. An expressway, the Eastern Distributor, is the fastest way to reach the city from the airport. There's a A$5 toll (the taxi driver pays the toll and adds the cost to your fare), but there is no toll on the road heading back to the airport. A 10 percent credit-card charge applies, and the Sydney airport charges a A$4.25 fee to catch a taxi from there. An **Uber** ride is a better deal, costing around A$30 from the international terminal to the city center.

international and domestic terminals. Single tickets on both cost A$6. The bus journey takes up to 10 minutes, the train 2 minutes. Buses run every 30 minutes from 6am to 9pm (more often in the morning peak period); the train is more frequent, and runs from 5am to midnight. Bus stops are on arrivals levels, at T1 Bus Bay 1 (near the McDonald's) and at T2 on the first roadway in the center of the terminal. **Qantas** and **Virgin Australia** offer seamless transfer services.

KST Airporter coaches (www.kst.com.au; ✆ **02/8339 0155**) travel to the city center from bus stops outside the terminals every 15 minutes. This service will drop you off (and pick you up) at hotels in the city, Kings Cross, and Darling Harbour. Pickups from hotels require at least 3 hours' advance notice; you can book online. One-way tickets cost A$17 adults and A$12 children 4–10; round-trip tickets cost A$32 adults and A$20 children.

In both terminals, you'll find luggage carts, wheelchairs, a post office (daily 7am–8pm), mailboxes, currency exchange, duty-free shops, restaurants, bars, stores, showers, luggage lockers, a baggage-hold service for larger items, ATMs, and tourist-information desks. You can rent mobile phones in the international terminal. **Smarte Carte** (at the southern end of the arrivals level) has luggage storage for A$13 a day for a small bag and A$16 for a suitcase or backpack. Luggage trolleys are free to use in the international arrival terminal but cost A$4 outside departure terminals (you'll need coins).

Between the Airport and the City Center
The airport is 8km (5 miles) from the city center. **Airport Link** (www.airport link.com.au) trains connect both terminals to the city stations of Central, Museum, St. James, Circular Quay, Wynyard, and Town Hall. You'll need to change trains for other Sydney stations. Unfortunately, the line has no dedicated luggage areas, and because it's also a commuter train to the city from

The iconic Sydney Opera House.

the suburbs, it gets very crowded during rush hours (around 7–9am and 4–6:30pm). If you have lots of luggage, it's probably best to take a taxi. The train takes 10 minutes to reach the Central Railway Station. Trains leave every 10 minutes and cost A$18 one-way for adults and A$14 for children from the international terminal. Round-trip tickets are available only if you want to return to the airport on the same day.

BY TRAIN

Central Station (⟨ **131 500** for Sydney Trains, or 132 232 for NSW Train-Link interstate trains) is the main city and interstate train station. It's at the top of George Street in downtown Sydney. All interstate trains arrive here, and it's a major Sydney Trains hub. Many city buses leave from neighboring Railway Square for such places as Town Hall and Circular Quay.

BY BUS

Greyhound coaches (⟨ **02/9212 9505**) operate from the Central Station Coach Terminal at the Western Forecourt of the station (Bays 5 and 6, up the escalators from Eddy Ave.).

BY CRUISE SHIP

Ships dock at the **Overseas Passenger Terminal** in The Rocks, opposite the Sydney Opera House, or the White Bay Cruise Terminal in the suburb of Rozelle, about 5km (3 miles) from the city center.

BY CAR

Drivers enter Sydney from the north on the Pacific Highway, from the south on the M5 and Princes Highway, and from the west on the Great Western Highway.

Visitor Information

The Sydney Visitor Centre, corner of Argyle and Playfair streets, The Rocks (www.bestof.com.au; ✆ **02/8273 0000**), is a good place to pick up maps, brochures, Youth Hostel Association (YHA) cards, and general tourist information. It is open from 9:30am to 5:30pm daily (closed Good Friday and Christmas Day). In Manly, find the **Hello Manly Booking and Information Centre** (www.hellomanly.com.au; ✆ **02/9976 1430**) at Manly Wharf (where the ferries come in). It's open Monday to Friday from 9am to 5pm; on weekends and public holidays, it's open 10am to 4pm. It's closed Christmas Day.

City of Sydney information kiosks at Circular Quay (corner of Pitt and Alfred sts.) and at Kings Cross (corner of Dixon and Goulbourn sts.) provide maps, brochures, and advice and are open daily (except Christmas Day) from 9am to 5pm.

A good website for events, entertainment, dining, and shopping is **www.sydney.com**.

City Layout

Sydney is one of the largest cities in the world, covering more than 1,730 sq. km (675 sq. miles) from the sea to the foothills of the Blue Mountains. Thankfully, the city center, or Central Business District (CBD), is compact. The jewel in Sydney's crown is its magnificent harbor, which empties into the South Pacific Ocean through headlands known as North Head and South Head. On the southern side of the harbor are the high-rises of the city center; the Sydney Opera House; a string of beaches, including Bondi; and the inner suburbs. Next to Circular Quay and across Sydney Cove from the Opera House is The Rocks, a cluster of small streets that was once part of a historic slum; it's now a tourist attraction. The Sydney Harbour Bridge and a tunnel connect the city center to the high-rises of the North Sydney business district and the affluent suburbs and beaches beyond.

Sydney Tower is the city's tallest structure and an easy-to-spot landmark.

MAIN ARTERIES & STREETS

The city's main thoroughfare, George Street, runs up from **Circular Quay,** past Wynyard train station and Town Hall, to Central Station. From Circular Quay to The Rocks, it's a 5- to 10-minute stroll; to Wynyard a

10-minute walk; and to Town Hall a 20-minute stroll. At the time of this writing, George Street was still a mass of construction work as a new light rail system, due to be completed in 2019, is being built. Other main streets running parallel to George include Pitt, Elizabeth, and Macquarie streets. **Macquarie Street** runs up from the Sydney Opera House, past the Royal Botanic Garden and Hyde Park. **Martin Place** is a pedestrian thoroughfare between Macquarie and George streets, about halfway between Circular Quay and Town Hall—in the heart of the city center. The easy-to-spot Sydney Tower, facing onto pedestrian-only **Pitt Street Mall** on Pitt Street, is the main city-center landmark. Roads meet at **Town Hall** from Kings Cross to the east and Darling Harbour to the west. From Town Hall to the near side of Darling Harbour it's about a 10-minute walk.

Sydney Neighborhoods in Brief

SOUTH OF SYDNEY HARBOUR

Circular Quay Tucked between the Harbour Bridge and the Sydney Opera House, this transport hub for ferries, buses, and trains is a good spot for a stroll, with outdoor restaurants and street performers. The Rocks, the Royal Botanic Garden, the Contemporary Art Museum, and the main shopping area (centered on Pitt and George sts.) are a short walk from here.

The Rocks This small historic area, a short stroll west of Circular Quay, is packed with colonial stone buildings, intriguing back streets, boutiques, pubs, tourist stores, restaurants, and hotels. It's the most exclusive place to stay in the city, with shops geared toward Sydney's yuppies and wealthy tourists. On weekends, a portion of George Street becomes The Rocks Market, selling souvenirs and crafts. There's a food market on Fridays. Check out www.therocks.com for event info.

Town Hall In the heart of the city, this area is home to the main department stores and two Sydney landmarks, the Town Hall and the Queen Victoria Building (QVB) shopping arcade. Nearby are Sydney Tower and the stores of Pitt Street Mall. Farther up George Street you'll find Sydney's Spanish district (enter at Liverpool St.) and Chinatown.

Darling Harbour Designed as a tourist precinct, Darling Harbour features Sydney's main convention, exhibition, and entertainment centers; a waterfront promenade; the Sydney Aquarium; an IMAX theater; the Australian Maritime Museum; the Powerhouse Museum; The Star casino; a food court; and plenty of shops. Nearby are the restaurants of Cockle Bay and King Street Wharf. To reach Darling Harbour, take a ferry from Circular Quay (Wharf 5) or the light rail from Central Station. Check out www.darlingharbour.com.

Kings Cross & the Suburbs Beyond "The Cross" is the city's red-light district—and also home to some of Sydney's best-known nightclubs and restaurants, along with backpacker hostels and some upscale hotels. The colorful main drag, Darlinghurst Road, is crammed with strip joints, prostitutes, and drunks—there's a heavy police presence and usually plenty of "ordinary" people around, but do take care. Beyond the Cross lie the waterfront neighborhoods of Elizabeth Bay, Double Bay, and Rose Bay (take train to the Edgecliff stop).

Paddington/Oxford Street This central-city neighborhood, centered on trendy Oxford Street, is known for its terrace houses, off-the-wall boutiques and bookshops, and restaurants, pubs, and nightclubs. It's also the heart of Sydney's large gay community and has lots of gay bars and dance spots. Take bus nos. 333, 380, or 397 from Circular Quay; no. 440 from Central Station; or nos. 333, 378, or 380 from Bondi Junction; or the train to Museum Station.

Darlinghurst Between grungy Kings Cross and upscale Oxford Street, this grimy, terraced area is home to some of Sydney's best cafes—though it's probably not wise to wander

Bronte Beach.

around here at night alone. Take the train to Kings Cross and head right from the exit.

Central The congested, polluted streets around Central Station has little to attract visitors beyond train and bus connections. The Sydney Central YHA (youth hostel) is here.

Glebe Young professionals and students come to this central-city neighborhood for the cafes, restaurants, pubs, and shops along the main thoroughfare, Glebe Point Road. It's a good place for budget-conscious travelers, only 15 minutes from the city. Take the light rail from Central Station or Darling Harbour.

Bondi & the Southern Beaches Some of Sydney's most glamorous surf beaches—Bondi, Bronte, and Coogee—lie along the South Pacific coast, southeast of the city center. Bondi has a wide sweep of beach (crowded in summer), some interesting restaurants and bars, and plenty of attitude—but no train station. It's a 40-minute bus ride (bus no. 333) from Circular Quay. (Buy ticket in advance at a newsstand or 7-Eleven store.) Bus no. 440 goes to Bronte from Railway Square; bus no. 373 travels to Coogee from Circular Quay.

Watsons Bay Known for The Gap—a section of dramatic sea cliffs—Watsons Bay has

several good restaurants and a nice beer garden. It's a terrific spot to spend a sunny afternoon. Take bus no. 324 from Circular Quay, or a ferry from Wharf 4.

NORTH OF SYDNEY HARBOUR

North Sydney You can see the giant clown face of Luna Park from Circular Quay, but North Sydney—across the Harbour Bridge—has little in the way of tourist attractions, being mostly a business area. Chatswood (take train from Central or Wynyard station) has some good suburban-type shopping.

The North Shore Across the Harbour Bridge, gorgeous Balmoral Beach, Taronga Zoo, and upscale boutiques are the attractions in Mosman. Take a ferry from Circular Quay (Wharf 2) to Taronga Zoo (10 min.) and a bus to Balmoral Beach (another 10 min.).

Manly Half an hour from Circular Quay by ferry, Manly is famous for its ocean beach and scores of cheap food outlets.

WEST OF THE CITY CENTER

Balmain Once Sydney's main shipbuilding area, in the last few decades Balmain has become trendy and expensive, with lots of restaurants and pubs. There's a popular Saturday market at the local church. Take bus nos. 441 or 442 from Town Hall or a ferry from Circular Quay.

Getting Around Sydney

State Transit operates the city's buses and ferry network; **Sydney Trains** runs the urban and suburban trains; and **Sydney Ferries** runs the public passenger ferries. Some private bus lines operate buses in the outer suburbs. In addition, a light rail line runs between Central Station and Wentworth Park in Pyrmont; an expansion is in the works and slated for completion in 2019.

Infoline (www.transportnsw.info; 🕾 **131 500**) is a one-stop search engine for bus, train, light rail, and ferry timetables. Public transit fares are subject to change, so the prices below should act only as a guide.

BY PUBLIC BUS

Buses are frequent and reliable and cover a wide area of metropolitan Sydney. For regular public buses, the minimum fare (which covers most short hops in the city) is A$2.60 for a 3km (1.8-mile) "section." The farther you go, the cheaper each section is. For example, the 44km (27-mile) trip to Palm Beach, way past Manly, costs A$5.60. Sections are marked on bus-stand signs, but if you're confused or in doubt, ask the bus driver.

Most buses bound for the northern suburbs, including night buses to Manly and the bus to Taronga Zoo, leave from Wynyard Park on Carrington Street, behind the Wynyard train station on George Street. Buses to the southern beaches, such as Bondi and Bronte, and the western and eastern suburbs leave from Circular Quay. Buses to Balmain leave from behind the QVB.

Buses run from 4:30am to around midnight during the week, less frequently on weekends and holidays. Some night buses to outer suburbs run throughout the night. You can buy single tickets onboard from the driver, if you don't have an Opal Card (see below).

BY SIGHTSEEING BUS

Bright red open-top **Big Bus Sydney** buses operate daily on two routes, around Sydney city and around Bondi Beach. The city circuit takes in 23 places of interest, including the Sydney Opera House, the Royal Botanic Garden, the State Library, Mrs. Macquarie's Chair, the Art Gallery of New South Wales, Kings Cross, Elizabeth Bay House, the QVB, Sydney Tower, the Australian Museum, Chinatown, Darling Harbour, and The Rocks. Bus stops are

---

Travel with an Opal Card

An electronic ticketing system, the **Opal Card** (www.opal.com.au, 🕾 **02/136 725**) is used for trains, buses, ferries, and light rail. While you can buy single tickets, these still use an electronic Opal Card. It is much cheaper to travel with an Opal Card. Buy your card at train stations, or from convenience stores, newsagents, and other shops (listed online).

There is no charge for the card, but you must pay a minimum value of A$10 for an adult card (or A$5 for a child's card). Then you top up the payment as needed at authorized retailers, train stations, online, by phone, or via the Opal app. On Sundays your card allows all-day travel for a maximum of A$2.60.

An open-top Sydney Big Bus sightseeing bus on George Street, the city's main drag.

identified by a distinctive red sign. The interval between services is about 15 to 20 minutes, and you can board the bus at any stop on the route. The first departure from Alfred Street (near the corner of Pitt St.) at Circular Quay is at 8:30am, and the last service returns you to Circular Quay at 7:30pm.

The Bondi route travels a 30km (19-mile) circuit around the eastern harborside bays and coastal beaches. The 10 stops along the way include Chinatown, Sydney Tower, Double Bay, Rose Bay, Bondi Beach, North Bondi, and Paddington's Oxford Street. The interval between the hop-on-hop-off services is around 30 minutes. The first departure is from Central Station (Stop A on Pitt St., bus bay 18) at 9:30am. Tickets, which allow you to do both the Sydney and Bondi tours, cost A$55 for adults, A$38 for children 5 to 16, and A$148 for a family of four for 24 hours; or A$75 adults, A$50 children, and A$200 families for 48 hours. If you stay on the bus, the full circuit of each tour will take around 90 minutes. When planning your itinerary, remember that some attractions, such as museums, close at 5pm. Buy tickets on board the bus. Call ℂ **02/9567 8400** for details or check out www.theaustralianexplorer.com.au.

BY FERRY

The best way to get a taste of a city that revolves around its harbor is to jump aboard a ferry. The main ferry terminal is at Circular Quay. For ferry information, call ℂ **131 500,** check out **www.transportnsw.info**, or visit the ferry information office opposite Wharf 4. One-way trips within the inner harbor (virtually everywhere except Manly) cost A$7.10 for adults and A$3.50 for children ages 4 to 15. Kids 3 and under travel free.

The ferry to Manly takes 30 minutes, and one-way tickets cost A$8.70 for adults and A$4.35 for children. It leaves from Wharf 3. Ferries run from 6am

The best—and cheapest—way to see Sydney Harbour is from the deck of a passenger ferry.

to midnight. You can also use your Opal Card on the privately run **Manly Fast Ferry** (www.manlyfastferry.com.au; ℂ **02/9583 1199**) which departs from Wharf 6 at Circular Quay. Tickets cost around A$18 adults and A$11 kids, round-trip, depending on the time of day. The first ferry leaves Circular Quay at 6:40am and the last at 7:30pm; the last fast ferry departs Manly at 7:50pm. Ferries operate every 25 minutes or so and the journey takes 18 minutes. Fast Ferry also offers a Harbour Beaches sightseeing ferry (Sat and Sun only) that goes from Manly to Watson's Bay and Rose Bay, for A$15 adults, half price for children, and A$38 for a family.

BY TRAIN

Sydney's publicly owned train system is a good news/bad news way to get around. The good news is that it can be a cheap and relatively efficient way to see the city; the bad news is that the system is limited. Many tourist areas—including Manly, Bondi Beach, and Darling Harbour—are not connected to the network. Though trains tend to run regularly, the timetable is unreliable. And many carriages aren't air-conditioned, so it can be really hot in summer.

Single tickets within the city center cost A$4.20 adults and A$2.10 children. Round-trip tickets cost twice as much. Weekly tickets are also available. Information is available from **Infoline** (www.transportnsw.info; or ℂ **131 500** in Australia).

BY METRO LIGHT RAIL

A system of trams runs on a 3.6km (2¼-mile) route between Central Station and Wentworth Park in Pyrmont. The route is currently being extended to a 12km (7½-mile) network that will have 19 stops, running from Circular Quay along George Street to Central Station, through Surry Hills to Moore Park, then to Kensington and Kingsford and Randwick. Services are expected to start running in early 2020; see www.sydneylightrail.transport.nsw.gov.au for updates. The current light rail line provides good access to Chinatown, Paddy's Markets, Darling Harbour, The Star casino and entertainment complex, and the Sydney Fish Markets; and from Pyrmont to inner-west suburbs such as Glebe and Leichhardt. Trams run every 10 minutes. The one-way fare is A$2.60 to A$4.30 for adults and A$1.30 to A$2.10 for kids 4 to 15, depending on the distance. You will need to buy an Opal Card (p. 54), even for a single trip. Round-trip tickets are available. Call ℭ **131 500** or check out www.transportnsw.info for details.

BY TAXI

Several taxi companies serve the city center and suburbs. All journeys are metered. If you cross either way on the Harbour Bridge or through the Harbour Tunnel, it will cost a few extra dollars (depending on the time of day). An extra 10 percent will be added if you pay by credit card.

In the city, taxis line up at stands such as those opposite Circular Quay and Central Station. They are also frequently found in front of hotels. A yellow light on top of the cab means it's vacant. Cabs can be hard to come by on Friday and Saturday nights and between 2 and 3pm every day, when cabbies are changing shifts after 12 hours on the road. Passengers must wear seatbelts in the front and back seats. The **Taxi Complaints Hotline** (ℭ **1800/648 478** in Australia) deals with problem taxi drivers. Taxis are licensed to carry up to four people.

The main taxi companies are **Taxis Combined Services** (www.taxiscombined.com.au; ℭ **133 300**), **Silver Service Fleet** (www.silverservice.com.au; ℭ **133 100**), **RSL Cabs** (www.rslcabs.com.au; ℭ **02/9581 1111**), **Legion Cabs** (www.legioncabs.com.au; ℭ **131 451**), **Premier Cabs** (www.premiercabs.com.au; ℭ **131 017**), and **St. George Cabs** (www.stgeorgecabs.com.au; ℭ **132 166**). **Uber** also operates in Sydney.

BY WATER TAXI

Water taxis operate 24 hours a day and are a quick, convenient way to get to waterfront restaurants, harbor attractions, and some suburbs. They can also be chartered for private cruises. Fares for a direct transfer are based on an initial flag-fall for the hire of the vessel and then a charge per person traveling. A 30-minute jaunt on Sydney Harbour costs A$20 adults, A$15 children 5 to 15. On most transfers, the more people traveling, the lower the fare per person. The main operators are **Yellow Water Taxis** (www.yellowwatertaxis.com.au; ℭ **1800/326 822** in Australia) and **Water Taxis Combined** (www.watertaxis.com.au; ℭ **02/9555 8888**).

BY CAR

Traffic restrictions, parking, and congestion can make getting around by car frustrating, but if you plan to visit some of the outer suburbs or take excursions elsewhere in New South Wales, renting a car will give you more flexibility.

The **National Roads and Motorists' Association (NRMA)** is the New South Wales auto club; for emergency breakdown service call ☏ **131 111.**

Tolls apply for some roads, including the Cross City Tunnel and Sydney Harbour Bridge; increasingly you must go through automatic toll booths using a prepaid electronic tag called an **E-Tag.** If you are renting a car, you may be provided with an E-Tag, but make sure to ask about how you pay. Drivers without E-Tags have 2 days to pay; call the **Roads and Traffic Authority** at ☏ **131 865** within 2 days for details on your payment options.

Car-rental agencies in Sydney include **Avis,** 395 Pitt St. (www.avis.com.au; ☏ **02/8255 1616**); **Budget,** 93 William St., Kings Cross (www.budget.com.au; ☏ **02/8255 9600**); **Europcar,** 818 George St. (www.europcar.com.au; ☏ **02/8255 9050**); **Hertz,** corner of William and Riley streets, Kings Cross (www.hertz.com.au; ☏ **02/9360 6621**); and **Thrifty,** 9A York St. (www. thrifty.com.au; ☏ **02/9276 7330**). All agencies also have desks at the airport. One of the best-value operations is **Bayswater Car Rental,** 180 William St., Kings Cross (www.bayswatercarrental.com.au; ☏ **02/9360 3622**), which has small cars from around A$40 a day, sometimes less.

[FastFACTS] SYDNEY

ATMs/Banks Banking hours are Mon–Fri 9am–5pm. Many banks, especially in the city center, are also open Saturday 9:30am–12:30pm. ATMs are easy to find in the city center and most are available 24 hrs.

Business Hours General office hours are Mon–Fri 9am–5pm. Shopping hours are usually 8:30am–5:30pm daily (9am–5pm Sat). Most stores stay open until 9pm on Thursday. Most city-center stores are open 10am–4pm on Sunday.

Dentists CBD Dental Practice, Level 2, 74 Castlereagh St. (www.cbdden tal.com.au; ☏ **02/9221 2453**), offers same-day emergency treatment. It's open by appointment Mon–Fri 8am–6pm. The **Sydney**

Dental Hospital is on 2 Chalmers St., Surry Hills (☏ **02/9293 3200**).

Doctors & Hospitals St. Vincent's Hospital is at Victoria and Burton sts. in Darlinghurst, near Kings Cross (☏ **02/8382 1111**). In the city center, the **V Health Plus** medical center (☏ **02/ 8188 2299**), 40 Park St. (corner of Pitt St.), is open Mon–Fri 8:30am–6pm, and the **Travellers' Medical & Vaccination Centre,** Level 7, the Dymocks Building, 428 George St. (www.travel doctor.com.au; ☏ **02/9221 7133**), administers travel-related vaccinations and medications Mon–Fri 9am–5pm (until 8pm Thurs), and 9am–1pm Sat. Appointments essential.

Embassies & Consulates All foreign embassies are based in Canberra. The following

consulates are in Sydney: **Canada,** Level 5, 111 Harrington St. (☏ **02/9364 3000**); **Britain,** Level 16, 1 Macquarie Place (☏ **02/ 9247 7521**); and **New Zealand,** 20 Bond St. (☏ **02/ 9270 5900.** The **US Consulate General** is in Melbourne (p. 113).

Emergencies Dial ☏ **000** to call the police, the fire service, or an ambulance. Call the **NRMA** for car breakdowns (☏ **131 111**). Other emergency lines include the **Poisons Information Centre** (☏ **131 126**), the **Rape Crisis Centre** (☏ **1800/424 017** in Australia), and the 24-hr. **Lifeline** counseling service (☏ **131 114**).

Mail & Postage The **General Post Office (GPO)** is at 1 Martin Place (☏ **02/ 9244 3711**). It's open

Mon–Fri 8:15am–5:30pm and Sat 10am–2pm. For the nearest post office, call ☏ **131 318** or find it online at www.auspost.com.au.

Newspapers & Magazines The *Sydney Morning Herald* is available throughout metropolitan Sydney. The daily *The Australian* is available nationwide. The metropolitan *Daily Telegraph* is a more casual read. A newcomer to the market is *The Saturday Paper,* an independent weekend newspaper. The *International Herald Tribune* and other U.S. and U.K. newspapers can be found at Circular Quay newspaper stands and most news dealers. The quarterly *Time Out Sydney* is a free guide to everything that's on in and around the city (find the online version at www.timeout.com/Sydney). It's handed out at major train stations, hotels, cafes, shops, and entertainment venues.

Pharmacies Most suburbs have pharmacies that are open late. For after-hours referral, contact the **Chemist Emergency Prescription Referral Service** (☏ **02/9467 7100**).

Police In an emergency, dial ☏ **000.** Make nonemergency police inquiries through the **City Central** police station (☏ **131 444,** or 02/9265 6499).

Safety Sydney is generally a safe city, but as anywhere else, it's good to keep your wits about you and your wallet hidden. Be wary in the evenings in Kings Cross, Redfern, around Central Station, and on the cinema strip on George Street near Town Hall station—the latter is a hangout for local gangs. Other places of concern are the back lanes of Darlinghurst, around the naval base at Woolloomooloo, and along the Bondi restaurant strip when sunburned drunken tourists spill out after midnight. If traveling by train at night, ride in the carriages next to the guard's van, marked with a blue light on the outside.

Wi-Fi Sydney has a widespread network of free Wi-Fi hot spots around the city center and even onboard Sydney Ferries.

WHERE TO STAY IN SYDNEY

The best location for lodging in Sydney is in The Rocks and around Circular Quay—a short stroll from the Sydney Opera House, the Harbour Bridge, the Royal Botanic Garden, and the ferry terminals.

Hotels around Darling Harbour offer good access to museums, the Sydney Aquarium, and The Star casino. Most Darling Harbour hotels are a 10- to 15-minute walk, or a short light rail trip, from Town Hall and the central shopping district.

More hotels are grouped around Kings Cross, Sydney's red-light district. Some hotels here are among the city's best; you'll also find a range of cheaper lodgings and hostels. Kings Cross can sometimes be unnerving (and noisy), especially on Friday and Saturday nights when the strip joints and nightclubs are jumping, but it's close to excellent restaurants and cafes around Kings Cross, Darlinghurst, and Oxford Street.

If you want to stay near the beach, check out the options in Manly and Bondi, though you should consider their distance from the city center and the lack of trains to these areas. A taxi to Manly from the city will cost around A$55 and to Bondi around A$35.

Almost all hotels offer nonsmoking rooms. Most moderately priced to expensive rooms will have tea- and coffee-making facilities and an iron and ironing board. Coffeemakers are rare in Australian hotels, which instead offer

Central Sydney Hotels

Adina Apartment Hotel Sydney Central **16**
Arts Hotel **19**
The Australian Hotel **5**
The Darling **13**
Fraser Suites Sydney **14**
Hotel 59 **22**
The Hughenden **20**
Hyatt Regency Sydney **10**
Kirketon Hotel Sydney **23**
The Langham **3**
The Lord Nelson Brewery Hotel **2**
Pier One Sydney Harbour **1**
Railway Square YHA **17**
The Russell **6**
Sir Stamford at Circular Quay **7**
Sofitel Sydney Darling Harbour **12**
Sydney Central YHA **15**
Sydney Harbour YHA – The Rocks **4**
The Tank Stream Hotel **8**
Travelodge Hotel Sydney **18**
Vibe Hotel Rushcutters **21**
Westin Sydney **9**
Woolbrokers Hotel **11**

KINGS CROSS

Hughes St.

Orwell St.

Earl St.

Victoria St.

Darlinghurst Rd.

St.

Keller.

Bayswater

Kings Cross Rd.

22

21

Surry St.

Broughham St.

Dowling St.

Stephen St.

McElhone St.

Kings Cross

Craigend St.

Nimrod St.

West St.

WOOLLOOMOOLOO

Wilson St.

Harmer St.

Cathedral St.

Kirketon Rd.

Darlinghurst Rd.

23

Victoria St.

Liverpool St.

DARLINGHURST

PADDINGTON

20

Hopewell St.

Bourke St.

Talbot Pl.

Forbes St.

Clapton Pl.

Thomson St.

Forbes St.

Bourke St.

Burton St.

West St.

Barcom Ave.

Boundary St.

1/4 mi

Sir John Young Crescent

The Domain

Palmer St.

Crown St.

Francis St.

Riley St.

Yurong Ln.

Stanley St.

Eastern Distributor

Crown St.

Foley St.

Oxford St.

Green Park

West St.

South Dowling St.

Oxford St.

Napier St.

Flinders St.

Clare St.

Albion St.

Fitzroy St.

19

0.25 km

Art Gallery Rd.

St. Marys Rd.

Phillip Park

Cook Park

William St.

St. Mary's Cathedral

College St.

Australian Museum

Yurong St.

Liverpool St.

St. Margaret's Hospital

0

0

Queens Square

St. James Rd.

St. James

Hyde Park

Anzac War Memorial

Museum

Nithsdale St.

Brisbane St.

Oxford St.

Campbell St.

Riley St.

Ann St.

SURRY HILLS

Waterloo St.

Albion Way

Albion St.

Commonwealth St.

Smith St.

Mary St.

Foveaux St.

King St.

Sydney Tower

Pitt Street Mall

Park St.

Elizabeth St.

Castlereagh St.

Wentworth Ave.

18

George St.

City Centre

Galeries Victoria

Town Hall

Pitt St.

Central St.

Goulburn St.

Campbell St.

Hay St.

Belmore Park

Pitt St.

Central Rail Station

To Sydney Airport

Central

Market St.

Queen Victoria Building

Town Hall

World Square

World Square

Eddy Ave.

York St.

St. Andrew's Cathedral

Bathurst St.

14

Lee St.

15

Clarence St.

Kent St.

Sussex St.

Liverpool St.

George St.

16 17

Pitt St.

Sussex St.

Dixon St.

Capitol Square

King St.

Harbour St.

Paddy's Markets

Quay St.

Sussex St.

Day St.

DARLING HARBOUR

Tumbalong Park

Her Majesty's Theatre

Ultimo Rd.

To Newtown

Slip St.

Darling Park

10

Wheat Rd.

Sydney Aquarium

Pyrmont Bridge

Darling Harbour (Tumbalong)

Cockle Bay

Sydney Exhibition Centre

Exhibition Centre

Darling Dr.

Pier St.

HAYMARKET

Powerhouse Museum

Harris St.

Hackett St.

National Maritime Museum

Pyrmont Bay

Murray St.

26

Harbourside

Harbourside Festival Marketplace

Convention

Sydney Convention Centre

12

Pyrmont St.

Pyrmont St.

William Henry St.

ULTIMO

To Glebe

Harris St.

Ada Pl.

Quarry St.

7

11

10

13

13

CityRail Stop

Light Rail Stop

Monorail Stop

Church

Information

Post Office

tea bags, instant coffee, small plastic milk cartons, and a kettle. Some smarter hotels have an in-room espresso machine.

MAKING A DEAL The prices given below for expensive hotels are mostly the **rack rates,** the recommended retail price, which guests can pay at the busiest periods if they book at short notice or walk in off the street. Check out **www.lastminute.com.au**, **www.wotif.com**, or a hotel's own website, for discounted rates. **Apartment hotels** may be worth considering, because you can save a bundle by cooking at least some of your own meals, and many also have free laundry facilities.

Most Australian hostels go beyond dorm-type accommodations and also offer private double rooms (some with en suite bathrooms) and a limited number of family rooms (sleeping four or five), making hostels a viable option for families and older travelers. Check **www.yha.com.au** for a full list of its eight Sydney hostels (some are listed in this section).

Around The Rocks & Circular Quay
EXPENSIVE

The Langham ★★★ This exclusive property, a 10-minute walk uphill from The Rocks and 15 minutes from Circular Quay (or a stroll down to Wynyard train station), is a turn-of-the-20th-century beauty competing for top-hotel-in-Sydney honors. It is also renowned for its personalized service. A multi-million-dollar refurbishment in 2014 created a more contemporary style, with a grand marble lobby and quiet guestrooms with huge bathrooms. Some rooms have city views; others look out over the harbor. The pool here is one of the best in Sydney. (Note the Southern Hemisphere constellations on the roof.) The Langham's day spa is one of the most exclusive in the city.

89–113 Kent St. www.langhamhotels.com. (© **02/9256 2222.** 98 units. A$450–A$563 double; A$600–A$3,000 suite. Parking A$60. Bus: nos. 339, 431, or 433. **Amenities:** Restaurant; bar; concierge; health club; chemical-free heated indoor pool; 24-hr. room service; sauna; lighted tennis court; free Wi-Fi.

Pier One Sydney Harbour ★★ Tucked just around the corner from Circular Quay, almost under the Harbour Bridge, Pier One is right on the waterfront (you can even arrive by boat at the private pontoon, if you wish). Some rooms offer harbor views, in both directions. Rooms are updated and contemporary, but may add interesting features, such as old timbers from the original Pier One Wharf, built in 1912. It's just far enough from the bustle of the city center to be in a world of its own but with all the benefits of being 5 minutes away.

11 Hickson Rd. www.pieronesydneyharbour.com.au. (© **02/8298 9999.** 189 units. A$280–A$400 double; A$530–A$1,280 suite. Valet parking A$60. Train, bus, or ferry: Circular Quay. **Amenities:** Restaurant; bar; babysitting; concierge; exercise room; room service; free Wi-Fi.

Sir Stamford at Circular Quay ★★★ This is one of my favorite Sydney hotels. It's plush and luxurious, but like all really great hotels the staff is friendly and the atmosphere relaxed rather than stuffy. It has a clubby European atmosphere, with gorgeous antique furniture, but the vibe is warm

The wonderfully located Pier One Sydney Harbour.

and welcoming. There's even a large mascot wombat (of the toy variety) called Morris who pops up in the most unexpected places (and can be with you for company, on request). The location is perfect, a short walk from Circular Quay and the Opera House, and just across the road from the Royal Botanic Garden. Rooms are large and luxurious, with good-size marble bathrooms. Most rooms have a small balcony. The rooms on the east side of the hotel have the best views across the Botanic Garden. Most rooms are accessible to wheelchairs.

93 Macquarie St. www.stamford.com.au/sscq. © **02/9252 4600.** 120 units. A$329–A$379 double; A$479–A$1,500 suite. Parking A$40. Train, bus, or ferry: Circular Quay. **Amenities:** Restaurant; bar; babysitting; concierge; exercise room; outdoor heated pool; room service; sauna; free Wi-Fi in-room (only if you book direct), in the business center, or for 30 min. in the lobby.

MODERATE

The Lord Nelson Brewery Hotel ★★★   Book a room upstairs in one of Sydney's oldest pubs (established in 1841) to be part of the city's living history. This attractive, three-story sandstone building is a busy pub on the ground floor, with hotel rooms on the second and third floors. The simple but stylishly outfitted rooms are compact, and some have walls made from convict-hewn sandstone blocks. The creaky floorboards, narrow corridors, wood fire, and boutique brewery in the bar add to Lord Nelson's colonial atmosphere without detracting from its essentially modern style. The smallest (and cheapest) of the rooms has a bathroom across the corridor; all the others have en suites.

19 Kent St. (at Argyle St.), The Rocks. www.lordnelsonbrewery.com. © **02/9251 4044.** 8 units. A$210 double with external bathroom; A$250 double with en suite bathroom. Rates include continental breakfast. No parking. Train or ferry: Circular Quay. **Amenities:** 2 restaurants; bar; free Wi-Fi.

The Russell ★★★   This is the coziest place to stay in The Rocks and perhaps in all of Sydney. It's more than 120 years old, and it shows its age wonderfully in the creaks of the floorboards. There are no harbor views, but all rooms provide immense character and are furnished in period style. Some have shared bathrooms (and all rooms have bathrobes in them). Single rooms are available for solo travelers. Guests have access to a sitting room with a small library and a balcony overlooking Circular Quay. The rooftop garden is another perfect spot for wonderful views of the harbor, with tables and chairs and sun umbrellas. A real find.

143A George St., The Rocks. www.therussell.com.au. ✆ **02/9241 3543.** 29 units, 19 with bathroom. A$169–A$209 double with shared bathroom; A$209–A$325 double with bathroom. Rates include continental breakfast. Parking nearby (A$25 for 24 hr. single entry). Train or ferry: Circular Quay. **Amenities:** Restaurant; lounge; free Wi-Fi.

INEXPENSIVE

The Australian Hotel ★   Rooms here are above one of Sydney's most historic pubs, but despite that, they are not noisy. Carry your bags up the narrow stairs and you'll find a charming—if somewhat frayed around the edges—little haven overlooking the action on the street. Each room has a double or queen bed, or twin beds, and the nine rooms share five bathrooms. The guest lounge, overlooking the street, has a TV, books and magazines, and nice little touches like free tea and coffee available all day, bowls of fruit, and a decanter of port. A second, quieter lounge is down another hallway. The Australian is clean, comfortable, and a bargain.

100 Cumberland St. (entry off Gloucester St.), The Rocks. www.australianheritagehotel. com. ✆ **02/9247 2229.** 9 units. A$149–A$159 double; A$299 family suite. Rates include continental breakfast. Train or ferry: Circular Quay. No parking. **Amenities:** Restaurant; bar; free Wi-Fi.

Sydney Harbour YHA–The Rocks ★★   The Sydney Harbour YHA offers basic, clean rooms at a very reasonable price for this sought-after part of the city. Some rooms have harbor views (if you crane your neck). All are air-conditioned, and even the dorms have private bathrooms. There are also some thoughtful design features, including an electric socket in each of the lockers, so you can securely charge your iPod/laptop/camera. It has a very large common area, and the roof terrace is an excellent place to hang out, particularly because of the fabulous views of the Opera House and the Sydney Harbour Bridge. *Note:* You do have to lug your luggage up a lot of steps to get to the building. There are also a couple of other YHA hostels worth considering (p. 66).

110 Cumberland St., The Rocks. www.yha.com.au. ✆ **02/8272 0900.** A$41–A$61 dorm; A$145–A$199 double; A$178–A$220 family room (sleeps 5). Train or ferry: Circular Quay. **Amenities:** Self-catering kitchen and dining area; Internet cafe; coffee bar; lounge; convenience store; free Wi-Fi.

In the City Center
EXPENSIVE
Adina Apartment Hotel Sydney Central ★★   Built in 1821, and once the parcels post office for Central Station next door, this Heritage-listed

property now offers elegant and roomy studios and apartments. My pick is the one-bedroom Premier apartments, which are on the higher levels of the hotel; some are corner rooms, which have wonderful round windows with views of the Central Station clock tower. There's no restaurant, but the hotel is surrounded by plenty of cafes and restaurants, and also offers a pantry service if you want to cook "at home."

2 Lee St., Haymarket. www.tfehotels.com. © **02/8396 9800.** 98 units. A$229–A$279 studio; A$259–A$289 1-bedroom apt; A$366–A$489 2-bedroom apt. Parking A$39. Train: Central. **Amenities:** Gym; Jacuzzi; outdoor heated pool; free Wi-Fi.

Fraser Suites Sydney ★★★
One of Sydney's most luxurious apartment hotels, Fraser Suites is just a few minutes' walk from the Queen Victoria Building and Darling Harbour. Choose from studios, one- and two-bedroom suites, or two- and three-bedroom penthouse suites. There are only seven apartments on each floor, and the views are to die for. Studios offer kitchenettes, while larger apartments have separate bedrooms, lounges, and full kitchen and laundry facilities. All rooms have Nespresso coffee machines, iPod docking stations, and a small study area. A buffet breakfast (A$32; A$14 kids) is available daily on the mezzanine floor, and room service is available for breakfast (6:30–10:30am) and dinner (6–11pm).

488 Kent St. www.sydney.frasershospitality.com. © **02/8823 8888.** 201 units. A$225 studio; A$280 1-bedroom suite; A$505 2-bedroom suite; A$999 penthouse. Self-parking A$42; valet parking A$52. Train: Town Hall. **Amenities:** Concierge; indoor heated pool, Jacuzzi; sauna; health club; free Wi-Fi.

Hyatt Regency Sydney ★★★
Opened in early 2017 after a A$250-million redevelopment, this super-swanky hotel is positioned between the city heart and Darling Harbour, across the street from the Sydney Aquarium and a short walk from Cockle Bay. It's one of the largest five-star properties in all of Australia, with 222 new rooms created, including suites and club rooms. Some rooms have views of Darling Harbour, and some have balconies. A highlight is the rooftop bar with harbor views.

161 Sussex St. www.sydney.regency.hyatt.com. © **02/8099 1234.** 892 units. A$270–A$405 double; A$540–A$567 suite. Parking A$70. Bus: no. 441. Train: Town Hall. **Amenities:** Restaurant; bar; concierge; 24-hr. gym; free Wi-Fi.

Westin Sydney ★★★
One of Sydney's most celebrated five-star hotels, the Westin is located in the center of the city, in the Martin Place pedestrian mall. Integrated into Sydney's original 19th-century General Post Office, the Westin has a charm that's modern and classic all at once. The large rooms have wonderfully comfortable beds and floor-to-ceiling windows. The hotel is home to several bars, restaurants, and clothing shops. Just steps from the central shopping streets and the Queen Victoria Building, and a 10- to 15-minute walk from both the Sydney Opera House and Darling Harbour, the hotel features an impressive seven-story atrium, a fabulous two-level health club, and an exclusive day spa.

1 Martin Place. www.starwoodhotels.com. © **02/8223 1111.** 416 units. A$280–A$490 double; A$3,220 suite. Parking A$68. Train: Martin Place. **Amenities:** Cafe; bar; babysitting; health club; day spa; free Wi-Fi.

MODERATE

The Tank Stream Hotel ★★   One of Sydney's newest hotels is situated on one of its most historic sites. Just a few minutes' walk from Circular Quay, the Sydney Opera House, Hyde Park, and Barangaroo, this modest but stylish hotel tells a terrific Sydney story. The Tank Stream is named for the freshwater stream that was the water source for Australia's first European colony in 1788. The hotel is built over the tank stream, and the hotel's wavelike forms reflect its position. Rooms are simply furnished and some are compact, but they are all you need and the location is hard to beat. The complimentary (non-alcoholic) minibar is a nice touch. Ask about underground tours of the original tank stream.

97–99 Pitt St. www.tankstreamhotel.com. ℂ **02/8222 1211.** 280 units. A$249–A$349 double. Train: Wynyard. **Amenities:** Restaurant; bar; free Wi-Fi.

Travelodge Hotel Sydney ★   This business-oriented hotel is cheap for Sydney, comfortable, and reasonably well located, making it a good option for travelers who just want to unpack and explore. The Ikea-style rooms include a kitchenette with a microwave and a queen bed or two twin-size beds. From here it's a short walk to Oxford Street, Town Hall, and Hyde Park.

27–33 Wentworth Ave. www.tfehotels.com. ℂ **1300/886 886** in Australia, or 02/8267 1700. 406 units. A$209–A$299 double. Parking (around corner) A$25. Train: Museum. **Amenities:** Restaurant; babysitting; health club; free Wi-Fi.

INEXPENSIVE

Sydney Central YHA ★★   This multiple-award-winning hostel is one of the biggest and busiest in the world, so book as far ahead as possible. The rooms are clean and basic, and come dorm-style for four, six, or eight people or as doubles (with private bathrooms). Family rooms (for up to 4 people) are also available. In the basement is a bar with pool tables and occasional entertainment. There's also an entertainment room with more pool tables and e-mail facilities, TV rooms on every floor, and a cinema. The YHA is accessible to travelers with disabilities.

There's also the **Railway Square YHA** at the corner of Upper Carriage Lane and Lee Street, or enter via the Henry Dean Plaza (ℂ **02/9281 9666**). The historic 1904 building adjoining "Platform Zero" at Central Railway Station has 64 beds in four- to eight-bed dorm rooms and 10 double rooms. Some dorm rooms are in old railway carriages. The facility has a sauna, pool, Internet cafe, tour desk, indoor and outdoor communal areas, and a self-catering kitchen.

11 Rawson Place (at Pitt St., outside Central Station). www.yha.com.au. ℂ **02/9281 9000.** 150 units. A$33–A$40 dorm bed; A$117–A$145 double/twin per room; A$160 family room (sleeps 4). Parking A$25. Train: Central. **Amenities:** Restaurant; bar; small heated outdoor pool; sauna; free Wi-Fi.

In Darling Harbour

EXPENSIVE

The Darling ★★★   Part of The Star casino complex, this chic hotel stands out from the crowd with splashes of color—purple sheets, even!—and luxurious amenities. All rooms have floor-to-ceiling windows; some boast views of the Sydney Harbour Bridge. The marble bathrooms have rain showers, bathtubs, and gorgeous Molton Brown products. Touch-controls from the bedside allow you to operate the window blinds, air-conditioning, and television (although sometimes these prove challenging!). It's an easy walk to anywhere in Darling Harbour, or across the Pyrmont Bridge to the city center.

80 Pyrmont St., Pyrmont. www.thedarling.com.au. © **1800/800 830** in Australia, or 02/9777 9888. 171 units. A$402–A$440 double; A$441–A$1,156 suite. Valet parking A$45–A$55. Bus: no. 389. Light rail: The Star. **Amenities:** 5 restaurants; 3 bars; outdoor heated pool; gym; spa; free Wi-Fi.

Sofitel Sydney Darling Harbour ★★★
From the moment you arrive, the "wow!" factor is strong at this beautiful hotel, one of Sydney's newest. All rooms are spacious, but for something special book a corner room, where the bathtub has one of the best views of Darling Harbour. Rooms are decorated in subtle colors without the blandness that besets so many contemporary hotels, and the beds are supremely comfortable. The Champagne Bar has stellar views of the city skyline. And of course, it all has a French flavor. The hotel is next door to the Sydney International Convention Centre and just a short walk across the Pyrmont Bridge to the city center.

12 Darling Dr., Pyrmont. www.sofitelsydneydarlingharbour.com.au. © **02/8388 8888.** 590 units. A$429–A$649 double; A$879–A$1,129 suite. Valet parking A$79. Bus: no. 389. Light rail: Convention Centre. **Amenities:** 1 restaurant; 3 bars; babysitting; outdoor pool; gym; spa; free Wi-Fi.

INEXPENSIVE

Woolbrokers Hotel ★
You'll find this friendly, circa-1886 Heritage building on the far side of Darling Harbour, next to the prominent Novotel hotel and hidden behind a monstrous parking garage. It's on a noisy road, so unless you're used to traffic avoid the rooms at the front. Rooms are simply furnished and come with a fridge and TV. Room no. 3 is one of the nicer choices. Family rooms are outfitted with a king-size bed and a pair of bunk beds. The hotel has 19 shared bathrooms, though some rooms have private bathrooms. Check the website for discounts. This is a good budget option, but note that there is no elevator or air-conditioning.

22 Allen St., Pyrmont. www.woolbrokershotel.com.au. © **02/9552 4773.** 27 units. A$94 double with shared bathroom; A$134 double with bathroom; A$154 family room (sleeps 4). Continental breakfast A$7.50. Parking A$16 (across the street). Bus: no. 501. Light rail: Convention Centre. **Amenities:** Guest laundry; free Wi-Fi.

In Kings Cross & Suburbs Nearby
INEXPENSIVE

Hotel 59 ★
This popular, well-priced, friendly B&B is well worth considering if you want to be near the Kings Cross action but far enough away to get some peace and quiet. It has two rooms for single travelers and three family rooms that can sleep two adults and two children. Rooms are well kept and comfortable, with private bathrooms and TVs. A flight of stairs and

the lack of an elevator might make Hotel 59 unsuitable for travelers with disabilities.

59 Bayswater Rd., Kings Cross. www.hotel59.com.au. © **02/9360 5900.** 9 units. A$130–A$145 double. Rates include breakfast. No parking. Train: Kings Cross. **Amenities:** Cafe; TV lounge; free Wi-Fi with most rates.

Kirketon Hotel Sydney ★ Popular among hip, fashionable types, this slightly offbeat boutique hotel in Darlinghurst offers rooms with modernist furniture and custom-made fittings, including mirrored headboards and sleek bathrooms hidden away behind mirrored doors. Standard rooms are quite compact and come with a double bed. Premium rooms have a queen-size bed. Superior and Executive rooms are quite large, with a king-size bed, and some have a small balcony overlooking the main road. For a quiet night, ask for a room away from the main road.

229 Darlinghurst Rd., Darlinghurst. www.kirketon.com.au. © **1800/332 920** in Australia, or 02/9332 2011. 40 rooms. A$149–A$199 double. Parking A$25. **Amenities:** Restaurant; bar; gym; free Wi-Fi.

Vibe Hotel Rushcutters Bay Sydney ★★ Compared with other hotels in its price bracket, this flagship Vibe Hotel on the far side of Kings Cross really is a bargain, especially when you book online. Standard rooms are a reasonable size, and I love the rooms' brightly accented and colorful—well, yes—vibe. All rooms have king-size beds (which split into twins if necessary), and families can get connecting rooms. The whole place underwent a major refurbishment in 2016, including the heated rooftop swimming pool and gym. The hotel has a good cafe, called **Curve.**

100 Bayswater Rd., Rushcutters Bay. www.tfehotels.com.au. © **02/8353 8988.** 258 units. A$149–A$172 double; A$246–A$449 suite. Parking A$25. Train: Kings Cross. **Amenities:** Restaurant; bar; concierge; gym; heated outdoor pool; free Wi-Fi.

Around Oxford Street & Darlinghurst
MODERATE

The Hughenden ★★ I love this boutique hotel, part of which is set in an 1870s mansion and full of antique furnishings. It's warm and comfortable with lots of sitting areas—including a den packed with books—and a permanent exhibition of illustrations from children's books. Hardly surprising given that one of the owners is children's book author Susanne Gervay. Guests are often writers and artists too, though you might run into cricket buffs, given the proximity to the Sydney Cricket Ground. Wander through to enjoy the artwork as well as the architecture, including lovely black marble fireplaces. It's in a great location, at the top end of Oxford Street and just across the road from Centennial Park. Another eight suites are located in a house across the street.

14 Queen St., Woollahra. www.thehughenden.com.au. © **02/9363 4863.** 45 units. A$152–A$276 double; A$326 suite; A$306 family room (sleeps up to 5). Rates include breakfast. Limited secured parking (A$33 per night). Bus: no. 440. **Amenities:** Restaurant; bar; guest lounge; free Wi-Fi.

INEXPENSIVE

Arts Hotel ★   This family-run hotel is right in the heart of the action in one of Sydney's most popular shopping, entertainment, restaurant, and gay pub and club areas. About half of the hotel's guests come from overseas, and it's popular with Americans during Mardi Gras. Rooms are simple, compact, and motel-like, but are fine for a few nights. Standard rooms and garden rooms (which are quieter) have two single beds or a queen-size bed. Art rooms are more up-market, with rainfall showerheads, hypoallergenic bedding, art on the walls, and other little luxury touches—and are offered as upgrades for bookings of 4 nights or more.

21 Oxford St., Paddington. www.artshotel.com.au. © **02/9361 0211.** 64 units. A$130–A$188 double. Limited free parking. Bus: no. 378 from Central Station or no. 380 from Circular Quay. **Amenities:** Breakfast cafe; bikes; gym; small heated outdoor pool; free Wi-Fi.

In Bondi

Bondi Beach is a good place to stay if you want to be close to the surf and sand. Two recommended backpacker hostels are good for budget-conscious travelers: **Surfside Backpackers,** 35a Hall St. (www.surfsidebackpackers.com.au; © **02/9365 4900**), offers four- to eight-person dorm rooms from A$38. Single, double, and family rooms are in a separate building (at higher rates). **Noah's Bondi,** 2 Campbell Parade (www.noahsbondibeach.com; © **02/9365 7544**), has a great ambience and modern four- to eight-person dorm rooms for A$21 to A$31 (doubles are A$65–A$75). Rates are higher in the summer peak season (Dec–Jan). Ask about weekly rates.

EXPENSIVE

Hotel Ravesis ★★   Right on Australia's most famous golden sands, this boutique property offers chic and modern minimalist rooms with white marble bathrooms and Juliet balconies. All rooms were renovated in 2017. Side View doubles are spacious and modern, but the Beach Front king rooms have the best ocean views. Four split-level suites have a bathroom downstairs, and a bedroom, lounge area, and private outdoor terrace on the second level. There is a lively bar downstairs (which can mean noise until late, especially on weekends) and a good restaurant.

Corner of Hall St. and Campbell Parade. www.hotelravesis.com. © **02/9365 4422.** 12 units. A$285–A$409 double; A$335–A$525 suite. Valet parking A$20. Bus: no. 333. **Amenities:** Restaurant; bar; room service; free Wi-Fi.

In Manly

If you decide to stay in Manly for a few days, consider buying a multiple-ride ferry ticket, which will save you a bit of money. But be warned that ferries from Sydney stop running at midnight. If you get stranded, you'll be facing an expensive taxi ride back.

Manly has several backpacker hostels that are worth checking out; the best of the bunch is **Manly Backpackers Beachside,** 28 Raglan St. (www.

manlybackpackers.com.au; © **1800/662 500** in Australia, or 02/9977 3411), which offers dorm beds from A$34 to A$50 and doubles from A$90 to A$159, depending on the time of year (pricier during peak summer period).

MODERATE

Manly Paradise Beachfront Motel and Apartments ★   The refurbished rooms are spacious, and some offer glimpses of the sea. The traffic can make it a little noisy in your room during the day, but you'll probably be on the beach anyway. Motel rooms come with queen, double, or twin beds, and the magnificent roomy apartments have everything you need, including a full kitchen with dishwasher, a washing machine and dryer, and two bathrooms (one with a tub). Sea views from the main front balcony are heart-stopping, and there's a pool on the rooftop.

54 N. Steyne, Manly. www.manlyparadise.com.au. © **1800/815 789** in Australia, or 02/9977 5799. 40 units. A$175–A$300 double (motel); A$350–A$535 2-bedroom apt; A$435–A$630 3-bedroom apt. Parking A$25 for motel; free for apts. Ferry: Manly. **Amenities:** Outdoor rooftop pool; free Wi-Fi.

At the Airport

MODERATE

Stamford Plaza Sydney Airport ★★   At the other end of the scale, this is Sydney's best airport hotel (just 7 min. from the terminals via the A$7 airport shuttle). It has the largest rooms, each with a king or two double beds, access to airport information, and a good-size bathroom with tub. Suites and deluxe rooms have airport views but all windows have been reinforced to keep out the aircraft noise!

Corner of O'Riordan and Robey sts., Mascot. www.stamford.com.au/ssa. © **02/9317 2200.** 315 units. A$209–A$259 double; A$259–A$809 suite. Parking A$30. **Amenities:** 2 restaurants; bar; babysitting; concierge; gym; Jacuzzi; outdoor rooftop pool; room service; sauna; free Wi-Fi (if booking direct).

INEXPENSIVE

Ibis Budget Sydney Airport ★   If all you want is a clean place to crash before an early flight, this no-frills hotel will do the job. This Ibis has almost no facilities, but it's next to a couple of fast-food joints and has an all-you-can-eat breakfast. Rooms are air-conditioned and have TVs. You can reach the airport via the Airport Shuttle, which costs A$7 (or walk there in 10 min.).

5 Ross Smith Ave., Mascot. www.accorhotels.com. © **02/8339 1840.** 200 units. A$114–A$164 double. Parking A$25 per day. **Amenities:** Breakfast room; free Wi-Fi.

WHERE TO EAT IN SYDNEY

Sydney is a gourmet paradise, boasting some of the world's best chefs. Asian and Mediterranean cooking have had a major influence on Australian cuisine, with spices and herbs finding their way into most dishes. Immigration has brought with it almost every type of cuisine, from African to Tibetan, Russian to Vietnamese.

Most moderate and inexpensive restaurants in Sydney are **BYO,** as in "bring your own" bottle (wine only), though some places also have extensive wine and beer lists. More moderately priced restaurants are also introducing corkage fees, which mean you pay anywhere from A$2 to A$10 per person for the privilege of having the waiter open your bottle of wine. Very expensive restaurants are usually fully licensed and don't allow you to BYO.

Sydney's **cheap eats** congregate in center-city areas such as Crown Street in Darlinghurst, and Glebe Point Road in Glebe. There are also inexpensive joints scattered among the more upscale restaurants in Kings Cross and along trendy Oxford Street.

Some restaurants add a surcharge on public holidays and Sundays, usually around 5 or 10 percent per person. Restaurants argue that it's difficult to get staff to work on these days, so they need to provide a cash incentive. In Australia, waiters rely on their wages rather than tips.

Smoking is banned in all Sydney restaurants, except at some with sidewalk tables or courtyards. Always ask before lighting up.

4

Sydney is a great place to try the Australian style of contemporary cuisine, which emphasizes fresh ingredients and a creative blend of European styles with Asian influences. And because a really great meal will stay in your mind long after your visit to Australia is over, I've included some of Australia's very top restaurants here. The prices may be high but are almost always well worth it, especially if you are looking for an experience rather than just a meal.

Breakfast is big in Australia, a favorite time of day to meet friends and linger over a hearty repast (albeit often a late one). As for coffee, Australians favor a range of Italian-style creations. Ask for a latte if you just want coffee with milk.

And remember that in Australia, the first course is called the entree and the second course the main.

Circular Quay, City Center & The Rocks
EXPENSIVE

Aria ★★★ CONTEMPORARY With front-row views of the Harbour Bridge and the Sydney Opera House, Aria stands in one of the most enviable spots in the city. The windows overlooking the water are huge, the atmosphere is elegant and buzzy, and many of the intimate tables have a stunning view. The food, created by one of Australia's great chefs, Matt Moran, is imaginative and mouthwatering. Some examples: guinea fowl with persimmon, mustard, and brown vinegar; or pink snapper with fungi, snake beans, ginger, and shallot. For lunch on weekdays, a set menu offers two or three courses (A$90 or A$120). Pre- and post-theater menus are available for the same prices from 5:30 to 7pm and after 10pm respectively. Reservations are essential.

1 Macquarie St. www.ariasydney.com. ℂ **02/9240 2255.** A$145 for 3 courses, A$170 for 4 courses. Seasonal 6-course tasting menu A$205, or A$320 with wine pairings. Mon–Fri noon–2:15pm and 5:30–10:30pm; Sat noon–1.30pm and 5–11pm; Sun noon–1:45pm and 5:30–10pm. Train, bus, or ferry: Circular Quay.

Central Sydney Restaurants

Aria **5**
Bennelong **6**
Bills **13**
Café Hernandez **15**
City Extra **3**
The Four in Hand **12**
Govinda's **14**
Harts Pub **2**
Love.fish Barangaroo **1**
Nick's Seafood
 Restaurant **9**
Otto Ristorante **7**
Sydney Cove Oyster Bar **4**
Tetsuya's **10**
The Taphouse **11**
Zaaffran **8**

You can get some really good food with a glass of wine or a schooner of beer on the side in several city pubs. Among the best is **The Four in Hand,** 105 Sutherland St., Paddington (www.fourinhand. com.au; ✆ **02/9326 2254**), which has a great restaurant and also does good bar meals, including hearty sandwiches and grilled steaks, with all main courses under A$30. **Harts Pub,** corner of Essex and Gloucester streets, The Rocks (www. hartspub.com; ✆ **02/9251 6030**), has a great range of craft beers, with gourmet and pub-grub offerings for A$20 to A$42. In Darlinghurst (Kings Cross), delve into the massive beer list at **The Taphouse,** 122 Flinders St. (www.taphousedarlo. com.au; ✆ **02/9360 0088**), and graze from the extensive menu; on Sundays, a roast dinner's on offer from noon on.

Bennelong ★★★ CONTEMPORARY   This is one of Australia's best restaurants, coupled with one of the world's best locations, in the Sydney Opera House. Executive chef Peter Gilmore and his team are creative but down-to-earth and that's reflected in the menu. There are several different areas in which to dine, from the casual Cured & Cultured in the beautiful Circle dining room (with those views of the Harbour Bridge) to the more formal lower level restaurant. Selections from the three-course dinner menu might include roasted quail with stone pot rice, fermented shiitake, sesame, and perilla; or wild Cape York barramundi with parsnip and hazelnuts and whole lemon puree. Pre- and post-theater sittings are offered (check website for details). Reservations are essential.

Sydney Opera House, Bennelong Point. www.bennelong.com.au. ✆ **02/9240 8000.** Lunch: 2 courses A$100, 3 courses A$135. Dinner: 3-course menu A$145. Bar tasting menu with 6 tasting plates A$65 in Cured & Cultured. Mon–Wed 5:30–9:30pm; Thurs 5:30–10:00pm; Fri–Sat noon–2:30pm and 5:30–10:00pm; Sun noon–2:30pm and 5:30–9:30pm. Train, bus, or ferry: Circular Quay.

Sydney Cove Oyster Bar ★★ SEAFOOD   Just before you reach the Sydney Opera House, you'll notice a couple of small shedlike buildings with tables and chairs set up to take in the stunning views of the harbor and bridge. This is where you'll find some of the best oysters in town. Oysters are A$54 for a dozen (A$27 for a half-dozen), but reliable mains, such as grilled barramundi or Atlantic salmon, tiger prawn linguini, or pasture-fed eye fillet steak, are also on the menu. Share a dozen oysters and follow up with more shellfish or tapas-style bites plus a bottle of crisp white wine or sparkling champagne. It's a perfect lunchtime spot on a sunny day.

Eastern Esplanade, Circular Quay East. www.sydneycoveoysterbar.com. ✆ **02/9247 2937.** Main courses A$36–A$59. Daily 11am–late. Train, bus, or ferry: Circular Quay.

Tetsuya's ★★★ JAPANESE/FRENCH FUSION   This is one of the world's best restaurants—it's that simple. To have a chance of getting a table, you need to book as early as possible, and you may be asked to reconfirm a few days before. Request a table next to the floor-to-ceiling windows with intimate views across a Japanese-inspired courtyard of maples and waterfalls. The service is impeccable and the food truly inspired—many diners consider this a once-in-a-lifetime experience. Chef Tetsuya Wakuda's signature dish is a confit of ocean trout served with a salad of celery, endive, apple, and ocean-trout roe.

529 Kent St. www.tetsuyas.com. ⓒ **02/9267 2900.** 9-course tasting menu A$230 per person. Tues–Fri 5:30–10pm; Sat noon–3pm and 6:30–10pm. Train: Town Hall.

MODERATE

City Extra ★ ITALIAN/AUSTRALIAN Because this place stays open around-the-clock, it's convenient if you get hungry at a ridiculous hour. It's also nicely situated, right next to the ferry terminals. The food varies in quality; if in doubt, stick to the burgers. It's always busy, and service can be a mixed bag too, but the plastic chairs and outdoor tables make it a pleasant enough spot for a quick bite at any time of the day or night. It has a kids' menu and free Wi-Fi.

Shop E4, Circular Quay. www.cityextra.com.au. ⓒ **02/9241 1422.** Main courses A$20–A$37. Open 24 hrs. Train, bus, or ferry: Circular Quay.

Love.fish Barangaroo ★★★ SEAFOOD One of the exciting dining options in Sydney's new Streets of Barangaroo precinct (p. 97), this indoor/outdoor waterside eatery combines great cocktails with delicious food (and a focus on sustainable seafood) and a helpful staff that can get you in and out quickly for a pre-theater meal. With seating for 160, it's a bustling place offering beautifully presented dishes—anything from oysters and champagne to an impressive seafood platter (A$160) to share.

Wulugul Walk, 23 Barangaroo Ave., Barangaroo. www.lovefishbarangaroo.com.au. ⓒ **02/8077 3700.** Main courses A$17–A$49. Mon–Fri noon–3pm and 5–11pm; Sat–Sun noon–11pm.

Darling Harbour
MODERATE

Nick's Seafood Restaurant ★ SEAFOOD This nice indoor and alfresco eatery overlooking the water on the same side as Darling Harbour (to the left of Sydney Aquarium if you're looking at the boats) offers good cocktails and plenty of seafood. The best seats are outside in the sunshine, where you can watch the world go by over a bottle of wine. A seafood platter for two (A$180) arrives piled with crab, prawns, mussels, fish, oysters, and lobster. A kids' menu for under 12s offers pasta, chicken, calamari, or fish with french fries and a soft drink, followed by ice cream for A$16. Nick's has another equally pleasant eatery on the other side of the Aquarium called **Nick's Bar & Grill,** and a sister establishment, **I'm Angus Steakhouse**—also at Cockle Bay Wharf—does good steaks, a great Guinness pie, and some seafood. The food and prices at all three places are similar, and they share the same phone number for bookings.

The Promenade, Cockle Bay Wharf (on the city side of Darling Harbour). www.nicks-seafood.com.au. ⓒ **1300/989 989.** Main courses A$32–A$68. Mon–Sat 11:30am–3pm and 5:30–10pm (11pm on Sat); Sun 11:30am–10pm. Ferry: Darling Harbour.

Zaaffran ★★ INDIAN Forget the dark interiors and exotic murals you usually find in an Indian restaurant; here are white surfaces, a glass-fronted wine cellar, and magnificent views of the water and the Sydney skyline from the far side of Darling Harbour. An outdoor terrace provides the best views. Chef Vikrant Kapoor, formerly the chef de cuisine at Raffles in Singapore, has revolutionized classic Indian cuisine on the menu here. Expect such delights as chicken *biryani,* baked in a pastry case and served with mint yogurt, or tiger prawns in coconut cream and turmeric broth, not to mention many interesting vegetarian options.

Level 2, Harbourside Centre, 10 Darling Dr. www.zaaffran.com. © **02/9211 8900.** Main courses A$20–A$30. Daily noon–2:30pm; Mon–Thurs 6–9:30pm; Fri–Sat 5:30–10:15pm; Sun 5:30–9:30pm. Ferry: Darling Harbour.

Woolloomooloo Wharf
EXPENSIVE

Otto Ristorante ★★ ITALIAN Recognized as one of Sydney's premier restaurants, Otto is all lush designer appointments and dim lighting, making it popular with local celebrities and socialites. Hence the price of the food, perhaps. Outside it's light and breezy, with nice views of a boardwalk and some harbor water. Menu possibilities include pumpkin- and ricotta-filled cappellacci with burnt sage butter, raisins, and pine nuts; or a pork cutlet with apple, walnuts, and prunes.

6 Cowper Wharf Rd. www.ottoristorante.com.au/sydney. © **02/9368 7488.** Main courses A$39–A$59. Daily noon–10pm. Bus: no. 311 from Circular Quay (or take a water taxi).

Vic's rosé veal T-bone salad at Otto Ristorante.

Kings Cross & Darlinghurst

INEXPENSIVE

Bills ★★★ CAFE   Strewn with flowers and magazines, this bright and airy place serves nouveau cafe–style food. It's so popular you might have trouble finding a seat. The signature breakfast dishes—including ricotta hotcakes with honeycomb butter and banana, and sweet corn fritters with roasted tomatoes, spinach, and bacon—are the stuff of legend. In fact, some of my friends think Bills serves the best breakfast in Sydney. Find other Bills cafes in Surry Hills (359 Crown St.; ☏ **02/9360 4762**) and Bondi Beach (79 Hall St.; ☏ **02/8412 0700**).

433 Liverpool St., Darlinghurst. www.bills.com.au. ☏ **02/9360 9631.** Main courses A$23–A$26. Mon–Sat 7:30am–3pm; Sun and public holidays 8am–3pm. Reservations Mon–Fri only. Train: Kings Cross.

Café Hernandez ★★ CAFE   The walls of this tiny, cluttered cafe are crammed with eccentric fake masterpieces, and the aroma of 20 types of coffee roasted and ground on the premises permeates the air. It's almost a religious experience for discerning central-city coffee addicts—and even better, it never closes! The Spanish espresso is a treat. Light meals are served: sandwiches, wraps, focaccias, and tortillas, as well as some sweet treats such as churros, Portuguese custard tarts, and Spanish rice pudding.

60 Kings Cross Rd., Potts Point. www.cafehernandez.com.au. ☏ **02/9331 2343.** Main courses A$5–A$10. Open 24 hr. Train: Kings Cross.

Govinda's ★★ VEGETARIAN   Simple vegetarian food—usually curries of some kind—coupled with a happy vibe and very cheap prices make this place a winner. Based in the Hare Krishna center, Govinda's serves buffet-style meals in a basic room of black-lacquer tables. The menu changes nightly but always includes a delicious Indian dahl soup, vegetable curry, penne pasta, lentil pie or potato au gratin, cauliflower pakoras, potato wedges, rice, papadums, and salads. It's BYO, doctrine-free, and very bohemian. After the meal, there's a recent-release movie (albeit on a different floor), which you watch prostrate on large futon-style chairs. It's hugely popular, so make a booking.

112 Darlinghurst Rd., Darlinghurst. www.govindas.com.au. ☏ **02/9380 5155.** Dinner A$23. Movie A$14 (if dining) or A$19. Wed–Sun 5:45–11pm. Train: Kings Cross.

In Bondi Beach

EXPENSIVE

Icebergs Dining Room & Bar ★★★ MEDITERRANEAN   Overlooking Bondi Beach and the sea baths at the Bondi Icebergs Club (famed for its year-round swimming), this is a truly fabulous place to dine. From its corner position on the cliffs, the Icebergs Bar looks directly across the beach and water, with floor-to-roof windows offering what is probably the best view in Sydney. The bar features lots of cushions and has a casual bar menu. The dining-room menu is Italian, with seafood featuring as well, and the service is faultless. Go for brunch on Sunday (10–11:30am); you won't be disappointed.

A tasting menu (A$140 per person) offers seven courses that will have you swooning.

1 Notts Ave. www.idrb.com. © **02/9365 9000.** Reservations essential. Main courses A$46–A$76. Tues–Sun noon–3pm and 6:30pm–midnight; Sun brunch 10–11:30am. Bus: no. 333.

INEXPENSIVE

Pompei's ★ ITALIAN   The formula is simple: Use good ingredients, like an organic tomato sauce, and you'll get good pizzas. In fact, some people think these are the best pizzas in Sydney. The pizzas have a huge range of interesting toppings, but Pompei's also offers a variety of other fare, including salads, antipasto, focaccia, and steaks. Don't miss the homemade gelato, the best in Sydney by far—try chocolate, tiramisu, or pistachio. The water views and outside tables are another plus. When it's busy, it can get cramped inside, and service can vary.

126–130 Roscoe St., at Gould St. www.pompeis.com.au. © **02/9365 1233.** Reservations recommended. Pizza A$21–A$25. Main courses A$24–A$34. Mon–Fri noon–11pm; Sat–Sun 11:30am–11pm. Bus: nos. 380 or 333 from the city.

EXPLORING SYDNEY

The only problem with visiting Sydney is fitting in everything you want to do and see. Of course, you won't want to miss the iconic attractions: the **Opera House** and the **Harbour Bridge.**

You should also check out the native wildlife in **Taronga Zoo,** stroll around the tourist precinct of **Darling Harbour,** and get a dose of Down Under culture at the **Australian Museum.** If it's hot, take your "cozzie" (swimsuit) and towel to **Bondi Beach** or **Manly.**

A classic view of Sydney, with the Opera House and the Harbour Bridge.

The best way to see Sydney Harbour is from the water. Several companies operate tourist craft (see "Harbor Cruises," p. 91), but it's easy enough just to hop on a regular passenger ferry (see "Getting Around," p. 55). The best ferry excursions are to the beachside suburb of **Manly** (return after dusk to see the lights ablaze around The Rocks and Circular Quay); to **Watsons Bay,** where you can have lunch and wander along the cliffs; to **Darling Harbour,** traveling right under the Harbour Bridge; and to **Mosman Bay,** to see the grand houses that overlook exclusive harbor inlets.

Sydney Harbour & The Rocks

Officially called Port Jackson, **Sydney Harbour** is the focal point of Sydney and one of the features—along with the beaches and easy access to surrounding national parks—that makes this city so special. It's entered through the **Heads,** two bush-topped outcrops (you'll see them if you take a ferry to Manly), beyond which the harbor laps at some 240km (149 miles) of shoreline before stretching out into the Parramatta River. Visitors are often awestruck by the harbor's beauty, especially at night, when the sails of the Opera House and the girders of the Harbour Bridge are lit up, and the waters are swirling with the reflection of lights from the abutting high-rises—reds, greens, blues, yellows, and oranges. During the day, it buzzes with green-and-yellow ferries pulling in and out of busy Circular Quay, sleek tourist craft, fully rigged tall ships, giant container vessels making their way to and from the wharves of Darling Harbour, and hundreds of white-sailed yachts.

The greenery along the harbor's edges is a surprising feature, thanks to the **Sydney Harbour National Park,** a haven for native trees and plants, and a feeding and breeding ground for lorikeets and other nectar-eating bird life. In the center of the harbor is a series of islands; the most impressive is the tiny isle supporting **Fort Denison,** which once housed convicts and acted as part of the city's defense.

The Rocks neighborhood is compact and close to the ferry terminals at Circular Quay. Sydney's historic district is hilly and crosscut with alleyways. Some of Australia's oldest pubs are here, as well as boutique restaurants, stores, and hotels. Pick up a walking map from the visitor center and make sure to get off the main streets to see the original working-class houses that survived development. Today, there are 96 heritage buildings in The Rocks. The oldest house is Cadmans Cottage, built in 1815, while the Dawes Point Battery, built in 1791, is the oldest remaining European structure. On Observatory Hill, you'll find the three remaining walls of Fort Phillip, built in 1804.

Museum of Contemporary Art (MCA) ★★★ MUSEUM Two MCA Collection Galleries (Level 2 and Level 1 South) feature the works of more than 150 Australian artists acquired since the founding of the MCA in 1989. This imposing sandstone museum, set back from the water on The

4

SYDNEY | Exploring Sydney

Central Sydney Attractions

Art Gallery of New South Wales 10
Australian Museum 17
Australian National
  Maritime Museum 16
Elizabeth Bay House 1
Hyde Park Barracks Museum 12
Luna Park 11
Museum of Contemporary Art 6
Museum of Sydney 7
Powerhouse Museum 19
The Rocks Discovery Museum 3
Royal Botanic Gardens 9
SEA LIFE Sydney Aquarium 15
Susannah Place Museum 5
Sydney Harbour Bridge 2
Sydney Jewish Museum 18
Sydney Observatory 4
Sydney Opera House 8
Sydney Tower 13
Wildlife Sydney Zoo 14

An installation at the Museum of Contemporary Art.

Rocks side of Circular Quay, also offers a changing program of exhibitions by Australian and international artists and is worth at least an hour (probably more!) of your time. Free guided tours are conducted at 11am and 1pm daily (and 7pm Wed and 3pm Sat–Sun), and there's also a program of free talks (check the website for details). The **MCA Café** (☏ **02/9250 8443,** open same hours) has good views of the harbor and Opera House.

140 George St., The Rocks. www.mca.com.au. ☏ **02/9245 2400.** Free. Mon–Tues, Thurs, Sun 10am–5pm; Wed, Fri–Sat 10am–9pm. Train, bus, or ferry: Circular Quay.

The Rocks Discovery Museum ★★ MUSEUM   Housed in a restored 1850s sandstone warehouse, this small but interesting museum is dedicated to telling the story of The Rocks from pre-European days to the present. Learn about the area's traditional landowners; the establishment of the English colony; the sailors, whalers, and traders who called the area home; and the 1970s union-led protests that preserved this unique part of Sydney.

Kendall Lane (off Argyle St.), The Rocks. www.therocks.com. ☏ **02/9240 8680.** Free. Daily 10am–5pm. Closed Good Friday and Christmas Day. Train: Circular Quay or Wynyard.

Susannah Place Museum ★★ MUSEUM   Entry to this small museum is by guided tour only, but don't let that put you off—it may enhance your visit. Contained in a terrace of four houses built in 1844, this museum is a real highlight of The Rocks area. It provides visitors with the opportunity to explore domestic working-class life from 1844 to 1990. The modest interiors and rear yards illustrate the restrictions of 19th-century inner-city life. The layers of paint, wallpapers, and floor coverings that have survived provide a valuable insight into the tastes of the working class. There's also a delightful little shop selling cordials, postcards, old-fashioned candies, and knickknacks.

58–64 Gloucester St., The Rocks. www.sydneylivingmuseums.com.au. ☏ **02/9241 1893.** Entry by guided tour only, A$12 adults, A$8 children, A$30 family of 4. Daily 2–5pm (last tour at 4pm). Closed Good Friday and Christmas Day. Bus, ferry, or train: Circular Quay.

Sydney Harbour Bridge ★★★ ICON One thing few tourists do—which is a shame—is to walk across the Harbour Bridge. The bridge, completed in 1932, is 1,150m (3,772 ft.) long and spans 503m (1,650 ft.) from the south shore to the north. It has pedestrian walkways, two railway lines, and an eight-lane road. The 30-minute walk from one end to the other offers excellent harbor views. From the other side, you can take a train from Milsons Point back to the city.

As you walk across, stop off at the **Pylon Lookout** (www.pylonlookout. com.au; ☎ **02/9240 1100**) at the southeastern pylon. Admission is A$15 for adults, A$8.50 for children ages 5 to 12. There are four levels inside the pylon, with displays about the bridge's history. On level two, there are observation balconies on both sides, and when you get to the top, 89m (292 ft.) above the water, you get panoramic views of Sydney Harbour, the ferry terminals of Circular Quay, and beyond. The Pylon Lookout is open daily from 10am to 5pm (closed Christmas Day).

Another very popular way of enjoying the wonderful views from the Bridge is to climb to the top. The Sydney BridgeClimb is an exhilarating achievement, and one you won't forget. **BridgeClimb,** 3 Cumberland St., The Rocks (www.bridgeclimb.com; ☎ **02/8274 7777**), offers three climbs. The **Bridge-Climb** takes you along the outer arch of the bridge on catwalks and ladders all the way to the summit. The **Discovery Climb** takes climbers into the heart of the bridge. You traverse the suspension arch and then wind your way through a tangle of hatchways and girders suspended above the traffic. You also climb between the arches to the summit. Both experiences take 3½ hours from check-in to completion. For those with limited time, the **BridgeClimb**

The Sydney BridgeClimb takes you along catwalks and ladders to the top of the bridge.

SEEING SYDNEY HARBOUR THROUGH
aboriginal EYES

Every visitor to Sydney should get out on the harbor with descendants of the original inhabitants of this most famous waterway. The **Tribal Warrior Association** is an Aboriginal-operated nonprofit organization that provides maritime training programs for Aboriginal youths, and also offers an Aboriginal perspective of Sydney Harbour in 2-hour **Aboriginal Cultural Cruises** ★★★ (www.tribal warrior.org; © **02/9699 3491**). Aboard the ketch *Mari Nawi* you will sail past the Royal Botanic Garden as your indigenous guide tells stories of the early Europeans and their hopeless farms, and the small-pox epidemic of 1789. You'll hear tales of the first Aboriginal tour guides, who took early settlers inland from the harbor,

and much more. The cruise stops at Clark Island, where visitors will see cave shelters with roofs stained black from ancient fireplaces, convict engravings, and a natural fish trap. Two Aboriginal guides, their bodies plastered in ghostly white ochre, beat a rhythm with hard-wood sticks and growl through a didgeri-doo as they beckon tourists to the Welcoming Ceremony. Then comes a repertoire of haunting songs, music, and dance. Cruises cost A$60 adults and A$40 children 4 to 14, A$180 for a family of four. Bookings are essential; tours run subject to minimum numbers and avail-ability. Cruises generally depart at 1pm April through October, at 3pm November through March.

Sampler (A$168 adults, A$143 children Mon–Fri; A$188 adults, A$158 children Sat–Sun) will take you to the halfway point of the climb, and takes only 90 minutes. Climbers wear "Bridge Suits" and are harnessed to a safety line; everyone must pass an alcohol breathalyzer test. You're not allowed to carry anything, even cameras (the guide will take photos of you at a couple of stops and at the summit). Daytime climbs cost A$303 for adults and A$203 for children ages 10 to 15. Dawn climbs cost A$388 adults, A$278 kids; twilight climbs cost A$368 adults, A$258 kids; night climbs cost A$263 adults, A$183 kids (bundle up, it can be cold up there!). Most climbs (except dawn climbs) cost A$30 more on weekends; prices also rise slightly between Christmas and early January. Children 7 and under are not allowed to climb. The **Sydney Harbour Bridge Visitor Centre,** where you set out from, has good displays featuring Sydney's famous icon. It's open daily 8am to 6pm.

Sydney Observatory ★★ OBSERVATORY   The city's only major observatory offers visitors a chance to see the southern skies through modern and historic telescopes. The best time to visit is during the night on a guided tour, when you can take a close-up look at the stars and planets. Two-hour night tours start at 6:30 and 8:30pm and must be booked in advance. There is also a tour at 9pm on Friday and Saturday. On weekends and school holidays, 30-minute guided tours run every hour from 10:15am, including a planetarium show and a telescope viewing. Schedules are subject to change, so check the times when you book. The planetarium and hands-on exhibits are also interesting. Daytime admission to the gardens and the exhibitions is free, but doesn't include the telescope towers, telescope viewings, and 3D theater. For A$330 you can also name a star after yourself or someone you love!

Observatory Hill, 1003 Upper Fort St., Millers Point. www.maas.museum/sydney-observatory. ℂ **02/9217 0111.** Daytime tours A$10 adults, A$8 children 4–15, A$26 family of 4. Guided night tours (reservations required) A$27 adults, A$20 children, A$80 families. Daily 10am–5pm. Closed Christmas Day, Boxing Day (Dec 26) and New Year's Eve. Train, bus, or ferry: Circular Quay.

Sydney Opera House ★★★ ICON/PERFORMING ARTS VENUE

Only a handful of buildings around the world are as architecturally and cultur-ally significant as the Sydney Opera House, a white-sailed construction caught mid-billow over the waters of Sydney Cove. But what sets it apart from some other famous buildings is that this is a working building, housing a full-scale performing-arts complex with four major performance spaces. The big-gest and grandest is the 2,690-seat **Concert Hall.** Come here to experience chamber music, symphonies, dance, choral performances, and even rock 'n' roll. The **Joan Sutherland Theatre** is smaller, seats 1,547, and books opera, ballet, and dance. The **Drama Theatre,** seating 544, and the **Playhouse,** seat-ing 398, specialize in plays and smaller-scale performances.

The history of the building is as intriguing as the design. The New South Wales Government raised the construction money with a lottery, and Danish architect Jørn Utzon won an international competition to design it. Following a disagreement, however, Utzon returned home without ever seeing his fin-ished project. Budgeted at A$7 million, by its completion in 1973 the project cost a staggering A$102 million, most raised through a series of lotteries. After a A$152-million upgrade in recent years, the Opera House has never looked better.

Guided tours of the Opera House last about an hour and are conducted daily from 9am to 5pm, except on Good Friday and Christmas Day. You may not get to see everything, because there's almost always some performance, practice, or setting up going on. Tour sizes are limited—reservations are essential—but it is worth planning for, as the tour is fascinating. Two-and-a-half-hour backstage tours, which include breakfast in the Green Room, require climbing up to 300 stairs (no children 9 and under).

The Tourism Services Department at the Sydney Opera House can book **combination packages,** including dinner and a show; a tour, dinner, and a show; or a champagne-interval performance. Prices vary depending on shows and dining venues. Visitors from overseas can buy tickets by credit card and pick them up at the box office on arrival. Advance purchases are a good idea, because performances are very popular.

The Opera House is where you will see performances by the Melbourne-based **Australian Ballet** during its Sydney season (www.australianballet.com.au). **Opera Australia** (www.opera.org.au; ℂ **02/9318 8200** for bookings) performs at the Joan Sutherland Theatre. The **Sydney Symphony Orchestra** (www.sydneysymphony.com; ℂ **02/8215 4600** box office) performs

For a thrill ride, you can board a 420-horsepower jet boat, which zooms about on three high-speed waterway tours at speeds of up to 40 knots (about 80kmph/50 mph), with huge 240-degree turns and instant stops. **Harbour Jet** (www.harbourjet.com; ☎ **1300/887 373** in Australia) offers a 35-minute Jet Blast ride costing A$80 for adults, A$50 for kids 14 and under, and A$210 for a family (book online for discounts). It leaves at 1, 2, and 3pm on weekends and noon Monday through Friday. Rides are fast and furious and pump with rock music. The boat leaves from the King Street Jetty 9 (near the Sydney SEA LIFE

Aquarium) at Darling Harbour.

Another option is **Oz Jet Boat** (www. ozjetboating.com; ☎ **02/9808 3700**), with departures every hour from the Eastern Pontoon at Circular Quay (on the walkway to the Opera House). These large red boats are a bit more powerful than the blue Harbour Jet ones, but you might not notice the difference. This company offers a 30-minute Shark Attack Thrill Ride for A$85 for adults, A$49 for kids 15 and under, and A$219 for a family of four. It leaves every hour from 11am to 4pm daily (5pm in summer). Kids must be at least 1.2m (3 ft., 11 in.) tall.

throughout the year in the Concert Hall. The main symphony season runs March through November, and there's a summer season in February.

Free performances take place outside on the Opera House boardwalks on Sunday afternoons and during festival times. The artists range from musicians and performance artists to school groups.

Bennelong Point. www.sydneyoperahouse.com. ☎ **02/9250 7250** for guided tours and information, or 02/9250 7777 box office. Box office Mon–Sat 9am–8:30pm; Sun 10am–6pm. Tours A$40 adults, A$22 kids, A$105 family of 4. Book online for discounts. Tours daily 9am–5pm (every 30 min.). Backstage tour A$175 starts daily at 7am, for 2½ hr., with breakfast. Train, bus, or ferry: Circular Quay.

Darling Harbour

Many tourists head to Darling Harbour for the cheap eateries and a few interesting shops, but Sydney's dedicated tourist precinct has much more to offer. See **www.darlingharbour.com** for current events.

Australian National Maritime Museum ★★ MUSEUM Australia owes almost everything to the sea, so it's not surprising that there's a museum dedicated to seafarers and ships, from Aboriginal vessels to submarines. Twice a year more names are added to the museum's migrant Welcome Wall, which celebrates the arrival of waves of migrants as part of Australia's maritime history. There are now more than 29,000 names from more than 200 countries on the wall. The museum's "Big Ticket" gives access to everything—the Australian navy destroyer *Vampire,* an Oberon Class submarine, the tall ship *James Craig,* and a replica of the *Endeavour,* the ship Captain James Cook commanded when he laid claim to Australia—as well as galleries, exhibitions, the Cape Bowling Green lighthouse, and the Kids on Deck program (Sun and school holidays). You'll find ships' logs and things to pull and tug at and clamber over—kids love it! Allow 2 hours.

2 Murray St., Darling Harbour. www.anmm.gov.au. © **02/9298 3777.** Free admission to permanent galleries; "Big Ticket" admission to galleries, exhibitions, ships, and Kids on Deck A$32 adults, A$20 children 4–15, A$79 families of 5. Additional fees for special exhibitions. Daily 9:30am–5pm (until 6pm Jan). Closed Christmas Day. Ferry: Darling Harbour. Bus: nos. 389 or 443.

Powerhouse Museum ★★★ MUSEUM Sydney's most interactive museum is also one of the largest in the Southern Hemisphere. Inside, you'll find displays, sound effects, and gadgets relating to the sciences, transportation, human achievement, decorative art, fashion, and social history, much of it with relevance or connections to Sydney and Australian exploration. There's also an Art Deco–style cinema, and exhibitions about global warming, steam trains and steam engines, and even about advertising. You could easily spend 2 or 3 hours discovering everything here. There's plenty to keep kids interested as well.

500 Harris St., Ultimo (near Darling Harbour). www.maas.museum/powerhouse-museum. © **02/9217 0111.** A$15 adults, free for children 15 and under. Daily 10am–5pm. Closed Christmas Day. Ferry: Darling Harbour.

SEA LIFE Sydney Aquarium ★ AQUARIUM Sharks, crocodiles, penguins, *dugongs* (sea cows), and platypuses are just some of the marine life you will encounter at this aquarium. The main attractions are the underwater walkways through two enormous tanks—one full of giant rays and gray nurse sharks and the other where you can see the seals. The sharks are fed at 11am and the Fairy Penguins at 3pm daily. The newest exhibit from late 2016 is Penguin Island, where you can raft though a sub-Antarctic environment populated with King and Gentoo penguins. Other exhibits include a section on the Great Barrier Reef, where thousands of colorful fish school around coral outcrops. A touch pool allows you to stroke baby sharks. Among many experiences and animal encounters, you can take a 20-minute behind-the-scenes tour of the Great Barrier Reef oceanarium in a glass-bottom boat (every 30 min. noon–4pm; A$57 adults, A$45 kids 4–15, no children 3 and under). You can also take the boat at shark-feeding time (11am) for about 30 minutes; the cost is slightly higher. Tour prices include general admission. Try to visit during the week, when it's less crowded. Allow around 2 hours.

Aquarium Pier, Darling Harbour. www.sydneyaquarium.com.au. © **02/8251 7800.** A$42 adults, A$30 children 4–15, A$136 families of 4; cheaper if booked online. Daily 10am–6pm (last entry 5pm). Train: Town Hall. Ferry: Darling Harbour.

Other Top Attractions

Art Gallery of New South Wales ★★★ MUSEUM This beautiful gallery, established in 1871, has a fine collection of international and Australian art that you should take time to see. Contemporary works are displayed in light-filled galleries with views of Sydney and the harbor, while colonial and 19th-century Australian art and European Old Masters are housed in the

Grand Courts. There are also dedicated galleries for Asian and Aboriginal and Torres Strait Islander art. The gallery hosts more than 30 temporary exhibitions each year, including the annual Archibald Prize for portraiture (late Mar–early June), in which you'll see plenty of famous Australian faces. Enter from the Domain parklands (across the road from the Royal Botanic Garden) onto the third floor (ground level) of the museum. Allow at least 1 hour, probably more if you are interested in any of the many free tours on offer.

Art Gallery Rd., The Domain. www.artgallery.nsw.gov.au. (C) **1800/679 278** in Australia, or 02/9225 1744. Free admission; prices vary for special exhibitions. Sun–Tues and Thurs–Sat 10am–5pm; Wed 10am–10pm. Closed Good Friday and Christmas Day. Tours of collection highlights daily 11am. Tours of Aboriginal galleries daily 10:30am. Bus: no. 441. Train: St. James.

Australian Museum ★★ MUSEUM   This is Sydney's premier natural history museum. Displays are presented thematically; the Aboriginal section, with traditional clothing, weapons, and everyday implements, is among the best. There are plenty of stuffed Australian mammals and birds, an insect display, and a mineral collection. Children are well catered to, with plenty of dinosaurs, mummies, and other wonderful things to observe.

1 William St. www.australianmuseum.net.au. (C) **02/9320 6000.** A$15 adults, free for children 15 and under, A$30 families of 4. Special exhibits extra. Daily 9:30am–5pm. Closed Christmas Day. Train: Museum, St. James, or Town Hall.

Elizabeth Bay House ★ HISTORIC HOME   Perched on a headland with some of the best harbor views in Sydney, this colonial mansion was built in 1835 and was considered "the finest house in the colony." You can tour the house and get a feeling for the history of that fledgling settlement.

7 Onslow Ave., Elizabeth Bay. www.sydneylivingmuseums.com.au. (C) **02/9356 3022.** A$12 adults, A$8 children, A$30 families. Fri–Sun 10am–4pm. Closed Good Friday and Christmas Day. Bus: no. 311 from Circular Quay. Train: Kings Cross.

Hyde Park Barracks Museum ★★ MUSEUM   If you don't know the terms "Lags and Swells," you will after meeting some convict characters at this museum, where a touchscreen interactive program brings to life some of the 50,000 convicts who passed through the Hyde Park Barracks between 1819 and 1848. These Georgian-style barracks, designed by the convict Francis Greenway (an architect), were built by convicts and inhabited by prisoners. They are among 11 convict sites in Australia that are World Heritage listed. These days they house relics from those days, including log books, settlement artifacts, and a room full of ships' hammocks in which you can lie and listen to fragments of prisoner conversation. If you are interested in Sydney's early beginnings, I highly recommend a visit. There are free audio tours available. Allow at least 1 hour.

Queens Sq., 10 Macquarie St. www.sydneylivingmuseums.com.au. (C) **02/8239 2311.** A$12 adults, A$8 children, A$30 families. Daily 10am–5pm. Train: St. James or Martin Place.

Museum of Sydney ★ MUSEUM   Free 30-minute tours, at 11am and 3pm daily, give a good introduction to this interesting museum. In a postmodern building near Circular Quay, encompassing the remnants of Sydney's first

Deals on Sightseeing

Several major Sydney attractions offer discounts if you buy passes to more than one of them. If you plan to visit the Sydney Eye Tower, SEA LIFE Sydney Aquarium, or Sydney Wildlife Zoo, check their websites for information on **Sydney Big Ticket** passes, which can be used for two, three, or four of the listed attractions. Once you visit your first attraction, you've got 30 days to visit the others on the pass. Prices start from A$50 adults and A$35 children 4–15 for two attractions and go up to A$70 adults and A$45 children for four attractions (that's A$17.50 per attraction for adults—compare that to the hefty A$42 you'd pay for the aquarium, for example). Buying tickets online also gives good savings (around A$8 for the aquarium). There's also the **Sydney Museums Pass,** which gives access to 12 museums and historic houses for A$24 adults, A$16 children 5–15, or A$50 for a family of four. Many of these museums cost A$12 adults—visit more than two and you're ahead! Buy online (www.sydneylivingmuseums.com.au) or at any of the attractions, which include the Museum of Sydney, Hyde Park Barracks Museum, Elizabeth Bay House, and others listed in this book.

Government House, the museum is certainly not what you might expect. No conventional showcase of history, it houses a collection of first-settler and Aboriginal objects, with multimedia displays that invite you to discover Sydney's past. Some of it is underfoot, in the archaeological digs exposed through "windows" in the paths. A forest of poles filled with hair, oyster shells, and crab claws in the courtyard, called *Edge of Trees,* represents first contact between Aborigines and the British. Modern . . . yes. And very interesting. There are plenty of reasons to linger, for a game of outdoor chess, perhaps, or just to lounge on the grassy areas.

37 Phillip St., (at Bridge St.). www.sydneylivingmuseums.com.au. ℂ **02/9251 5988.** A$12 adults, A$8 children 14 and under, A$30 families. Daily 10am–5pm. Closed Good Friday and Christmas Day. Train, bus, or ferry: Circular Quay.

Sydney Jewish Museum ★★★ MUSEUM   A major permanent exhibition developed in consultation with Holocaust survivors, many of whom are volunteer guides at the museum, gives voice to their history. One of the most moving aspects of any visit to this museum has always been the chance to talk to Holocaust survivors. Another permanent exhibition here is *Serving Australia,* which showcases the contribution that Jewish servicemen and women have made to the Australian armed forces. The museum also has a shop, a resource center, a small theater, and a kosher cafe. Allow 1 to 2 hours. Plan to visit in the afternoon to avoid large school groups.

148 Darlinghurst Rd. (at Burton St.), Darlinghurst. www.sydneyjewishmuseum.com.au. ℂ **02/9360 7999.** A$15 adults, A$9 children, free for kids 9 and under, A$32 families of 4. Free 45-min. guided tours Mon–Fri 1pm, Sun noon and 2pm. Mon–Thurs 10am–4:30pm; Fri 10am–3pm; Sun 10am-4pm. Closed Sat and Jewish holidays. Train: Kings Cross.

Sydney Tower ★ OBSERVATION TOWER The Sydney Tower is hard to miss—it resembles a giant steel pole skewering a golden marshmallow. Standing 309m (984 ft.) tall, the tower offers stupendous 360-degree views across Sydney and as far as the Blue Mountains. At the top is a revolving restaurant and bar, and an indoor viewing platform called the Sydney Tower Eye. (Don't be too concerned if you feel the building tremble slightly, especially in a strong wind—it's built to do that.) The ticket price includes admission to a 4D cinema, where you can watch a film about Sydney with footage of the harbor, coastline, famous landmarks, and events. The **Sydney Tower Skywalk** is a heart-stopping experience and definitely not for those who are afraid of heights. You don a special suit, walk out onto a glass-floored platform 260m (853 ft.) above the city floor and walk around the building. The views are breathtaking (even between your feet!). You are harnessed to a safety rail, so there's no chance of falling off, and well-informed guides offer a helping hand to the nervous. Each Skywalk lasts about 90 minutes. Cameras aren't allowed for safety reasons, but the guide will take group or individual shots that you can buy. No children age 7 and under allowed on the Skywalk.

100 Market St. (another entrance on Pitt St. Mall). www.sydneytowereye.com.au. ✆ **1800/258 693** in Australia, or 02/9333 9222. A$28 adults, A$19 children 4–15. Mid-Apr–early Oct daily 9am–9:30pm (last entry 8:30pm); Oct–Apr 9am–10pm (last entry 9pm). Closed Christmas Day. Skywalk A$70 adults, A$49 kids 8–15. Train: St. James or Town Hall.

Kangaroos, Koalas & Other Aussie Wildlife

See p. 87 for SEA LIFE Sydney Aquarium.

Featherdale Wildlife Park ★★★ WILDLIFE VIEWING If you have time to visit only one wildlife park in Sydney, make it this one. The selection of Australian animals is excellent, and, most important, the animals are very well cared for. You could easily spend a couple of hours here, despite the park's compact size. You'll have the chance to hand-feed friendly kangaroos and wallabies and get a photo taken next to a koala. The **Reptilian Pavilion** houses 30 native species of reptiles in 26 realistic exhibits. If you are heading to the Blue Mountains (p. 100) on a bus tour, choose one that stops off here. Allow 1½ hours to get here by public transport or 45 minutes by car from the city center.

217 Kildare Rd., Doonside. www.featherdale.com.au. ✆ **02/9622 1644.** A$32 adults, A$17 children 3–15, A$58–A$88 families. Daily 9am–5pm. Closed Christmas Day. Train: Blacktown station; then bus no. 729.

Koala Park Sanctuary ★ NATURE CENTER In all, around 55 koalas roam within the park's leafy boundaries (it's set in 4 hectares/10 acres of rainforest). Free koala feeding sessions take place at 10:20 and 11:45am, and 2 and 3pm daily (and you can have your photo taken with them too!). There are wombats, dingoes, kangaroos, wallabies, emus, and native birds here as well. Live sheep shearing takes place at 10:30am and 2:30pm daily. Allow 1½ hours to get here by public transport from the city center or about 30 minutes to drive.

84 Castle Hill Rd., West Pennant Hills. www.koalapark-sanctuary.com.au. ℭ **02/9484 3141.** A$28 adults, A$15 children 4–14. Daily 9am–5pm. Closed Christmas Day. Train: Pennant Hills station via North Strathfield (45 min.). Cross over railway line and join Glenorie Bus routes 651 to 655. The bus takes about 10 min. to Koala Park.

Taronga Zoo ★★★ ZOO   Taronga has the best views of any zoo in the world. Set on a hill, it looks out over Sydney Harbour, the Opera House, and the Harbour Bridge. It's easiest on the legs to explore the zoo from the top down (admission includes a trip on the cable car from the ferry pier to the main entrance). The big attractions are the fabulous chimpanzee exhibit, the gorilla enclosure, and the Nocturnal Houses, where you can see some of Australia's unique marsupials, including the platypus and the cute bilby. There's an interesting reptile display, a couple of impressive Komodo dragons, a scattering of indigenous beasties—including a few koalas, echidnas, kangaroos, dingoes, and wombats—and lots more. Animals are fed at various times during the day. An "Aboriginal Discovery Tour" is offered Monday, Wednesday, and Friday at 9:45am; it takes around 2 hours and costs A$99 adults and A$69 children, including zoo entry (advance bookings essential). Despite the steep entry price, the zoo can get crowded on weekends, so it's a good idea to plan your visit for a weekday or go early in the morning on weekends. Allow around 3 hours.

Bradley's Head Rd., Mosman. www.taronga.org.au/taronga-zoo. ℭ **02/9969 2777.** A$47 adults, A$27 children 4–15. Sept–Apr daily 9:30am–5pm; May–Aug daily 9:30am– 4:30pm. Ferry: Taronga Zoo. Lower zoo entrance is at ferry terminal.

Wildlife Sydney Zoo ★★ ZOO   Not to be confused with Taronga Zoo (Sydney's premier outdoor zoo; see above), this inner-city attraction has a big collection of Australian creatures, including kangaroos, a cassowary, snakes, wallabies, Tasmanian devils, birds, butterflies, and a large saltwater crocodile. You'll find koalas lazing around in the rooftop garden. The Wild Discovery Zone was designed especially for kids, with hands-on animal encounters. You walk through eight themed Australian habitats. No elephants or giraffes here, but it might not matter! Behind-the-scenes tours run daily at 10am and 3pm. You can also take a "Wild Flight" across the aviary in a harness, or get up close with a koala.

Aquarium Pier, Darling Harbour. www.wildlifesydney.com.au. No phone. A$42 adults, A$30 kids 3–15. Daily 10am–5pm (last entry 4pm). Ferry: Darling Harbour.

ORGANIZED TOURS

For details on the **Sydney Big Bus** sightseeing buses, see "Getting Around," p. 54.

Harbor Cruises

The best thing about Sydney is the harbor, and you shouldn't leave without taking a cruise. **Captain Cook Cruises,** departing Wharf 6, Circular Quay (www.captaincook.com.au; ☏ **02/9206 1111**), offers several harbor excursions on its sleek vessels, with commentary along the way. One-hour afternoon "High Tea Cruises" cost A$59, and there's a range of breakfast and dining cruises as well. The popular 1-hour, 15-minute "Harbour Highlights Cruise" costs A$35 for adults and A$19 for children 4 to 15 and runs daily at 2:30pm from Circular Quay. Whale-watching cruises run from mid-May to early November and cost A$85 adults, A$49 children 4 to 15. Check the website for special deals. Captain Cook Cruises has ticket booths at Wharf 6, Circular Quay (daily 8:30am–7pm), at King Street Wharf 1 (Mon–Fri 9am–7:30pm, Sat–Sun 4–7:30pm) and at Pier 26, Darling Harbour (daily 8:30am–5pm). A "Zoo Express" cruise (A$69 adults, A$39 kids) includes entry to Taronga Zoo and departs from Darling Harbour, Circular Quay, or Manly.

Yellow Water Taxis (www.yellowwatertaxis.com; ☏ **1300/326 822** in Australia, or 02/9556 9200) offers a 15-minute mini-tour by small water taxi from its bases at King Street Wharf in Darling Harbour and Circular Quay Jetty 1. This tour is good for a quick look at Sydney's famous harbor and a great way to travel to or from Darling Harbour and Circular Quay. These "snapshot" tours depart every 30 minutes and cost A$20 for adults, A$15 for children 4 to 12 years of age, and A$55 for a family of four. A 45-minute Harbour Highlights Tour includes Darling Harbour, the Sydney Opera House, Royal Botanic Garden, and harbor-front mansions, with a commentary. This tour costs A$45 for adults, A$30 for kids, and A$120 for a family of four.

Check websites or pop into a ticket office at Darling Harbour or Circular Quay, because cruise options, departure times, and prices change frequently.

Walking Tours

If you want to learn more about Sydney's early history, book an excellent guided tour with **The Rocks Walking Tours,** based at Clocktower Square, corner of Argyle and Harrington streets (www.rockswalkingtours.com.au; ☏ **02/9247 6678**). Walks leave daily at 10:30am and 1:30pm. The 1½-hour tour costs A$32 for adults, A$15 for children ages 5 to 16, and A$79 for families of four.

Culture Scouts (www.culturescouts.com.au; ☏ **02/9016 5531**) runs interesting walking tours that focus on art, food, and conversation (think galleries, cafes, bars, street art, and boutiques) in the inner suburbs Chippendale, Redfern, Darlinghurst, Surry Hills, Ultimo, and Newtown. Tours last 2 to 3 hours, go at a gentle pace, and can be tailor made if you wish. All tours cost A$95 per person; they're not recommended for kids 14 and under. Two-hour street art tours (A$59 per person) run twice a month on Saturday mornings.

Motorcycle Tours

Wild Ride Australia (www.wildride.com.au; ☏ **1300/738 338** in Australia) runs Harley-Davidson tours of Sydney, the Blue Mountains, and beyond. A 1-hour ride (you sit on the back of the bike) around the city or Bondi costs A$130. A 1½-hour ride through the city and out to Bondi costs A$160. A 3-hour trip to the northern beaches costs A$250. Full-day trips cover the Blue

Mountains and the Hawkesbury region. If you love motorcycles and want to rent one for a self-guided or guided tour, contact **Bikescape** (www.bikescape. com.au; © **1300/736 869** in Australia, or 02/8123 0917).

ESPECIALLY FOR KIDS

Sydney is a great city to visit with kids. It's got a load of zoos and wildlife viewing experiences (p. 90), and several engaging attractions with hands-on and interactive displays, including the Australian National Maritime Museum (p. 86), Powerhouse Museum (p. 87), SEA LIFE Sydney Aquarium (p. 87), and the Australian Museum (p. 88). There are many different options for getting out onto the waters of famous Sydney Harbour, from short water taxi rides (p. 57) to high-speed jet boats (p. 86). Older kids may love the thrill of a BridgeClimb (p. 83) or a Skywalk at Sydney Tower (p. 90). Add in a day at the beach and you've got a vacation they'll long remember.

Luna Park ★ AMUSEMENT PARK   The huge smiling clown face and the fairground attractions, which are visible from Circular Quay, make up one of Australia's most iconic attractions. It's fun for kids, with traditional theme-park amusements rather than high-tech rides. It has a carousel, bumper cars, a Ferris wheel, and the like. Many rides are suitable for small children, too. You buy tickets at booths inside the park. The best way to get here is either to walk over the Sydney Harbour Bridge from The Rocks or to catch a train from the city center to Milsons Point. Leave some time for a walk along the foreshore of Sydney Harbour, right beneath the bridge. Hours vary, so check online before setting out.

1 Olympic Dr., Milsons Point. www.lunaparksydney.com.au. © **02/9922 6644,** or 02/9033 7676 for information. Free admission. Ride passes based on height: unlimited ride pass A$25 small child; A$45 big kids; A$55 adults. Other prices and deals available. Expect higher prices during school holidays, but better rates if booked online. Mon 11am–4pm; Fri–Sat 11am–11pm; Sun 10am–6pm. During school holidays: Sun–Thurs 10am–6pm; Fri–Sat 10am–10pm. Ferry or train: Milsons Point.

OUTDOOR ACTIVITIES

Hitting the Beach

One of the big bonuses of visiting Sydney in the summer (Dec–Feb) is that you get to experience the beaches in their full glory. Most major city beaches, such as Manly and Bondi, have lifeguards on patrol, especially during the summer. They check the water conditions and are on the lookout for **"rips"**— strong currents that can pull a swimmer far out. Always swim in the area between the red and yellow flags that mark the patrolled area. Fiberglass surfboards must be used outside the flags. (Expect a warning from the loudspeakers and a fine if you fail to do this.)

SOUTH OF SYDNEY HARBOUR

Sydney's most famous beach is **Bondi ★★★**. The beach, sadly, is cut off from the cafe and restaurant strip that caters to beachgoers by a busy road that

One of the first things visitors ask before they hit the water in Australia is: "Are there sharks?" The answer is yes, but fortunately they are rarely spotted inshore—you are far more likely to spy a migrating whale. In reality, the chance of a shark attack is very small. Some beaches—such as the small beach next to the Manly ferry wharf—have permanent shark nets, while others rely on portable nets that are moved from beach to beach. Shark attacks are most likely in early morning and at dusk—avoid swimming at these times.

More common off Sydney's beaches are **"blue bottles"**—small blue jellyfish, often called "stingers" in Australia (and Portuguese man-o'-war elsewhere). You'll often find these creatures (which are not the same as the stingers in north Queensland) washed up on the beach. Be on the lookout for warning signs erected on the shoreline. Minute stinging cells that touch your skin can cause minor itching. You might be hit by the full force of a blue bottle if it wraps its tentacles around you, which causes a severe burning sensation almost immediately. Wearing a T-shirt in the water reduces the risk somewhat. If you are stung, rinse the area liberally with seawater or fresh water to remove any tentacles stuck in your skin. To combat intense pain, take a hot shower. In the unlikely event that you experience breathing difficulties or disorientation, seek medical attention immediately.

pedestrians must cross to reach the sand. On summer weekend evenings, it's popular with young men driving souped-up cars and strutting their stuff. To reach Bondi Beach, take the train to Bondi Junction, and then transfer to bus no. 380 or 333 (a 15-min. bus journey). The no. 333 bus takes about 40 minutes from Circular Quay.

If you're facing the water at Bondi, to your right is a scenic cliff-top trail that takes you to **Bronte Beach ★★★** (a 20-min. walk) via gorgeous little **Tamarama ★★★**, nicknamed "Glamourama" for its trendy sun worshippers. Bronte has better swimming; Tamarama is known for its dangerous rips and is often closed to swimming. To go straight to Bronte, catch bus no. 378 from Circular Quay or pick up the bus at the Bondi Junction train station.

Clovelly Beach ★★★, farther along the coast, is blessed with a large rock pool carved into a rock platform that's sheltered from the force of the Tasman Sea. This beach is accessible for visitors in wheelchairs on a series of ramps. To reach Clovelly, take bus no. 339 from Circular Quay.

The cliff walk from Bondi will eventually bring you to **Coogee ★★**, which has a pleasant strip of sand with a couple of hostels and hotels nearby. To reach Coogee, take bus no. 373 or 374 from Circular Quay.

NORTH OF SYDNEY HARBOUR

On the North Shore you'll find **Manly ★★★**, a long curve of golden sand edged with Norfolk Island pines. The best way to reach Manly is on a ferry from Circular Quay. Follow the crowds through the pedestrian Corso to the main ocean beach, ignoring the two small beaches on either side of the ferry terminal.

4

Facing the ocean, head to your right along the beachfront and follow the coastal path to small and sheltered **Shelly Beach ★★★**, a nice area for snorkeling and swimming. This is one of Sydney's nicest walks. Follow the path up the hill to the car park. Here, a track cuts up into the bush and leads toward a firewall, which marks the entrance to the Sydney Harbour National Park and offers spectacular ocean views across to Manly and the northern beaches.

The best harbor beach is at **Balmoral ★★★**, a wealthy suburb with some good cafes and restaurants. Reach Balmoral on the ferry to Taronga Zoo and then a 10-minute ride on a connecting bus from the ferry wharf, or catch the bus from the stop outside the zoo's top entrance.

Surfing

Bondi Beach and **Tamarama** are the best surf beaches on the south side of Sydney Harbour. **Manly, Narrabeen, Bilgola, Collaroy, Long Reef,** and **Palm** beaches are the most popular on the north side. Most beach suburbs have surf shops where you can rent a board.

At Bondi Beach, **Lets Go Surfing,** 128 Ramsgate Ave. (www.letsgo surfing.com.au; ✆ **02/9365 1800**), rents surfboards for A$20 for 1 hour or A$40 all day. You can hire wet suits for A$10 to A$15. Lets Go also offers surfing lessons for individuals or groups. A 2-hour session in a small group costs A$85 per person; 1-hour private lessons cost A$140.

In Manly, **Manly Surf Guide** (www.manlysurfguide.com; ✆ **0412/417 431** mobile) rents (and delivers) surfboards for A$40 a day. **Manly Surf School** (http://manlysurfschool.com; ✆ **02/9932 7000**) offers 2-hour small-group surf classes for A$70 adults and A$55 children. The more lessons you take, the cheaper it is. For A$120 you get a full day's outing that includes pickup from the city, lessons, and surfing at various places on the northern beaches.

Surfing on Bondi Beach.

Escaping a Rip

Plenty of tourists get into real trouble on Sydney's beaches each year by being caught in a rip tide—a fast current that moves away from the shore (but that will not pull you under the water). If this happens, the most important thing to do is not to panic. If you can't stand up and are being pulled out to sea, try to attract attention by raising a hand in the air. Whatever you do, don't try to battle it out with the rip by swimming against it back to shore. You will quickly become exhausted; this is how people drown. Keep calm, and swim parallel to the beach. If you run out of energy, float on your back. If you swim parallel to the beach you will be pulled a little farther out to sea—it won't take you far out—but before long you should be out of the rip and able to swim back to the beach. Never swim outside of the area marked by yellow and red flags on a beach patrolled by lifeguards. If there are no lifeguards around, it's safest not to swim.

If you're already proficient, consider a 1-day trip to the Royal National Park with **Waves Surf School** (www.wavessurfschool.com.au; ✆ **1800/616 667** in Australia, or 02/9641 2358). Trips cost A$99, and include lunch. Waves also offers a 2-day surfing trip to Seal Rocks, north of Sydney, for A$295, as well as 4- and 5-day trips farther afield.

Parks & Gardens

If you have time to spend in one of Sydney's green spaces, make it the **Royal Botanic Garden** ★★★ (www.rbgsyd.nsw.gov.au; ✆ **02/9231 8111**), next to the Sydney Opera House. Open daily (7am–dusk), these lovely informal gardens were laid out in 1816 on the site of a farm that supplied food for the colony. The gardens have a scattering of duck ponds and open spaces, with several areas dedicated to particular plant species. These include the rose garden, the cacti and succulent display, and the central palm and rainforest groves. Try to spot the thousands of large fruit bats, which chatter and bicker among the rainforest trees. Free 90-minute guided walks are run daily at 10:30am and also at 1pm Monday to Friday (Mar–Nov only). **Aboriginal Heritage Tours** (A$41 adults; children 7 and under free) run at 10am Wednesday, Friday, and Saturday. **Mrs. Macquarie's Chair** ★★, along the coast path, offers superb views of the Opera House and the Harbour Bridge. The "chair" bears the name of Elizabeth Macquarie (1788–1835), the wife of Governor Lachlan Macquarie. The sandstone building dominating the gardens nearest the Opera House is **Government House.** The gardens are open most days from 10am to 4pm, and the house is usually open Friday through Sunday and on public holidays, except Good Friday and Christmas Day (✆ **02/9228 4111** to check times and closures). Entrance is free, but you'll need a ticket from the gatehouse (bring photo ID) to tour the house. Tours run every 30 minutes from 10:30am to 3pm and take about 45 minutes. Note that the house is sometimes closed for official functions.

In the center of the city is **Hyde Park** ★, a favorite with lunching businesspeople. Here you will find the **Anzac Memorial** to Australian and

New Zealand troops killed in action, and the **Archibald Fountain,** complete with spitting turtles and sculptures of Diana and Apollo.

Another Sydney favorite is the giant **Centennial Park** ★★★ (www.centennialparklands.com.au; ☎ **02/9339 6699**). The park has five main entrances, but the easiest one from the city is at the top of Oxford Street. Opened in 1888 to celebrate the centenary of European settlement, today the park encompasses huge lawns, several lakes, picnic areas with barbecues, cycling and running paths, and a cafe. It's open from sunrise to sunset. The visitor information desk is open 9am to 4pm weekdays, 9am to 2pm weekends.

The harborside **Barangaroo Reserve** ★★★ (www.barangaroo.com; ☎ **1300/966 480** in Australia, or 02/9255 1700) is a spectacular 6-hectare (15-acre) parkland on the headland opposite Luna Park. Opened in 2015 and still a work in progress, half of the Barangaroo precinct is public space with a 2km (1¼-mile) waterfront walkway lined with restaurants and cafes; the rest of the 22-hectare (54-acre) space comprises retail and apartment development. The parkland is planted with 74,000 native plants and landscaped with sandstone blocks, forming a natural amphitheater to be used for concerts and other events. Barangaroo was a key figure in local Aboriginal culture in early colonial times (and the wife of Bennelong, for whom Bennelong Point, site of the Sydney Opera House is named). **Aboriginal Cultural Tours** of the site run daily at 10:30am for about 90 minutes and cost A$37 adults, A$22 children. Barangaroo is an easy walk from Circular Quay, either along the harbor-front or along Argyle Street. The closest train station is Wynyard, and there's a ferry terminal at Barangaroo South.

Biking

The best place to cycle in Sydney is Centennial Park. Rent bikes from **Centennial Park Cycles,** 50 Clovelly Rd., Randwick (www.cyclehire.com.au; ☎ **02/9398 5027**), which is 200m (656 ft.) from the Musgrave Avenue entrance. Bikes cost A$15 for the first hour, A$20 for 2 hours, A$30 for 4 hours, and A$50 for a full day. Extra days cost just A$15 each.

Bonza Bike Tours (www.bonzabiketours.com; ☎ **02/9247 8800**), at 30 Harrington St., The Rocks, runs guided bike tours of the city. A half-day city tour costs A$119 adults, A$99 kids, or A$349 families, including a bike and helmet. They also offer a tour of Manly and another that goes across Sydney Harbour Bridge. You can rent bikes from them for A$15 an hour, A$30 a half-day, or A$40 a day.

Kayaking

Natural Wanders (www.naturalwanders.com.au; ☎ **0427/225 072** mobile) takes paddlers out on Sydney Harbour. Tours start from Lavender Bay, near Luna Park; this is the only kayaking company that takes you under Sydney Harbour Bridge. Group tours run on weekends only, but if you'd like a private tour, owner Patrick Dibben will take you during the week too. A 3½-hour paddle costs A$120 and takes you from Lavender Bay west, across the

Bondi Icebergs Club features an ocean-fed public pool.

Harbour and south to explore Balmain, then north to land at Berry Island before returning to Lavender Bay (about 10–12km/6–7 miles). Private tours cost A$190 for one person or A$160 each for two or more people. These tours usually go under Sydney Harbour Bridge and past the Opera House and stop on a beautiful beach in a bushland setting before returning. Check the website for tour options. You must be 15 years or older, have a good level of fitness, and be able to swim.

Swimming

With all that ocean, why bother with a pool? Well, Sydney has some great pools that you might want to try just for their settings. The **Bondi Icebergs Club,** 1 Notts Ave. (www.icebergs.com.au; ℂ **02/9130 4804**), at Bondi Beach, has an Olympic-size ocean tidal pool built into the rocks with the ocean lapping into it. It also has a children's pool. Entrance costs A$7 for adults, A$5 for kids, or A$20 for a family of five. Towel hire is A$3.50. The pool is open from 6am (6:30am Sat–Sun) until 6:30pm Friday through Wednesday (it's closed Thursday for cleaning). *Be warned:* This is a true ocean pool, so the water is sometimes very cold (hence the name of the club!).

There are fabulous views across Sydney Harbour from the outdoor **Andrew (Boy) Charlton Swimming Pool,** the Domain, Mrs. Macquaries Road, near the Royal Botanical Garden (www.abcpool.org; ℂ **02/9358 6686**). It also has a learner's pool and a toddler's pool. Entry is A$6.50 adults, A$4.90 kids, A$18 family of four. It's open 6am to 7pm daily September to April.

Yachting

Sydney by Sail (www.sydneybysail.com.au; ℂ **02/9280 1110**), based at Darling Harbour and run by former Olympic yachtsman Matt Hayes, offers day sails on Sydney Harbour. A skippered, 3-hour afternoon sail leaving at 1pm costs A\$175 for adults and A\$80 for kids 13 and under, or A\$475 for a family of four. You can help sail, or just relax.

SYDNEY SHOPPING

You'll find plenty of places to keep your credit cards in action in Sydney. Most shops of interest to the visitor are in **The Rocks** and along **George and Pitt streets** (including the shops below the Sydney Tower and along Pitt Street Mall). Other precincts worth checking out are **Mosman,** on the North Shore; **Double Bay,** in the eastern suburbs, for boutique shopping; **Chatswood,** for its shopping centers; and various **weekend markets** (see box, below). For really trendy clothing, walk up Oxford Street to **Paddington** or head to **Surry Hills,** and for alternative clothes, go to **Newtown.** If you are looking for trendy surf- and swimwear, the main drags at **Bondi Beach** and **Manly Beach** offer plenty of choices.

Don't miss the **Queen Victoria Building (QVB),** on the corner of Market and George streets. This ornate Victorian shopping arcade, built 1893–1898, has around 200 boutiques—mostly men's and women's fashion—on four levels. Here you'll find fashion-statement stores featuring the best of Australian design, including Oroton, Country Road, and David Lawrence. The arcade is open 24 hours, but the shops do business Monday through Saturday from 9am to 6pm (Thurs to 9pm) and Sunday from 11am to 5pm.

The **Strand Arcade** (between Pitt Street Mall and George St.), built in 1892, has small boutiques, food stores, and cafes, and the Downtown Duty Free store on the basement level. Labels to look for include Scanlan Theodore, Leona Edmiston, and Megan Park. Nearby on **Pitt Street Mall** you'll find a few shops and a Westfield Shopping Centre full of fashion boutiques.

Oxford Street runs from the city to Bondi Junction through Paddington and Darlinghurst and is home to countless stylish clothing stores. You could spend anywhere from 2 hours to an entire day making your way from one end to the other. Detour down **William Street,** once you get to Paddington, to visit trendy boutiques including the luxury recycled goods of Di Nuovo.

The two big department store names in Sydney are David Jones and Myer. **David Jones** (www.davidjones.com) is the city's largest department store, selling everything from fashion to designer furniture. You'll find the women's section on the corner of Elizabeth and Market streets, and the men's section on the corner of Castlereagh and Market streets. The food section offers expensive delicacies. **Myer** (www.myer.com.au; ℭ **1800/811 611** in Australia) is similar, but the building is newer and flashier. It's on the corner of George and Market streets.

Nearer to Circular Quay is **Chifley Plaza** (at Hunter and Elizabeth sts.), home to a selection of the world's most famous and stylish international brands.

SYDNEY'S street markets

Sydney has many good markets worth a look for quirky gifts or souvenirs and to soak up the local vibe, especially on weekends.

Closest to the city is **The Rocks Market** (www.therocks.com), held every Saturday and Sunday (with a smaller "foodies" market on Fri.). This touristy market has more than 100 vendors selling everything from crafts, housewares, and posters to jewelry and curios. George Street in The Rocks is closed to traffic from 10am to 4pm to make it easier to stroll around.

Paddy's Markets (www.paddysmarkets.com.au) are a Sydney institution, with hundreds of stalls selling everything from cheap clothes and plants to chickens. It's open Wednesday to Sunday, 10am to 6pm. Above Paddy's Markets is **Market City,** which has three floors of fashion stalls, food courts, and specialty shops, and a huge Asian-European supermarket. Paddy's is at the corner of Thomas and Hay streets, Haymarket, near Chinatown.

Balmain Market (www.balmain market.com.au), held from 9am to 3pm on the second and fourth Saturday of each month, has about 140 vendors selling crafts, jewelry, and knickknacks. Take the ferry to Balmain (Darling St.); the market is a 10-minute walk up Darling Street, on the grounds of St. Andrew's Church.

Bondi Markets (www.bondimarkets.com.au) is a nice place to stroll around on Sunday and discover upcoming young Australian designers. This market specializes in clothing and jewelry, new, secondhand, and retro. It's open Sunday from 9am to 4pm at the Bondi Beach Public School, Campbell Parade.

Paddington Markets (www.paddingtonmarkets.com.au) is a Saturday-only market where you'll find 150 stalls offering everything from essential oils and designer clothes to New Age jewelry and Mexican hammocks. Expect things to be busy from 10am to 4pm. Take bus no. 380 or 333 from Circular Quay and follow the crowds. It's held in the grounds of St. John's Church, Oxford Street, on the corner of Newcombe Street.

A DAY TRIP TO THE BLUE MOUNTAINS ★★★

Katoomba: 114km (71 miles) W of Sydney; Leura: 107km (66 miles) W of Sydney; Blackheath: 114km (71 miles) W of Sydney; Wentworth Falls: 103km (64 miles) W of Sydney.

The **Blue Mountains** offer breathtaking views, rugged tablelands, sheer cliffs, deep, inaccessible valleys, enormous chasms, colorful parrots, cascading waterfalls, historic villages, and stupendous walking trails. In 2000, UNESCO classified it as a World Heritage Site.

Although the Blue Mountains are where Sydneysiders now go to escape the humidity and crowds of the city, in the early days of the colony the mountains kept at bay those who wanted to explore the interior. In 1813, three explorers—Gregory Blaxland, William Charles Wentworth, and William Lawson—managed to conquer the cliffs, valleys, and dense forests and cross the mountains to the plains beyond. There they found land the colony urgently needed for grazing and farming. The **Great Western Highway** and **Bells Line of Road** are the access roads through the region today—winding and steep in places, they are surrounded by the Blue Mountains and Wollemi national parks.

This area is known for its spectacular scenery, particularly the cliff-top views into valleys of gum trees and across to craggy outcrops that tower from the valley floor. It's colder up here than in the city, and clouds can sweep in and fill the canyons with mist in minutes, while waterfalls cascade down sheer drops, spraying the dripping fern trees that cling to the gullies. A day tour may only scratch the surface but should give you a glimpse into why Sydneysiders love it. The Blue Mountains are also one of Australia's best-known adventure playgrounds, where rock climbing, caving, abseiling (rappelling), bushwalking, mountain biking, horseback riding, and canoeing are practiced year-round.

There are four main towns in the Blue Mountains. **Katoomba** (pop. 11,200) is the largest and the focal point of the Blue Mountains National Park. It's an easy 1½- to 2-hour trip from Sydney by train, bus, or car.

Leura (3km/2 miles west of Katoomba) is known for its gardens, its attractive old buildings (many holiday homes for Sydneysiders), and its cafes and restaurants. Just outside Leura is the **Sublime Point Lookout,** which has spectacular views of the **Three Sisters** (p. 103) in Katoomba. From the southern end of Leura Mall, a cliff drive takes you all the way back to **Echo Point** in Katoomba; along the way you'll enjoy stunning views across the Jamison Valley.

The pretty town of **Wentworth Falls** (7km/4½ miles east of Katoomba) has numerous crafts and antiques shops, but the area is principally known for its 281m (922-ft.) waterfall, situated in **Falls Reserve.** On the far side of the falls is the **National Pass Walk**—one of the best in the Blue Mountains. It's cut into a cliff face with overhanging rock faces on one side and sheer drops on the other. The views over the Jamison Valley are spectacular. The track takes you down to the base of the falls to the **Valley of the Waters.** Climbing up out of the valley is quite a bit more difficult, but just as rewarding.

Blackheath (14km/8½ miles northwest of Katoomba) is the highest town in the Blue Mountains at 1,049m (3,441 ft.). Take the Cliff Walk from **Evans Lookout** to **Govetts Leap** for magnificent views over the **Grose Valley** and **Bridal Veil Falls.** The 1½-hour trek passes through banksia, gum, and wattle forests, with wonderful views of mountain peaks and valleys.

Essentials

ARRIVING   By car from central Sydney, take Parramatta Road and turn off onto the M4 motorway (around 2 hr. to Katoomba). Another route is via the Harbour Bridge to North Sydney, along the Warringah Freeway (following signs to the M2). Then take the M2 to the end and follow signs to the M4 and the Blue Mountains. This takes around 1½ hours.

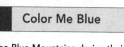

Color Me Blue

The Blue Mountains derive their name from the ever-present blue haze, caused by light striking the droplets of eucalyptus oil that evaporate from the leaves of the dense surrounding forest.

Frequent rail service connects Sydney to Katoomba and Blackheath from Central Station; contact **Sydney Trains** (www.sydneytrains.info; ℓ **131 500**) for details. The trip takes around 2 hours. Trains leave almost hourly. An adult round-trip ticket costs around A$15 (less in off-peak hours).

VISITOR INFORMATION You can pick up maps, walking guides, and other information and book accommodations at **Blue Mountains Tourism,** Echo Point Road, Katoomba (www.visitbluemountains.com.au; ℓ **1300/653 408** in Australia). The information center is an attraction itself, with glass windows overlooking a gum forest, and cockatoos and lorikeets feeding on seed dispensers. It's open 9am to 5pm daily (closed Christmas Day).

The **Blue Mountains Heritage Centre,** end of Govetts Leap Road, Blackheath (www.nationalparks.nsw.gov.au; ℓ **02/4787 8877**), run by the National Parks and Wildlife Service, offers detailed information about the Blue Mountains National Park. It's open daily from 9am to 4:30pm (closed Christmas Day).

Another good website is **www.bluemts.com.au.**

GETTING AROUND The best way to get around the Blue Mountains without a car is the **Blue Mountains Explorer** bus (www.explorerbus.com.au; ℓ **1300/300 915** in Australia). The double-decker "hop-on, hop-off" bus leaves from outside the Katoomba train station about every 30 minutes between 9:45am and 4:45pm and stops at 29 attractions, resorts, galleries, and tearooms in and around Katoomba and Leura. Tickets cost A$50 for adults, A$25 for children, and A$125 for a family; other passes include rides on the Scenic Railway and the Skyway (see "Exploring the Blue Mountains," below), and entry to the Waradah Aboriginal Centre.

Tours

Many private bus operators offer day trips from Sydney, but it's important to shop around. Some offer a guided coach tour, during which you just stretch your legs occasionally, while others let you get your circulation going with a couple of longish bushwalks. Remember, this will be a long day, leaving at 7 or 8am and returning to the city about 6pm.

Sydney Tours-R-Us (www.sydneytoursrus.com.au; ℓ **02/9498 4084**) runs minicoaches to the Blue Mountains, stopping off at Sydney Olympic Park on the way. Then you see all the major sights in the mountains and come home via ferry from Parramatta to Circular Quay. The trip costs A$135 for adults and A$100 for kids ages 4 to 12 (lunch is A$15 extra). The tour includes a stop at Featherdale Wildlife Park (p. 90).

Blue Mountains Walkabout (www.bluemountainswalkabout.com; ℓ **0408/443 822** mobile) is owned and operated by Evan Yanna Muru, an Aboriginal. This guided walk follows a traditional walkabout song line for about

> **Timing Is Everything: When to Visit**
>
> If you can, try to visit the Blue Mountains on **weekdays,** when most Sydney-siders are at work and prices are lower. Note that the colder winter months (June–Aug) are the busiest season.

3.5km (2 miles), exploring part of the Blue Mountains wilderness for a full day (about 2 hr. walking and 4 hr. of relaxation and activities). You'll see ancient art, ceremonial sites, and artifacts, and hear Dreamtime stories. Also included is ochre-bark and body painting, bush-tucker tastings, wildlife viewing, sandstone cave exploring, and bathing in a crystal-clear billabong (pool) below a waterfall. You should be reasonably fit. Bring wet-weather gear, good boots or walking shoes, lots of water, and lunch. The trek costs A$95 per person (no kids 6 and under). The walk begins in the Blue Mountains on Faulconbridge Railway Station platform at 10:50am. Take the train from Central Station in Sydney (see "Arriving," p. 50). You can get the 4:30pm train back to the city.

Exploring the Blue Mountains

Almost every other activity in the Blue Mountains costs money, but bushwalking (hiking) is the exception. There are some 50 walking trails, ranging from routes you can cover in 15 minutes to the 3-day **Six Foot Track.** The staff at the national park and tourist offices will be happy to point you in the right direction.

The most visited and photographed attraction in the Blue Mountains is the rock formation known as the **Three Sisters.** For the best vantage point, head to **Echo Point Road,** across from the Blue Mountains Tourism office. Or try Evans Lookout, Govetts Leap, or Hargreaves Lookout, all at Blackheath.

Four attractions in one are offered at **Scenic World** (www.scenicworld. com.au; ℰ **1300/759 929** in Australia, or 02/4780 0200). The **Scenic Railway,** the world's steepest, consists of a carriage on rails that is lowered 415m (1,361 ft.) into the Jamison Valley at a maximum incline of 52 degrees. It's *very* steep and quite a thrill. The trip takes only a few minutes; at the bottom is the 2.4km (1½-mile) **Scenic Walkway,** a boardwalk through forests of ancient tree ferns. Another way to get down is on the **Scenic Cableway,** not to be confused with

The famous Three Sisters rock formation in Blue Mountains National Park.

The Legend of the Three Sisters

The Aboriginal Dreamtime legend has it that three sisters (Meehni, Wimlah, and Gunnedoo) lived in the Jamison Valley as members of the Katoomba tribe. These beautiful young women had fallen in love with three brothers from the Nepean tribe, yet tribal law forbade them to marry. The brothers were not happy with this law and so decided to capture the three sisters, which caused a major tribal battle. As the lives of the three sisters were in danger, a witch doctor from the Katoomba tribe took it upon himself to turn the three sisters into stone to protect them from any harm. He had intended to reverse the spell later, but was killed in the battle and the sisters were doomed to remain in their magnificent rock formation forever.

the **Scenic Skyway,** a different form of cable car that travels 270m (885 ft.) above—and across—the Jamison Valley, between two cliffs. A ticket that includes all four attractions costs A$39 adults, A$21 children 4 to 13, and A$99 families of up to seven (you can't buy separate tickets for any of the attractions). Scenic World is open 9am to 5pm daily. You'll find it on Violet Street (corner of Cliff Dr.), Katoomba.

If you are driving back to Sydney, take the Bells Line of Road through Bilpin and stop off at the wonderful **Blue Mountains Botanic Garden** (www.bluemountainsbotanicgarden.com.au; ℂ **02/4567 3000**) at Mount Tomah. (Look for a large sign on your right about 10 min. before you get to Bilpin.) An adjunct of Sydney's Royal Botanic Garden, it is well worth a stop.

Where to Eat in the Blue Mountains

Katoomba Street has many ethnic dining choices, whether you're hungry for Greek, Chinese, or Thai. Restaurants in the Blue Mountains are generally more expensive than equivalent places in Sydney.

Conservation Hut Cafe ★ CAFE This pleasant cafe is in the national park on top of a cliff overlooking the Jamison Valley. It's a good place for a bit of lunch on the balcony after the Valley of the Waters walk, which leaves from outside. In addition to lighter meals like soup or a steak sandwich, dishes may include a beef ragout with penne or a Thai-style chicken curry. It has vegetarian and great breakfast/brunch options, too. There's a nice log fire inside in winter. Children are welcome.

Fletcher St., Wentworth Falls. www.conservationhut.net.au. ℂ **02/4757 3827.** Main courses A$14–A$27. Daily 9am–4pm (closed Christmas Day).

Elephant Bean ★★ CAFE This groovy little cafe is a good stop for lunch or a coffee. The menu changes weekly and has a strong vegetarian/vegan slant, so you might find dishes such as a hearty vegetable soup, hand-made gnocchi, or a vegetable curry (but there are a few options for meat-lovers). Monthly exhibitions by local artists add interest to the walls.

159 Katoomba Rd., Katoomba. www.facebook.com/pg/theelephantbean. ℂ **02/4782 4620.** Main courses A$12–A$19. Mon–Sat 7am–4pm; Sun 7am–3pm; Thurs–Sun 6pm–late.

MELBOURNE

I t's rare to find anyone who lives in Melbourne who doesn't adore it. I've lived there, and I love it too, and I hope this chapter illustrates the many reasons why. Victoria's capital, Melbourne (pronounced *Mel*-bun), is a cultural melting pot. For a start, more people of Greek descent live here than in any other city except Athens, Greece. Multitudes of Chinese, Italian, Vietnamese, and Lebanese immigrants have all left their mark. Almost a third of Melburnians were born overseas or have parents who were born overseas. With such a diverse population—and with trams rattling through the streets and stately European-style architecture surrounding you—it is sometimes easy to think you are somewhere else.

Melbourne's roots can be traced back to the 1850s, when gold was discovered in the surrounding hills. British settlers took up residence and prided themselves on coming freely to their city, rather than having been forced here in convict chains. The city grew wealthy and remained a conservative bastion until World War II, when another wave of immigration, mainly from southern Europe, made it a more relaxed place.

With elegant tree-lined boulevards and a lively cafe culture, Victoria's capital maintains a distinctly European feel. Expect wonderful architecture, both old and new, and green spaces like the Royal Botanic Gardens. Wander down atmospheric laneways, often adorned with street art. This cosmopolitan city is also Australia's culture capital, with vibrant dining, shopping, and nightlife.

In fact, Melbourne, which has a population of around 4.9 million, is at the head of the pack when it comes to shopping, restaurants, fashion, music, and nightlife. It frequently beats other state capitals in bids for major concerts, plays, exhibitions, and sporting events. Oh, and everyone wears black.

5

ESSENTIALS
Arriving
BY PLANE
Qantas (www.qantas.com.au; ℂ 131 313 in Australia) and **Virgin Australia** (www.virginaustralia.com.au; ℂ 136 789 in Australia) both fly to Melbourne from all state capitals and some regional centers. Qantas's discount arm, **Jetstar** (www.jetstar.com.au;

$ⓒ$ **131 538** in Australia) flies to and from Townsville, Hamilton Island in the Whitsundays, Uluru, and various other cities around the country. Jetstar also flies between Avalon Airport, about a 50-minute drive outside Melbourne's city center, and Sydney. Low-cost carrier **Tigerair** (www.tigerair.com.au; $ⓒ$ **1300/174 266** in Australia, or 07/3295 2104 in Australia) has its hub in Melbourne, and from there flies to Sydney, Hobart, Cairns, Townsville, Brisbane, and the Gold Coast in Queensland, as well as several other cities.

Melbourne Airport's international and domestic terminals (www.melbourneairport.com.au) are at Tullamarine, 22km (14 miles) northwest of the city center (often referred to as Tullamarine Airport). There are four passenger terminals. The international terminal (T2) and Qantas (T1) and Virgin Australia (T3) terminals are all under one roof. A separate domestic terminal (T4) is home to Jetstar, Tigerair, and Regional Express (REX). The travelers' information service desk, on the ground floor of the international arrivals hall (T2), is open from 7am until midnight daily. The international terminal has snack bars, a restaurant, currency-exchange facilities, duty-free shops, and showers (on the first floor). ATMs are available at both terminals. Baggage carts are free in the international baggage claim hall but cost A$4 in the parking lot, departure lounge, or domestic terminal; baggage storage, available in the international terminal, costs A$9 to A$26 per day, depending on the size of your bag (open 5am to 12:30am daily; photo ID required).

There are three airport hotels: **Parkroyal Melbourne Airport** ($ⓒ$ **03/8347 2000**), **Holiday Inn Melbourne Airport** ($ⓒ$ **03/9933 5111**), and **Ibis Budget Melbourne Airport** ($ⓒ$ **03/8336 1811**), all within 5 minutes' walk of the terminals. The Parkroyal offers a A$25 "lounge" package (available 6am–11pm) giving access to its pool, gym, and sauna for 3 hours, plus free Wi-Fi in the bar. Transiting passengers can book rooms for 3 to 8 hours (7am–7pm only), starting at A$89. A 5-minute drive away are the **Quest Melbourne Airport** (www.questmelbourneairport.com.au; $ⓒ$ **03/8340 8400**), an apartment hotel in the Melbourne Airport Business Park, and **Mantra Tullamarine** (www.mantrahotels.com/mantra-tullamarine-hotel; $ⓒ$ **03/9093 6500**), which runs a free shuttle.

Between the Airport and the City

Avis (www.avis.com.au; $ⓒ$ **03/8855 5333**), **Budget** (www.budget.com.au; $ⓒ$ **03/9241 6366**), **Europcar** (www.europcar.com.au; $ⓒ$ **03/9241 6800**), **Hertz** (www.hertz.com.au; $ⓒ$ **03/9338 4044**), **Thrifty** (www.thrifty.com.au; $ⓒ$ **03/9241 6100**) and **Redspot** (www.redspot.com.au; $ⓒ$ **03/9334 5455**) all have airport rental desks. The Tullamarine freeway to and from the airport joins with the CityLink, an electronic tollway system. Drivers need a CityLink pass. Check with your car-rental company.

The distinctive red **Skybus** (www.skybus.com.au; $ⓒ$ **03/9600 1711**) runs between the airport and Melbourne's Southern Cross station in Spencer Street every 10 minutes, 24 hours a day, every day. Buy tickets from Skybus desks outside the baggage claim areas or at the information desk in the international terminal. Returning to the airport, a free Skybus hotel shuttle will pick you up

Making Waves at the Airport

By mid-2019, Melbourne's newest attraction, Australia's first urban surf park, is expected to open near Melbourne Airport. At press time, construction was underway on the huge lagoon that will pump waves of up to 2m out for eager surfers. Puts a whole new meaning on waving goodbye! The park will also have food outlets and bars, a surf pro-shop, gymnasium and skate ramps. See www.urbnsurf.com.

at your hotel to connect with the larger airport-bound bus at Southern Cross railway station in the city center; you must book this in advance. It operates from 6am to 10:30pm weekdays and 7am to 7pm Saturday and Sunday, except Christmas Day. Skybus also operates from the airport to Southbank Docklands on the city fringe, and to the suburb of St Kilda, 6:30am to 7pm daily, every 30 minutes weekdays and every hour Saturday and Sunday. One-way **tickets** cost A$19 for adults to either the city or Southbank/Docklands, and A$37 round-trip. Tickets for children age 4 to 16 cost A$9 one-way or A$18 round-trip, but if you buy online, up to four children travel free on your adult ticket. The trip takes about 30 minutes from the airport to Southern Cross station and about an hour to St Kilda, but allow extra time (at least 15 minutes) for your return journey.

Skybus also operates the **Avalon City Express** transfer service to Avalon Airport for Jetstar flights. One-way fares from Avalon Airport are A$22 for adults and A$10 for children 4 to 14 to Southern Cross station, more to other central business district (CBD) locations and other suburbs.

A **taxi** to the city center takes about 30 minutes and costs around A$65.

BY TRAIN

Interstate trains arrive at **Southern Cross Railway Station,** Spencer and Little Collins streets (5 blocks from Swanston Street, in the city center). You may hear locals refer to it as Spencer Street Station. Taxis and buses are available here.

The **Sydney–Melbourne *XPT*** travels between Australia's two largest cities daily; trip time is 11 hours. For more information, contact **NSW Trainlink** (www.transportnsw.info; ☎ **132 232** in Australia, or 02/4907 7501). **V/Line** (www.vline.com.au; ☎ **1800/800 007** in Australia, or 03/9662 2505) services also connect Melbourne with destinations around Victoria and other capital cities.

BY BUS

Several bus companies connect Melbourne with other capitals and regional areas of Victoria. Among the biggest are **Greyhound Australia** (www.greyhound.com.au; ☎ **1300/473 946** in Australia, or 03/8667 8701). Coaches serve Melbourne's **Transit Centre,** 58 Franklin St., 2 blocks north of the Southern Cross Railway station on Spencer Street. Trams and taxis serve the station; **V/Line buses** (www.vline.com.au; ☎ **1800/800 007** in Australia), which travel all over Victoria, depart from the Spencer Street Coach Terminal.

BY CAR

You can drive from Sydney to Melbourne along the Hume Highway (a straight trip of about 9½ hr.). Another route is along the coastal Princes Highway, for which you will need a minimum of 2 days, with stops. For information on all aspects of road travel in Victoria, contact the **Royal Automotive Club of Victoria** (www.racv.com.au; 🕿 **137 228** in Australia, or 03/8832 7980).

Visitor Information

The first stop on any visitor's itinerary should be the **Melbourne Visitor Centre,** Federation Square, Swanston and Flinders streets (www.whatson. melbourne.vic.gov.au; 🕿 **03/9658 9658**). The center serves as a one-stop shop for tourism information, accommodations and tour bookings, public transport information, and ticket sales. Also here are an ATM, Internet terminals, and interactive multimedia providing information on Melbourne and Victoria. The center is open daily from 9am to 6pm (10am–5pm Good Friday; closed Christmas Day). The **Melbourne Greeter Service** also operates from the Melbourne Visitor Centre. This service connects visitors to enthusiastic local volunteers who offer free 2- to 4-hour orientation tours of the city at 9:30am daily. Book at least 24 hours in advance (🕿 **03/9658 9658** Mon–Fri, 03/9658 9942 Sat–Sun, or online). The Melbourne Visitor Centre also operates a staffed information booth in **Bourke Street Mall,** between Swanston and Elizabeth streets, open daily 9am to 5pm (closed Good Friday and Christmas Day). In the central city area (mainly along Swanston Street), also look for Melbourne's **City Ambassadors**—volunteers who give tourist information and directions. They'll be wearing bright red shirts.

Good websites about the city include the official tourism site, **www.visit melbourne.com**, and the locally run **www.onlymelbourne.com.au**. Also worth a look is the official City of Melbourne site, **www.melbourne.vic.gov.au**.

Melbourne City Layout

Melbourne is on the Yarra River and stretches inland from Port Phillip Bay, which lies to its south. On a map, you'll see a distinct central oblong area surrounded by Flinders Street to the south, Latrobe Street to the north, Spring Street to the east, and Spencer Street to the west. Cutting north to south

---

Half-Price Tickets

Buy tickets for entertainment events, including opera, dance, and drama, on the day of the performance from **Half-Tix** in the Melbourne Town Hall administration building on Swanston Street (right next to the Town Hall). The booth is open Monday from 10am to 2pm, Tuesday through Thursday 11am to 6pm, Friday 11am to 6:30pm, and Saturday 10am to 4pm (also selling for Sunday shows). Tickets must be purchased in person and in cash. Available shows are displayed on the booth door and on the website, www.halftixmelbourne.com.

St Kilda Pier.

through its center are the two main shopping thoroughfares, Swanston Street and Elizabeth Street. Cross streets between these major thoroughfares include Bourke Street Mall, a pedestrian-only shopping promenade. If you continue south along Swanston Street and over the river, it turns into St Kilda Road, which runs to the coast. Melbourne's various urban "villages," including South Yarra, Richmond, Carlton, and Fitzroy, surround the city center. The seaside suburb of St Kilda is known for its diverse restaurants.

Melbourne Neighborhoods in Brief

At more than 7,695 sq. km (2,971 sq. miles), Melbourne is one of the biggest cities in the world by area, with a population of about 4.9 million. Below are the neighborhoods of most interest to visitors.

City Center   Made up of a grid of streets north of the Yarra River, the city center—bounded by Flinders, Latrobe, Spring, and Spencer streets—offers good shopping and a charming cafe scene; in recent years an active nightlife has sprung up with the opening of a swath of funky bars and restaurants playing live and recorded music to suit all ages. The gateway to the city is the Flinders Street Station, with its dome and clock tower, flanked by the Federation Square precinct (p. 129).

Chinatown   Centering on Little Bourke Street, between Swanston and Exhibition streets, Australia's oldest permanent Chinese settlement dates from the 1850s, when a few boardinghouses catered to Chinese prospectors lured by gold rushes. Plenty of cheap restaurants crowd its alleyways.

Southgate & Southbank   This flashy entertainment district on the banks of the Yarra River opposite Flinders Street station (linked by pedestrian bridges) is home to the huge Crown Casino (p. 128), as well as myriad restaurants, bars, cafes, nightclubs, cinemas, and designer shops. On the city side of the river is the Melbourne Aquarium (p. 134). All are a 10-minute stroll from Flinders Street Station. Tram: 8 from Swanston Street.

The River District   Southeast of the center, the muddy-looking Yarra River runs past the Birrarung Marr parkland and Royal Botanic Gardens (p. 139); nearby are the Arts Centre, the National Gallery of Victoria, and the Melbourne Cricket Ground. It is accessible by the free City Circle Tram.

Docklands Near the city center, at the rear of the Spencer Street station, this industrial area has become the biggest new development in Melbourne. NewQuay on the waterfront has a diverse range of restaurants, shops, and cinemas, along with the 52,000-seat Etihad Stadium, where Melbourne dominates Australian Rules football. Docklands is accessible by the free City Circle Tram.

Carlton North of the center, this rambling suburb is known for Italian restaurants along Lygon Street, with varying food quality but lots of outdoor seating. Melbourne University is in Carlton, so there's a healthy student scene. From Bourke Street Mall, it's a 15-minute walk to Lygon Street. Tram: 1 or 22 from Swanston Street.

Fitzroy A ruggedly bohemian place 2km (1¼ miles) north of the city center, Fitzroy is filled with students and artists; it's popular for people-watching and amazing street art. Its hub is Brunswick Street, lined with cheap restaurants, busy cafes, late-night bookshops, art galleries, and pubs. Around the corner on Johnston Street, a growing Spanish quarter has tapas bars, flamenco restaurants, and Spanish clubs. Tram: 11 from Collins Street.

Richmond One of Melbourne's earliest settlements, noted for its historic streets and back lanes, Richmond today is a multicultural quarter lying east of the city center. Victoria Street is reminiscent of Ho Chi Minh City, with Vietnamese sights, sounds, aromas, and restaurants. Bridge Road is a discount-fashion precinct. Tram: 48 or 75 from Flinders Street; 70 from Princes Bridge; 109 from Bourke Street.

St Kilda Once Melbourne's red-light district, this shabby-chic bayside suburb (6km/3¾ miles south of the city center) now has the city's highest concentration of restaurants, from glitzy to cheap, as well as superb cake shops and delis. The Esplanade hugs a beach with a vintage pier and a lively Sunday arts-and-crafts market. Check out Luna Park, one of the world's oldest fun parks, built in 1912. Tram: 10 or 12 from Collins Street; 15 or 16 from Swanston Street; 96 from Bourke Street.

South Yarra/Prahran This posh part of town abounds with boutiques, cinemas, nightclubs, and galleries. Chapel Street has upscale eateries and designer fashions; Commercial Road is popular with the LGBTQ community. Off Chapel Street in Prahran, Greville Street is full of boutiques and music outlets. Tram: 8 or 72 from Swanston Street.

South Melbourne One of the city's oldest working-class districts, South Melbourne is known for its historic buildings, old-fashioned pubs and hotels, and markets. Tram: 12 from Collins Street; 1 from Swanston Street.

Williamstown Bypassed by developers, this waterfront suburb preserves a rich architectural heritage. Parts of Ferguson Street and Nelson Place look just like English High Streets, and on The Strand is a line of seaside bistros and a World War II warship museum. Ferry: From Southgate, or St Kilda Pier.

Getting Around Melbourne
BY PUBLIC TRANSPORTATION

Trams are the major form of transport in the city; you will probably only use a train or bus if you are going into the suburbs. Melbourne's transport system uses an electronic ticketing system called **myki,** a reusable smart card to pay for your travel. The card costs A$6, then you put money on it for travel. You "touch on" and "touch off" at an electronic machine on board the tram or bus, or as you enter the train station. When your myki balance gets low, just top up your card. A 2-hour trip in Zones 1 and 2, which will allow you to travel on all trams and trains within the city and close surrounding suburbs from rooms here are stylish and contemporary. Studios have queen-size beds or two singles, plenty of hardwood, soft lighting, and neutral tones with red accents. Superior rooms have king-size beds and lovely polished-wood floorboards, and deluxe rooms have wonderful views across to the Botanic Gardens through large bay windows. The hotel also boasts a worthy restaurant and a bar with an open fire.

26 Flinders St. www.hotellindrum.com.au. ✆ **03/9668 1111.** 59 units. A$265–A$365 double; A$385 suite. Public parking next door (discounted for guests). Train: Flinders St. **Amenities:** Restaurant; bar; nearby health club; room service; free Wi-Fi.

The Hotel Windsor ★★ One of Australia's grandest and most historic hotels, the Windsor has over the past few years, after a long debate over planning issues, been undergoing a controversial A$330-million redevelopment and restoration, expected to be completed in 2020. But it's still business as usual, as guests settle in to the opulent rooms and sit down to "high tea" each afternoon, as has been the custom for 130 years. The Windsor opened in 1883, an upper-crust establishment that oozed sophistication, and has hosted the rich, famous, and glamorous ever since. The hotel holds a special place in Australia's history as the setting for the drafting of the country's Constitution in 1898. The redevelopment adds a 26-story tower (and 152 guest rooms) behind the heritage building. Many guest bedrooms have striking views of Parliament House and the Treasury Gardens. I'd suggest you stay there as soon as you can!

103 Spring St. www.thehotelwindsor.com.au. ✆ **03/9633 6000.** 180 units. A$269–A$359 double; A$409–A$709 suite. Valet parking A$55–A$65 per night. Train: Parliament. **Amenities:** Restaurant; 2 bars; babysitting; concierge; health club; room service; free Wi-Fi.

Quest Grand Hotel Melbourne ★★ This majestic, Heritage-listed six-story building—originally home to the Victorian railway administration—is striking for its remarkable scale and imposing Italianate facade. Building started in 1887, and it became a hotel in 1997. Studios have plush carpets and full kitchens with dishwashers; one-bedroom loft suites have European-style espresso machines and a second TV in the bedroom, and some have great views over the new Docklands area beyond—though rooms are whisper-quiet. All vary in size; some have balconies (mostly on the 6th floor). Many of the suites are split-level, with bedrooms on the second floor.

33 Spencer St. www.grandhotelmelbourne.com.au. ✆ **03/9611 4567.** 94 units. A$189–A$209 studio; A$219–A$329 apt. Parking A$45. Tram: 48 or 75 from Flinders St. **Amenities:** Restaurant; bar; babysitting; concierge; golf course nearby; exercise room; Jacuzzi; heated indoor swimming pool (with retractable roof); room service; sauna; free Wi-Fi.

MODERATE

Ibis Melbourne Hotel and Apartments ★ The Ibis Melbourne is a good deal, next door to a tram stop, close to the bus station, *and* a short walk from the central shopping areas and Queen Victoria Market. Rooms in this mid-range hotel are spacious, immaculate, and bright (if somewhat bland and

5:30am to midnight (when transportation stops), costs A$4.30; the daily fare of A$8.60 allows unlimited travel. On weekends and public holidays, pay the off-peak rate of A$6.30 per day. A **7-day myki pass** will cost A$43 to travel in Zones 1 and 2. You can get cards at Flinders Street or Southern Cross stations, at the MetShop, or at most 7-Eleven convenience stores, and top them up through the **Public Transport Victoria** website (www.ptv.vic.gov.au) or at the call center (✆ **1800/800 007**); or top up as little as A$1 at myki machines in train stations and at selected tram platforms and bus interchanges.

Money-Saving Transit Passes

Visitors to Victoria can buy a **myki Explorer** card, which gives 1 day's unlimited travel as well as discounts on entry to 16 major attractions around the city and region. Buy this at the Melbourne Visitor Centre (p. 108) or Skybus terminal at Melbourne Airport or Southern Cross station. It costs A$15 adults or A$7.50 children, and you can top it up for another day.

You can pick up a free route map from the Melbourne Visitor Centre, Federation Square, or from the **PTV Hub** at Southern Cross station (www.ptv.vic.gov.au; ✆ **1800/800 007** in Australia), open Monday through Friday from 7am to 7pm, and weekends and public holidays (except Christmas Day) 9am to 6pm. There's another hub at 750 Collins St., Docklands, open from 8am to 6pm weekdays only (closed Sat–Sun and public holidays).

BY TRAM

Melbourne has the oldest tram network in the world. Trams are an essential part of the city, a major cultural icon, and a great non-smoggy way of getting around. Several hundred trams run over 325km (202 miles) of track.

Trams stop at numbered tram-stop signs, sometimes in the middle of the road (so beware of oncoming traffic!). To get off the tram, press the button near the handrails or pull the cord above your head.

A **free tram zone** operates in the inner city center, bounded by Spring, Flinders, and La Trobe streets, running along Victoria, William, and Elizabeth streets (around the Victoria Market) and to Docklands. Drivers announce when you are leaving the free zone. If you are staying in the free zone, you don't need to "touch on" with your myki, but if you are beginning or ending your trip outside the free zone, you must do so.

There is also a free **City Circle Tram** (tram no. 35) that travels a circular route between all the major central attractions and past shopping malls and arcades. The trams run in both directions every 12 minutes between 10am and 6pm (and until 9pm Thurs–Sat), except on Good Friday and Christmas Day. The trams run along all the major corridors including Flinders and Spencer streets.

BY BUS

Melbourne's bus services generally only serve the far-flung suburbs where trams don't reach. If you're looking for a bus tour, see **Melbourne City Sightseeing Tours** (p. 137).

A Quirky Melbourne Road Rule

There is one rule about turning right from the left lane at certain major intersections in the downtown center and in South Melbourne: In order to leave the left lane free for trams and through traffic, you must pull into the left lane opposite the street you are turning into, and make the turn when the traffic light in the street you are turning into becomes green. Luckily, these intersections are signposted.

BY TAXI

Cabs are plentiful in the city, but it may be difficult to hail one in the city center late on Friday and Saturday night. Major taxi ranks can be found in Queen Street (between Little Collins and Bourke streets), outside Flinders Street station, at Bourke Street (near Russell St.) and on King Street (near Flinders St.). Otherwise, order one by phone: Taxi companies include **Silver Top** (℃ **131 008** in Australia) and **13CABS** (Yellow) (℃ **132 227** in Australia). **Uber** also operates in Melbourne. Note that from 10pm to 5am, anywhere in Victoria, you must prepay your fare. The driver estimates the fare at the start of the journey, gives you a receipt, and then adjusts it according to the meter reading (plus any fees such as road tolls) at the end of your trip.

BY CAR

Driving in Melbourne can be challenging. Roads can be confusing, there are trams everywhere (you must always stop behind a tram if it stops, because passengers usually step directly into the road), and there's a general lack of parking and expensive hotel valet parking. It's better to avoid driving and get on a tram instead. For road rules, pick up a copy of the Victorian Road Traffic handbook from bookshops or from a **Vic Roads** office (℃ **131 171** in Australia for the nearest office).

If you plan to travel beyond Melbourne, wait to pick up your rental car until the day you're leaving the city. (See p. 106 for car rental companies.) Most car rental offices in the city center are on Franklin Street.

[FastFACTS] MELBOURNE

ATMs/Banks Banks are open Monday through Thursday from 9:30am to 4pm, and Friday from 9:30am to 5pm. Most ATMs operate 24 hr. and are found throughout the CBD.

Business Hours In general, stores are open daily from 9am to 5:30pm; many stay open until 9pm on Fridays, and on Saturdays and Sundays hours are often 10am to 4pm. Shops are generally not open on Good Friday and Christmas Day.

Dentists The **Royal Dental Hospital of Melbourne** (℃ **1800/833 039** in Australia, or 03/9341 1000), at 720 Swanston St.,

Carlton, offers emergency services 8:15am–9:15pm Mon–Fri and 8:45am–9:15pm weekends and public holidays.

Doctors & Hospitals The emergency department at the **Royal Melbourne Hospital,** 300 Grattan St., Parkville (℃ **03/9342 7000**), is open 24 hours. The

Traveller's Medical & Vaccination Centre, Second Floor, 393 Little Bourke St. (www.traveldoctor.com.au; ℃ **03/9935 8100**), offers full vaccination and travel medical services. It is open 9am–5pm Mon–Fri (until 8pm Thurs), Sat by appointment.

Embassies & Consulates The following English-speaking countries have consulates in Melbourne: **United States,** Level 6, 553 St Kilda Rd. (℃ **03/9526 5900**); **United Kingdom,** Level 17, 90 Collins St. (℃ **03/9652 1600**); and **New Zealand,** Level 4, 45 William St. (℃ **03/9678 0201**).

Emergencies In an emergency, call ℃ **000** for

police, ambulance, or the fire department.

Mail & Postage The **General Post Office (GPO)** at 250 Elizabeth St. (℃ **131 318** in Australia) is open Mon–Fri 8:30am–5:30pm, Sat 9am–5pm.

Newspapers & Magazines Melbourne's daily newspapers are *The Age* and the *Herald-Sun.* Both have Sunday versions as well.

Pharmacies (Chemist Shops) The **Mulqueeny Pharmacy,** 99 Swanston St. (℃ **03/9654 8569**), is open Mon–Fri 8am–8pm, Sat 9am–6pm, Sun 11am–6pm. The **Mulqueeny Midnight Pharmacy,** 416 High St., Windsor (℃ **03/9510 3977**), is open daily 9am–midnight.

Safety St Kild[...] coming up in the[...] walking there al[...] still isn't wise. Pa[...] gardens can also[...] night, as can the[...] around the King[...] nightclubs in the[...]

Wi-Fi The **Sta[...] of Victoria,** 328[...] St. (www.slv.vic.g[...] ℃ **03/8864 700[...]** wireless Internet[...] of the library an[...] stations in all re[...] rooms. It is ope[...] Thurs 10am–9p[...] Sun 10am–6pm.[...] Wi-Fi is availabl[...] bourne CBD at [...] and the Bourke[...] Queen Victoria [...] South Wharf Pro[...] the Melbourne [...] and Exhibition C[...]

WHERE TO STAY IN MELBOURNE

Getting a room is easy enough on weekends, when business travele[...] home. You need to book well in advance, however, during the city[...] events (say, the weekend before the Melbourne Cup, and during [...] Prix and the Australian Open). Hostels in the St Kilda area ten[...] quickly in December and January.

You'll feel right in the heart of the action if you stay in the city ce[...] seems to buzz all day (and night). Otherwise, the inner-city subu[...] exciting satellites, with good street life, restaurants, and pubs—and [...] tram ride from the city center. Transportation from the airport to the[...] a little more expensive and complicated than to the city center, how[...]

The **Best of Victoria** booking service, Federation Square (www[...] visitorcentres.com.au/vic; ℃ **03/9928 0000**), open daily 9am to 6[...] Christmas Day), can help you book accommodations after you arrive[...] They also have a desk in the Arrivals Hall at Melbourne Internation[...]

In the City Center
EXPENSIVE
Hotel Lindrum ★★ This gorgeous hotel has always felt qui[...] to me; perhaps the billiard room has something to do with it. Th[...]

Melbourne Hotels & Restaurants

HOTELS ■

The Blackman **21**
The Cullen **22**
Georgian Court Guest House **20**
Hotel Lindrum **19**
The Hotel Windsor **10**
Ibis Melbourne Hotel
 & Apartments **2**
Ibis Styles Kingsgate Hotel **32**
Jasper Hotel **3**
The Larwill Studio **1**
The Nunnery **9**
The Olsen **23**
Quest Grand Hotel
 Melbourne **33**

RESTAURANTS ◆

Babka Bakery **8**
Bamboo House **13**
Barbarella **29**
Becco **11**
Brunetti **5**
Café Segovia **30**
Chocolate Buddha **24**
Flower Drum **16**
Grossi Florentino **14**
Hopetoun Tea Rooms
 Winter Garden **28**
Il Bacaro **17**
Il Solito Posto **18**
Journal Café **27**
Koko **34**
Marios **7**
MoVida **25**
MoVida Aqui **31**
Mr Tulk **4**
Pellegrini's Espresso Bar **12**
Shakahari **6**
Supper Inn **15**
Young & Jackson **26**

MELBOURNE'S art hotels

Some of Melbourne's most interesting boutique hotels belong to the **Art Series Hotel Group** (www.artseries hotels.com.au), which themes its hotels to well-known Australian artists. The flagship is **The Olsen ★★★**, at Chapel Street and Toorak Road, South Yarra (📞 **03/9040 1222**), named for John Olsen, regarded as Australia's greatest living painter. It has 224 spacious rooms and claims to have the world's largest glass-bottom swimming pool, suspended over the street. Rates start from A$259 to A$319 double per night for a studio suite. It's a little bit out of the city center, but there's a tram almost on the doorstep, and I vote it one of my favorite hotels. **The Cullen ★★**, a 115-room boutique hotel at 164 Commercial Rd., Prahran (📞 **03/9098 1555**), is named for the controversial artist Adam Cullen and has a rooftop cocktail bar and two restaurants. Room rates range from A$229 to A$279 double. **The Blackman ★★**, named for Sydney artist John Blackman and housed within the Heritage-listed Airlie House (backed by a modern high-rise annex), is at 452 St Kilda Rd. (📞 **03/9039 1444**) and has 209 rooms, with rates ranging from A$249 to A$299 double. North of Melbourne's city center, **The Larwill Studio ★★**, 48 Flemington Rd., Parkville (📞 **03/9032 9111**), is dedicated to artist David Larwill, and has rooms from A$169 to A$229.

Each hotel features a major artwork commissioned especially for the hotel foyer by the naming artist: The Cullen has one from Adam Cullen's *Ned Kelly* series, and the Olsen's spectacular glass lobby features Olsen's 6m (19-ft.) mural *The Yellow Sun and Yarra*. Prints and a photographic history of each artist's life adorn guestroom walls and public spaces; the architecture, interior design, linens, and stationery also reflect the artist's style. If you like the concept, there are Art Series hotels in other Australian cities: **The Schaller** in Bendigo, **The Johnson** in Brisbane, and **The Watson** in Adelaide, if your travels take you there. Visit the Art Series website for links to all properties.

colorless); the whole hotel was refurbished in 2015. All apartments come equipped with kitchenettes and bathtubs.

15–21 Therry St. www.ibis.com. 📞 **03/9666 0000**. 250 units. A$149 double; A$179 1-bedroom apt; A$269 2-bedroom apt. Parking A$25. Tram: 19, 57, 59. **Amenities:** Restaurant; bar; free Wi-Fi.

Jasper Hotel ★★ Looking sharp and welcoming after a A$7-million upgrade completed in 2014, this is a good choice for an inner-city boutique hotel. There are 16 suites on the hotel's second level, some of which open out onto a guest courtyard with walled gardens and artificial grass. Levels 2 and 3 also have small executive lounges with free refreshments (and check out the hallways' star-spangled ceilings). Some rooms have balconies overlooking Elizabeth Street. The Jasper Kitchen restaurant sources most of its produce from the Queen Victoria Market, just outside the back door; the more casual Spiked@Jasper opens at 4pm. Hotel guests get free entry to the nearby Melbourne City Baths swimming pool.

489 Elizabeth St. www.jasperhotel.com.au. 📞 **03/8327 2777**. 90 units. A$164–A$264 double; A$274 suite. Parking nearby (around A$35 per day). Tram: 19, 57, 59. Train: Melbourne Central. **Amenities:** 2 restaurants; bar; gym; room service; free Wi-Fi.

INEXPENSIVE

Ibis Styles Kingsgate Hotel ★   A 10-minute walk from the city, this interesting hotel resembles a terrace building from the outside, but inside it's a maze of corridors and rooms. At the time of writing the hotel was undergoing renovation of its guest rooms, due for completion in mid-2020, which means there may be some daytime noise issues from time to time. The least expensive economy rooms have double beds (no twins); these rooms are small but a good value if you just want somewhere to sleep. Standard rooms have double or twin beds. The 21 family rooms have double beds and one or two singles. There's a 24-hour reception desk, free luggage-storage facilities, and a guest laundry.

131 King St. www.kingsgatehotel.com.au. © **1300/734 171** in Australia, or 03/9629 4171. 171 units. A$86–A$111 double; A$106–A$136 family room. Parking at nearby Southern Cross Station, A$25 per day. Tram: 19, 57, 59. **Amenities:** Restaurant (breakfast only); bar; free Wi-Fi.

In East Melbourne

INEXPENSIVE

Georgian Court Guest House ★   The appearance of the comfortable Georgian Court, set on a beautiful tree-lined street, hasn't changed much since it was built in 1910. The sitting and dining rooms have high ceilings and offer old-world atmosphere. The guest rooms are simply furnished, and some are in need of a refurbishment; others have already been refreshed. Some have en suite bathrooms; others have private bathrooms in the hallway. One room comes with a queen-size bed and Jacuzzi. The Georgian Court is a 15-minute stroll through the Fitzroy and Treasury Gardens from the city center and is also close to the fashion shops of Bridge Road.

21 George St., East Melbourne. www.georgiancourt.com.au. © **03/9415 8225.** 31 units. A$90–A$129 double; A$129–A$159 family room. Rates include breakfast. Free parking. Tram: 75 from Flinders St., or 48 from Spencer St. **Amenities:** Free Wi-Fi.

In Fitzroy

MODERATE/INEXPENSIVE

The Nunnery ★★   This former convent offers smart budget accommodations—and something a little more upmarket—a short tram ride from the city center, close to the restaurants and nightlife of Brunswick and Lygon streets in nearby Carlton. The informal, friendly 1860s main building has high ceilings, handmade light fittings, polished floorboards, marble fireplaces, and a hand-turned staircase. There's also a clever and rather irreverent play on its past in the decor. It's well suited to couples and families. The Guesthouse next door, built in the early 1900s, is also comfy, stylish, and decorated with tasteful furnishings and artwork; its seven rooms share three bathrooms. The Nunnery, former home of the Daughters of Charity, also offers dorm rooms with 4, 8, or 12 beds. *Note:* There are no elevators.

116 Nicholson St., Fitzroy. www.nunnery.com.au. © **1800/032 635** in Australia, or 03/9419 8637. 30 units, all with shared bathroom. A$155–A$225 double family room; A$31–A$36 per person bunk rooms. Guesthouse: A$110–A$140 double. Rates include breakfast. Free parking (reservation required). Tram: 96. **Amenities:** Kitchen; free Wi-Fi.

In St Kilda

EXPENSIVE

Novotel Melbourne St Kilda ★   Ask for a room with a view at this sleek contemporary seaside hotel; the best of them overlook St Kilda beach, the pier, and Port Phillip Bay. Standard rooms have a queen or king bed, a small desk, and minibar; some have a Jacuzzi. This well-located property is a 2-minute walk to the beach, Luna Park, and Acland Street shopping—and on Sundays you're right across the street from the St Kilda arts-and-crafts markets that line the Esplanade.

16 The Esplanade. www.novotel.com. ℂ **03/9525 5522.** 211 units. A$199–A$244 double; A$399 1-bedroom penthouse; A$274 family room (sleeps 4). Parking A$25. Tram: 16, 96. **Amenities:** Restaurant; bar; outdoor heated pool; fitness center; Wi-Fi (A$10/24hr.).

MODERATE

Tolarno Hotel ★★   Quirky Tolarno is in the middle of St Kilda's cafe and restaurant strip and just a short stroll from the beach. Set in the former private residence and gallery of artist Mirka Mora, the rooms and corridors of this modern, colorful property are adorned with 150 contemporary works by Melbourne artists, many of them by Mora, for whom the hotel's restaurant is named. Rooms vary but the deluxe doubles in the front of the building, with balconies overlooking the main street, are the most popular. These rooms are larger than the standard rooms, but if you are a light sleeper you might prefer something away from the noise of the trams running by. Superior doubles come with microwaves, and two have Japanese baths. Suites have a separate kitchen and lounge, but no balcony. The hotel restaurant is a pasta bar, open for lunch and dinner, serving "traditional Italian with a twist." If that's not to your taste, there are plenty of other options right on Fitzroy Street, the heart of St Kilda's restaurant strip.

42 Fitzroy St. www.tolarnohotel.com.au. ℂ **03/9537 0200.** 37 units. A$104–A$154 double; A$215–A$275 suite. Free street parking or A$10 in the building opposite. Tram: 16 from Swanston St., 12 from Collins St., or 96 from Flinders St. **Amenities:** Restaurant; bar; babysitting; bikes; concierge; room service; free Wi-Fi.

WHERE TO EAT IN MELBOURNE

Melbourne's ethnically diverse population ensures a healthy selection of international cuisines. Chinatown, in the city center, is a fabulous hunting ground for Chinese, Malaysian, Thai, Indonesian, Japanese, and Vietnamese fare, often at bargain prices. Carlton has plenty of Italian restaurants, but some of the outdoor eateries on Lygon Street target unsuspecting tourists with overpriced and disappointing fare; avoid them. Richmond is crammed with Greek and Vietnamese restaurants, and Fitzroy has cheap Asian, Turkish, Mediterranean, and vegetarian food. To see and be seen, head to Chapel Street or Toorak Road in South Yarra, or travel to St Kilda, where you can join the throng of Melburnians dining out along Fitzroy and Acland streets.

5

WHERE TO EAT IN MELBOURNE | Where to Eat in Melbourne

Most of the cheaper places in Melbourne are strictly BYO (bring your own wine or beer). Smoking is banned in Melbourne cafes and restaurants, so don't even think about lighting up.

For restaurant locations, see map on p. 115.

In the City Center
EXPENSIVE
Becco ★★ ITALIAN   Tucked away on a quiet lane, this favorite of Melburnians consistently lives up to its many accolades. The simplicity of the surroundings—terrazzo floors, white tablecloths, views of the lane—belie the sophistication of this stylish restaurant. The cuisine mixes Italian flavors with

5

MELBOURNE | Where to Eat in Melbourne

119

Australian flair. Try the veal saltimbocca, one of the tasty pasta dishes, or the specials, which your waiter will fill you in on. If you prefer something lighter, there's a bar menu of equally tempting dishes.

11–25 Crossley St., near Bourke St. www.becco.com.au. ℭ **03/9663 3000.** Main courses A$28–A$70. Mon–Fri noon–3pm; Mon–Sat 6–11pm.

Grossi Florentino ★★★ ITALIAN Under the management of the Grossi family, this is probably the best Italian restaurant in Melbourne, with three dining options. The casual bistro, the Grill, is downstairs, right next to the Cellar Bar where a bowl of pasta on the bar menu is less than A$26, but the upstairs, outfitted with chandeliers and murals reflecting the Florentine way of life, is reserved for fine dining. With such innovative dishes as pasta with wild boar ragu, the food is not traditional Italian, but everything has a distinctive Italian twist to it. Seafood and steak dishes are also on the menu. Save room for dessert: perhaps buttermilk panna cotta with white chocolate and caramel, or the cheese plate to share? On weekdays, two-course lunch specials are available in the restaurant for A$65.

80 Bourke St. www.grossiflorentino.com. ℭ **03/9662 1811.** Main courses A$26–A$58. Mon–Fri noon–3pm; Mon–Sat 6–11pm (cellar bar opens at 7:30am for breakfast Mon–Sat). Tram: 86, 96.

Koko ★★ JAPANESE Though you'll find plenty of sushi and noodle bars around Chinatown, there's nothing quite like raw fish with a bit of panache. Koko's decor is contemporary-traditional, with a goldfish pond in the center of the main dining room and wonderful views over the city. There are separate teppanyaki grills and screened tatami rooms where you sit on the matted floor. Koko has a vast and changing seasonal menu that includes a variety seafood dishes (think grilled crayfish with soy salt), or you can opt for a set menu to take the agony out of choosing. A large selection of sakes aids digestion. The A$50 lunch special includes a selection of hot and cold dishes, as well as sashimi and miso soup, green tea ice cream, and a glass of wine, beer, or soft drink.

Level 3, Crown Towers, Southbank. www.crownmelbourne.com.au/koko. ℭ **03/9292 5777.** Main courses A$40–A$115. Daily noon–2:30pm; Sun–Thurs 6–10pm; Fri–Sat 6–10:30pm.

MODERATE

Bamboo House ★★ CHINESE/CANTONESE Esteemed by both the Chinese community and local business big shots, this restaurant is worth writing home about. Service here is a pleasure; the waiters will help you construct a feast from the myriad Cantonese and northern Chinese dishes. Order ahead to get a taste of the signature dish, Szechuan tea-smoked duck. Other popular dishes include pan-fried beef dumplings and spring-onion pancakes.

47 Little Bourke St. www.bamboohouse.com.au. ℭ **03/9662 1565.** Main courses A$22–A$44. Mon–Fri noon–3pm (except public holidays); Mon–Sat 5:30–11pm; Sun 5:30–10pm. Tram: 35, 86, 96.

Chocolate Buddha ★★ JAPANESE This place offers mostly organic produce, including some organic wines. Based mostly on Japanese-inspired noodle, ramen, and soba dishes to which the kitchen adds meat, chicken, or seafood, it's casual yet satisfying dining. The best way to eat here is to order dishes to share. The food is creative, and the view across the square to the Yarra River and Southbank is a delight at dusk. It can get very crowded, so book ahead if you can.

Federation Sq., corner of Flinders and Swanston sts. www.chocolatebuddha.com.au. ✆ **03/9654 5688.** Main courses A$15–A$26. Daily noon–11:30pm. Train: Flinders St.

Flower Drum ★★★ CANTONESE   Praise pours in from all quarters for this upscale restaurant just off Little Bourke Street, Chinatown's main drag. Take a slow elevator up to the restaurant, which has widely spaced tables (perfect for politicians and businesspeople to clinch their deals). Take note of the specials— the chefs are extremely creative and use the best ingredients they find in the markets each day. A smart idea is to put your menu selections into the hands of the waiter. The signature dish is Peking duck, and the seafood dumplings in soup is a great starter. Or, you can order more unusual dishes, such as abalone (at a price: A$1,700 per kg) or pearl meat. The atmosphere is clubby and a bit old-fashioned; the service is impeccable. But be prepared to pay for the privilege.

17 Market Lane. www.flowerdrum.melbourne. ✆ **03/9662 3655.** Main courses A$18–A$42. Mon–Sat noon–3pm and 6–11pm; Sun 6–10:30pm. Tram: 86, 96.

Il Bacaro ★★ ITALIAN   Walk into Il Bacaro and you'll experience a little piece of Venice. Dominated by a horseshoe-shaped bar, it's jam-packed with small tables and weaving waiters carrying interesting dishes such as rabbit tortellini or braised goat with porcini mushrooms, pickled carrots, silverbeet, and truffled pecorino. The pasta dishes and the risotto of the day always go down well, as do the side salads. It's often crowded at lunch with businesspeople digging into the excellent wine list.

168–170 Little Collins St. www.ilbacaro.com.au. ✆ **03/9654 6778.** Main courses A$27–A$48. Mon–Sat noon–3pm; Mon–Thurs 6–10:30pm; Fri–Sat 6–11pm. Tram: 11, 12, 48, 86, 96, 109.

5

MELBOURNE | Where to Eat in Melbourne

Spanish tapas and a convivial vibe draw crowds to MoVida.

Il Solito Posto ★★ ITALIAN This below-ground restaurant consists of two parts. The casual bistro or *caffeteria* has a blackboard menu offering good pastas, soups, and salads. Then there's the sharper and more upmarket trattoria, with an a la carte menu of northern Italian dishes offering the likes of slow-braised lamb in white wine, chili, garlic, herbs, fresh peas, and tomato; as well as steak, fish, and veal dishes. It's open for breakfast, lunch, and dinner. You'll find the coffee excellent, too.

113 Collins St., basement (enter through George Parade). www.ilsolitoposto.com.au. ✆ **03/9654 4466.** Main courses A$28–A$34 in bistro, A$23–A$46 in trattoria. Mon–Fri 7:30am–1am; Sat 9am–1am. Tram: 11, 12, 48, 109.

MoVida ★★★ SPANISH Barcelona-born chef and co-owner Frank Camorra has made MoVida one of the most talked-about restaurants in Melbourne. His restaurant reflects the spirit of Spain, relaxed and fun, with seriously good food and good wine. Melburnians flock here, and it's truly one of those places I was tempted to keep a secret (if that's possible, considering that everyone talks about how great it is). MoVida offers a choice of tapas (small individual dishes) or *raciones* (plates to share among two or more people, or a larger dish for one). Specials are available every night to keep the regulars happy. So successful was the first MoVida that there's also now **Next Door,** which is . . . you guessed it, next door. And if you have a group (up to six people), or you want to dine outdoors, there is **MoVida Aqui,** at level 1, 500 Bourke St. (entry off Little Bourke St.), which has a huge casual dining area and a terrace and serves the same great food. Be sure to book a table.

1 Hosier Lane. www.movida.com.au. ✆ **03/9663 3038** (for all restaurants). Tapas A$3.80–A$9; *raciones* (main courses) A$18–A$38; banquet menu (10 dishes) A$80 per person. Daily noon–late. Train: Flinders St.

Young & Jackson ★★ PUB   Melbourne's oldest and most famous pub—it's a great place to stop in for a drink at the bar or a meal in the stylish upstairs restaurant or bistro areas. It has fairly standard pub food (burgers, schnitzel, ribs, and so on) in the cafe downstairs and at the rooftop bar, but offerings are more refined in the restaurant. It's a landmark on the corner opposite Federation Square and Flinders Street Station. Head upstairs to see the nude *Chloe,* the famous painting brought to Melbourne from Paris for the Great Exhibition in 1880, which has a special place in the hearts of customers and Melburnians. The pub, which was built in 1853 and started selling beer in 1861, has a few years on *Chloe,* which was painted in Paris in 1875.

At the corner of Flinders and Swanston sts. www.youngandjacksons.com.au. © **03/9650 3884.** Main courses A$24–A$40. Bar meals available 10am–late. Restaurant: daily noon–2:30pm; Sun–Thurs 5:30–9pm; Fri–Sat 5:30–10pm. Train: Flinders St.

INEXPENSIVE

Hopetoun Tea Rooms Winter Garden ★ CAFE   The first cup of tea served in this Melbourne institution left the pot in 1892. With its green-and-cream Regency wallpaper and marble tables, the Tea Rooms cater to a loyal clientele of little old ladies and students, with the odd tourist or businessperson thrown into the mix. At times, there are long queues waiting for a table, but most people think it's worth it. There's a full lunch menu, but really you should come for tea or coffee and very good cakes. Try the chocolate strawberry Swiss roll. Scones, croissants, pasta, and grilled food are also available. Traditional "High Tea" at A$55 per person can be taken between 10am and 3pm.

Block Arcade, 280–282 Collins St. www.hopetountearooms.com.au. © **03/9650 2777.** Main courses A$14–A$26; sandwiches A$13–A$19. Mon–Sat 8am–5pm; Sun 9am–5pm. Tram: 11, 12, 48, 109.

Supper Inn ★★ CANTONESE   Head here if you get the Chinese-food munchies late at night. It's a friendly place with a mixed crowd of locals and tourists chowing down on such dishes as steaming bowls of *congee* (rice-based porridge), dumplings, barbecued suckling pig, mud crab, pepper squid, or stuffed scallops. Everything here is the real thing.

15 Celestial Ave. © **03/9663 4759.** Main courses A$11–A$40. Daily 5:30pm–2:30am. Train: Melbourne Central.

In Carlton
INEXPENSIVE

Brunetti ★★ ITALIAN   Don't be daunted by the crowds around the cake counters—and there *will* be crowds! This is a real Italian/Melbourne experience. If you can get past the mouthwatering array of excellent cakes, the cafe menu offers authentic Italian cuisine, done very well. The open kitchen allows you to watch the chefs in action; there's a wood-fired pizza oven (imported from Italy) and a traditional *gelatieri* (ice-cream maker) at work. Or pop in for breakfast. If you can't get to Carlton, there's the cafe-style **Brunetti City Square** at Swanston Street and Flinders Lane in the city, and another on level three of the Myer department store (p. 140). Or you can check out their cafe at Terminal 4 at Melbourne Airport before you leave town!

380 Lygon St. www.brunetti.com.au. 📞 **03/9347 2801.** Main courses A$16–A$23. Sun–Thurs 6am–11pm; Fri–Sat 6am–midnight. Tram: 1, 15, 21, or 22 going north on Swanston St.

Shakahari ★ VEGETARIAN/VEGAN   Good vegetarian or vegan food isn't just a meal without meat; it's a creation in its own right. At Shakahari you're assured a creative meal that's not at all bland. The large restaurant is quite low-key, and there's a lovely courtyard out the back. The signature satay dish—skewered, lightly fried vegetables and tofu pieces with a mildly spicy peanut sauce—is a perennial favorite. Also available are curries, croquettes, green papaya salad, a pasta dish, and a fragrant laksa. A second restaurant, **Shakahari Too,** is located in South Melbourne (📞 **03/9682 2207**).

201–203 Faraday St. www.shakahari.com.au. 📞 **03/9347 3848.** Main courses A$22–A$23. Mon–Sat noon–3pm; Mon–Fri 6–9:30pm; Sat–Sun 6–10:30pm. Tram: 1, 8, 16, or 96 (or any traveling north along Swanston St.).

In Fitzroy
MODERATE

Marios ★★★ ITALIAN   Opened in 1986 by two Italian-Australian friends, both named Mario, this place has ambience, groovy decor, and impeccable service. And after 30 years in business, there's little here you can fault, including the food. Offerings include a range of cakes and pastas (like gnocchi with pancetta, peas, basil, tomato, and shaved Parmesan), and breakfast is served all day. The art on the walls, all by local artists, is always interesting—and for sale. The coffee is excellent (just don't ask for skim, decaf, or anything other than the real deal). You can also buy a jar of Marios' marmalade to take home for A$8.

303 Brunswick St. www.marioscafe.com.au. 📞 **03/9417 3343.** Main courses A$16–A$32. Mon–Sat 7am–10:30pm; Sun & public holidays 8am–10:30pm. Tram: 112 from Collins St.

In St Kilda
EXPENSIVE

Cicciolina ★★★ CONTEMPORARY   It's difficult enough to get a table at this wonderful but understated place without encouraging more people to line up, but I'd be depriving you of a terrific night out if I kept quiet. Cicciolina is intimate, crowded, and well run and has superb but simple food. Although you cannot book for dinner (there's a waitlist after 6pm), you may have to wait an hour or so for a table. Have a drink in the Back Bar, and they'll call you when your table is ready; I assure you it will be worth it for delights such as roasted organic saltbush lamb rump with marjoram baby beets, roasted garlic puree and pickled kohlrabi, or a simple linguini with Tasmanian salmon, braised leek, baby spinach, lemon and olive oil (my eternal favorite). If you're not into the wait, Cicciolina accepts reservations for lunch.

130 Acland St. www.cicciolinastkilda.com.au. ℭ **03/9525 3333.** Main courses A$32–A$48. Mon–Sat noon–11pm; Sun noon–10pm. Reservations for lunch only. Tram: 16 from Swanston St., or 94 or 96 from Bourke St.

MODERATE/EXPENSIVE

Donovans ★★ CONTEMPORARY   Watching the sun go down over St Kilda Beach from the veranda at Donovans (with glass in hand) is a perfect way to end the day. Owners Gail and Kevin Donovan's much-loved restaurant—housed in a 1920s bathing pavilion—is a place that many of their loyal customers see as being welcomed into their home (or at least their beach house). Lots of comfy cushions, a log fire, coffee-table books, and the sound of jazz and breakers on the beach create a wonderful atmosphere. The menu includes a mind-boggling array of dishes, many big enough for two. Try the seafood linguine or perhaps an old-fashioned chicken pie with mushrooms and vegetables. The bombe Alaska for two is legendary. There's also a children's menu.

40 Jacka Blvd. www.donovanshouse.com.au. ℭ **03/9534 8221.** Main courses A$26–A$68. Daily noon–10:30pm. Tram: 16, 94, or 96.

INEXPENSIVE

Babu Ji ★★ INDIAN   This very popular Indian eatery is fun and noisy and focuses on good food and good service. The menu offers curries of all kinds and Indian street food. On Sundays, there's a A$28 "thali" all-you-can-eat meal offer (cash only), and there are set menus for A$49 (four courses) and A$69 (six courses) per person. Pair your meal with a craft beer (grab your own from the good selection in the fridge; everything is A$9) or glass of

---

Pay What You Think

With a novel approach that not surprisingly has become a hit, the vegetarian restaurant **Lentil as Anything** (www.lentilasanything.com) has a menu without prices. Here you eat—then pay "as you feel" (or for some people, what they can afford) for the meal and service. The food is organic, with lots of noodles and veggies, plus tofu, curries, and stir-fries. Before you leave, you put your money in a box. The original restaurant is at 41 Blessington St., St Kilda (ℭ **0424/345 368** mobile; daily noon–9pm). A second outlet at the Abbotsford Convent, 1 St. Heliers St., Abbotsford (ℭ **03/9419 6444**), is open daily from 9am to 11:30am, noon to 3pm, and 5 to 9pm. To avoid long waits, you can now book a table at Abbotsford (for a fee of A$15 per person). Cash only.

wine—BYO with A$10 per bottle corkage fee, or buy it there. Takeout service available.

The George Building, 4–6 Grey St. www.babuji.com.au. Reservations for parties of 4 or more only. Main courses A$15–A$25. Sat–Sun 11:30am–2:30pm; Sun–Wed 5:30–9:30pm; Thurs–Sat 5:30–10pm. Closed Christmas Day, Dec 31, and Jan 1. Tram: 16 from Swanston St. or 96 from Bourke St.

Ichi Ni ★★ JAPANESE   Join Melbourne's beautiful people at one of the city's most popular *izakaya* (Japanese gastropub), a great place for a casual meal with a view of Port Phillip Bay. Take a booth inside, or a table on the deck (heated in winter), for the full experience—sharing is best—of yakitori, sashimi, sushi, and Japanese-style tapas dishes. The prices are great, the atmosphere lively, and the service good—a fine combination that keeps me coming back.

12 The Esplanade. www.ichini.com.au. ✆ **03/9534 1212.** Main courses A$10–A$25. Daily noon–10:30pm. Tram: 16, 94, or 96.

EXPLORING MELBOURNE

Visitors to Melbourne come to experience the contrasts of old-world architecture and the exciting feel of a truly multicultural city. This is a wonderfully compact city, with all the major attractions within easy reach of the city heart. Most visitors also venture to the bayside suburb of St Kilda, an easy tram ride away.

The Arts Centre ★★ PERFORMING ARTS CENTER   The spectacular 162m-high (531½-ft.) spire that glitters atop the Theatres Building of the Arts Centre, on the banks of the Yarra River, crowns the city's leading performing arts complex. Beneath it, the State Theatre, the Playhouse, and the Fairfax Studio present performances that are the focal point of culture in Melbourne. The Arts Centre has been the hub of Melbourne's cultural world for more than 30 years, and you can see some of that history in the changing themed exhibitions of costumes, photographs, and memorabilia. The **State Theatre,** seating 2,085 on three levels, can accommodate elaborate stagings of opera, ballet, musicals, and more. The **Playhouse** is a smaller venue that often books the Melbourne Theatre Company. The **Fairfax** is more intimate still and is often used for experimental theater or cabaret. Adjacent to the Theatres Building is **Hamer Hall,** home of the Melbourne Symphony Orchestra and often host to visiting orchestras. Many international stars have graced this stage, known for its excellent acoustics. Make sure you book ahead, as Melburnians love this place, and performances are often sold out. You can do a guided Theatres and Exhibition Tour daily (except Sun) at 11am. The tour takes an hour, and costs A$20 adults and A$15 children 17 and under, and includes morning tea. On Sundays at 11am, the Backstage Tour takes about 90 minutes and costs A$25 per person (not suitable for children 11 and under).

100 St Kilda Rd. www.artscentremelbourne.com.au. ✆ **1300/182 183** for tickets. Ticket prices vary depending on the event. Box office (in the Theatres Bldg.): Mon–Sat 9am–8:30pm; Sun 10am–5pm. Train: Flinders St. Tram: 1, 3, 3a, 5, 6, 16, 64, 67, 72.

Melbourne Attractions

DOCKLANDS

Southern Cross
Station

CITY CENTER

CHINATOWN

SOUTHBANK

Yarra River

St. Patrick's Cathedral

Princess Theatre

Parliament

State Library of Victoria

Melbourne Central

Myer Store

David Jones

St. Francis

St. Paul's Cathedral

Flinders Street Station

Federation Square

City Square

The Arts Centre

St. Johns

Princes Bridge

Queens Bridge

Sandridge Bridge

Kings Bridge

Rod Laver Arena

To Melbourne Cricket Ground

National Tennis Centre

Fitzroy Gardens

Treasury Gardens

Parliament Gardens

Carlton Gardens

Flagstaff Gardens

Alexandra Gardens

Birrarung Marr

Southbank Promenade

Victoria Parade

Brunswick St.

Gisborne St.

To Fitzroy

Nicholson St.

Spring St.

Albert St.

La Trobe St.

Lonsdale St.

Little Lonsdale St.

Bourke St.

Little Bourke St.

Collins St.

Little Collins St.

Flinders St.

Flinders Ln.

Exhibition St.

Russell St.

Swanston St.

Elizabeth St.

Queen St.

William St.

King St.

Spencer St.

Collins St.

Market St.

A'Beckett St.

Franklin St.

Anthony St.

Peel St.

Queen St.

Macarthur St.

St. Andrews Pl.

Cathedral Pl.

Landsdowne St.

Wellington Parade

Wellington Parade South

Treasury Pl.

George Parade

Jolimont Rd.

Boathouse Dr.

Alexandra Ave.

CITY Rd.

Southern Cross

To Carlton

To Fitzroy

To South Yarra

1/4 mi

0   0.25 km

The Arts Centre **15**
Birrarung Marr **18**
Cooks' Cottage **7**
Crown Casino **13**
Eureka Skydeck **14**
Federation Square **10**
Fitzroy Gardens **6**
The Ian Potter Centre **9**
La Trobe's Cottage **21**
Melbourne Museum **4**
Melbourne Zoo **2**
National Gallery of Victoria International **16**
National Sports Museum **19**
Old Melbourne Gaol **3**
Parliament House Victoria **5**
Polly Woodside **11**
Queen Victoria Market **1**
Royal Botanic Gardens **20**
SEA LIFE Melbourne Aquarium **12**
Shrine of Remembrance **17**
Treasury Gardens **8**

The Eureka Skydeck offers 360-degree, glassed-in views from high above Melbourne.

Cooks' Cottage ★ HISTORIC HOME   Built in 1755 by the parents of explorer Captain James Cook, this golden-brick cottage was moved to Melbourne from Great Ayton, in Yorkshire, England, in 1934 to mark Victoria's centenary. Inside, it's spartan and cramped, not unlike a ship's cabin. Displays provide the opportunity to learn about Cook's voyages of discovery around the world.

Fitzroy Gardens, off Wellington Parade. www.melbourne.vic.gov.au/cookscottage. © **03/9658 9658.** A$6.50 adults, A$3.50 children 5–15, A$18 family of 4. Daily 9am–5pm. Closed Christmas Day. Tram: 48, 75, or 35 (City Circle).

Crown Casino ★ CASINO   Australia's largest casino is a plush affair that's open 24 hours. You'll find all the usual roulette and blackjack tables and so on, as well as an array of gaming machines. This is also a major venue for international headline acts, and some 25 restaurants and 11 bars are on the premises, with more in the extended Southgate complex.

8 Whiteman St. (at Clarendon St.), Southbank. www.crownmelbourne.com.au. © **03/9292 8888.** Daily 24 hr., except on Christmas Day, Good Friday, and Anzac Day (Apr 25) when it is closed 4am–noon. Tram: 12, 96, 109.

Eureka Skydeck ★ OBSERVATION DECK   The vertigo-challenging Skydeck is the highest public vantage point in the Southern Hemisphere. On the 88th floor of the Eureka Tower, a viewing deck gives a 360-degree panorama of the city from 297m (935 ft.) above the ground. But there's more adrenaline-pumping action than just the view: A huge glass cube called the Edge is actually a 6-ton horizontal elevator, which emerges from inside the walls of Skydeck carrying 12 passengers out over the tower's east side. As the opaque glass cube reaches its full extension, the reinforced, 45-millimeter-thick (1¾-in.) glass becomes clear, giving passengers uninterrupted views below, above, and to three sides. All this is accompanied by recorded sounds of creaking chains and breaking glass—just to scare you more! Actually, it's not as scary as it sounds, and the ride is only 4 minutes long. For an extra A$5.50 on your admission price, you can return at night for a look at the city all lit up.

Eureka Tower, Riverside Quay, Southbank. www.eurekaskydeck.com.au. © **03/9693 8888.** A$22 adults, A$15 children 4–16, A$37–A$59 families (extra child A$12); additional A$12 adults, A$8 children for the Edge. Daily 10am–10pm (last entry 9:30pm); 10am–5:30pm on Christmas Day and New Year's Eve (last entry 5pm). Tram: 58.

Federation Square ★★ PUBLIC PLAZA   You have to get into Federation Square, physically, to appreciate it. The controversial design—Melburnians either love it or hate it (I fall into the former category)—has given the city a gathering place, and you only have to visit on the weekends to see that it works. A conglomerate of attractions is centered on a large open piazza-style area cobbled with misshapen paving. Here you'll find the **Ian Potter Centre** (see below) and the **Australian Centre for the Moving Image (ACMI),** which has two state-of-the-art cinemas and large areas where visitors can view movies, videos, and digital media. It has a one-stop visitor center (see "Visitor Information," p. 108), and there are many cafes and coffee shops throughout the precinct. It's worth visiting "Fed Square" just to see the architecture, made up of strange geometrical designs, and the glass Atrium. Lots of events happen in the square's 450-seat amphitheater, including theatrical performances and free concerts. Other events take place on the plaza and along the banks of the Yarra River. There's free Wi-Fi anywhere in the square. Free 50-minute guided tours are run Monday through Saturday at 11am.

Flinders St. (at St Kilda Rd.). www.fedsquare.com.au. © **03/9655 1900.** Free; charges for some special events and exhibitions. Outdoor spaces open 24 hr. Tram: City Circle.

Art in the Streets

Melbourne's street art is some of the best in the world. Often tucked away in laneways or where you'd least expect them, these massive colorful murals—often covering whole walls and multi-story buildings—are among the city's most popular attractions and worth seeking out. Some of the best known in the city center are in **Hosier Lane** (off Flinders St.), **Union Lane** (off the Bourke Street Mall), **Centre Place** (off Degraves St.), and **Croft Alley**—but these spots are being outshone lately by others in the suburb of **Fitzroy,** north of the city. Head there by tram to take a walk around Johnston, Gertrude, and Brunswick streets, remembering to head into the alleys as well. You'll also find some good street art in **St Kilda.** To see the best street art, and possibly even meet some of the artists and see them at work, take a 3½-hour walking tour from **Melbourne Street Art Tours** (www.melbournestreettours.com; © **03/9328 5556**), run by street artists. Tours cost A$69 (half price for kids 15 and under).

The Ian Potter Centre ★★★ GALLERY   This fascinating gallery, featuring 20 rooms dedicated to Australian art, is in the heart of Federation Square. Part of the National Gallery of Victoria (NGV), it contains the country's largest collection of Australian art, including works by Sidney Nolan, Russell Drysdale, and Tom Roberts, as well as Aborigines and Torres Strait Islanders. Some 20,000 objects are stored here, although only about 800 are on display at any one time. Aboriginal art and colonial art collections are the centerpieces of the gallery, but you will find modern paintings here, too. Temporary exhibitions include anything from ceramics to shoes. Free tours are run daily.

Federation Sq. (corner of Flinders St. and St Kilda Rd.). www.ngv.vic.gov.au. ℂ **03/8620 2222.** Free. Daily 10am–5pm. Closed Christmas Day, and until 1pm on Anzac Day (Apr 25). Tram: City Circle. Bus: City Explorer.

Melbourne Museum ★★★ MUSEUM   This museum is Australia's largest and one of its most interesting. For me, the highlight is **Bunjilaka,** the Aboriginal Cultural Centre, which gives an insight into the Victorian Koori people. Other highlights of the museum include a genuine blue-whale skeleton, an indoor rainforest, and a brilliant insect and butterfly collection with lots of real-life exhibits, including revolting cockroaches, ant colonies, and huge spiders (kids love these creepy-crawlies). Apart from that, there are interactive exhibits and science displays and social history, including a stuffed racehorse called Phar Lap. Check out the brightly colored **Children's Museum,** which will bring hours of enjoyment to the little ones. Allow 2 hours, more if you would like to tour the adjacent **Royal Exhibition Building,** a magnificent piece of 19th-century architecture, with soaring domed ceilings and colonnaded galleries. Tours of the building, built in 1879 and used as the venue for the first Commonwealth Parliament of Australia in 1901, run at 2pm daily and cost A$10 adults and A$7 children. Worth every cent.

11 Nicholson St., Carlton. www.museumsvictoria.com.au. ℂ **131 102** in Victoria, or 03/8341 7777. A$15 adults, free for children 15 and under. Daily 10am–5pm. Closed Good Friday and Christmas Day. Tram: 86, 96, or 35 (City Circle).

Melbourne Zoo ★★ ZOO   Built in 1862, this is one of the oldest zoos in the world and makes a great day out with kids. Some 3,000 animals reside here, including kangaroos, wallabies, echidnas, koalas, wombats, and platypuses. Rather than being locked in cages, most animals are in almost natural surroundings or well-tended gardens. Don't miss the butterfly house, with its thousands of colorful occupants flitting around; the free-flight aviary; the lowland gorilla exhibit; and the treetop orangutan exhibit. Allow at least 90 minutes if you just want to see the Australian natives, and around 4 hours for the entire zoo.

Elliott Ave., Parkville. www.zoo.org.au. ℂ **1300/966 784.** A$36 adults, A$18 children 4–15. Entry free for children Sat–Sun, public holidays, and school holidays. Daily 9am–5pm. Tram: 55 north on William St. to stop 25; 19 from Elizabeth St. to stop 16 (then a short walk to your left, following signposts). Train: Royal Park Station.

Playing with kangaroos at Melbourne Zoo.

National Gallery of Victoria International ★★ GALLERY The NGV International is a showcase for Australia's finest collections of international art. On display are Gainsboroughs and Constables, as well as paintings by Bonnard, Delacroix, Van Dyck, El Greco, Monet, Manet, Magritte, and Rembrandt. Architecturally, the building itself is a masterpiece, with high ceilings, fabulous lighting, and great open spaces. Free tours are run daily.

180 St Kilda Rd. www.ngv.vic.gov.au. ✆ **03/8620 2222.** Free; fees for some temporary exhibitions. Daily 10am–5pm. Closed Christmas Day, and until 1pm on Anzac Day (Apr 25). Tram: Any tram from Swanston St. to Victorian Arts Centre.

National Sports Museum ★★★ MUSEUM In a nation that's quite frankly sports-mad, you really can't miss this outstanding and interesting museum, located within the Melbourne Cricket Ground (MCG). It tells Australia's sporting story from its early beginnings to the present, celebrating memorable moments and achievements in just about every sport you can think of, from basketball and boxing to hockey, rugby, tennis, and everything in between. It also includes the Australian Cricket Hall of Fame, the Sport Australia Hall of Fame, and the Champions Racing Gallery. The huge collection includes Australia's first-ever Olympic gold medal, Ian Thorpe's swimsuit, and the Malvern Star bicycle that Hubert Opperman rode in his record-breaking 24-hour cycling marathon in Sydney in 1940. Recognition has been given to Australia's first Paralympic gold medalist and first female Paralympian in the Paralympic display. There's lots of interactive areas, and even room for kids to bowl a ball or two. Allow 1 hour (more if you are a real sports fanatic).

During MCG major event days, including the AFL Grand Final, Day 1 of the Boxing Day Test, and Anzac Day football, access to the museum (at half-price) is restricted to patrons holding an event ticket. Opening hours when events are being held within the MCG arena vary, so check the website.

Tours of the MCG run daily from 10am to 3pm and take about 75 minutes. Tickets include admission to the museum. Tours leave from Gate 3 in the Olympic Stand on non-event days only.

Gate 3, Melbourne Cricket Ground, Yarra Park, East Melbourne. www.nsm.org.au. ℃ **03/9657 8879.** A$25 adults, A$14 children 5–15, or A$60 families of 4 for museum only; A$35 adults, A$18 children, or A$76 families for museum and MCG tour. Daily 10am–5pm (last admission 4:30pm). Closed Good Friday and Christmas Day. Bus: Melbourne City Tourist Shuttle. Tram: 75 or 70 from the city center. Train: Jolimont.

Old Melbourne Gaol ★★★ HISTORIC SITE   This is number one on my list of favorite Melbourne attractions. Roaming the Old Melbourne Gaol complex is a fascinating way to spend a few hours. Start off at the spooky old prison, with its stone walls, tiny cells, and bizarre collection of death masks and artifacts of 19th-century prison life. Among the 135 hangings that took place here was that of notorious bushranger Ned Kelly, in 1880. The scaffold where he was hanged still stands, and his gun, as well as a replica suit of homemade armor (similar to those used by his gang), is on display. Profiles of former prisoners give a fascinating insight into what it was like to be imprisoned here, before the jail finally closed in 1924.

After exploring the jail, move next door for a guided interactive tour of the former City Watch House. The lockup, which operated from 1908 to 1994, is just across the road from the scene of one of Melbourne's most notorious crimes, the 1986 bombing of the Russell Street police station. There's role-playing involved for everyone, but it can be quite challenging for children. During holiday times, you can also visit the adjacent former Magistrate's Court and take part in a reenactment of Ned Kelly's trial.

Three tours give the brave a chance to explore the gaol by night, and they are not for the fainthearted. Ghost tours and equally chilling "hangman" tours run by candlelight and last for an hour. Check the website for session days and times. A Night in the Watch House tours, set in the cellblock, run for 1 hour, are conducted in the dark, and are not for anyone under 16 years old. Tickets for all night tours cost A$38 per person. Ghost and hangman's tours are not recommended for children 11 and under.

Old Melbourne Gaol, where bushranger Ned Kelly was hanged.

377 Russell St. www.oldmelbournegaol.com. au. ℃ **03/9663 7228.** A$28 adults, A$15 children, A$48-A$65 families. Daily 9:30am–5pm. Closed Good Friday and Christmas Day. Tram: 30 or 35 (City Circle) to corner of Russell and Latrobe sts.

Exploring Melbourne

MELBOURNE

Kid-friendly tours and hands-on fun aboard the historic tall ship *Polly Woodside*.

Parliament House Victoria ★ HISTORIC SITE   Now the home of Victoria's Parliament, this monument to Victorian (as in Queen Victoria) pride and power was built in 1856, a neoclassical statement of empire with ranks of fluted columns and a grand sweep of sandstone steps. During the Australian Federation (1900–27), it was used as the national parliament. When the state government is in session—generally on Tuesday afternoon and all day Wednesday and Thursday March through July, and again from August through November (there's a break between sessions)—you can view the proceedings from the public gallery. Call ahead or check the website, as sitting times do vary. During non-sitting times, both the opulent Upper House and the less ornate Lower House chambers are open to the public by guided tour. In addition to regular tours, free architecture tours are held at 2pm on the last Friday of the month. Finally, there's a guided tour that finishes with High Tea in the Strangers Corridor, weekdays from 2:30 to 4pm. The cost is A$47 per person.

Spring St. www.parliament.vic.gov.au. © **03/9651 8568.** Free. Mon–Fri 9am–5pm. Free 1-hr. guided tours Mon–Fri at 9:30, 10:30, 11:30am, 1:30, 2:30, and 3:30pm when Parliament is not in session; 20-min. "Express Tours" Mon–Fri at 1 and 4pm. Reservations required for 1-hr. tours for groups of 6 or more and for architecture tours. Train: Parliament.

Polly Woodside ★★ VINTAGE SHIP   The historic tall ship *Polly Woodside* sits beside the original Dockside sheds, and is beloved by generations of Melburnians for its many fun diversion and hands-on activities for kids. The exhibit includes six zones with interactive displays about life at sea, the crew, navigation, maritime language, and Melbourne's docks (you can even try your hand at loading coal onto a robot ship!). Launched in 1885 in Ireland, the ship sailed to all corners of the globe between 1885 and 1904, rounding the infamous Cape Horn 16 times. After World War II, the ship was towed back to Melbourne and worked as a coal supply ship for the next 20 years. Tours are offered throughout the day, and the first Sunday of the month is "Pirate Day" for kids, from 11am to 3pm.

21 South Wharf Promenade, South Wharf. www.pollywoodside.com.au. © **03/9699 9760.** A$16 adults, A$9.50 children, A$30–A$43 families. Sat–Sun 10am–4pm (last entry 3:15pm); daily during Victorian school holidays. Closed Christmas Day, Boxing Day (Dec 26), New Year's Day, and Easter. Tram: 96, 109, or 12.

Queen Victoria Market ★ MARKET   This Melbourne institution—the "Vic Market"—covers several blocks. Ignore the hundreds of stalls selling everything from live rabbits to bargain clothes. There's a lot of junk here, and the crowds can be awful. The indoor food section, particularly the interesting delicatessen section, is the best part of the markets. The 90-minute **Queen Vic Market Ultimate Foodie Tour** explores the market's food and heritage and is well worth doing. It departs Tuesday, Thursday, and Saturday at 9 and 11am, and costs A$69 adults; the tour includes generous tastings and a A$5 shopping voucher. Bookings (online) are essential. **Night markets** are held every Wednesday from 5 to 10pm in winter (June–Aug) and 5:30 to 10pm in summer (Nov–late Feb, except the last week of Dec).

Btw. Peel, Victoria, Elizabeth, and Therry sts. on the northern edge of the city center. www.qvm.com.au. © **03/9320 5822.** Tues and Thurs 6am–2pm; Fri 6am–5pm; Sat 6am–3pm; Sun 9am–4pm. Closed Mon and public holidays. Tram: 35 (City Circle) or any tram traveling north along William or Elizabeth sts.

SEA LIFE Melbourne Aquarium ★ AQUARIUM   The Melbourne Aquarium's prize exhibit is an Antarctica display featuring King and Gentoo penguins playing in the pool (with underwater viewing) and sliding across the snow-covered ice. These beguiling birds are Australia's only collection of sub-Antarctic penguins. The aquarium also features a reef exhibit, a crocodile

Fit for a King—Or a Governor

Northwest of the city center, the sprawling parklands called **King's Domain** surround **Government House,** residence of Victoria's governor. Free tours of the Government House gardens run on the third Thursday of every month at 11am. Online registration is essential (www.governor.vic.gov.au/government-house/tours/monthly-garden-tours). Also worth a visit is historic **La Trobe's Cottage** (www.nationaltrust.org.au/places/la-trobes-cottage; © **03/9656 9889**), Victoria's first Government House, which was built in England and transported to Australia brick by brick in 1836. The cottage is open on Sundays from 2 to 4pm, October through April. Admission is A$5 adults, A$4 children, A$12 families. Across Birdwood Avenue, stop by the **Shrine of Remembrance,** a memorial to servicemen lost in Australia's wars. It's designed so that at 11am on Remembrance Day (Nov 11), a beam of sunlight hits the Stone of Remembrance in the Inner Shrine. Note the eternal flame in the forecourt.

Queen Victoria Market.

exhibit, some jellyfish displays, and a 2.2-million-liter (581,000-gal.) ocean-arium walk-through tank with larger fish, sharks, and rays. You can arrange to dive with the sharks (A$299 per person; must be 15 years or older). Bookings are required; call ✆ **03/9923 5911.**

Corner of Flinders and Kings sts. www.melbourneaquarium.com.au. ✆ **03/9923 5999.** A$42 adults, A$30 children 4–15, A$69–A$99 families (cheaper if booked online). Daily 9:30am–6pm (last admission 5pm). Tram: 35 (City Circle).

Outlying Attractions

Healesville Sanctuary ★★★ NATURE PRESERVE   Opened in 1921 to preserve endangered species and educate the public, this sanctuary out in Healesville (70km/43 miles northwest of the city) is a prime spot for seeing native animals in almost-natural surroundings. Walk through the peppermint-scented gum forest, which rings with the chiming of bellbirds, and see wedge-tailed eagles, dingoes, koalas, wombats, reptiles, and more. The platypus show at 11:15am daily (and again at 1:30pm Sat–Sun) is a great chance to get up close to these elusive creatures. The sanctuary played a major role in saving and rehabilitating the hundreds of animals injured or displaced by the bushfires that devastated parts of Victoria in 2009; you can visit the Wildlife Health Centre to see veterinarians caring for injured or orphaned wildlife. The sanctuary has a gift shop, a cafe, and picnic grounds.

Badger Creek Rd., Healesville. www.zoo.org.au. ✆ **03/5957 2800.** A$36 adults, A$18 children 4–15, A$91–A$118 families (Mon–Fri only). Children free Sat–Sun, public holidays, and Victorian school holidays. Daily 9am–5pm (last admission 3:30pm). Train from Flinders St. station to Lilydale; then bus no. 685 to Healesville and bus no. 686 toward Badger Creek, which will stop at the sanctuary.

Eternally popular Puffing Billy scenic railway.

Puffing Billy Railway ★★★ VINTAGE TRAIN Generations of Austra-lians have clambered aboard the Puffing Billy steam train to chug over a 13km (8-mile) track from Belgrave to Emerald and Lakeside. Passengers ride on open carriages and enjoy lovely views as the train passes through forests and fern gullies and over a National Trust–classified wooden trestle bridge. Trips take around an hour each way, and there's time to walk around the lake before the return journey. Special "Steam and Cuisine" fares are available daily: choose from a cheese platter and dessert for A$79 adults or A$71 children, or a three-course lunch (and perhaps a glass of wine) in a "first class" enclosed carriage with white tablecloths for A$103 adults, A$93 children (excluding drinks). Dinner trains also run, usually only once a month, with three courses for A$103 per person (no children 4 and under). Other special trains—jazz nights, murder themes, and so on—also run; check the website for details. Trains do not run on days of total fire ban.

Belgrave Station, Belgrave. www.puffingbilly.com.au. ✆ **03/9757 0700.** Round-trip fares A$57–A$75 adults, A$30–A$38 children 4–16, A$114–A$150 families of 6 (depend-ing on how far you travel). Closed Christmas Day. Train from Flinders St. station in Melbourne to Belgrave (1 hr.); Puffing Billy station is a 5-min. walk away.

Werribee Mansion ★★★ HOUSE MUSEUM I never tire of visiting this stately 60-room Italianate mansion, just a 30-minute drive along the Princes Freeway from Melbourne, at Werribee Park. Dubbed "the palace in the paddock," it was built in 1877 and is surrounded by 132 hectares (326 acres) of magnificent formal gardens and bushland. Get the audio tour (A$6.30) for further insight as you wander around the house. Be sure to mean-der through the interesting and extensive contemporary sculpture garden. There's a cafe on-site.

K Rd., Werribee. www.werribeepark.com.au. ✆ **131 963.** A$10 adults, A$7.40 children 4–15, A$32 families of 4. Nov–mid-Apr daily 10am–5pm; mid-Apr–Oct Mon–Fri 10am–

4pm, Sat–Sun and public holidays 10am–5pm. Closed Christmas Day. Train from Flinders St. station to Werribee (45 min.); then bus no. 439. The **Werribee Park Shuttle** (www.werribeeparkshuttle.com.au; ℂ **03/9748 5094**) leaves the National Gallery of Victoria, 180 St Kilda Rd., daily at 9:30am and costs A$35 adults, A$25 children 10–14, A$20 children 4–9 (reservations essential).

Werribee Open Range Zoo ★ ZOO   Part of Zoos Victoria, which runs the Melbourne Zoo, this Werribee facility also has a collection of Aussie animals, but the main focus is on its open range section, where you will see giraffes, hippos, rhinoceros, lions, zebras, and more. The zoo also has one of the largest gorilla exhibits in the world, home to the silverback Motaba and his two sons. Access to the zoo's open-range area is strictly by a 40-minute guided tour on a safari bus. On busy days, it might pay to spend the extra money to take a small group tour in an open-sided jeep, as you'll get a better view and better photo opportunities. The zoo also has a walk-through section featuring African cats, including cheetahs, and monkeys. If you've been to Africa, you may find little to excite you, but kids love it, and it's crowded with families.

K Rd., Werribee. www.zoo.org.au/werribee. ℂ **1300/966 784** in Australia, or 03/9731 9600. A$36 adults, A$18 children 4–15, A$91–A$118 families (Mon–Fri only). Children free Sat–Sun, public holidays, and school holidays. Daily 9am–5pm (last entry at 3:30pm). Safari tours run regularly all day. Take train from Flinders St. station to Werribee, then bus no. 439. The **Werribee Park Shuttle** (www.werribeeparkshuttle.com. au; ℂ **03/9748 5094**) leaves the National Gallery of Victoria, 180 St Kilda Rd., daily at 9:30am and costs A$35 adults, A$25 children 10–14, A$20 children 4–9 (bookings essential).

Organized Tours

Melbourne City Sightseeing Tours (www.citysightseeing.melbourne; ℂ **03/8353 2578**) offers a range of tours on open-top double-decker buses. It's a hop-on, hop-off service to 23 stops around the city center and St Kilda, with an audio commentary. A 24-hour pass costs A$23 adults, A$15 kids age 4-14, or A$70 families of 6. A 48-hour pass costs A$45 adults or A$25 children.

Melbourne for Kids

Melbourne is a terrific family-friendly city, with lots to do that will keep kids of all ages amused and entertained. In the city center, the **Melbourne Museum** (p. 130) has a special children's section, and the historic ship *Polly Woodside* (p. 133) has lots of interactive fun for kids. Hop on a bike from **Melbourne Bike Share** (p. 139) and ride along the riverfront paths or through the **Royal Botanic Gardens** (p. 139). Animal lovers will love **Melbourne Zoo** (p. 130), hand-feeding the wildlife at **Healesville Sanctuary** (p. 135), the touch-tanks at **SEA LIFE Melbourne Aquarium** (p. 134), or seeing the waddling little penguins on **Phillip Island** (p. 141). Older kids will like the **National Sports Museum** (p. 131) and the spooky **Old Melbourne Gaol** (p. 132), as well as the sky-high thrill of the **Eureka Skydeck** (p. 128). For a big day out, take the train to Ballarat to step back in time at **Sovereign Hill** (p. 152) and discover what life was like in the gold rush days.

Tickets can also be bought to combine entry to major attractions such as the Old Melbourne Gaol, a river cruise, Melbourne Zoo, the Eureka Skydeck, and more.

Melbourne River Cruises (www.melbcruises.com.au; © **03/8610 2600**) offers boat trips up and down the Yarra River, lasting 1 to 2 hours. It's a great way to get a feel for the city, and the tours include commentaries. A 2-hour Melbourne Highlights tour or a tour from the city to Williamstown costs A$35 adults, A$18 kids, or A$85 families. Call ahead to confirm cruise departure times, because they change. Cruises depart from Berth 5, on the South Bank Promenade.

Real Melbourne Bike Tours (www.rentabike.net.au/bike-tours.htm; © **0417/339 203** mobile) can help you find your bearings and discover some of hidden Melbourne—the back streets and bluestone lanes, markets, cafes, arcades, and bike paths. Run by former journalist Murray Johnson, tours are fun and interesting. The cost is A$110 adults and A$79 children ages 12 to 18, or A$299 for a family of four, and includes bike hire, helmet, and guided tour, plus coffee, cake, and lunch along the way. Tours leave at 10am (or other times by arrangement) from Rentabike at Federation Square and return around 2pm. Tours can be customized to suit your needs and interests. Bookings are essential.

Sports Lovers Tours (www.melbournesportstours.com.au; © **03/8802 4547**) are designed for passionate sports fans or those who just want to get into the spirit of some local sporting action. Half- and full-day tours cater to all tastes and include visits to the National Sports Museum (p. 131), behind the scenes at the Melbourne Cricket Ground or Rod Laver Arena, Flemington Racecourse, and the Albert Park Formula 1 track. Other options include attending an Aussie Rules football game with a local host who can explain the

Melbourne River Cruises offers boat tours on the Yarra River.

rules, or a horse-racing themed tour for fans of the Melbourne Cup. Tour prices range from A$115 per person for a 5-hour tour to A$149 for a full day.

Outdoor Activities

Birrarung Marr, along the Yarra River east of Federation Square on Batman Avenue (www.melbourne.vic.gov.au/parks; ℭ **03/9658 9658**), is Melbourne's newest major parkland. *Birrarung* means "river of mists" in the Woiwurrung language of the Wurundjeri people who originally inhabited the area; *marr* relates to the side of the river. The wide-open spaces and large, sculptured terraces were designed to host some of Melbourne's top events and festivals throughout the year, and the terraces provide views of the city, Southbank, King's Domain, and the Yarra River.

The **Royal Botanic Gardens,** 2km (1¼ miles) south of the city on Birdwood Avenue, off St Kilda Road (www.rbg.vic.gov.au; ℭ **03/9252 2429**), are the best gardens in Australia and well worth a few hours of wandering. More than 40 hectares (99 acres) are lush and blooming with some 12,000 plant species from all over the world. Don't miss a visit to the oldest part of the garden, the Tennyson Lawn, with its 120-year-old English elm trees. Other special corners include a fern gully, camellia gardens, an herb garden, rainforests packed with fruit bats, and ponds full of ducks and black swans. A hop-on, hop-off "Garden Explorer" tour operates year-round from 10am to 3pm daily, offering a golf-buggy style transport (with commentary) and stops around the gardens. It costs A$10 adults, A$8 children 5 to 17, and A$25 for a family of four. Buy tickets at the visitor center or from the driver. Aboriginal Heritage Walks, in which you will learn about traditional uses of plants for food, tools, and medicine, are run daily (except Sat) at 11am, and are well worth doing. The tour takes about 90 minutes and costs A$35 adults, A$12 children. The gardens are open daily from 7:30am to sunset. Admission is free. To get there, catch the no. 8 tram and get off at stop 21. Allow at least 2 hours.

Extensive bicycle paths wind through the city and suburbs. **Melbourne Bike Share,** Melbourne's public bike hire (www.melbournebikeshare.com. au; ℭ **1300/711 590**), has 50 bike stations and 600 bikes at locations around the city. You can't miss the racks of bright blue bikes. You can pay for a bike with Visa or MasterCard (limit of two bikes per credit card). Your card swipe will also take a A$50 security deposit, which will be refunded after return of the bikes. You pay a daily rate of A$3 (or A$8 for a week) and the first 30 minutes of usage are free; then you pay A$2 for 30 minutes (up to your first hour), A$7 for 90 minutes, and A$10 for every half-hour after that. The daily rate makes the bike-share system one of the cheapest transport options in town, but only if you have the bike for less than about 2 hours. If you need a bike for longer than that, it's probably cheaper to rent a bike elsewhere. Bike helmets are compulsory by law, and come free when you hire a bike. You must be 16 years or older to use the bike-share system. Melbourne Bike Share has a range of suggested bike tours that you can download from the website.

MELBOURNE SHOPPING

Ask almost any Melburnian to help you plan your time in the city, and he or she will advise you to shop until you drop. All Australia regards Melbourne as a shopping capital—it has everything from fashion houses to major department stores and unusual souvenir shops. So even if you're also visiting Sydney, save your money until you get to Melbourne, and then indulge!

Start at the magnificent city arcades, such as the **Block Arcade** (between Collins and Little Collins sts), which has more than 30 shops, including the historic **Hopetoun Tea Rooms** (p. 123), and the **Royal Arcade** (stretching from Little Collins St. to the Bourke Street Mall). Then hit the courts and lanes around **Swanston Street** and the huge **Melbourne Central shopping complex** between Latrobe and Lonsdale streets.

Department store giants **David Jones** (www.davidjones.com.au; ℂ **03/9643 2222**)—or DJs, as it's affectionately known—and **Myer** (www.myer.com.au; ℂ **03/9661 1111**) both have stores in the city center. DJs spans 2 blocks separated into men's and women's stores and has a vast and tantalizing food hall. Myer, the grand dame of Melbourne's department stores, is in hot competition with David Jones. It has household goods, perfume, jewelry, and fashions, as well as a food section. Both stores are on the Bourke Street Mall.

High-fashion boutiques line the eastern stretch of **Collins Street,** between the Grand Hyatt and the Hotel Sofitel. Collins Street features most international labels, as well as shoe heaven **Miss Louise,** 205 Collins St. (www.misslouise.com.au; ℂ **03/9654 7730**). Nearby Flinders Lane has earned style status with the likes of **Christine,** 181 Flinders Lane (www.christineaccessories.com; ℂ **03/9654 2011**), where women are reputed to sometimes faint over the accessories. Down the road is **Little Collins Street,** another fashion hot spot with lots of local labels.

Next, fan out across the city, taking in **Chapel Street** in South Yarra for its Australian fashions and the **Jam Factory** (500 Chapel St., South Yarra), a series of buildings with a range of shops and food outlets as well as 16 cinema screens. Get there on tram no. 8 or 72 from Swanston Street.

Shop 'til You Drop

For an easy way to shop—with local guidance—take a tour with Jessica Lothian, either to Melbourne's outlet stores or to hunt out designer styles. **Melbourne Shopping Experiences** (www.melbourneshoppingexperiences.com.au; ℂ **03/8822 4568**) offers small group tours for some retail therapy. Jess will help you explore back-street warehouses, pop-up sales, and discount shopping streets such as Swan Street and Bridge Road. Tours operate Monday to Saturday, 9am to 5pm, and cost A$94 adults, A$71 children 13 and under (not recommended for under-10s). The tour includes lunch and a glass of bubbles, and is adapted to fit the interests of the group. Pickups from city hotels on request.

There's also **Toorak Road** in Toorak, for Gucci and other high-priced, high-fashion names; **Bridge Road** in Richmond, for budget and outlet fashion stores; **Lygon Street** in Carlton, for Italian fashion, footwear, and accessories; and **Brunswick Street** in Fitzroy, for a more alternative scene.

DAY TRIPS FROM MELBOURNE
Phillip Island: Penguins on Parade ★★★
139km (86 miles) S of Melbourne

Phillip Island's **penguin parade,** which happens every evening at dusk, is one of Australia's most popular animal attractions. There are other, less crowded places in Australia where watching homecoming penguins feels less staged, but at least the guides and boardwalks protect the little ones and their nesting holes from the throngs. Nevertheless, the commercialism of the penguin parade puts a lot of people off—busloads of tourists squashed into a sort of amphitheater hardly feels like being one with nature. But Phillip Island also offers nice beaches, good bushwalking, fishing, and Seal Rocks.

ESSENTIALS
ARRIVING   Most visitors come to Phillip Island on a day trip from Melbourne and arrive in time for the penguin parade and dinner. Several tour companies run day trips. Among them are **Gray Line** (www.grayline.com.au; ℗ **1300/858 687** in Australia), which operates a number of different tours, including daily "penguin express" trips for those who are short of time. The express tour departs Melbourne at 4:30pm and returns around 11:30pm. Tours cost A$143 for adults and A$72 for children, and can be booked online. Upgrades to premium seating at the penguin parade and various other options are available.

If you're driving yourself, Phillip Island is an easy 2-hour trip from Melbourne along the South Gippsland Highway and then the Bass Highway. A bridge connects the island to the mainland.

V/Line (www.vline.com.au; ℗ **136 196** in Australia) runs a bus from Melbourne to Cowes, but does not take you to any of the attractions on Phillip Island. Once on the island, you need to hire a car, take a tour, or rent a bicycle to get around. The parade is 15km (9½ miles) from the center of Cowes.

VISITOR INFORMATION   There are two information centers on the island. The **Phillip Island Information Centre** is at 895 Phillip Island Rd., Newhaven, just a few kilometers onto the island, and is open daily from 9am to 5pm (6pm Dec–Jan) and closed Christmas Day. The **Cowes Visitor Information Centre** is at Thompson Avenue (corner of Church St.), Cowes, and is open daily 9am to 5pm (except Christmas Day). The centers share the toll-free number ℗ **1300/366 422** in Australia, and the website www.visitphillipisland.com.

DISCOUNT PASSES   A **4 Parks Pass** gives discounted entry to Phillip Island's top attractions: the **Koala Conservation Centre,** the **Penguin**

Parade, Churchill Island Heritage Farm, and the **Antarctic Journey** (all covered below). The pass costs A$59 adults, A$29 children ages 4 to 15; it can be purchased online (www.penguins.org.au) or at any of the attractions. A variety of other passes are also available; see the website for details.

EXPLORING PHILLIP ISLAND

Visitors approach the island from the east, passing through the town of **Newhaven.** The main town on the island, **Cowes** (pop. 4,000), is on the north coast. The penguin parade and other nature attractions are on the far southwest coast, on Phillip Island's Summerland Peninsula. The peninsula ends in an interesting rock formation called the **Nobbies,** a strange-looking outcropping that can be reached at low tide by a basalt causeway. You'll get some spectacular views of the coastline and two offshore islands from here. On the farthest of these islands is a population of up to **12,000 Australian fur seals,** the largest colony in Australia. This area is also home to thousands of nesting silver gulls. Bring your binoculars, or for a closer view take a 1-hour speedboat ride with **Wild Ocean EcoBoat Tours** (www.penguins.org.au; ✆ **03/5951 2800**) to the seal colony for A$85 adults, A$65 children, or A$235 for a family of 4 (or combine with a 4 Parks Pass, Penguin Parade ticket, or other attractions). Boats leave from the Cowes jetty, on The Esplanade. The modern Nobbies Centre provides boardwalks and a cafe, as well as the **Antarctic Journey** attraction (see below).

On the north coast of the island, you can explore **Rhyll Inlet,** an intertidal mangrove wetland inhabited by wading birds such as spoonbills, oystercatchers, herons, egrets, cormorants, and the rare bar-tailed godwit and whimbrel. Birders will also love **Swan Lake,** another breeding habitat for wetland birds.

Elsewhere, walking trails lead through heath and pink granite to **Cape Woolamai,** the island's highest point, where there are fabulous coastal views. From September through April, the cape is home to thousands of short-tailed shearwaters (also known as mutton birds).

PHILLIP ISLAND ATTRACTIONS

Antarctic Journey ★ NATURAL HISTORY MUSEUM   Covering three levels, this high-tech attraction at the Nobbies Centre showcases the natural world of Phillip Island and the Antarctic landscape and wildlife to its far south—whales, sharks, penguins, and the like. Expect lots of multimedia displays, immersive virtual reality experiences, sensory learning activities, and hands-on interactive stations.

Nobbies Centre, Phillip Island. www.penguins.org.au. ✆ **03/5951 2800.** A$18 adults, A$9 children 4–15, A$45 family of 4; also included in 4 Parks Pass (p. 141). Daily 10am–2 hrs. before sunset. 20-min. guided tours at 11am, 1, and 3pm daily.

Churchill Island Heritage Farm ★ OUTDOOR MUSEUM/FARM   On adjacent Churchill Island, connected by causeway to Phillip Island, visitors can roam this tranquil working farm, a recreation of Victoria's oldest agricultural settlement, worked continuously since the 1850s. Daily farming demonstrations include cow milking and sheep shearing; the dog herding demonstrations are particularly fun.

246 Samuel Arness Dr., Churchill Island, Newhaven. www.penguins.org.au. ℂ **03/5951 2800.** A$13 adults, A$6.50 children, A$32.50 family of 4; also included in 4 Parks Pass (p. 141). Daily 10am–5pm.

Koala Conservation Centre ★★ NATURE CENTER Koalas were introduced to Phillip Island in the 1880s, and at first they thrived in the predator-free environment. However, overpopulation, the introduction of foxes and dogs, and the clearing of land for farmland and roads have taken their toll. Though you can still see a few koalas in the wild, the best place to find them is at this sanctuary, set up for research and breeding purposes. Visitors can get quite close to them, especially on the elevated boardwalk, which lets you peek into their treetop homes. Around 4pm, the ordinarily sleepy koalas are on the move—but this is also the time when tour buses converge on the place, so it can get crowded.

Fiveways, Phillip Island Tourist Rd., Phillip Island. www.penguins.org.au. ℂ **03/5952 1610.** A$13 adults, A$6.50 children 4–15, A$33 families of 4; also included in 4 Parks Pass (p. 141). Daily 10am–5pm, slightly later in summer (2–6pm on Christmas Day).

National Vietnam Veterans Museum ★★ MUSEUM Phillip Island may seem an unusual place to find a national museum, but it's definitely worth a stop. Dedicated to the Australian veterans of the Vietnam War, the collection includes about 6,000 artifacts, including marbles used in Australia's conscription lottery, uniforms, vehicles, and weapons. Four galleries tell the story of Australia's involvement in the war: a Remembrance Gallery and separate Air, Ground, and Naval Operations galleries. There is also a large exhibit telling the Vietnamese story, and by the time you visit there may be a new life-size diorama showing a Viet Cong tunnel system. The big-ticket item is a Bell AH-IG HueyCobra helicopter gunship, one of only three in Australia, and the museum is also restoring a Canberra bomber, the only surviving example of its kind in the world. There's a moving audiovisual on Australia's involvement in the war from 1962 to 1972. You can have a coffee in the **Nui Dat Café** or buy books and memorabilia from the shop.

25 Veterans Dr., Newhaven. www.vietnamvetsmuseum.org. ℂ **03/5956 6400.** A$15 adults, A$12 veterans, A$10 children 5–15, A$40 families of 5. Daily 10am–5pm. Closed Good Friday, Christmas Day, Boxing Day (Dec 26), New Year's Day, and from noon on Christmas Eve.

Phillip Island Penguin Reserve ★★ NATURE ATTRACTION The penguin parade takes place every night at dusk, when hundreds of Little Penguins appear at the water's edge, gather in the shallows, and waddle up the beach toward their burrows in the dunes. They're the smallest of the world's 17 species of penguins, standing just 33 centimeters (13 in.) high, and the only penguins that breed on the Australian mainland. **Photography is banned,** because it scares the penguins; smoking and touching the penguins are also prohibited. Wear a sweater or jacket, because it gets chilly after the sun goes down. A kiosk selling food opens an hour before the penguins turn up. Reservations for the parade are essential during busy holiday periods such as Easter and in summer.

For a better experience, exclusive small-group tours give you a closer view of the penguins. **Penguins Plus** allows you to watch the parade from a board-walk in the company of rangers, while an **Underground Viewing** option allows you to watch up-close from indoors. The **Ultimate Adventure Tour** for groups of only 10 people (no children 15 and under) takes you to a secluded beach away from the main viewing area to watch penguins coming ashore. Other options include ranger-guided tours a few hours before the penguins appear, or a behind-the-scenes tour with researchers, ending with

The Phillip Island penguin parade is a nightly event.

front-row seats on the viewing platform. In school holidays, 30-minute tours run specially for families, at a very affordable A$11 adults and A$5.25 for children.

Summerland Beach, Phillip Island Tourist Rd., Ventnor. www.penguins.org.au. © **03/5951 2820.** A$26 adults, A$13 children 4–15, A$68 families of 4; also included in 4 Parks Pass (p. 141). Penguins Plus A$53 adult, A$26 children, A$131 families; Underground Viewing A$65 adults, A$34 children, A$169 families of 4; VIP Tour (no children 11 and under) and Guided Ranger Tour (no children 11 and under) A$83; Ultimate Adventure Tour A$93; Penguin Research Tour A$103. Visitor center opens daily at 10am (2pm on Christmas Day).

The Mornington Peninsula ★★

80km (50 miles) S of Melbourne

The Mornington Peninsula, a scenic 40km (25-mile) stretch of windswept coastline and hinterland, is one of Melbourne's favorite day-trip and weekend-getaway destinations—and not just because it's a popular wine-producing region. The peninsula's fertile soil, temperate climate, and rolling hills produce excellent wine, particularly pinot noir, shiraz, and chardonnay. Many wineries offer cellar-door tastings; others have excellent restaurants.

ESSENTIALS

ARRIVING From Melbourne, you can drive to the Mornington Peninsula in about an hour. There are two toll roads, but taking the toll-free Neapean Highway, and then the Point Nepean Road, is just as easy. Getting there by public transport is a time-consuming process, and does not solve the problem of how to get around once you are there.

VISITOR INFORMATION The **Mornington Peninsula Visitor Information Centre,** 359 Point Nepean Rd., Dromana (www.visitmornington peninsula.org; ✆ **03/5950 1579**), has plenty of maps and information on the area and can also help book accommodations. It's open daily from 9am to 5pm (except Christmas Day and Good Friday), and from 1 to 5pm on Anzac Day (Apr 25).

EXPLORING THE MORNINGTON PENINSULA

As you're driving south from Melbourne, stop in the gateway city of Mornington to check out the **Mornington Peninsula Regional Gallery,** 350 Dunns Rd. (www.mprg.mornpen.vic.gov.au; ✆ **03/5950 1580**), which exhibits the work of well-known Australian artists. It's open every day except Monday, from 10am to 5pm; admission is A$4 adults, A$2 children. A little farther down the coast, just past Dromana, drive up to the summit at **Arthurs Seat State Park** for glorious views of the coastline. Continue on B110 toward Point Nepean, stopping off at the town of **Sorrento** to spot pelicans on the jetty or visit the town's many galleries.

There are lovely beaches all around the peninsula, but some of the best face onto the Bass Strait, along the southwest coast from Portsea to Cape Schank. Take the timbered boardwalk and stairs to the beach at **Cape Schanck,** keeping an eye out for gray kangaroos, southern brown bandicoots, echidnas, native rats, mice, reptiles, bats, and many forest and ocean birds. The Cape Schanck lighthouse has a small museum, and there are numerous interconnecting walking tracks providing access to some remote beaches. You can get more information on this and all the other Victorian national parks from www. parkweb.vic.gov.au or by calling ✆ **131 963.**

East of Cape Schank, there are also some fine beaches around Point Leo and Shoreham. Kids in particular should enjoy a stop at Australia's oldest maze, **Ashcombe Maze & Lavender Gardens,** 15 Shoreham Rd., Shoreham (www.ashcombemaze.com.au; ✆ **03/5989 8387**). In addition to the big hedge maze, there is also a rose maze comprised of 1,200 rose bushes, and the gardens are huge. It also has a pleasant cafe with indoor and outdoor dining. The park is open daily from 9am to 5pm, except Christmas Day; admission is A$19 for adults, A$10 for children 4 to 15, and A$52 to A$66 for families.

For fabulous wildlife viewing, take a night tour of **Moonlit Sanctuary,** 550 Tyabb-Tooradin Rd., Pearcedale (www.moonlitsanctuary.com.au; ✆ **03/5978 7935**), at the northern end of the peninsula. The sanctuary is open daily from 10am to 5pm (except Christmas Day), but the best way to see Australia's nocturnal animals is on a guided evening tour. The bushland tour will enable you to see animals such as the eastern quoll, the red-bellied pademelon, and the southern bettong, all of which are extinct in the wild on Australia's mainland. Night tours must be booked in advance (at least by 3pm on the day of your visit). I highly recommend this—it's a wonderful way to see and interact with animals and birds you'd never see during daylight hours. Day admission is A$24 adults, A$12 children 4 to 17, and A$64 families of four (extra children A$8). Night-time admission and guided tour is A$50 adults, A$30 children, A$19 children 3 and under, or A$150 for a family of four (extra children A$25). Night tours begin at dusk, with times varying throughout the year; call ahead for current times.

WHERE TO EAT ON THE MORNINGTON PENINSULA

The Portsea Hotel ★★ BISTRO   The large restaurant at this Tudor-style pub on the seafront is very popular, and the outdoor beer garden overlooking the sea is hard to beat on a sunny day. This lovely sprawling old hotel, completely renovated in 2018, has a large terrace area at the back so you can enjoy the sea views from a sheltered spot. The bistro menu features plenty of choices for steak-lovers, vegetarians, and diners looking for something a bit different. Daily seafood specials change according to the local catch of the day. There's also a kids' menu. After dining, it's an easy walk down the stairs through the sand dunes to the beach below (keep your eye out for dolphins).

3746 Point Nepean Rd., Portsea. www.portseahotel.com.au. (℗ **03/5984 2213.** Main courses A$17–A$41. Sun–Fri noon–9pm; Sat noon–9:30pm.

The Macedon Ranges ★★

Some of Victoria's finest gardens dot the hills and valleys of the Macedon Ranges, just an hour northwest from Melbourne. In bygone times, the wealthy swapped the city's summer heat for the cooler climes of Macedon. Their legacy of "hill station" private gardens and impressive mansions, along with the region's 40 cool-climate wineries and gourmet foods, are enough reason to visit. The best times to visit the Macedon Ranges for the gardens are April (autumn) and November (spring).

ESSENTIALS

ARRIVING & GETTING AROUND   The Macedon Ranges are less than an hour's drive from Melbourne along the Calder Freeway, a continuation of the Tullamarine Freeway. Follow the signs toward Bendigo until you reach Gisborne, and then move off the freeway. **V/Line** (www.vline.com.au; (℗ **136 196** in Australia) trains from Melbourne to Bendigo pass through the Macedon Ranges, stopping at stations including Macedon, Woodend, Kyneton, and Malmsbury.

VISITOR INFORMATION   There are two visitor information centers in the region: the **Woodend Visitor Centre,** 711 High St., Woodend ((℗ **03/5427 2033**), and the **Kyneton Visitor Information Centre,** 127 High St., Kyneton ((℗ **03/5422 6110**). Both share the same telephone information line ((℗ **1800/244 711**) and are open daily 9am to 5pm (except Christmas Day and Good Friday). The website **www.visitmacedonranges.com** is also a good source of information.

ORGANIZED TOURS   With more than 40 vineyards and 20 cellar doors in the region, wine buffs who want to sample the product should consider a tour. **Victoria Winery Tours** (www.winetours.com.au; (℗ **1800/946 386** in

Australia, or 03/5428 8500) runs small-group (minimum 2 people) day tours from Melbourne, visiting four or five wineries. Pickup in Melbourne is at 9am, returning by about 5:30pm. The A$180 cost per person includes morning tea and lunch.

EXPLORING THE MACEDON RANGES

Swinging northward through the region, the Calder Freeway passes the main towns of Macedon, Woodend, Kyneton, and Malmsbury. Some private homestead gardens are open to the public, including two in **Mount Macedon: Duneira** (www.duneira.com.au; ℂ **03/5426 1490**) and **Tieve Tara** (www.gardensoftievetara.com.au; ℂ **0418/337 813** mobile). It pays to call ahead to check times and access (the gardens are often closed in winter). Entry fees apply.

After the gold rush of the 1850s, **Woodend** became a resort town with guesthouses, gardens, a racecourse, a golf club, and hotels. Reminders of those days are found in the historical buildings and clock tower on High Street. Cafes, boutiques, and galleries abound. Stop in for a beer at the family-run **Holgate Brewhouse,** in the historic Keatings Hotel on High Street (www.holgatebrewhouse.com; ℂ **03/5427 2510**). They produce a range of draught beers, and you can buy "tastings" until you decide on your favorite. The beer is brewed using just four ingredients—malt, hops, yeast, and pure Macedon Ranges water. It's open daily noon 'til late (except Christmas Day).

For many visitors, however, Woodend's chief draw is the **Hanging Rock Recreation Reserve,** South Rock Road, Woodend (ℂ **1800/244 711** in Australia, or 0418/373 032 [mobile] for the ranger), where the ghost of Miranda—the fictional schoolgirl who vanished at Hanging Rock in author Joan Lindsay's evocative 1967 novel *Picnic at Hanging Rock*—is never far away. Peter Weir's 1975 film of the novel cemented its fame, but the natural beauty of the area overshadows its slightly spooky reputation. You can climb the rock, walk the tracks, and explore caves like the Black Hole of Calcutta and the Cathedral. You can take a guided tour (night tours are offered in summer). The Hanging Rock Discovery Centre explains the geology and history of the area and revisits the book and movie. The reserve is also home to lots of wildlife including koalas, kangaroos, sugar gliders, echidnas, and wallabies. It's open daily 9am to 5pm (except Christmas Day). Admission is A$10 per car or A$4 per pedestrian.

A 15- or 20-minute drive north of Woodend brings you to **Kyneton,** where you can stroll along Piper Street for antiques, homewares, cafes, a heritage pub, and more. The **Kyneton Farmers' Market** is held at Saint Paul's Park in Piper Street on the second Saturday of the month from 8am to 1pm. Near Kyneton, **Bringalbit** (www.bringalbit.com.au; ℂ **03/5423 7223**) is another private homestead garden worth checking out.

The hamlet of **Malmsbury** may be small but it offers some compelling reasons to drive this far north. First is the **Malmsbury Botanic Gardens,** next to the Town Hall, designed to take advantage of the Coliban River valley and a billabong that was transformed into a group of ornamental lakes. The

5-hectare (12-acre) gardens have a superb collection of mature trees; it's also a popular spot for barbecues, and at Apple Hole you'll find kids leaping into the river from a rope swing. At quiet times, you may even spot a platypus. But Malmsbury's most famous landmark may be the **bluestone railway viaduct** built by 4,000 men in 1859. At 25m (82 ft.) high, with five 18m (59-ft.) spans, it is one of Australia's longest stone bridges and is best viewed from the gardens. I also like to pop in to **Tin Shed Arts** (75 Mollison St. East, ✆ **03/5423 2144**), a spacious gallery near the Town Hall that displays contemporary and traditional art from both local artists and well-known names from around Australia. It always has something interesting and unexpected—paintings, mixed media, sculpture, and craftwork. It's open Friday to Monday 10am to 5pm. The gallery is next door to the **Malmsbury Bakery** (✆ **03/5423 2369**), a local institution where you'll find plenty of tempting hot pies, bread, and pastries. The gallery and bakery share a website: www.malmsburybakeryand-gallery.com.au.

WHERE TO EAT IN THE MACEDON RANGES

Pizza Verde Woodfire Kitchen ★★ PIZZA   If you like your pizza thin and crisp, made from organic or gluten-free flour, and adorned with tasty organic toppings, then this Piper Street pizzeria in Kyneton is the place for you. Some unlikely combinations include the "green" pizza—topped with zucchini, ricotta, mint, garlic, and lemon (with optional chili)—or the potato-topped pizza with caramelized onion jam and pancetta. Some have the traditional tomato base, others an olive-oil base. There are also meatballs, chicken wings, and other wood-fired dishes for those who don't want pizza.

62 Piper St., Kyneton. www.pizzaverde.com.au. ✆ **03/5422 7400**. Main courses A$18–A$26. Kids' pizzas (until 5pm) A$9. Wed–Fri 5pm–late; Sat–Sun noon–3pm and 5pm–late.

Daylesford ★★★

108km (67 miles) NW of Melbourne

Daylesford can be a terrific day trip from Melbourne or can easily be combined with a trip to the Macedon Ranges (see above). Part of "spa country," this village is a bit of a trendy getaway for Melburnians. Along the main street, you'll find small galleries, homewares shops, and some smart foodie outlets.

ESSENTIALS

ARRIVING   From Melbourne, take the CityLink toll road (the M2) north toward Melbourne Airport. Take the Calder Highway turnoff toward Bendigo (M79) and continue until you see the turnoff to Daylesford (C792); then follow the signs. The road will take you through Woodend, Tylden, and Trentham. At Trentham take the C317 to Daylesford. When you arrive in Daylesford, turn right at the roundabout as signposted to get to Hepburn Springs.

VISITOR INFORMATION   The **Daylesford Visitor Information Centre,** 98 Vincent St. (www.visithepburnshire.com.au; ✆ **1800/454 891** in Australia, or 03/5321 6123), features an interpretive display about the area's mineral waters. It's open daily from 9am to 5pm, except Christmas Day.

EXPLORING DAYLESFORD

Australians have been heading to Hepburn Springs, on the edge of Daylesford, to "take the waters" since 1895, and the region now has about a dozen or so day spas. The original, and most famous, is **Hepburn Bathhouse & Spa** (www.hepburnbathhouse.com; ✆ **03/5321 6000**). Not everyone likes the slick, modern, and rather cold new extension that has replaced the elegant old wooden building, but sink into the hot pools and it's easy to forget what the exterior looks like. There's traditional communal bathing in the Bathhouse and the Sanctuary, or you can book in to the Spa (in the original bathhouse building; reservations essential) for the usual range of therapies and treatments. The complex includes an aroma steam room, salt therapy pool, relaxation pool, and "spa couches" submerged in mineral water (which I didn't find very comfortable). The complex is on Mineral Springs Reserve Road and is open Monday to Thursday 9am to 6:30pm, Friday 9am to 8pm, Saturday 8am to 9pm, and Sunday 8am to 6:30pm. Closed Christmas Day. Tuesday to Thursday Bathhouse entry for 2 hours costs A$37 adults, A$24 children 2 to 16, and A$115 for a family of four; Friday to Monday and on public holidays it's A$47 adults, A$27 children, and A$148 families. Towel rental is A$5. Entry to the Bathhouse and Sanctuary is A$79 Tuesday to Thursday and A$99 Friday to Monday and public holidays, including towel and robe rental. A 30-minute private mineral bath at The Spa costs from A$99 to A$109 depending on the day of the week.

On the hill behind Daylesford's main street is **The Convent** (www.convent gallery.com.au; ✆ **03/5348 3211**), a historic 19th-century mansion, complete with twisting staircases. The Convent comprises a restaurant, a gallery, gardens, a chapel, and shops, as well as a small museum that speaks to its origins as a private home, which later became the Holy Cross Convent and Boarding School for Girls. After years of dereliction, it reopened as a gallery in 1991, but the nuns' infirmary and one of the "cells," or bedrooms, were left unrestored. You'll find it on the corner of Hill and Daly streets. It's open daily 10am to 4pm (3pm on New Year's Eve), closed Good Friday, Easter Monday, Christmas Day, Boxing Day (Dec 26), and New Year's Day. Admission is A$5 per person. Take time to wander through the lovely gardens, with their sculptures and bench seats.

Just outside Daylesford is **Lavandula** (www.lavandula.com.au; ✆ **03/5476 4393**), a Swiss-Italian lavender farm that has a rustic trattoria-style cafe and a cobblestone courtyard with a cluster of farmhouse buildings. Swiss immigrants ran a dairy farm here in the 1860s; today you can see the process of lavender farming and buy lavender products. Free tours of the restored stone farmhouse are run daily at noon, 2, and 4pm. The lavender is in full bloom in December, with harvesting in January. Lavandula is at 350 Hepburn-Newstead Rd., Shepherds Flat, about 10 minutes' drive north of Daylesford. From September to May (except Dec 23–26) it is open Friday to Tuesday from 10:30am to 5:30pm; from June through August it is open only on Saturday, Sunday, public holidays, and school holidays. Admission is A$4 adults, A$1 school-age children.

WHERE TO EAT IN DAYLESFORD

The Lake House ★★★ CONTEMPORARY   Treat yourself to one of Australia's best restaurants while you're in Daylesford. Set on the edge of Lake Daylesford, on 2.4 hectares (6 acres) of beautiful gardens, the Lake House is the creation of Alla and Allan Wolf-Tasker. Alla is the executive chef, and Allan's vibrant artworks adorn the walls of the light-filled restaurant overlooking the lake (with adjoining accommodation, if you can't tear yourself away). The restaurant is renowned for its commitment to local and seasonal produce, and the menu changes daily. If—like me—you are tempted by tastes not often on offer at city restaurants, you will relish the offerings on the lunch menu: for example, a shared plate of cured, smoked, or sashimi-style seafood, with fennel salad and watercress and mustard crème fraiche; or dry-aged Macedon Ranges duck with raddichio, fig, and macadamias. Walk it off on the track around the lake!

King St., Daylesford, VIC 3460. www.lakehouse.com.au. ℭ **03/5348 3329.** Lunch and dinner A$95–A$130 for 2 to 4 courses; 8-course tasting menu A$165. Daily noon–2:30pm and 6–9pm.

Ballarat ★★★

113km (70 miles) W of Melbourne

History buffs will love Ballarat. Victoria's largest inland city (pop. 100,000) is synonymous with two major events in Australia's past: the gold rush of the 1850s and the birth of Australian democracy in the early 20th century. It all started with gold; in 1851 two prospectors found gold nuggets scattered on the ground at a place known as, ironically, Poverty Point. Within a year, 20,000 people had drifted into the area, and Australia's gold rush had begun.

In 1858, the second-largest chunk of gold discovered in Australia (the Welcome Nugget) was found, but by the early 1860s, most of the easy diggings were gone. Larger operators continued digging until 1918, but by then Ballarat had developed enough industry to survive without mining. Today, you can still see the gold rush's effects in the impressive buildings, built from the miners' fortunes, lining Ballarat's streets.

ESSENTIALS

ARRIVING   From Melbourne, Ballarat is a 1½-hour drive on the Great Western Highway. **V/Line** (www.vline.com.au; ℭ **136 196** in Victoria, or 03/8608 5011) runs trains between the cities every day; the trip takes about 90 minutes.

Several companies offer day trips from Melbourne, one of which is **AAT Kings** (www.aatkings.com; ℭ **1300/228 546** in Australia). A full-day tour costs A$169 for adults and A$85 for children ages 2 to 15.

VISITOR INFORMATION   The **Ballarat Visitor Information Centre** is at 225 Sturt St., in the Ballarat Town Hall (www.visitballarat.com.au; ℭ **1800/446 633** in Australia, or 03/5337 4337). It is open daily from 9am to 5pm (except Christmas Day).

A eureka **MOMENT**

The story that is central to Ballarat's history, and many of its attractions, is that of the **Eureka Uprising** in 1854. The story goes like this: After gold was discovered, the government introduced gold licenses, charging miners even if they came up empty-handed. The miners had to buy a license every month, and corrupt gold-field police (many of whom were former convicts) instituted a vicious campaign to extract the money. When license checks intensified in 1854, resentment flared. Prospectors began demanding political reforms, such as the right to vote, parliamentary elections, and secret ballots. The situation exploded when the Eureka Hotel's owner murdered a miner but was set free by the government. The hotel was burned down in revenge, and more than 20,000 prospectors joined together, burned their licenses in a huge bonfire, and built a stockade over which they raised a flag. Troops arrived at the "Eureka Stockade" the next month, but only 150 miners remained. The stockade was attacked at dawn, with 24 miners killed and 30 wounded. The uprising forced the government to act: The licenses were replaced with "miners' rights" and cheaper fees, and the vote was introduced to Victoria. It was a definitive moment in Australia's history, and the Eureka flag (see below) is still a potent (and often controversial) symbol of nationalism.

EXPLORING BALLARAT

Art Gallery of Ballarat ★★★ GALLERY   Founded in 1884, this is Australia's oldest regional gallery and houses a fine collection of Australian art, including paintings from the Heidelberg School and a stunning collection of 20th-century modernists. It also hosts interesting contemporary exhibitions on popular themes (there is usually a fee for these). Free guided tours at 2pm daily. 40 Lydiard St. N. www.artgalleryofballarat.com.au. ℂ **03/5320 5858.** Free. Daily 10am–5pm. Closed Christmas Day and Boxing Day (Dec 26).

Ballarat Botanical Gardens ★★★ GARDEN   The gold-rich citizens of Ballarat bestowed magnificent gifts on these delightful gardens from its early days, including the collection of 12 marble statues that now stand in the conservatory, the elegant Statuary Pavilion and its contents—including the wonderful *Flight from Pompeii*—and a statue of William Wallace near the gardens' entrance. Other highlights include Prime Ministers Avenue, lined with bronze busts of Australia's 29 former PMs, and the striking Australian Ex-Prisoners of War Memorial at the southwestern end of the gardens. One of the greatest attractions is an avenue of 70 giant redwoods, planted about 130 years ago. Free guided tours run every Sunday at 11am and on request by advance booking. The gardens' cafe overlooks Lake Wendouree. Wendouree Parade. www.ballaratbotanicalgardens.com.au. ℂ **03/5320 5135.** Free. Daily 7:30am–9pm (Oct–Apr) and 7:30am–6pm (May–Sept). Conservatory daily 9am–4:30pm. Bus: 16.

Blood on the Southern Cross ★★★ ENTERTAINMENT   This breathtaking sound-and-light show re-creates the Eureka Uprising, one of the most important events in Australia's history (see box, above). You will be outdoors, so bring something warm to wear because it can get chilly at night. It's stirring stuff, and the reenactment does the story justice. The 90-minute show is full of surprises.

Sovereign Hill, Bradshaw St. www.sovereignhill.com.au. ℂ **03/5337 1199.** Reservations required. A$60 adults, A$32 children 5–15, A$162 families of 4. Package with daytime entry to Sovereign Hill and dinner (see below), A$153 adults, A$77 children, A$408 families. Ask about packages with overnight accommodations. 2 shows nightly (times vary seasonally).

Eureka Centre – Home of the Eureka Flag ★★ MUSEUM The highlight of a visit to Ballarat—especially after you've learned the story of the Eureka Uprising (see "A Eureka Moment," above)—is the sight of the beautiful and now fragile blue-and-white flag made from petticoat fabric by the women of the uprising and enshrined here. The former museum on the site of the 1854 Eureka Stockade was at press time being "reimagined," but remains open for visitors to view the flag. It also has a cafe and gardens.

102 Stawell St. S. (at Eureka St.). ℂ **03/5333 0333.** A$12 adults, A$8 children 6–15, A$35 families. Daily 10am–5pm. Closed Christmas Day.

The Gold Museum ★ MUSEUM A 4.4kg (nearly 10-lb.) gold nugget—known as "Goldasaurus"—is the latest highlight in this surprisingly interesting small museum. Found by a local prospector, it is one of many curious objects you will discover here, as well as a large collection of gold nuggets found at Ballarat, displays of alluvial deposits, gold ornaments, coins, and the history of gold mining in the area.

Bradshaw St. (opposite Sovereign Hill). ℂ **03/5337 1107.** A$14 adults, A$7.20 children 5–15, A$36 family of 6. Free with entry to Sovereign Hill (see below). Daily 9:30am–5:30pm. Closed Christmas Day.

Sovereign Hill ★★★ MUSEUM Ballarat's history comes to life at Sovereign Hill, long described as Australia's best outdoor museum, which transports you back to the 1850s and the heady days of the gold rush. Living in the gold-rush times wasn't all beer and skittles, as Sovereign Hill's latest multimillion-dollar underground exhibit—the multisensory experience "Trapped"—conveys, depicting an 1882 mining disaster as a tale of bravery, love, and loss. More than 40 reproduction buildings, including shops and businesses on Main Street, sit on the 25-hectare (62-acre) former gold-mining site. There are also tent camps around the diggings on what would have been the outskirts of town. Sovereign Hill has a lot to see and do, so expect to spend at least 4 hours here. The township bustles with actors in period costumes going about their daily business. You can pan for real gold, ride in horse-drawn carriages, and watch potters, blacksmiths, and tanners make their wares. Don't miss the gold pour at the smelting works, or the redcoats as they parade through the streets. On top of Sovereign Hill are the mineshafts and pithead equipment. The guided tour of a typical underground gold mine takes around 45 minutes and

The Sovereign Hill living history museum illuminates Victoria's 1850s gold-rush era.

costs A$7.50 for adults, A$4 for children, and A$20 for a family of six. A restaurant and several cafes and souvenir stores are scattered around the site.

Bradshaw St. www.sovereignhill.com.au. © **03/5337 1199.** A$57 adults, A$26 children 5–15, A$103–A$144 families. Daily 10am–5pm. Closed Christmas Day. A free bus meets the 9:16am train (the "Goldrush Special" from Melbourne's Southern Cross railway station) when it arrives at Ballarat Station and takes visitors direct to Sovereign Hill. Return service connects with the 3:52pm (4:13pm on Sat–Sun) train back to Melbourne.

WHERE TO EAT IN BALLARAT

Eclectic Tastes ★★ CAFE   This unusual cafe, spread out over five rooms, serves up all-day breakfast, lunch, coffee, and snacks. Menu offerings may include simple sweet corn fritters, a roast cauliflower salad, or Eclectic's own take on *yum cha* (similar to dim sum), with pork dumplings, chicken, and bok choy gyozas, prawn toast, and an Asian-style salad. You'll find this smart little cafe opposite the Ballarat Cemetery near the shores of Lake Wendouree (a bit off the beaten track but worth the effort). There's a kids' menu, too.

2 Burnbank St. www.eclectictastes.com.au. © **03/5339 3391.** Main courses A$18–A$27. Mon–Fri 7am–4:30pm; Sat–Sun 8am–4pm.

Oscar's ★ CONTEMPORARY   This cafe and bar inside one of Ballarat's historic old pubs is in the heart of the town, walking distance from shopping, the art gallery, and many other attractions. The former gold rush–era hotel has an appealing open-plan restaurant, with a courtyard and bar. It's open for breakfast, lunch, and dinner, and you can get snacks all day. Meals include Italian favorites (pizzas, lasagna, risotto, pasta), as well as steaks, a Thai green curry, salads, and gluten-free dishes. Something for everyone (including kids).

18 Doveton St. S. www.oscarshotel.com.au. © **03/5331 1451.** Main courses A$23–A$35. Daily 7am–10pm.

BRISBANE

risbane is one of those cities that seems always to be changing, without ever losing its essential heart and character. It's that most Australian of cities—big-hearted, blue-skied, and with a down-to-earth attitude that soon rubs off on you. Brisbane will most likely be your first port of call in Queensland, and you can even reach the southernmost part of the Great Barrier Reef on a day trip from here.

Brisbane (pronounced *Briz*-bun), "Brizzie" to locals, functions on a very human scale. It's a place where you can cuddle koalas, join bronzed urbanites on the beaches on the weekend, and sunbathe by the Brisbane River while gazing up at gleaming skyscrapers. Beyond landmarks such as the 1920s City Hall and the Treasury Building's graceful colonnades, Brisbane's most iconic experiences seem to all take place out of doors—strolling through the Brisbane City Gardens, adventure-climbing on Story Bridge, taking in the city skyline from the gently revolving Wheel of Brisbane, cuddling koalas at the Lone Pine Koala Sanctuary. Even its top arts and entertainment complexes—the Queensland Cultural Centre and South Bank Parklands—are built as open-air malls with lots of plazas and alfresco gathering places.

The city center and surrounding suburbs represent fusion cuisine at its finest, particularly nightlife hotspot Fortitude Valley, which serves the world on a plate—everything from Spanish tapas to Thai—in chic lounge-style restaurants.

On the city river bank, opposite South Bank and adjacent to the Treasury Casino and Hotel, a major redevelopment to be called **Queen's Wharf** will transform the city over the next 4 years. It will include five new hotels, three residential towers, around 50 new restaurants, cafes, and bars, and a riverfront outdoor cinema. A pedestrian bridge will link the precinct to South Bank.

ESSENTIALS

Arriving

BY PLANE   About 30 international airlines serve Brisbane from Europe, North America, Asia, and New Zealand. From North America, you can fly direct from Los Angeles to Brisbane on Qantas, but from other places you will likely fly to Sydney first, then take a connecting flight to Brisbane, or come via Auckland, New Zealand.

Qantas (www.qantas.com.au; ℂ **131 313** in Australia) operates daily flights from Sydney, Melbourne, Darwin, Alice Springs, Cairns, Townsville, Bundaberg, Hamilton Island, Gladstone, Rockhampton, and several other towns. **Jetstar** (www.jetstar.com.au; ℂ **131 538** in Australia) has daily service from the Queensland centers of Cairns, Townsville, Proserpine, and Hamilton Island, as well as Sydney, Melbourne, Hobart, Launceston, and other Australian cities. **Virgin Australia** (www.virginaustralia.com.au; ℂ **136 789** in Australia) offers direct services from all capital cities as well as Alice Springs, Launceston, Cairns, Townsville, Hamilton Island, and Proserpine in the Whitsundays, Bundaberg, Gladstone, and other centers. **Tigerair** (www.tigerair.com; ℂ **1300/174 266** in Australia, or 07/3295 2104) flies from Sydney, Melbourne, Darwin, and Cairns, as well as other cities.

Brisbane International Airport (www.bne.com.au) is 16km (10 miles) from the city, and the domestic terminal is 2km (1¼ miles) farther away. There is a free inter-terminal bus, or you can catch the train (p. 158) for A$5. A taxi between terminals costs about A$15. The arrivals floor of the international terminal, on Level 2, has a check-in counter for passengers transferring to domestic flights and an information desk to meet all flights, help with flight inquiries, dispense tourist information, and make hotel bookings. **Travelex** currency-exchange bureaus are on the departures and arrivals floors.

There are three airport hotels, two at the domestic terminal and one at the Skygate precinct close to the international terminal. **Pullman Brisbane Airport** (www.pullmanhotels.com/Pullman/Airport-Hotel; ℂ **07/3188 7300**) and the **Ibis Brisbane Airport Hotel** (www.ibisba.com.au; ℂ **07/3188 7373**) are on Dryandra Drive, a 3-minute walk to the domestic terminal. The hotels adjoin and share some facilities. **Novotel Brisbane Airport** (www.novotel brisbaneairport.com.au; ℂ **07/3175 3100**) is in the Skygate shopping precinct, with shuttle buses running from the terminals. All three hotels offer a day rate (9am–5pm), which includes a room, free Wi-Fi, and use of the pool and other facilities. At the Ibis, the rate is A$85, at the Novotel it's A$145 and at the Pullman A$155.

Avis (www.avis.com.au; ℂ **07/3633 8666**), **Budget** (www.budget.com.au; ℂ **07/3000 1030**), **Europcar** (www.europcar.com.au; ℂ **07/3874 8150**), **Hertz** (www.hertz.com.au; ℂ **07/3860 4522**), **Thrifty** (www.thrifty.com.au; ℂ **07/3000 8600**), and local company **Red Spot Rentals** (www.redspot.com.au; ℂ **07/3860 5766**) have desks on Level 2. On levels 2, 3, and 4 you will find ATMs, free showers, and baby-changing rooms. The domestic terminal has a Travelex currency-exchange bureau, ATMs, showers, and the big four car-rental desks. Luggage lockers are available at both terminals, for between A$10 and A$14 per day, depending on size.

Between the Airport and the City

Con-x-ion (www.con-x-ion.com; ℂ **1300/910 943** in Australia) runs a shuttle between the airport and city hotels and the Brisbane Transit Centre every 30 minutes from 5am to 11pm. The one-way cost is A$20 per person; round-trip A$38. The trip takes about 40 minutes. No public buses serve the airport. A

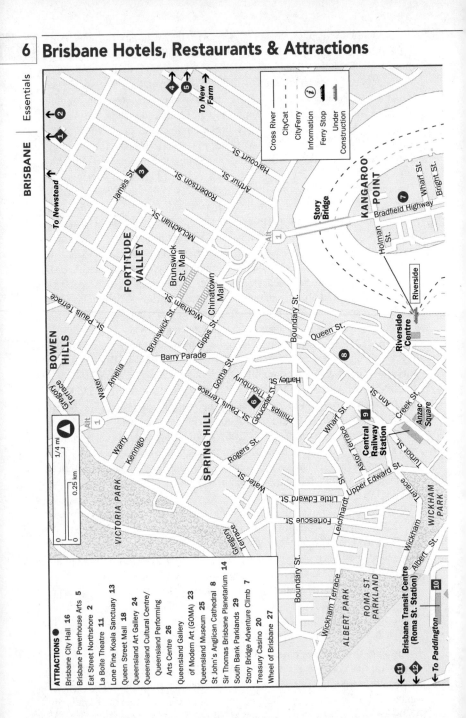

Cross River
CityCat
CityFerry
Information
Ferry Stop
Under Construction

To New Farm
To Newstead

Harcourt St.
Arthur St.
Robertson St.
James St.
Mclachlan St.

FORTITUDE VALLEY

Brunswick St. Mall
Brunswick St.
Wickham St.
Chinatown Mall
Gipps St.

Barry Parade

Story Bridge
Bradfield Highway
KANGAROO POINT
Wharf St.
Bright St.
Holman St.

Riverside
Riverside Centre

Boundary St.
Queen St.

BOWEN HILLS
Gregory Terrace
St. Pauls Terrace

Water St.
Amelia
Warry
Kennigo

St. Pauls Terrace
Gotha St.
Gloucester St.
Phillips St.
Thornbury
Hartley St.
Wharf St.
Ann St.

Queen St.

SPRING HILL
Rogers St.
Water St.
Little Edward St.
Leichhardt
Upper Edward St.
Astor Terrace
Turbot St.
Creek St.
Anzac Square

Central Railway Station

VICTORIA PARK

1/4 mi
0.25 km

Fortescue St.
Gregory Terrace
Boundary St.
Wickham Terrace
Terrace
Wickham

WICKHAM PARK

ALBERT PARK
ROMA ST. PARKLAND
Albert St.

To Paddington
Brisbane Transit Centre (Roma St. Station)

ATTRACTIONS ●

Brisbane City Hall **16**
Brisbane Powerhouse Arts **5**
Eat Street Northshore **2**
La Boite Theatre **11**
Lone Pine Koala Sanctuary **13**
Queen Street Mall **18**
Queensland Art Gallery **24**
Queensland Cultural Centre/
Queensland Performing
Arts Centre **26**
Queensland Gallery
of Modern Art (GOMA) **23**
Queensland Museum **25**
St John's Anglican Cathedral **8**
Sir Thomas Brisbane Planetarium **14**
South Bank Parklands **29**
Story Bridge Adventure Climb **7**
Treasury Casino **20**
Wheel of Brisbane **27**

156

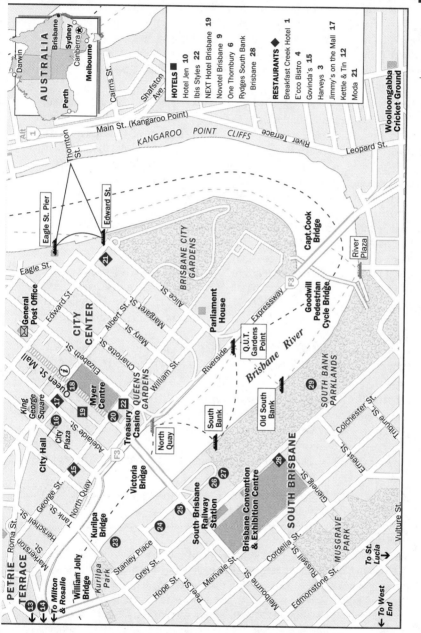

taxi to the city costs around A$50, plus a A$3.40 airport fee for departing taxis.

Airtrain (www.airtrain.com.au; © **1800/119 091** in Australia, or 07/3216 3308), a rail link between the city and Brisbane's domestic and international airport terminals, runs every 15 minutes from around 5am (6am Sat–Sun) to 10pm daily. Fares from the airport to city stations are A$18 per adult one-way, A$34 round-trip; children ages 14 and under travel free. The trip takes about 20 minutes.

BY TRAIN Queensland Rail (www.queenslandrailtravel.com.au; © **1300/131 722** in Australia, or 07/3606 6630) operates long-distance trains north from Brisbane along the coast. The swish Spirit of Queensland takes about 24 hours between Brisbane and Cairns and costs A$390 for an airline-style "rail bed" seat, and includes meals. The high-speed Tilt Train takes about 4½ hours from Brisbane to Bundaberg or 7½ hours to Rockhampton. NSW Trainlink (www.transportnsw.info; © **131 500** in Australia) runs daily train services to Brisbane from Sydney. The trip takes around 14½ hours, with the final 3½ hours (from the town of Casino, south of the Queensland border) by bus. Fares vary but cost around A$91 for an adult economy seat or A$130 for a first-class seat. A sleeper costs around A$216.

All intercity and interstate trains pull into the city center's **Brisbane Transit Centre at Roma Street,** often called the Roma Street Transit Centre. From here, most city and Spring Hill hotels are a few blocks' walk or a quick cab ride away. The station has food outlets, showers, tourist information, and lockers.

Queensland Rail CityTrain (© **131 230** in Queensland) provides daily train service from the Sunshine Coast and plentiful service from the Gold Coast.

BY BUS All intercity and interstate coaches pull into the Brisbane Transit Centre (see "By Train," above). **Greyhound Australia** (www.greyhound.com.au; © **1300/473 946** in Australia, or 07/3736 2610) serves the city several times daily. A one-way Cairns-Brisbane ticket costs around A$328; the trip takes nearly 30 hours. The Sydney-Brisbane trip takes about 17 hours and costs around A$190 one-way.

BY CAR The Bruce Highway from Cairns enters the city from the north. The Pacific Highway enters Brisbane from the south.

Visitor Information

The **Brisbane Visitor Information Centre** (www.visitbrisbane.com.au; © **07/3006 6290**) is in the Regent Theatre building in the Queen Street Mall, between Edward and Albert streets. It's open Monday through Thursday from 9am to 5:30pm, Friday 9am to 7pm, Saturday 9am to 5pm, Sunday 10am to 5pm. It's closed Christmas Day, Anzac Day (Apr 25) and Good Friday. There are also visitor information centers at the airport, and at South Bank Parklands (p. 172).

Post Office Square, a shopping and leisure area in downtown Brisbane.

City Layout

The **city center**'s office towers shimmer in the sun on the north bank of a curve of the Brisbane River; across the river lie the **South Bank Parklands** and the **Queensland Cultural Centre,** known as South Bank. At the tip of the river's curve lie the lush **Brisbane City Gardens** (sometimes called the City Botanic Gardens); across from them, on the eastern side of the south bank, rise the 30m (98-ft.) sandstone cliffs of **Kangaroo Point**. Two pedestrian bridges link South Bank with the city: **Kurilpa Bridge** links Tank Street, in the city center, with the Gallery of Modern Art at South Bank, and the **Goodwill Bridge** links South Bank with the City Gardens. To the west 5km (3 miles), Mount **Coot-tha** (pronounced *Coo*-tha) looms out of the flat plain.

MAIN ARTERIES & STREETS   It's easy to find your way around central Brisbane once you know that the east-west streets are named after female British royalty, and the north-south streets are named after their male counterparts. The northernmost is Ann, followed by Adelaide, Queen, Elizabeth, Charlotte, Mary, Margaret, and Alice. From east to west, the streets are Edward, Albert, George, and William, which becomes North Quay, flanking the river's northeast bank.

   Queen Street, the main thoroughfare, becomes a pedestrian mall between Edward and George streets. **Roma Street** exits the city diagonally to the northwest. **Ann Street** leads all the way east into Fortitude Valley. The main street in Fortitude Valley is **Brunswick Street**, which runs into New Farm.

Brisbane Neighborhoods in Brief

City Center This is where Brisbane residents eat, shop, and socialize. Queen Street Mall, in the heart of town, is popular with shoppers and moviegoers, especially on weekends and Friday night (when stores stay open until 9pm). The Eagle Street financial and legal precinct has restaurants with great views of the river and Story Bridge. Much of the city's surviving colonial architecture is here, too. Strollers, bike riders, and in-line skaters shake the summer heat in the green haven of the Brisbane City Gardens at the business district's southern end.

Fortitude Valley "The Valley," as locals call it, was once one of the sleazier parts of town. Today, it is a stamping ground for street-smart young folk who meet in restored pubs and eat in cool cafes. The lanterns, food stores, and shopping mall of **Chinatown** are here, too. On weekends, you'll find Brisbane's only alternative market, Valley Markets in the Brunswick Street and Chinatown malls (take Turbot St. from the city center). Venture a little farther to the trendy boutiques and cafes of James Street.

New Farm Always an appealing suburb, New Farm is an in-spot for cafe-hopping. Merthyr Street is where the action is,

especially on Friday and Saturday nights. From the intersection of Wickham and Brunswick streets, follow Brunswick southeast for 13 blocks to Merthyr.

Paddington This hilltop suburb, a couple of miles northwest of the city, is one of Brisbane's most attractive. Brightly painted Queenslander cottages line the main street, Latrobe Terrace, as it winds west along a ridge top. Many of the houses have been turned into shops and cafes, where you can browse, enjoy coffee and cake, or just admire the charming architecture.

Milton & Rosalie Park Road, in Milton, is not quite a little bit of Europe, but it tries hard—right down to a replica Eiffel Tower above the cafes and shops. Italian restaurants line the street, buzzing with office workers who down espressos at alfresco restaurants, scout interior-design stores for a new objet d'art, and stock up on European designer rags.

West End This small inner-city enclave is alive with ethnic restaurants, cafes, and a few interesting housewares or fashion stores. Most action centers on the intersection of Vulture and Boundary streets, where Asian grocers and delis abound.

Getting Around Brisbane
BY PUBLIC TRANSPORTATION

TransLink operates a single network of buses, trains, and ferries. For timetables and route inquiries, call **TransInfo** (www.translink.com.au; ✆ **131 230**). It uses an integrated ticket system, and the easiest place to buy your tickets is on the buses and ferries or at the train stations. You can also buy tickets and pick up maps and timetables at the Queen Street bus station information center (in the Myer Centre, off Queen Street Mall) and the Brisbane Visitor Information Centre in the Queen Street Mall. Tickets and electronic go cards are also sold at some inner-city newsdealers and convenience stores.

A trip in a single sector or zone on the bus, train, or ferry costs A$4.70. A single ticket is good for up to 2 hours on a one-way journey on any combination of bus, train, or ferry. When traveling with a parent, kids 4 and under travel free, and kids 5 to 14 and students pay half fare. If you plan on using public transport a lot, it is worth investing in a **go card,** which gives discounted rates (you can also buy online and just top up the card balance as you need it). This reduces the price of a one-zone one-way trip to A$3.25 or less, depending on the time of day. You will probably not need to travel farther than four zones on the transport system. This will cost you less than A$12. On weekends and public holidays, it's cheaper to buy an **off-peak ticket.** The off-peak ticket is also available on weekdays, but to use it you'd have to plan your sightseeing around the fact that it cannot be used before 8:30am or between 3:30 and 7pm. You might also like to buy a **seeQ card,** specially designed for visitors, which offers 3 or 5 consecutive days' travel on all public transport services (including to the Gold Coast), including two Airtrain trips. seeQ cards cost A$79 adults and A$40 children for 3 days or A$129 adults and A$65 children for 5 days.

BY PUBLIC BUS

Buses operate from around 5am to 11pm Monday through Friday, with less service on weekends. On Sunday, many routes stop around 5pm. Most buses depart from City Hall at King George Square, Adelaide, or Ann Street. The **Loop** is a free bus service that circles the city center, with distinctive red buses running on two routes, stopping at convenient places including Central Station, Queen Street Mall, Brisbane City Gardens, Riverside Centre, and King George Square. Look for the red bus stops. They run every 10 minutes Monday through Friday, from 7am to 6pm.

BY FERRY

The fast **CityCat** ferries run to many places of interest, including South Bank and the Queensland Cultural Centre; the restaurants and Sunday markets at the Riverside Centre; and New Farm Park, not far from the cafes of Merthyr Street. They run every half-hour between the University of Queensland to the south of the city center, and Hamilton to the north (a route of around 20km/12 miles). Slower but more frequent CityFerry service (the **Inner City** and **Cross**

One of Brisbane's speedy CityCat ferries.

River ferries) has stops at points including the south end of South Bank Parklands, Kangaroo Point, and Edward Street right outside the Brisbane City Gardens. Ferries run from around 6am to 10:30pm daily. Two hours on the CityCat takes you the entire length of the run (and there's free Wi-Fi on board too!).

BY TRAIN

Brisbane's suburban rail network is fast, quiet, safe, and clean. Trains run from around 5am to midnight (until about 11pm on Sun). All trains leave Central Station, between Turbot and Ann streets at Edward Street.

BY BICYCLE

CityCycle (www.citycycle.com.au; ℭ **1300/229 253**) has 150 bike parking stations across central Brisbane, with bright yellow bikes and helmets (compulsory by law) to rent. You can hire a bike between 5am and 10pm daily and return it to the station at any time. You can buy a casual subscription for A$2 a day, and the first 30 minutes on a bike is free. After that, usage charges start from A$2 for 30 minutes and then A$5 for every 30 minutes, to a maximum of A$97—so unless you are only planning a short ride, it's cheaper to hire a bike elsewhere.

BY CAR OR TAXI

Brisbane's grid of one-way streets can be confusing, so plan your route before setting out. Apart from that, it's easy to get around, and a car is useful here (Brisbane's a sprawling place and quite hilly too). Brisbane's biggest parking lot is at the Myer Centre (66 Elizabeth St.), open 24 hours (ℭ **07/3229 1699**). Most hotels and motels have free parking for guests. Most car rental companies (see p. 155 for contact information) have outlets in the city center.

For a taxi, call **Yellow Cabs** (ℭ **131 924** in Australia) or **Black and White Taxis** (ℭ **133 222** in Australia). There are taxi stands at each end of Queen Street Mall, on Edward Street and on George Street (outside the Treasury Casino).

[FastFACTS] BRISBANE

ATMs/Banks Banks are open Mon–Thurs 9:30am–4pm, until 5pm Fri. ATMs are easy to find in the city center and are open 24 hrs.

Business Hours Brisbane shops are open Mon–Thurs 9am–6pm, Fri 9am–9pm (except in Paddington, where shops are open until 9pm Thurs), Sat 9am–5:30pm, and Sun 10am–6pm. Some

restaurants close Monday night, Tuesday night, or both; bars are generally open from 10 or 11am until midnight.

Dentists **Maven Dental,** 171 Moray St., New Farm (ℭ **07/3358 1333**), is open 8am–7pm Mon–Thurs, and 9am–5pm Fri–Sat. For after-hours emergencies, call for recorded info on whom to contact.

Doctors & Hospitals The **Royal Brisbane Hospital** is about a 15-minute drive from the city at Herston Road, Herston (ℭ **07/3636 8111**). The **Travel Doctor** (www.thetravel doctor.com.au; ℭ **07/3221 9066**) is on Level 5, 247 Adelaide St., between Creek and Edward streets. It's open Mon–Fri 8am–4:30pm (except Wed

10am–6:30pm), and Sat 8:30am–12:30pm.

Embassies & Consulates The United States, Canada, and New Zealand have no representation in Brisbane; see chapter 4, "Sydney," for those countries' nearest offices. The **British Consulate** is at Level 9, 100 Eagle St. (℡ **07/3223 3200**); it's open Mon–Fri 9am–5pm.

Emergencies Dial ℡ **000** for fire, ambulance, or police help in an emergency. This is a free call from a private or public telephone. **Lifeline** (℡ **131 114**) is a 24-hour emotional crisis counseling service.

Mail & Postage The General Post Office is at 261 Queen St., opposite Post Office Square. It is open Mon–Fri 7am–6pm and Sat 9am–12:30pm.

Newspapers & Magazines The *Courier-Mail* (Mon–Sat) and the *Sunday Mail* are Brisbane's daily newspapers. Another good news source is the online newspaper *Brisbane Times* (www.brisbanetimes.com. au). The free weekly *Brisbane News* magazine is a good guide to dining, entertainment, and shopping.

Pharmacies (Chemist Shops) The **Queen Street Pharmacy,** 141 Queen St. (on the mall) (℡ **07/3221 4585**), is open Mon–Thurs 7am–9pm, Fri 7am–9:30pm, Sat 8am–9pm, Sun 8:30am–7pm, and public holidays 9am–7:30pm.

Police Dial ℡ **000** in an emergency, or ℡ **131 444** for police headquarters. Police are stationed 24 hours a day at 67 Adelaide St. (℡ **07/3224 4444**).

Safety Brisbane is relatively crime free, but as in any large city, be aware of your personal safety, especially when you're out at night. Stick to well-lit streets and busy precincts.

Wi-Fi Brisbane has plenty of public Wi-Fi, with hotspots throughout the city center and suburbs. If you need access to a computer, try the **State Library of Queensland,** Stanley Place, South Bank (www.slq.qld. gov.au; ℡ **07/3840 7666**).

WHERE TO STAY IN BRISBANE

Expensive

NEXT Hotel Brisbane ★★★   This is one of my favorite Brisbane hotels. Not just for the location—up an escalator at the top of the Queen Street Mall—and fabulous city and river views, but for service that is casual, friendly, and efficient. NEXT opened in 2015 after a major redevelopment transformed one of the city's old hotels into one of its smartest. And I don't just mean the sleek contemporary look of it: This is Australia's first hotel to use smart technology that lets guests control just about everything. You can even use your smartphone as your room "key." Don't have a smartphone? That's okay, there's one in the room for you to use. Add to this an outdoor terrace bar overlooking the 20-m lap pool, "sleep pods" if you're in transit, and four free items each day from the mini-bar. Seems they've thought of everything.

72 Queen St. www.silverneedlehotels.com/next. ℡ **1800/303 186** in Australia, or 07/3222 3222. 304 units. A$189–A$209 double. Valet parking A$45. Train: Central. **Amenities:** Restaurant; bar; babysitting; concierge; gym; outdoor pool; room service; free Wi-Fi.

Novotel Brisbane ★★   This well-appointed contemporary hotel, a short walk from Brisbane's main shopping areas, is popular among families and business travelers. Rooms and suites are modern, stylish, and spacious, with interesting abstract artworks. The lap pool is very inviting and offers terrific city views. For dining, you can choose among **The Restaurant,** the more casual **Bar Astor** bistro, or an all-day menu in **The Bar.**

200 Creek St. www.novotelbrisbane.com.au. ✆ **1300/656 565** in Australia, or 07/3309 3309. 296 units. A$149–A$559 double. Parking A$35–A$45. Train: Central. **Amenities:** 2 restaurants; bar; babysitting; concierge; gym; outdoor pool; room service; sauna; Wi-Fi (A$10/24 hr.).

Rydges South Bank Brisbane ★★★ Right in the heart of the South Bank cultural precinct, this is a perfect spot for theater- or museum-goers. After a A$30-million refurbishment in 2017, this hotel is sparkling again. All rooms have new beds and a selection of pillows, and those above the sixth floor have views of the city skyline, the river (1 block away), Mount Coot-tha, and the Wheel of Brisbane. Some rooms have balconies. The main action is in the Soleil Pool Bar, where Brisbane's beautiful people gather at cocktail hour; look up for changing images on the ceiling. **Bacchus Restaurant** is fine dining at its best, and puts on a lavish breakfast buffet.

9 Glenelg St. www.rydges.com. ✆ **07/3364 0800.** 304 units. A$449–A$649 double. Valet parking A$35 per day. Train: South Brisbane. **Amenities:** Restaurant; bar; concierge; gymnasium; outdoor heated pool; room service; sauna; free Wi-Fi.

Moderate

Hotel Jen ★ Linked to the Brisbane Transit Centre by a covered walkway, this is a great choice if you plan to arrive in Brisbane by bus or Airtrain. This is a quirky hotel with lots to discover, from the sixth-floor sky garden (ask for a tour to see the beehives) to the excellent Asian-style restaurant. Some rooms overlook the city, others the green Roma Street Parklands next door (get up early for the Wednesday morning boot camp). Rooms all have espresso machines and fridges. Despite the proximity to the train station, a good night's sleep is ensured, as all the windows are double-glazed. It's a 5-minute walk to the Queen Street Mall.

159 Roma St. www.hoteljen.com. ✆ **07/3238 2222.** 191 units. A$129–A$199 double. Train: Roma St. **Amenities:** Restaurant; bar; 24-hr gymnasium; sauna; free Wi-Fi.

Ibis Styles ★★ This bright and breezy inner-city hotel is a great budget choice, appealing to travelers of all ages. Opened in 2016, it is one of the most colorful hotels I've stayed in; each floor is painted in vivid pink, green, purple, or blue (easy to remember which floor you are staying on!). Standard rooms are small, but the beds are comfortable and rooms all have city, river, or South Bank views. If you're not going to spend much time in your room, it's a great choice. The Queen Street Mall is just around the corner.

40 Elizabeth St. www.ibisstylesbrisbaneelizabeth.com.au. ✆ **1300/656 565** in Australia, or 07/3337 900. 386 units. A$119–A$149 double. Parking (at the Myer Centre next door) A$20–A$38. Train: Central. Bus: Downtown Loop. **Amenities:** Restaurant; bar; babysitting; small exercise room; free Wi-Fi.

One Thornbury ★★ In the lovely inner-city suburb of Spring Hill, this heritage cottage is a stylish boutique bed-and-breakfast where you will feel

Kettle & Tin ★★ CAFE   I've been a fan of this cute cafe, with its picket fence outside, since my daughter took me here for lunch. In the Paddington cafe strip, it's a converted cottage, opened up for tables on the veranda or tucked away in its few rooms. My favorite time to come now—along with lots of locals—is for weekend brunch. I love the Vietnamese crepe with pork and prawns but there's more traditional fare if you prefer. At night, shared plates are on offer—and if you go on Thursday night you might get involved in the trivia quiz.

215 Given Terrace, Paddington. www.kettleandtin.com.au. ℓ **07/3369 3778.** Main courses A$18–A$23. Mon–Tues 7am–3pm; Wed–Sat 7am–10pm; Sun 7am–7pm. Bus: 377.

EXPLORING BRISBANE

Many of Brisbane's attractions are outdoors or nature-based, and many are free, making it a popular destination for families. The riverfront provides its own attractions, with much of the city turned towards it, with bikeway and walking paths providing terrific views.

Brisbane City Hall ★★★ HISTORIC ARCHITECTURE   The imposing Brisbane City Hall, built in the 1920s in Italian Renaissance style, was once the city's tallest building, standing at the heart of the city center. Free 45-minute guided tours are offered daily at 10:30 and 11:30am, and 1:30 and 2:30pm. Tours are hugely popular and numbers are limited, so it's essential to book your spot. This is still a working civic building, so at times some of the rooms and features are not open. Separate free tours are run to the top of the **Clock Tower** every 15 minutes daily from 10:15am to 4:45pm. You cannot book ahead for these tours, and it pays to arrive early, because the vintage elevator only holds seven passengers. You'll need to get a ticket from the **Museum of Brisbane** reception counter on Level 3, and then wait your turn. The museum is also well worth spending time in; it provides an insight into the history and essence of Brisbane. Changing exhibitions relate the stories, events, and ideas that have shaped the city. This is a beautiful building—don't miss it!

City Hall, King George Sq. www.museumofbrisbane.com.au. ℓ **07/3339 0845.** Free. Sat–Thurs 10am–5pm; Fri 10am–7pm. Closed New Year's Day, Good Friday, Christmas Day, and Boxing Day (Dec 26), and until 1pm Anzac Day (Apr 25). Train: Roma St. or Central. Bus: The Loop.

Brisbane Powerhouse Arts ★★ ARTS CENTER   A former electricity powerhouse, this massive brick factory is now a dynamic space for exhibitions, contemporary performance, and live art. The building retains its character, an industrial mix of metal, glass, and stark surfaces etched with 20 years of graffiti. It's a short walk from the New Farm ferry terminal along the riverfront through New Farm Park. **Farmers markets** operate every Saturday morning, and there's a restaurant/cafe/bar overlooking the river.

119 Lamington St., New Farm. www.brisbanepowerhouse.org. ℓ **07/3358 8600.** CityCat to New Farm Park.

right at home. A courtyard garden, a house cat called Sassy, and rooms with espresso machines and bathrobes all add up to a great feeling of comfort. Owner Geof Harland is on hand to cook breakfast and help with directions or anything you need. There's a two-bedroom suite on the top floor (no elevator); the rest are roomy doubles. It's about 5 minutes' walk to Chinatown and 15 minutes to the city center.

1 Thornbury St., Spring Hill. www.onethornbury.com. ℓ **07/3839 5334.** 6 units. A$149–A$179 double; A$199 suite. Rates include breakfast. Limited parking. Bus: 196. **Amenities:** Bar; free Wi-Fi.

WHERE TO EAT IN BRISBANE

Brisbane has a sophisticated dining scene. Stylish bistros and cafes line the riverfront at South Bank; cute cafes are plentiful in Paddington; Asian eateries are a good choice in West End; and in Fortitude Valley, you'll find Chinatown. A street lined with upscale but laid-back restaurants, many with a Mediterranean flavor, sits under the kitschy replica Eiffel Tower on Park Road in Milton, and in the city center you can find slick waterfront restaurants at Eagle Street Pier and Riverside. The intersection of Albert and Charlotte streets buzzes with inexpensive, good-quality cafes.

Expensive

e'cco bistro ★★★ CONTEMPORARY   *E'cco* means "here it is" in Italian, and that's the philosophy behind the food at this award-winning bistro, considered one of Australia's best. It serves simple food, done exceptionally well and with passion. A move to new premises in 2018 has enabled different styles of dining (although the food remains at the high standard regulars expect), with the inclusion of an outdoor bar and dining area with a more casual menu. Dishes include such delights as braised short rib with smoked

Eat Street

Brisbane foodies love this vibrant outdoor market designed to emulate the street food stalls of Asia. **Eat Street Northshore** (www.eatstreetmarkets. com.au; ℓ **1300/328 787** in Australia) unleashes the aromas of exotic foods every Friday and Saturday from 4 to 10pm and Sunday from noon to 8pm, at Hamilton Wharf on Brisbane's North Shore. Around 180 shipping containers have been transformed into kitchens and cafes, and it's all very industrial chic. There's also live music and other entertainment and design galleries. Bars serve craft beers, cocktails, and other cool drinks, and there's every type of cuisine from Thai to Turkish, noodles and dumplings to tacos, seafood, or salads, or even a good old Aussie (gourmet) pie. You'll find it by heading to Macarthur Avenue, Hamilton, where there's parking for 1,200 cars, but a better way to get there is by CityCat to North Shore Hamilton, or take bus no. 305 from George Street, in the city, or no. 300 from Adelaide Street, outside City Hall. There's an entry fee of A$3 per person (over 12 years old).

Sup at the Summit

A teahouse of some kind has been on top of Mount Coot-tha for more than a century. Part 19th-century Queenslander house and part modern extension, the **Summit** restaurant (www.brisbanelookout.com; (℃) **07/3369 9922**) has wraparound covered decks with views of the city and Moreton Bay. A changing menu features local produce and wines. The sunset dinner menu—A$43 for three courses if you finish by 7pm—is available starting at 5pm. After your meal, enjoy the observation deck—the city lights provide a glittering panorama. On Sundays, high tea is served from 3 to 5pm (A$35 per person or A$45 with a glass of champagne). Reservations are recommended for Friday, Saturday, and Sunday evenings. The Summit is open daily 11:30am to midnight (closed for lunch New Year's Day, Good Friday, and Boxing Day [Dec 26]; closed for dinner Christmas Day). For breakfast (starting at 8am Mon–Fri and 7am Sat–Sun) or lighter fare (served from 11am daily), there's also the casual **Kuta Café** (no bookings taken). To get to the summit, take bus no. 471 from Adelaide Street, in the city; if you're driving, take Upper Roma Street from the city center, then Milton Road 3.5km (2¼ miles) west to the Western Freeway roundabout at Toowong Cemetery. Veer right onto Sir Samuel Griffith Drive, and follow the road about 3km (2 miles) up the mountain. A taxi from the city will cost about A$30.

Jerusalem artichoke and shiitake; or suckling pig with porchetta, beans, and chimichurri. The bistro is enormously popular, so reservations are advisable (although less imperative at lunch).

63 Skyring Terrace, Newstead. www.eccobistro.com. (℃) **07/3831 8344.** Main courses A$40–A$115. 6-course tasting menu A$89 (or A$160 with wine pairings). Tues–Sat noon–3pm and 5:30–10pm. Bus: 60.

Moda ★★★ CONTEMPORARY Whether you choose the more formal and private mezzanine floor or the relaxed courtyard dining area (my pick), you're sure to enjoy this Spanish-flavored restaurant. Owner-chef Javier Codina has combined his Catalan, French, and Italian influences with fresh (often organic) Queensland produce to make some marvelous dishes. The menu changes often, but you might find something like Spanish-style Wagyu short ribs, or white rabbit ragout with saffron pappardelle and truffle pecorino. If you're there for Friday lunch (or order ahead), you can sample Javier's wonderful paella (A$39). Plates meant to be shared with two or four diners are a good choice, for A$46 or A$78, or Javier's three-course "table experience" for A$89 per person. *Fair warning:* The wine list is expensive.

12 Edward St. www.modarestaurant.com.au. (℃) **07/3221 7655.** Main courses A$29–A$45. Thurs–Fri noon–late; Mon–Wed and Sat 6pm–late. Bus: All Edwards St. buses.

Moderate

Breakfast Creek Hotel ★★ STEAKHOUSE Built in 1889 and listed by the National Trust, this Renaissance-style pub is fondly known as the Brekky Creek—or simply the Creek—and is considered a Brisbane icon. The quintessentially Queensland establishment is famed for its gigantic steaks

(choose your own), served with baked potato (or chips), coleslaw, sal a choice of mushroom, pepper, or chili sauce, and for serving beer " wood" (from the keg). The pub's **Spanish Garden Steakhouse** and the **horn beer garden** are always popular, and an outdoor dining area over Breakfast Creek. The **Substation No. 41** bar, created in the shell of a der electricity substation next to the hotel, makes the most of its exposed b walls and soaring ceilings. The 4.5m-long (15-ft.) wooden bar is just the pla to sip the latest cocktail.

2 Kingsford Smith Dr. (at Breakfast Creek Rd.), Albion. www.breakfastcreekhotel.com (℃) **07/3262 5988.** Main courses A$33–A$59. Daily 10am–late. (Substation No. 41 daily noon–late.) Bus: 300 or 322. Wickham St. becomes Breakfast Creek Rd.; the hotel is just off the route to the airport.

Harveys ★★ CONTEMPORARY In the heart of trendy James Street, take a table in this modern, light-filled restaurant and prepare for something wonderful. Chef/owner PJ McMillan has a strong local following for his deceptively simple dishes. Personally, I can never go past the Asian chicken salad, with coriander, mint, peanuts, coconut, and tamarind dressing—and it always seems that half the other patrons are having it, too. Service is friendly and attentive, and the coffee's good, too!

31 James St., Fortitude Valley (next to the Centro Cinemas). www.harveys.net.au. (℃) **07/3852 3700.** Main courses A$28–A$44. Mon–Fri 7am–3pm; Sat–Sun 7:30am–3pm; Tues–Sat 5:30pm–late. Closed public holidays. Train: Brunswick St.

Jimmy's on the Mall ★★ INTERNATIONAL/CAFE FARE Jimmy's is a Brisbane institution, at the heart of the city's shopping precinct and open around-the-clock. The food here is consistently good, which is why the place is always busy and takes no reservations. On the lower level, the vertical gardens that decorate the eatery's walls open up to the passing shopping trade, while upstairs you can take a bar-style table overlooking the mall, or a booth. The downstairs menu focuses on Asian fusion and includes wok dishes such as pad Thai noodles or satay chicken; the upstairs menu adds pizzas (try the pescatore). An open kitchen adds to the lively atmosphere.

Queen Street Mall, at Albert St. www.jimmysonthemall.com.au. (℃) **07/3077 7126.** Main courses A$20–A$44. Daily 24 hrs. Train: Central.

Inexpensive

Govinda's ★★ VEGETARIAN Tasty, cheap vegetarian food is served up at this Hare Krishna restaurant. That means a buffet of vegetable curry, *dahl* (lentil) soup, papadums, koftas, and other tasty stuff with a north-Indian influence. And it's a stimulant-free zone, so don't come expecting alcohol, tea, or coffee—you're likely to get something like homemade ginger-and-mint lemonade instead. Check the website for details about Govinda's other locations, in Fortitude Valley and the inner suburb of West End.

358 George St. www.brisbanegovindas.com.au. (℃) **07/3210 0255.** A$13 all-you-can-eat; A$10 students. No credit cards. Mon–Fri 7am–8pm; Sat 11am–8pm. Bus: 360, 470, 475, 476.

La Boite Theatre ★★ THEATER   This well-established innovative company performs contemporary Australian plays and some classics in the 400-seat Roundhouse Theatre, ensuring an intimate theater experience. Tickets typically cost A$30 to A$60. Located in the Queensland University of Technology precinct, it offers an affordable night out and some cutting-edge productions.

6 Musk Ave., Kelvin Grove. www.laboite.com.au. ℂ **07/3007 8600.** Take bus no. 390 from the city to Kelvin Grove Rd., and get off at stop 12.

Lone Pine Koala Sanctuary ★★ WILDLIFE VIEWING   This is the best place in Australia to cuddle a koala—and one of the few places where koala cuddling is still allowed. Banned in New South Wales and Victoria, holding a koala is legal in Queensland under strict conditions that ensure that each animal is handled for less than 30 minutes a day—and gets every third day off! When it opened in 1927, Lone Pine had just two koalas, Jack and Jill; it is now home to more than 130. You can cuddle them anytime and have a photo taken holding one (for an extra A$25); once you've paid, you can have some photos taken using your own camera, too. Lone Pine isn't just koalas— you can also hand-feed kangaroos and wallabies and get up close with emus, snakes, baby crocs, parrots, wombats, Tasmanian devils, skinks, lace monitors, frogs, bats, turtles, possums, and other native wildlife. There is a currency exchange, a gift shop, a restaurant, and a cafe. Picnic and barbecue facilities are also available.

The nicest way to get to Lone Pine is a cruise down the Brisbane River aboard the **MV** *Mirimar* (www.mirimarcruises.com.au; ℂ **0412/749 426**), which leaves the Cultural Centre at South Bank Parklands at 10am. The 19km (12-mile) trip to Lone Pine takes 75 minutes and includes commentary. You have 3 hours to explore before returning, arriving in the city at 3:30pm. The round-trip fare is A$78 for adults, A$48 for children ages 3 to 13, and A$215 for families of five, and includes entry to Lone Pine. A shorter, faster "express" cruise also runs daily at 11am, allowing half an hour less at Lone Pine and costing A$30 adults each way (and not including entry). Cruises run daily except Anzac Day (Apr 25) and Christmas Day.

Jesmond Rd., Fig Tree Pocket. www.koala.net. ℂ **07/3378 1366.** A$36 adults, A$22 children 3–13, A$60–A$85 families. Daily 9am–5pm; Anzac Day (Apr 25) 1:30–5pm. By car (20 min. from city center), take Milton Rd. to the roundabout at Toowong Cemetery, and then Western Fwy. toward Ipswich. Signs point to Fig Tree Pocket and Lone Pine. Bus: nos. 430 or 445 from the city center. A taxi from the city center will cost about A$40.

Queen Street Mall ★ SHOPPING DISTRICT   Brisbane's inner-city shopping centers on **Queen Street Mall,** which has around 500 stores. Fronting the mall at 171–209 Queen St., the three-level **Wintergarden** shopping complex (www.wgarden.com.au; ℂ **07/3229 9755**) houses upscale jewelers and Aussie fashion designers. Farther up the mall at 91 Queen St. (at Albert St.) is the **Myer Centre** (www.themyercentre.com.au; ℂ **07/3223 6900**), which has Brisbane's biggest department store and five levels of moderately priced stores, mostly fashion. The gorgeous **Brisbane Arcade,** 160 Queen St. (www.brisbanearcade.com.au; ℂ **07/3231 9777**), runs through to Adelaide Street, and abounds with jewelers and the boutiques of local Queensland designers. Across from the Edward Street end of the mall, at 255 Queen St., is a smart fashion and lifestyle shopping precinct, **MacArthur Central** (www.macarthurcentral.com; ℂ **07/3007 2300**), right next door to the General Post Office on the block between Queen and Elizabeth streets. This is where you'll find top designer labels, Swiss watches, galleries, and accessory shops. On Edward and Adelaide streets, you'll find more chic shopping at **Queens-Plaza** (www.queensplaza.com.au; ℂ **07/3234 3900**). There are also weekly **farmers markets** in the Queen Street Mall (at the Victoria Bridge/George Street end) on Wednesdays from 8am to 6pm.

Queen St. www.queenstreetmall.com.au.

Queensland Cultural Centre ★★★ ARTS CENTER   This modern complex stretching along the south bank of the Brisbane River houses many of the city's performing-arts venues as well as the state art galleries, museum, and library. With plenty of open plazas and fountains, it is a pleasing place to wander or just sit and watch the river and the city skyline. It's a 7-minute walk from town, across the Victoria Bridge from the Queen Street Mall.

The **Queensland Performing Arts Centre** (www.qpac.com.au; ℂ **136 246** for bookings Mon–Sat 9am–8:30pm) houses the 2,000-seat Lyric Theatre for musicals, ballet, and opera; the 1,800-seat Concert Hall for orchestral performances; the 850-seat Playhouse theater for plays; and the 315-seat Cremorne Theatre for theater-in-the-round, cabaret, and experimental works. The complex has a restaurant and a cafe. Resident companies include the **Queensland Theatre** (www.queenslandtheatre.com.au), which offers eight or nine productions a year, from the classics to new Australian works; **Opera Queensland** (www.operaq.com.au), which performs a lively repertoire of traditional as well as modern works, musicals, and choral concerts; and the **Queensland Symphony Orchestra** (www.qso.com.au), which provides classical music lovers with a diverse mix of orchestral and chamber music, with the odd foray into fun material, such as movie themes, pop, and gospel music. It schedules about 30 concerts a year.

The **Queensland Art Gallery ★★★** (www.qagoma.qld.gov.au; ℂ **07/3840 7303**) is one of Australia's most attractive galleries, with vast light-filled spaces and interesting water features inside and out. It is a major player in the Australian art world, attracting blockbuster exhibitions of works by the likes of Renoir, Picasso, and van Gogh, and showcasing diverse modern Australian painters, sculptors, and other artists. It also has an impressive collection of Aboriginal art. The adjacent **Queensland Gallery of Modern Art (GOMA) ★★★** houses collections of modern and contemporary Australian, Indigenous Australian, Asian, and Pacific art, and also gives a stunning sense of light and space. Admission is free to both galleries, and both run regular free tours that take around 30 to 40 minutes. Tours of each gallery's collection highlights are held

Queensland's own *Muttaburrasaurus* is on display at the Queensland Museum.

daily at 11am and 1pm. The galleries are open daily 10am to 5pm; closed Good Friday, Christmas Day, Boxing Day (Dec 26) and until noon on Anzac Day (Apr 25).

Stanley Place, South Brisbane.

Queensland Museum ★★★ MUSEUM Fossils that are 50 million years old—including a frog, snail, crocodile, and fish—are just some of the many fascinating "lost creatures" on show at this interesting and eclectic museum. Displays range from natural history specimens to insects, dinosaurs—including Queensland's own *Muttaburrasaurus*—and more. Children will love the blue whale model that greets you at the entrance. The museum also has a cafe and gift shop. Admission is free, except to the Sciencentre and to any special exhibitions. At press time, the Sciencentre was closed for redevelopment (re-opening late 2018), so expect something special when you get there!

Grey St. (at Melbourne St.), next to the Queensland Art Gallery. www.qm.qld.gov.au. ⓒ **07/3840 7555.** Daily 9:30am–5pm; closed Good Friday, Christmas Day, and Boxing Day (Dec 26), and until 1:30pm on Anzac Day (Apr 25). Free. Ferry: South Bank (CityCat) or Old South Bank (Inner City Ferry). Bus: Numerous buses from Adelaide St. (near Albert St.). Train: South Brisbane.

St. John's Anglican Cathedral ★★ CHURCH Brisbane's stunning neo-Gothic Anglican cathedral took more than a century to complete, but the result has been worth the wait. Plagued by lack of funding throughout its history, the building was finally completed in 2009, making it one of the last Gothic-style cathedrals to be completed anywhere in the world, with stonemasons using traditional medieval building techniques. Volunteer guides are on hand to point out some of the details that make this cathedral uniquely

Queensland—such as the carved possums on the organ screen and the hand-stitched cushions.

373 Ann St. (btw. Wharf and Queen sts.). www.stjohnscathedral.com.au. ℭ **07/3835 2222.** Daily 9:30am–4:30pm. Closed to visitors, except for services, Anzac Day (Apr 25), Christmas Day, and some other public holidays. Train: Central Station.

Sir Thomas Brisbane Planetarium & Cosmic Skydome ★★

PLANETARIUM   Digital multimedia systems that present real-time digital star shows and computer-generated images in the Cosmic Skydome theater are a popular feature here for all ages. The fascinating 40-minute astronomical show includes a re-creation of the Brisbane night sky using a Zeiss star projector. Show times vary, and there are also special shows designed for kids ages 6 and under. Check the website for details.

Brisbane Botanic Gardens, Mt. Coot-tha Rd., Toowong. www.brisbane.qld.gov.au/planetarium. ℭ **07/3403 2578.** A$16 adults, A$9.60 children 14 and under, A$43 families of 4. Tues–Thurs 10am–4pm; Fri 10am-7:30pm; Sat 10:45am–7:30pm; Sun 10:45am–4pm. Closed Mon (except school holidays) and public holidays. Bus: nos. 471, 598, or 599.

South Bank Parklands ★★★ SHOPPING/ENTERTAINMENT

CENTER   Follow the locals' lead and spend some time at this delightful 16-hectare (40-acre) complex of parks, restaurants, cafes, shops, playgrounds, street theater, and weekend markets. There's a manmade beach lined with palm trees, with waves and sand, where you can swim, stroll, and cycle the meandering pathways. From the parklands it's an easy walk to the museum, art gallery, and other parts of the adjacent **Queensland Cultural Centre** (p. 170). Hop on the **Wheel of Brisbane** (www.thewheelofbrisbane.com.au; ℭ **07/3844 3464**)

The manmade beach at South Bank Parklands.

for a 13-minute ride in an air-conditioned enclosed gondola, where you get a 360-degree bird's-eye view of Brisbane from 60m (197 ft.) up; it costs A$20 for adults, A$14 for children 4 to 12, and A$57 for family of four. The buzzing outdoor **Collective Markets** (www.collectivemarkets.com.au) is illuminated by fairy lights at night; it's open Friday 5 to 9pm, Saturday 10am to 9pm, and Sunday 9am to 4pm. The South Bank Parklands are a 7-minute walk from town.

South Bank. www.visitbrisbane.com.au/South-Bank. © **07/3156 6366** for Visitor Centre. Free. Park daily 24 hr.; Visitor Centre daily 9am–5pm (closed Good Friday and Christmas Day, open from 1pm on Anzac Day [Apr 25]). Train: South Brisbane. Ferry: South Bank (CityCat or Cross River Ferry). Bus: Numerous routes from Adelaide St. (near Albert St.), including nos. 100, 111, 115, and 120, stop at the Queensland Cultural Centre; walk through the Centre to South Bank Parklands.

Story Bridge Adventure Climb ★★★ ACTIVITY Brisbane seems to have a fascination with building bridges across its wide river. There are 15 (at last count), but the most interesting is the Story Bridge, built in 1940. If you are over 10 years old, at least 130 centimeters (just over 4 ft., 3 in.) tall, and accompanied by an adult (if you are under 16), you can "climb" this overgrown Meccano set. The Story Bridge Adventure Climb peaks at a viewing platform on top of the bridge, 44m (143 ft.) above the roadway and 80m (262 ft.) above the Brisbane River. On Sunday mornings, you can also rappel down to the park below from the top of the bridge. You'll be rewarded with magnificent 360-degree views of the city, river, and Moreton Bay and its islands, not to mention interesting stories from your guide. Don't be scared—you'll love it!

170 Main St. (at Wharf St.), Kangaroo Point. www.storybridgeadventureclimb.com.au. © **07/3188 9070.** Day climbs A$129 adults, A$110 children; night climbs A$139 adults, A$118 children; dawn climbs, twilight climbs, and abseil climbs (Sat only) A$159 adults, A$135 children. Ferry: Holman St.

Treasury Casino ★ CASINO This lovely heritage building—built in 1886 as, ironically enough, the state's Treasury offices—houses a modern casino. Three levels of 100 gaming tables offer roulette, blackjack, baccarat, craps, sic bo, and traditional Aussie two-up. Open 24 hours, the casino has more than 1,600 gaming machines, six restaurants, and five bars. DJs bring music to **LiveWire Bar** on Friday, Saturday and Sunday nights, or you can relax in the clubby atmosphere of **Ryan's on the Park.** A massive 10-block redevelopment of the George Street precinct around the casino is currently taking place, but once you're inside you'd never know it.

159 William St. (corner of Queen St.). www.treasurybrisbane.com.au. © **07/3306 8888.** Must be 18 years old to enter; neat, casual attire required (no beachwear or flip-flops). Closed from 3am Good Friday, Christmas Day, and from 3am until 1pm Anzac Day (Apr 25). Train: Central or South Brisbane, and then walk across the Victoria Bridge.

ORGANIZED TOURS

RIVER CRUISES The best way to cruise the river, in my view, is aboard the fast **CityCat ferries** ★★★. Board at Riverside and head downstream under the Story Bridge to New Farm Park, past Newstead House to the restaurant row at Brett's Wharf, or cruise upriver past the city and South Bank for only a few dollars. For more information, see "Getting Around," earlier in this chapter.

Kookaburra River Queen paddlewheelers (www.kookaburrariverqueens. com; © 07/3221 1300) run sightseeing cruises Thursday through Saturday afternoons, giving around 2 hours on the river. The cost is A$30 adults, A$20 for children 4 to 12 on Thursday and Friday, or A$40 adults and A$30 children on weekends. For those who'd like to dine as they cruise, 90-minute lunch cruises cost A$49 adults and A$20 kids on Thursday and Friday, or A$69 adults and A$20 children on Saturday and Sunday. Dinner cruises run on Thursday, Friday, and Saturday for A$69 adults and A$20 children. The boat departs from the Eagle Street Pier (parking is available under the City Rowers tavern on Eagle St.) at 7pm. On weekend lunch cruises there's live jazz. Or you can take a High Tea cruise on Saturday or Sunday at 1pm, for A$49 adults and A$20 children (ages 4-12).

WALKING TOURS   The best walking tours in town are run by the **Brisbane Greeters** (www.visitbrisbane.com.au)—and even better, they're free. You get your own personal tour guide (or you can join a group), often a local with a particular area of expertise or interest in some aspect of the city. You can choose from tours that look at architecture, arts and culture, history, and more, or at a particular neighborhood or precinct. Guides are volunteers with a passion and enthusiasm for the city, and you'll learn a lot along the way. Some tours combine bicycling using the CityCycle bikes (p. 162). But really, it's up to you to decide what to do and how long the walk will be. You'll likely see the Greeters in their bright red shirts out and about in the city. Tours start from the Visitor Information Centre in the Queen Street Mall, and last

The *Kookaburra River Queen* paddlewheeler.

Gasps of delight and wonder are the norm aboard Captain Kerry Lopez's whale-watching boat, and Australia's only female whale-watching captain never tires of hearing them. Lopez's purpose-built vessel, the MV *Eye-Spy*, carries up to 320 passengers out into Moreton Bay between June and November for one of the most awesome sights you may ever see. When I traveled with them, we witnessed the antics of 17 humpback whales as they breached and displayed in the waters around the boat. It was an amazing, unforgettable experience.

Brisbane Whale Watching ★★★ (www.brisbanewhalewatching.com.au; ℰ **07/3880 0477**) will organize your 30-minute transfers from city hotels to the departure point in the northern suburb of Redcliffe. If you choose to drive yourself, there's free all-day parking near the jetty. Tours depart daily at 10am, returning around 2:30 to 3pm. The trip onto the bay features excellent educational commentary about the whales while Kerry and her crew keep a lookout for these gentle giants of the deep. Prices are A$135 adults, A$125 seniors and students, A$95 children 4 to 14, or A$365 for a family of four, including lunch and morning and afternoon tea. Transfers from Brisbane hotels are an extra A$30 per person.

The best part? There's a guarantee you'll see a whale—or you can take another cruise for free.

Brisbane Whale Watching offers tours in Moreton Bay.

anywhere from 1 to 4 hours. Try to book at least 48 hours ahead. Book online or at the Visitor Information Centre.

Free guided walks of the **Brisbane City Gardens** at Alice Street leave from the rotunda at the Albert Street entrance Monday through Saturday at 11am and 1pm (except public holidays and mid-Dec to mid-Jan). They take about 1 hour. Bookings are not necessary.

Prepare for shivers up your spine when you take one of Jack Sim's **Ghost Tours ★** (www.brisbaneghosttours.com.au; ✆ **0401/666 441** mobile), which relive Brisbane's gruesome past. His 90-minute "Haunted Brisbane" walking tours depart from the Queen Street Mall at 7:30pm Thursday and Sunday (A$26 for adults, A$15 for kids 5–17, or A$65 for a family of four). On Friday and Saturday nights, you can take a 2-hour tour of the historic and haunted Toowong cemetery (A$45 for adults, A$25 for children 10–17). Or choose from a range of other spooky tours. Reservations are essential; some tours are not suitable for children 11 and under.

A DAY TRIP TO THE GREAT BARRIER REEF ★★★

Brisbane is south of the most southern parts of the Great Barrier Reef (see chapter 7), but it is still possible to experience the Reef in a day trip to **Lady Elliot Island,** off the coast near Bundaberg (384km/238 miles north of Brisbane). If you are pressed for time before heading south or to Central Australia and Uluru, this is an excellent option.

Lady Elliot (www.ladyelliot.com.au; ✆ **1800/072 200** in Australia) is a small coral cay ringed by a lagoon filled with coral and marine life. Reef walking, snorkeling, and diving are the main reasons people come to this coral cay, but you can snorkel and reef walk only for the 2 to 3 hours before and after high tide, so your day-trip activities will be reliant on nature to some extent.

Keep in mind that you will not be able to dive and fly on the same day. But the snorkeling on Lady Elliot is a wonderful experience (and the island has accommodations if you wish to stay longer or do some diving; see p. 234). You will see beautiful corals, brightly colored fish, clams, sponges, urchins, and anemones, and with luck, green and loggerhead turtles (which nest on the beach Nov–Mar) and manta rays. Whales migrate through these waters from June through September.

Be aware that Lady Elliot is a sparse, grassy island rookery, not a sandy tropical paradise. Some find it too spartan; others relish chilling out in a beautiful, peaceful spot with reef all around. Just be prepared for the smell and constant noise of the birds.

Lady Elliot's own airline, **Seair,** offers a day-trip package from Brisbane for A$849 adults and A$449 children ages 3 to 12. In addition to the flights, the price includes snorkel gear, a glass-bottom-boat ride, lunch, and guided activities (and the Reef tax).

Your day trip begins with an early pickup (around 6:30am) from your Brisbane hotel to drive to the northern Brisbane suburb of Redcliffe for the coastal scenic flight. The flight takes about 80 minutes. Seair operates a fleet of 9- and 13-seat aircraft. All you need to take is a daypack with swimwear, camera, sunscreen, and footwear suitable for getting wet (no more than 10kg [22 lb.] in luggage). Take some cash too, in case you decide to buy an underwater camera or a small souvenir from the resort gift shop.

You'll have around 5 hours to explore the island and Reef. You can take an island orientation tour, a guided reef walk at low tide (if possible), a snorkeling lesson in the resort pool (if you need it), and a glass-bottom-boat or guided snorkel tour, and even feed the fish in the lagoon fish pool.

All snorkel equipment (mask, snorkel, fins, and wetsuit) is provided, along with towels and reef-walking shoes. Storage lockers are available, as are resort shower facilities. A hot and cold buffet lunch includes fresh prawns, champagne, wine, beer, and soft drinks.

You'll be boarding your light plane for the return trip at 2:30pm, arriving back at your Brisbane hotel at around 4:45pm—but you'll feel like you've been gone much longer. Such is the magic of a day on the Great Barrier Reef!

CAIRNS & THE GREAT BARRIER REEF

F ish out your flippers and prepare to dive! Or snorkel. Beneath the aqua blue waters off Queensland's northern coast lie the jewels of the deep—gardens of coral, inhabited by colorful reef fish. Welcome to Australia's most famous natural attraction, the Great Barrier Reef. And while the Reef is by no means the only thing worth seeing in a state that's two and a half times the size of Texas, it is the focus of this chapter. There are many gateways to the Reef along the Queensland coast, but Cairns is the major center; most commercial boat tours depart from here.

White sandy beaches grace nearly every inch of coastline in Queensland, and a string of islands and coral reefs dangles just offshore. Cairns, set between rainforest hills, sugarcane fields, and the Coral Sea, still has few options for direct arrivals; for most people, Brisbane or Sydney will be their first stop before heading to the far north of Australia's east coast. In Cairns, a harbor full of boats awaits to take you to the Reef. An hour north, the village of **Port Douglas** provides another point of departure for the Reef.

Departing from Airlie Beach on the Whitsunday Coast, you'll be tempted by one tropical island after another; a cluster of 74 makes up the **Whitsunday** and **Cumberland** groups. These idyllic islands are laced by coral reefs rising out of calm, blue waters teeming with colorful fish—warm enough for swimming year-round.

Townsville boasts 320 days of sunshine a year and marks the start of the Great Green Way—an area of lush natural beauty on the way to Cairns—for those who choose to drive. Townsville is also the home to the Great Barrier Reef Marine Park Authority.

ESSENTIALS

Visitor Information

The **Tourism & Events Queensland** website at **www.queensland. com** is a great resource on traveling and touring the state, including the Great Barrier Reef, and on this site you can select information

In recent years, parts of the Great Barrier Reef have been affected by changing environmental factors that cause coral to degrade and, in some cases, die. One of the major problems on the reef is coral bleaching, caused by heat stress resulting from rising sea temperatures. Other stressors can also cause bleaching, including freshwater inundation (low salinity) and poor water quality from sediment or pollutant run-off from agriculture, mining, and other coastal development. Tour operators are well aware of the best places to see healthy coral, so you can still have the experience you expect—but of course, things can change in a relatively short time. Get there while you can still see some of the glory of the Reef.

specifically designed for travelers from your country. In Australia, call **Go Queensland** (www.goqueensland.com.au; ✆ **138 833** in Australia) to book online or speak to a Queensland travel specialist.

When to Go

Winter (June–Aug) is high season in Queensland; the water can be chilly—at least to Australians—but its temperature rarely drops below 72°F (22°C). April through November is the best time to visit the Great Barrier Reef, because although southeast trade winds can sometimes make it a tad choppy at sea, this is peak visibility time for divers. December through March can be uncomfortably hot and humid, particularly as far north as the Whitsundays, Cairns, and Port Douglas.

Getting Around
BY PLANE

This is the fastest way to cover the most ground in such a big state. **Qantas** (www.qantas.com.au; ✆ **131 313** in Australia) and its subsidiaries **Qantas-Link** and **Jetstar** (www.jetstar.com.au; ✆ **131 538** in Australia) serve most coastal towns from Brisbane, and a few from Cairns. **Virgin Australia** (www.virginaustralia.com; ✆ **136 789** in Australia) serves Brisbane, Cairns, Townsville, Gladstone, Bundaberg, and Proserpine and Hamilton Island in the Whitsundays, as well as other centers.

BY TRAIN

Queensland Rail (www.queenslandrailtravel.com.au; ✆ **1300/131 722** in Australia) operates two long-distance trains along the coast north from Brisbane, a 24-hour trip aboard the **Spirit of Queensland** to Cairns or about five hours less on the **Tilt Train** to Bundaberg and Rockhampton. See the "Getting Around" section in chapter 10 for more details.

BY CAR

The Bruce Highway travels along the coast from Brisbane to Cairns. It is mostly a narrow, two-lane highway, with the scenery varying from eucalyptus bushland to sugarcane fields.

Safe Swimming

All the northern beaches have small, netted enclosures for safe swimming from October through May, when deadly stingers (box jellyfish) render all mainland beaches in north Queensland off-limits.

Tourism Queensland (see "Visitor Information," p. 178) publishes regional motoring guides, but all you are likely to need is a state map from the **Royal Automobile Club of Queensland (RACQ)** (www. racq.com.au; © 131 905 in Australia). A large range of touring maps is available online, and the website is brimming with advice about driving in Australia. For recorded road-condition reports, call © **131 940.** Brisbane-based online specialist map shop **World Wide Maps & Guides** (www.worldwidemaps.com.au) offers a wide range of Australia maps, atlases, and street directories.

Exploring the Great Barrier Reef

First, a few facts: The Great Barrier Reef is the only living thing on earth that's visible from the moon; at 348,700 sq. km (135,993 sq. miles), it's bigger than the United Kingdom and more than 2,000km (1,240 miles) long, stretching from Lady Elliot Island off Bundaberg to Papua New Guinea. It's home to 1,500 kinds of fish, 400 species of corals, 4,000 kinds of clams and snails, and who knows how many sponges, starfish, and sea urchins; the Great Barrier Reef region is listed as a World Heritage Site and contains the biggest marine park in the world.

There are three kinds of reef on the Great Barrier Reef—*fringing, ribbon,* and *platform.* **Fringing reef** is the stuff you see just off the shore of islands and along the mainland. **Ribbon reefs** create "streamers" of long, thin reef along the outer edge of the continental shelf and are only found north of Cairns. **Platform** or **patch reefs** can be up to 16 sq. km (10 sq. miles) of coral emerging off the continental shelf all the way along the Reef's length. Platform reefs, the most common kind, are what most people think of when they refer to the Great Barrier Reef. Island resorts in the Great Barrier Reef Marine Park are either "continental," meaning part of the Australian landmass, or "cays," crushed dead coral and sand amassed on the reef tops over time by water action.

The rich colors of the coral can be seen best with lots of light, so the nearer the surface, the brighter and richer the marine life. That means snorkelers are

The Reef Tax

Every passenger over 4 years old must pay a A$6.50 daily **Environmental Management Charge (EMC),** commonly called the "reef tax," every time they visit the Great Barrier Reef. This money goes toward the management and conservation of the Reef. Your tour operator will collect it from you when you pay for your trip (or it may be included in the tour price).

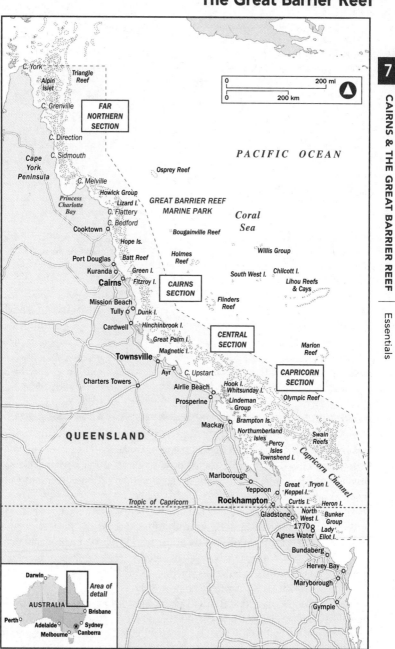

DIVING the reef

Divers have a lot to choose from: dive boats that make 1-day runs to the Outer Reef, boats that offer overnight stays, live-aboard dive boats that make excursions that last up to a week, or staying on an island. As a general rule, on a typical 5-hour day trip to the Reef, you will fit in about two dives. The companies listed in this book give you an idea of the kinds of trips available and how much they cost. Prices quoted include full gear rental; knock off about A$20 if you have your own gear. It is recommended that you only dive with members of **Dive Queensland.** The website, **www.dive-queensland.com.au,** has more information on diving in Queensland.

Many dive companies in Queensland offer instruction, from initial open-water certification all the way to dive-master level, rescue-diver, and instructor level. To take a course, you will need to have a medical exam done by a Queensland doctor. (Your dive school will arrange it; it usually costs between A$45 and A$70.) You can find out more about dive medicals on **www.divemedicals.com.au**. You will also need two passport photos for your certificate, and you must be able to

swim! Courses usually begin every day or every week. Some courses take as little as 3 days, but 5 days is regarded as the best. Open-water certification usually requires 2 days of theory in a pool, followed by 2 or 3 days on the Reef, where you make four to nine dives. Prices vary but are generally around A$600 for a 4-day open-water certification course, or A$700 for the same course as a live-aboard.

Divers Den (www.diversden.com.au; ✆ 07/4046 7333) has been in operation since 1974 and claims to have certified more than 55,000 divers. Courses range from 4-day open-water courses (from A$665 per person) to 6-day courses on a live-aboard boat, which cost from A$1,290 per person, and include all meals on the boat, all gear, a wetsuit, and transfers from your city hotel. Prices include reef tax, port and administration charges, and fuel levy. New courses begin every day of the week.

Virtually every Great Barrier Reef dive operator offers dive courses. Most island resorts offer them, too. You will find dive schools in Cairns, Port Douglas, Townsville, and the Whitsundays.

in a prime position to see it at its best. Snorkeling the Reef can be a wondrous experience. Green and purple clams, pink sponges, red starfish, purple sea urchins, and fish from electric blue to neon yellow to lime green are truly magical sights.

Apart from the impressive fish life around the corals, the Reef is home to large numbers of green and loggerhead turtles, one of the biggest dugong (relative of the manatee) populations in the world, sharks, giant manta rays, and sea snakes. In winter (June–Aug), humpback whales gather in the warm waters south of the Reef around Hervey Bay and as far north as Cairns to give birth to calves. This is what you've come to see!

For most people, the Great Barrier Reef means the Outer Reef, the network of reefs that are an average of 65km (40 miles) off the coast (about 60–90 min. by boat from the mainland). You can snorkel the Reef, dive, ride a semisubmersible, or fly over it.

If your Reef cruise offers a guided **snorkel tour** or "snorkel safari," take it. Some include it as part of the price, but even if you pay an extra A$30 or so, it is worth it. Most safaris are suitable for beginners and advanced snorkelers and are led by guides trained by marine biologists. Snorkeling is easy to master, and crews on cruise boats are always happy to tutor you.

A day trip to the Reef also offers a great opportunity to go **scuba diving**—even if you have never dived before. Every major cruise boat listed in this book and many dedicated dive boats offer introductory dives ("resort dives") that allow you to dive without certification to a depth of 6m (20 ft.) with an instructor. You will need to complete a medical questionnaire and undergo a 30-minute briefing on the boat.

Find out more about the Reef from the **Great Barrier Reef Marine Park Authority** (www.gbrmpa.gov.au; ✆ **07/4750 0700**).

Choosing a Gateway to the Reef

Think carefully about where to base yourself. The main gateways, north to south, are **Port Douglas, Cairns, Townsville,** the **Whitsunday Islands, Gladstone** (for Heron Island), and **Bundaberg** (for Lady Elliot Island). The Reef is generally about 90 minutes away by high-speed catamaran from any of these towns, except **Townsville,** which is about 2½ hours away. The quality of the coral is equally good anywhere along the coast.

Cairns is the stepping-off point for exploring the Great Barrier Reef.

7

CAIRNS & THE GREAT BARRIER REEF

Essentials

Reef Health & Safety Warnings

Coral is very sharp, and coral cuts get infected quickly and badly. If you cut yourself, ask the staff on your cruise boat for immediate first aid as soon as you come out of the water.

The sun and reflected sunlight off the water can burn you fast. Remember to put sunscreen on your back and the back of your legs, especially around your knees and the back of your neck, and even behind your ears—all places that rarely get exposed to the sun but will be exposed as you swim facedown. Apply more when you leave the water. If you can, use a sunscreen that does not contain Oxybenzone (also known as BP-3 or Benzophenone-3), a chemical that scientists believe causes damage to coral reefs. However, labels don't always list all ingredients in these products so the safest way to be sure is to cover up wearing a wetsuit or sunsuit (known in Australia as a "rashie").

The major launching points for day trips to the Reef are Port Douglas, Cairns, Townsville, and the Whitsundays. Day-trip options for each are outlined in their dedicated sections of this chapter.

Many people stay in Cairns simply because of its easy international airport access. The Whitsundays, however, have the added attractions of dazzling islands to sail among; beautiful island resorts offering a wealth of watersports and other activities; and a large array of diving, fishing, and day cruises. You can snorkel every day off your island or join a sailing or cruise day trip to a number of magnificent fringing or inner shelf reefs much nearer than the main Outer Reef.

If you are a nonswimmer, choose a Reef cruise that visits a coral cay, because a cay slopes gradually into shallow water and the surrounding coral. The **Low Isles** at Port Douglas; **Green Island, Michaelmas Cay,** or **Upolu Cay** off Cairns; and **Heron Island,** off Gladstone, are all good locations. Swimmer supports are available so nonswimmers can snorkel, too.

CAIRNS ★★

346km (215 miles) N of Townsville; 1,807km (1,120 miles) N of Brisbane

Cairns is the only place on earth where two World Heritage–listed sites—the Wet Tropics Rainforest and Great Barrier Reef—are side by side. Explore the reef and offshore islands and slip into the distinctive pace, heat, and style of a truly tropical city.

This is the departure point for the large-scale Reef boats that take hundreds of people out every day. Many smaller operators offer a more intimate experience, some on sailing boats. Offshore, **Michaelmas Cay** and **Upolu Cay** are two pretty coral sand blips in the ocean, 30km (19 miles) and 25km (16 miles) off Cairns, surrounded by reefs. Michaelmas is vegetated and is home to 27,000 seabirds; you may spot dugongs (cousins of manatees) off Upolu. Michaelmas and Upolu are great for snorkelers and introductory divers.

ATTRACTIONS ●
Cairns Aquarium **7**
Skyrail Rainforest Cableway **11**
Tjapukai **12**

HOTELS ■
Cairns Plaza Hotel **9**
Coral Tree Inn **8**
Ellis Beach Oceanfront
   Bungalows **13**
Novotel Cairns Oasis Resort **6**
Pullman Reef Hotel Casino **1**
Reef House Palm Cove **14**
The Reef Retreat **15**
Rydges Esplanade Resort **10**

RESTAURANTS ◆
Caffiend **4**
Candy **3**
L'Unico **18**
NuNu **16**
Ochre Restaurant **2**
Perrotta's
   at the Gallery **5**
Vivo Bar & Grill **17**

   Cairns Esplanade offers top-to-bottom-dollar shopping plus an array of food halls, but its sparkling jewel is the man-made **lagoon** on the Esplanade, where you can cool off from the heat. There's plenty to do on days when the Reef's not on your radar.

Essentials
ARRIVING
BY PLANE **Qantas** (www.qantas.com.au; ⓒ **131 313** in Australia) has direct flights to Cairns from Sydney, Brisbane, Townsville, Hamilton Island, Melbourne, Darwin, Uluru, and Alice Springs. **Virgin Australia** (www. virginaustralia.com.au; ⓒ **136 789** in Australia) flies to Cairns direct from Brisbane, Sydney, and Melbourne. **Jetstar** (www.jetstar.com.au; ⓒ **131 538** in Australia) flies from the Gold Coast, Perth, and Adelaide. **Tigerair** (www. tigrair.com.au; ⓒ **1300/174 266** in Australia, or 07/3295 2104) flies to Cairns from Brisbane, Melbourne, and Sydney. **Regional Express**, also known as Rex (www.rex.com.au; ⓒ **131 713** in Australia, or 02/6393 5550) flies

between Cairns and Townsville. Some international carriers serve Cairns from various Asian cities and New Zealand.

Cairns Airport (www.cairnsairport.com.au; ℂ **07/4080 6703**) is 8km (5 miles) north of downtown. A 5-minute walk along a covered walkway connects the international terminal with the domestic terminal.

Between the Airport and the City Center

Sun Palm Transport (www.sunpalmtransport.com.au; ℂ **07/4099 1191**) provides transfers from the airport to the city center. The one-way fare is A$15 adults to Cairns; kids 11 and under travel free with an adult (extra children A$7.50). Sun Palm also offers a **free Airport Connect** bus service from the airport to connect you to the Sunbus public transport network on Sheridan Street in the city center. From there, you can jump on a Sun Bus service to the northern beaches for just a couple of dollars. To catch Airport Connect back to the airport, wait at the C9 bus stop on Sheridan Street (opposite the Tobruk Pool) and hail the driver of the Sun Palm Transport bus. Pre-bookings can be made 24 hours ahead.

A taxi from the airport costs around A$30 to the city, A$55 to Trinity Beach, A$75 to Palm Cove, and A$200 to Port Douglas. Call **Cairns Taxis** (ℂ **131 008** in Australia). An airport fee of A$4.40 is added to all pickups at the domestic and international terminals.

Avis (www.avis.com.au; ℂ **07/4033 9555**), **Budget** (www.budget.com.au; ℂ **07/4033 9777**), **Europcar** (www.europcar.com.au; ℂ **07/4034 9088**), **Hertz** (www.hertz.com.au; ℂ **07/4035 9299**), **Thrifty** (www.thrifty.com.au; ℂ **07/4033 9800**), and **Redspot** (www.redspot.com.au; ℂ **07/4034 9052**) all have car-rental offices at the domestic and international terminals. (For rental offices in Cairns city, see "Getting Around By Car," below).

BY TRAIN   Long-distance trains operated by **Queensland Rail** (www.queenslandrailtravel.com.au; ℂ **1300/131 722** in Australia, or 07/3606 6630) run from Brisbane several times a week. The 160kmph (100-mph) **Spirit of Queensland** takes about 24 hours to make the trip between Brisbane and Cairns. Trains leave Brisbane at 3:45pm on Monday, Tuesday, Wednesday, Friday, and Saturday; southbound runs depart Cairns at 9am on Monday, Wednesday, Thursday, Friday, and Sunday. The trains feature luxury business-class seating (A$390), with an entertainment system for each seat, including movie and audio channels, as well as lie-flat airline-style "railbeds" (A$519).

BY BUS   **Greyhound Australia** (www.greyhound.com.au; ℂ **1300/473 946** in Australia, or 07/4033 4811 in Cairns) buses pull into Trinity Wharf Centre in the center of town. Buses travel from the south via all towns and cities on the Bruce Highway; they also run from the west, from Alice Springs and Darwin, via Tennant Creek on the Stuart Highway, and the Outback mining town of Mount Isa to Townsville, where they join the

> ### Croc Alert!
>
> Dangerous crocodiles inhabit Cairns' waterways. Do not swim in or stand on the bank of any river or stream.

Bruce Highway and head north. The 48-hour Sydney-Cairns trip costs about A$513; the 29-hour trip from Brisbane is around A$350.

BY CAR From Brisbane and all major towns in the south, you'll approach Cairns on the Bruce Highway. To reach the northern beaches or Port Douglas, take Sheridan Street in the city center, which becomes the Captain Cook Highway.

VISITOR INFORMATION

Tourism Tropical North Queensland (TTNQ) closed its official visitor information center in mid-2018, saying there were enough places in the city for visitors to get information and most visitors now use online booking agencies. Instead, TTNQ is working on "innovative technology" to deliver future information to visitors. Stay tuned. One source visitors can use to get information on tours and make bookings is the **Cairns Visitor Centre** (www.cairns visitorcentre.com.au; © **07/4036 3341**)—but there is no physical office to drop in to.

CITY LAYOUT

The focal point of the city is the **Esplanade,** which has a 4,000-sq.-m (43,000-sq.-ft.) man-made saltwater swimming lagoon, with a wide sandy beach, and surrounding parkland with public artworks and picnic areas. Suspended over the mud flats and providing a platform for birding, a boardwalk runs 600m (1,968 ft.) along the waterfront and is lit at night. A walkway links the Esplanade to the **Reef Fleet Terminal,** the departure point for Great Barrier Reef boats.

Downtown Cairns is on a grid 5 blocks deep, bounded in the east by the Esplanade and in the west by **McLeod Street,** where the train station and the Cairns Central shopping mall are situated.

Heading 15 minutes north from the city along the Captain Cook Highway, you come to the **northern beaches:** Holloway's Beach, Yorkey's Knob, Trinity Beach, Kewarra Beach, Clifton Beach, Palm Cove, and Ellis Beach.

GETTING AROUND

BY BUS Sunbus (www.sunbus.com.au; © **07/4057 7411**) buses depart Cairns City Mall at the intersection of Lake and Shields streets. Buy all tickets and passes on board, and try to have correct change. The standard fare is A$1.20, or you can travel all day in one zone for A$4.60. Bus nos. 110 and 111 travel to Trinity Beach and Palm Cove. Routes and timetables change, so check with the driver. Most buses run from around 7am until almost midnight.

BY CAR As well as the car rental desks in the airport, listed above, **Avis** (www.avis.com.au; © **07/4048 0522**), **Budget** (www.budget.com.au; © **07/4048 8166**), **Europcar** (www.europcar.com.au; © **07/4033 4800**), and **Thrifty** (www.thrifty.com.au; © **07/4051 8099**) have offices in Cairns city as well. One long-established local outfit, **Sugarland Car Rentals** (© **07/4052 1300**), has reasonable rates. **Britz Campervan Rentals** (© **1300/738 087** in

Australia, or 07/4032 2611) and **Maui Rentals** (✆ **1800/827 821** in Australia, or 07/4032 2065) rent motor homes.

BY TAXI   Call Cairns Taxis (✆ **131 008**).

Where to Stay in Cairns & the Northern Beaches

High season in Cairns includes 2 weeks at Easter, the period from early July to early October, and the Christmas holiday through January. Book ahead in those periods. In low season (Nov–June), many hotels offer discounts or negotiate fees. Cairns has a good supply of affordable accommodations, both in the heart of the city and along the northern beaches. You don't have to stay in Cairns city if you don't have a car—most tour and cruise operators provide transfers.

EXPENSIVE

Pullman Reef Hotel Casino ★★   This stylish seven-story hotel is a block from the water, with Trinity Inlet views from some rooms, and city/hinterland outlooks from others. All the rooms have lots of natural light, high-quality amenities, robes, and small balconies with smart timber furniture. The **Cairns Wildlife Dome** (p. 194) and **Reef Casino** are attached to the hotel. Be aware that there are two Pullman hotels in Cairns (the other is in the next street), which can be confusing even to your taxi driver! The **Tamarind** restaurant is one of Cairns' best dining spots, for breakfast *or* dinner.

35–41 Wharf St. www.pullmanhotels.com/2901. ✆ **07/4030 8888.** 128 units. A$323–A$443 double; A$573–A$1,173 suite. Rates include breakfast. Valet parking A$15, free self-parking. **Amenities:** 4 restaurants; 4 bars; babysitting; concierge; health club; Jacuzzi; small outdoor rooftop pool; room service; sauna; free Wi-Fi.

The Reef House Palm Cove – MGallery by Sofitel ★★★   The old colonial-style Reef House has a romantic feel about it—the white walls are swathed in bougainvillea, the beds are draped in mosquito netting, and rooms have white wicker chairs. Verandah Spa rooms have a Jacuzzi on the balcony; overlook the pool, waterfalls, and lush gardens; and have extra touches, such as bathrobes, and balconies within earshot of the ocean. One-, two-, and four-bedroom apartments are also available. Every night at sunset, all the candles throughout the resort are lit, and Brigadier's Punch is served to guests in an old tradition. The beachfront restaurant, on a covered wooden deck beneath towering paperbark trees, is a favorite for locals and tourists alike for its ocean views and gentle breezes.

99 Williams Esplanade, Palm Cove. www.reefhouse.com.au. ✆ **07/4080 2600.** 69 units. A$245–A$359 double; A$661 2-bedroom apt. Limited free parking; ample street parking. Bus: no. 110. **Amenities:** 2 restaurants; bar; babysitting; concierge; 3 small heated outdoor pools; room service; spa; free Wi-Fi.

MODERATE

Cairns Plaza Hotel ★★   The harbor views at this five-story complex are better than those at most of the more luxurious hotels in Cairns. Two blocks

Overnighting on the Reef

The **Spirit of Freedom** (www.spiritof freedom.com.au; ☏ **07/4047 9150**) in Cairns offers a chance to "sleep on the Reef" aboard the 36m (120-ft.) *Spirit of Freedom*, a sleek, modern motor yacht with electronic stabilizers, a widescreen TV with DVD player, comfortable lounge areas, sun decks, and 11 luxury double or quad shared cabins, each with an en suite bathroom. You will visit the popular Cod Hole and Ribbon Reef and on longer trips venture into the Coral Sea.

A 3-day, 3-night trip will cost A$1,820 to A$2,645 depending on your choice of cabin and ends with a 193km (120-mile) one-way, 1-hour, low-level flight from Lizard Island back to Cairns. You will fit in up to 11 dives. Prices include meals and pickup from your Cairns accommodations. Allow A$130 extra for equipment rental. Additional 4- and 7-day cruises are offered, the latter a combination of both shorter trips.

from town, the accommodations are a good size, with fresh, appealing furnishings and modern bathrooms. Suites and studios have kitchenettes. If your balcony does not have a water vista, you overlook a nice aspect of the city or mountains instead. This is a great place for families, because most rooms sleep three or four, and if you need more space and privacy, you can book a connecting suite and standard room. A children's playground is located just across the street.

145 The Esplanade (at Minnie St.). www.cairnsplaza.com.au. ☏ **07/4051 4688.** 60 units. A$180–A$210 double; A$280 suite. Limited free parking. **Amenities:** Restaurant (breakfast only); bar; babysitting; Jacuzzi; small outdoor pool; room service; free Wi-Fi (restaurant/lobby and 6th floor only).

Novotel Cairns Oasis Resort ★
The large pool, complete with swim-up bar and a little sandy beach, is the focus of this attractive six-story resort. All the contemporary-style rooms have balconies with views over the tropical gardens, the mountains, or the pool. The suites, with a large Jacuzzi bathtub, could well be the best-value suites in town.

122 Lake St. www.novotelcairnsresort.com.au. ☏ **07/4080 1888.** 314 units. A$179–A$233 double; A$279 suite. Parking A$9. **Amenities:** Restaurant; 2 bars; babysitting; concierge; gym; lagoon pool; kids' pool; room service; spa; broadband Internet (A$12/hr.; A$25/24 hr.).

The Reef Retreat ★★
Tucked back one row of buildings from the beach is this little gem—a collection of contemporary studios and suites built around a swimming pool in a grove of palms and silver paperbark trees. All the rooms have cool tile floors and smart teak and cane furniture. The studios are a terrific value and much larger than the average hotel room. Some suites have two rooms; others have a Jacuzzi and a kitchenette outside on the balcony. Rooms also have iPod docks. There's a barbecue and a Jacuzzi on the grounds, but no elevator.

10–14 Harpa St., Palm Cove. www.reefretreat.com.au. ☏ **07/4059 1744.** 36 units. A$149–A$169 double; A$164–A$349 suite. Free parking. Bus: no. 110. **Amenities:** Jacuzzi; heated saltwater pool; free Wi-Fi.

Rydges Esplanade Cairns Resort ★★ Despite its lack of glitz, this 14-story hotel has been the lodging of choice for a number of movie stars on location in Cairns. A 20-minute waterfront walk from downtown, the hotel offers a range of units, from hotel rooms to penthouse apartments. The one- and two-bedroom apartments face the sea; hotel rooms have sea or mountain views. Kitchenettes are in studios and apartments only. Rooms are spacious, but bathrooms are not. Out back are cheaper studios and apartments, with upgraded furnishings; in front is a pool and sun deck. Family rooms include a queen bed and separate "kids zone" with bunk beds, each featuring a personal 15-inch TV linked to an Xbox. On-site are a masseuse and a tour desk.

207–209 Abbott St. (at Kerwin St.). www.rydges.com. ⓒ **07/4044 9000.** 240 units. A$139–A$242 double; A$242 family room; A$229–A$259 2-bedroom apt. Free covered parking. Bus stop about 100m (328 ft.) from the hotel. **Amenities:** 2 restaurants; 3 bars; airport transfers; babysitting; bikes; concierge; health club; Jacuzzi; 3 outdoor pools; room service; sauna; 2 lit tennis courts; free Wi-Fi.

INEXPENSIVE

Coral Tree Inn ★ The focal point of this airy, modern resort-style motel—a 5-minute walk from the city center—is the friendly communal kitchen that overlooks the palm-lined saltwater pool and paved sun deck. It's a great spot to cook a steak or reef fish on the free barbecue and join other guests at the big shared tables. The smallish, basic-but-neat motel rooms have painted brick walls, terra cotta tile or carpeted floors, and new bathrooms with marble-look laminate countertops. In contrast, the eight suites, which have kitchenettes, are huge and stylish—and some of the best-value rooms in town. All rooms have a balcony or patio; some overlook the commercial buildings next door, but most face the pool. Ask about packages that include cruises and other tours.

166–172 Grafton St. www.coraltreeinn.com.au. ⓒ **07/4031 3744.** 58 units. A$149 double; A$200 family room; A$157 suite. Limited free parking; ample street parking. **Amenities:** Restaurant; bar; airport shuttle; babysitting; bike rental; outdoor saltwater pool; free Wi-Fi.

Ellis Beach Oceanfront Bungalows ★★ Set on what is arguably the loveliest of the northern beaches, about 30 minutes from Cairns, these bungalows and cabins sit under palm trees between the Coral Sea and a backdrop of mountainous rainforest. Lifeguards patrol the beach, and there are stinger nets in season as well as a shady pool and a toddlers' wading pool. You'll have plenty of privacy, and rooms are basic but pleasant. As you sit on your veranda and gaze at the ocean, keep an eye out for dolphins. Each bungalow and cabin sleeps two or four and has kitchen facilities (with microwave, fridge, and freezer), but cabins have no en suite bathrooms (they have use of the communal facilities at the campground in the same complex). Beachfront bungalows are the priciest; those behind them are slightly cheaper. The property has a laundry, coin-operated barbecues, and public phone you can use (but no phone in your room). No Wi-Fi.

Captain Cook Hwy., Ellis Beach. www.ellisbeach.com. ℂ **1800/637 036** in Australia, or 07/4055 3538. 15 units. A$95–A$115 double cabin; A$150–A$190 double bungalow. 2-night minimum stay; 3-night minimum June–Sept. **Amenities:** Restaurant; 2 outdoor pools.

Where to Eat in Cairns

For cheap eats, head to the Esplanade along the seafront; it's lined with cafes, pizzerias, fish-and-chips shops, food courts, and ice-cream parlors. The northern beaches—particularly Palm Cove—also have some great restaurants (sometimes with prices to match!).

EXPENSIVE

NuNu ★★★ CONTEMPORARY   With an absolute-beachfront location under the palm trees, this Palm Cove favorite offers the kind of food that makes you drag your eyes from the view to your plate. Dining fare includes some bold choices, such as pork belly in a pineapple and turmeric curry, cinnamon-roasted lamb, or the pricey (A$125) Queensland mud crab with a chili tamarind sauce. The menu changes seasonally, and you can always count on some surprises. To savor a bit of everything, there are four-course and seven-course tasting menus (A$89 and A$129 per person respectively). You could easily settle in here for hours.

1 Veivers Rd., Palm Cove (in the Alamanda Resort). www.nunu.com.au. ℂ **07/4059 1880.** Main courses A$15–A$125. Daily 7am–4pm and 5pm–late. Bus: no. 110.

MODERATE

L'Unico ★★ ITALIAN   Ask for a table on the veranda, overlooking Trinity Beach's esplanade and the sea. This smart but relaxed Italian place has a great

Creative cuisine and a beachfront setting at NuNu.

vibe and terrific staff. A wood-fired oven produces pizzas with unexpected toppings (such as lamb with caramelized onion, tomato, and spinach), and the kitchen makes good use of local ingredients in all dishes (angel-hair pasta with Moreton Bay bugs—that's seafood—with chili, garlic, and white wine is one of my favorite dishes here). The cocktail bar offers a bar menu throughout the day, and there's a kids' menu, too.

75 Vasey Esplanade, Trinity Beach. www.lunico.com.au. © **07/4057 8855.** Main courses A$18–A$46. Fri-Tues 8-11am; daily noon–3:30pm and 5:30–9:30pm. Bus: no. 110.

Ochre Restaurant ★★ GOURMET BUSH TUCKER   With a fabulous waterfront location, this Cairns institution is the place to visit if you want a taste of crocodile or kangaroo. You could accuse this restaurant/bar of using weird and wonderful Aussie ingredients as a gimmick, but the diners who have flocked to Ochre for more than a decade know good food when they taste it. Daily specials are big on fresh local seafood, and the regular menu changes often. There may be ingredients you've never heard of—but this is a place to be adventurous! Try salt-and-native-pepper crocodile and prawns with Vietnamese pickles and lemon aspen sambal, chargrilled kangaroo sirloin with a quandong chili glaze, sweet potato fritter and bok choy, or wallaby with lemon aspen couscous and pea puree. It can be very busy, and you may have to wait for a table, but the food is very good.

1 Marlin Parade, Cairns. www.ochrerestaurant.com.au. © **07/4051 0100.** Main courses A$19–A$42. Australian game platter A$54 per person; seafood platter A$76 per person; 4-course set menu A$70 per person (minimum 2 people). Daily 11:30am–9:30pm.

Vivo Bar and Grill ★★★ CONTEMPORARY   White-painted colonial style, complete with wooden shutters and a wide veranda, this is an inviting choice, looking through the palm trees to the water. Choose from some tempting pasta dishes (such as spanner crab linguine) or something more exotic like a mild red duck curry. A fixed-price dinner menu—two courses ($39) or three courses ($49), including a glass of wine—changes every week, with a choice of dishes for entree, main, and dessert. There's a seafood platter for two for A$95. The restaurant is also open for breakfast. Cocktails and tapas are served daily from 3 to 5pm. A children's menu is available.

49 Williams Esplanade, Palm Cove. www.vivo.com.au. © **07/4059 0944.** Main courses A$30–A$48. Daily 7am–10pm. Bus: nos. 110 or 111.

INEXPENSIVE

Caffiend ★★ CAFE   Tucked away between an alley full of street art and an arcade, this atmospheric little cafe is easy to miss. I first found this place after being tipped off by a friend, and headed here for what I'd been told was the best coffee in Cairns (it's roasted in house). The menu was so appealing I ended up staying for lunch! Terrines, salads, soups, a big BLT, coffee-infused beef tacos, and other delicious eats are on a menu that changes monthly, but don't forget to check the specials board. The breakfast menu offers some unusual dishes, such as miso-infused scrambled eggs, and pan-fried mushrooms with buffalo feta. There's live music at lunchtime on Sundays.

Shop 5, 78 Grafton St., Cairns. www.caffiend.com.au. © **07/4051 5522.** Main courses A$15–A$22. Daily 7am–3pm.

Candy ★★ CAFE   Huge murals and dangling chandeliers give this quirky little cafe/bar an offbeat but sophisticated feel. A tip from a local—and yes, the coffee here is good—led me to this standout on the Grafton Street cafe strip. Candy is a popular breakfast spot, offering the usual range of eggs, avocado on toast with feta cheese, sweet corn fritters, and pancakes. For lunch, you might go for something like the Candy Burger or a Southern Fried Chicken Burger, or a healthy Garden of Eden salad with beetroot, pumpkin, asparagus, and more.

70 Grafton St., Cairns. www.facebook.com/candycairns. © **07/4031 8816.** Main courses A$9–A$20. Mon–Sat 6am–5pm; Sun 6:30am–5pm.

Perrotta's at the Gallery ★★ CONTEMPORARY   Locals flock here for brunch and lunch, particularly on weekends, and you can team a meal here with a visit to the Cairns Regional Art Gallery next door. Breakfast differs from the usual, offering delights such as strawberry ricotta pancakes with pistachios and lemon syrup. The all-day menu includes bruschetta, burgers, pizza, salads, and pasta, or mains such as fish tacos (Spanish mackerel with avocado and Italian-style coleslaw), or spaghetti with prawns—and perhaps a vanilla-bean panna cotta with mango for dessert.

Abbott and Shields sts., Cairns. www.perrottasatg.com. © **07/4031 5899.** Breakfast A$5–A$23; main courses A$19–A$28. Daily 6:30am–10pm.

Exploring Cairns

Many of the Cairns region's attractions lie outside the city center. Apart from the Reef, there is a string of white sandy beaches just 15 minutes north of the city center. **Trinity Beach,** 15 minutes from the airport or 25 minutes from the city center, is secluded, elegant, and scenic. The most upscale is **Palm Cove,** 20 minutes from the airport or 30 minutes from the city. If you're staying in Cairns, also check out activities in and around Port Douglas (p. 205). Many tour operators in Port Douglas offer transfers from Cairns. Ask about packages that include discounted entry when you visit several of Cairns' attractions, such as Tjapukai Aboriginal Cultural Park, Cairns Tropical Zoo, Skyrail, and Kuranda Scenic Rail.

Cairns Aquarium ★★ AQUARIUM   Opened in late 2017, this world-class aquarium is dedicated to the animals and habitats found only in Australia's Wet Tropics and the Great Barrier Reef, the area surrounding Cairns. The 16m-high (52-ft.) building houses—over three levels—15,000 animals from 10 different ecosystems and 71 habitats in Tropical North Queensland. There is a program of talks throughout the day, where you can also touch some of the creatures on display; other experiences include shark dives, river monster snorkeling, and fish feeding (all at extra cost). Twenty-minute behind-the-scenes tours run several times a day and cost A$10 per person. The **Aqua-Luna restaurant** (accessible from Abbott Street) has its own 70,000-liter shark tank to keep you mesmerized while eating.

5 Florence St. www.cairnsaquarium.com.au. ✆ **07/4044 7300.** A$42 adults, A$28 children 3–14, A$88-A$126 families. Sat–Thurs 9am–5pm; Fri 9am–7pm; last entry 1 hr. before closing).

Cairns ZOOM and Wildlife Dome ★★ WILDLIFE VIEWING/ ATTRACTION   Here, 200 animals—including a large saltwater crocodile named Goliath—are housed in a 20m-high (66-ft.) glass dome on the rooftop of the Pullman Reef Hotel Casino (p. 188). Birds soar overhead, and you can get up close with koalas, lizards, frogs, pademelons, turtles, and snakes. There are wildlife presentations and free, guided tours throughout the day. For A$40 (pay when you buy your entry ticket), you can have a photo taken with a koala, snake, or baby croc. Thrill-seekers can zipline through the dome, "climb" around its exterior, or do other adrenaline-charged activities (for an extra cost).

35–41 Wharf St. www.cairnszoom.com.au. ✆ **07/4031 7250.** A$24 adults, A$12 children 4–14, A$60 family. Tickets are valid for reentry for up to 4 days. Daily 9am–6:15pm (last entry 5pm). Closed Christmas Day.

Skyrail Rainforest Cableway ★★★ ATTRACTION/RIDE   This magnificent feat of engineering is one of Australia's top tourist attractions. Six-person gondolas leave every few seconds from Cairns for the 7.5km (4½-mile) journey to the rainforest village of Kuranda (p. 201). The view of the coast as you ascend is so breathtaking that even those afraid of heights should find it worthwhile. As you rise over the foothills of the coastal range, watch the lush green of the rainforest take over beneath you. Looking back, you have

The Cairns Wildlife Dome tops the Pullman Reef Hotel Casino.

Packaging Your Day Trip

Several options exist for a 1-day Cairns adventure. A package combining one-way travel on Skyrail (see above) and a trip back on the Kuranda Scenic Railway (p. 202) is A$126 for adults, A$63 for children 4 to 14, and A$315 for families of four with round-trip transfers from Cairns or the northern beaches. A package including the Skyrail, the Scenic Railway, and entry to the Tjapukai Aboriginal cultural park (see below) is A$188 for adults, A$105 for kids, and A$481 for families of four, including transfers. An option including the Sky-rail, Scenic Railway, and Rainforestation Nature Park (p. 204) is A$189 for adults, A$94 for kids, and A$471 for families of four, including transfers. In most cases, these packages represent convenience rather than savings. Book them through Skyrail, Queensland Rail, or Tjapukai.

spectacular views over Cairns and north toward Trinity Bay. On a clear day, you can see . . . if not forever, then at least to Green Island. For even better views—looking down, between your feet through the glass floor, take a Diamond View gondola. This slightly more expensive option (A$20 extra per adult, A$10 per child one-way) also gives you a dedicated boarding queue—and shorter wait—at all stations. If you're really fearless, the Canopy Glider is an open-air option, where for A$100 extra per person (one-way) four passengers and a ranger guide travel in an open gondola.

There are two stops during the 90-minute trip, at Red Peak and Barron Falls. After about 10 minutes, you reach Red Peak. You are now 545m (1,788 ft.) above sea level, and massive kauri pines dominate the view. You must change gondolas at each station, so take the time to stroll around the board-walks for the ground view of the rainforest. Free, guided walks are run regularly through the day. On board again, you continue on to Barron Falls station, built on the site of an old construction camp for workers on the first hydroelectric power station on the Barron River in the 1930s. A rainforest information center is here, as well as boardwalks to the lookouts for wonderful views of the Barron Gorge and Falls. From Barron Falls station, the gondola travels over the thick rainforest of the range. As you reach the end of the trip, the gondola passes over the Barron River and across the Kuranda railway line into the station. Don't worry if it rains on the day you go—one of the best trips of several I've made on Skyrail was in a misty rain, which added a new dimension to the rainforest.

Tip: For a wonderful day trip from Cairns I strongly recommend that you combine Skyrail with a trip on the Kuranda Scenic Rail (p. 202). The best way is to take the train from Cairns in the morning and return on Skyrail in the afternoon—for the views going down the range.

Cairns Western Arterial Rd. and Captain Cook Hwy., Smithfield. www.skyrail.com.au. © **07/4038 5555.** Round-trip ticket A$102 adults, A$51 children, A$255 families, including transfers from Cairns or northern beaches hotels. Daily 9am–5:15pm. Closed Christmas Day. You must make a reservation to travel within a 15-min. time frame. Last boardings at 2:45pm for a round-trip or 3:30pm for a one-way journey. Bus: no. 123.

Tjapukai ★★ INTERACTIVE ENTERTAINMENT Tjapukai (pronounced Jab-oo-guy) offers indigenous experiences in an all-weather venue. This Aboriginal cultural park uses cutting-edge theater technology and an open-plan glass design to showcase the park's rainforest. Two state-of-the-art theater spaces—History and Hero's Walk—and a restaurant and outdoor bar complement the interactive cultural village, where you can try fire-making, didgeridoo playing, and boomerang and spear throwing, and learn about bush foods, medicines, and hunting techniques. In addition to Aboriginal culture, Torres Strait Islander dance is part of the Tjapukai experience. Allow 2 to 3 hours to see everything (although you could spend longer here). Start in the Creation Theatre, where performers use the latest in illusion, theatrics, and technology to tell the story of the creation of the world according to the spiritual beliefs of Tjapukai people. Move on through the Magic Space museum and gallery section of the complex to the History Theatre, where a 20-minute film relates the history of the Tjapukai people since the arrival of white settlers 120 years ago.

Art of My People is a performance that explains the varying styles of Australian Indigenous art, including the role of totems, body painting traditions, and differing types of artistic expression used to identify tribes, languages, dialects, and geographical landscapes. A gallery stocks the work of Aboriginal artists and crafts workers.

Night Fire by Tjapukai tours include interactive time in the Magic Space museum, a Creation Show performance, and an outdoor Serpent Circle—a show featuring tap sticks for each guest to use, a join-in *corroboree* (an Aboriginal nighttime dance), and a ceremony involving fire and water. A buffet dinner and dance show follow, where you get the chance to meet the dancers.

4 Skyrail Dr., Caravonica (beside the Skyrail terminal). www.tjapukai.com.au. © **07/4042 9999.** A$62 adults, A$42 children 5–14, A$166 families. Daily 9am–4:30pm. Night Fire tours (daily 7–9:30pm) A$151 adults, A$93 children, including transfers to/from Cairns. Closed Christmas Day. Bus: no. 123. Tjapukai shuttle: A$21 adults, A$12 children, and A$24 families.

Outlying Attractions

Hartley's Crocodile Adventures ★★★ ENTERTAINMENT Hartley's is the original Australian croc show and quite possibly the best. Its fantastic natural setting is a 2-hectare (5-acre) lagoon surrounded by melaleuca (paperbark) and bloodwood trees that is home to 23 estuarine crocs. The best time to visit is for the 3pm "croc attack" show, when you can witness the saltwater crocodile "death roll" during the 45-minute performance. At 11am you can see these monsters being hand-fed or hear an eye-opening talk on the less-aggressive freshwater crocs.

You can also have a **"Big Croc Experience,"** where you get to pole-feed a large crocodile yourself—and believe me, this is the way to feel the sheer power of these creatures as they tug the chicken off the pole. Available twice

Wildlife Passes

Wildlife enthusiasts who plan to visit several of the attractions in the Cairns region can save a few dollars by buying a **Four Park Pass,** which gives entry to the Cairns ZOOM & Wildlife Dome, the Wildlife Habitat at Port Douglas, and two Kuranda attractions (see "Day Trip from Cairns to Kuranda," p. 201): the Rainforestation Nature Park and the Australian Butterfly Sanctuary (all owned by the same local family). The discounted price of A$90 adults, A$45 children, and A$225 for a family of four is a savings of A$38 per adult or A$95 per family. The pass is valid for 6 months and doesn't have to be used on consecutive days. Buy it at any of the participating parks. A **Kuranda Wildlife Experience pass** offers discounted admission to Birdworld, the Kuranda Koala Gardens, and the Australian Butterfly Sanctuary (p. 203). It can be bought on arrival at any of the three sanctuaries for A$50 adults, A$25 for children 4 to 15.

a day at 10:30am and 1pm (bookings essential), you'll be one of six adults (16 and over) to take part in each group (but your friends and family can come along to watch). The cost is A$130 per person. There are tours of the croc farm at 10am and 1:30pm; at 2pm there is a snake show; 4:30pm is koala-feeding time. Cassowaries are fed at 9:30am and 4:15pm. There are also croc- and snake-handling opportunities and heaps of other interesting things to see and do.

Captain Cook Hwy. (40km/24 miles north of Cairns; about 100m off the highway). www. crocodileadventures.com. © **07/4055 3576.** A$39 adults, A$20 children 4–15, A$98 families of 4 (admission good for 3 days). Daily 8:30am–5pm. Closed Christmas Day.

Day Trips from Cairns to the Reef ★★★

For an introduction to the Great Barrier Reef, most visitors take one of the large-scale tour boats. These motorized catamarans can carry up to 300 passengers each and tie up at their own private, permanent pontoons anchored to a platform reef. The boats are air-conditioned and have a bar, videos, and educational material, as well as a marine biologist who gives a talk on the Reef's ecology en route. The pontoons have glass-bottom boats for passengers who don't want to get wet, dry underwater viewing chambers, sun decks, shaded seats, and often showers. But be aware that you will be in a crowded environment. And if you are prone to seasickness, make sure you take some preventive measures before you set out!

An alternative is to go on one of the many smaller boats. These typically visit two or three Reef sites rather than just one. There are usually no more than 20 passengers on board, so you get more personal attention. Another advantage is that you will have the coral pretty much all to yourself. The drawbacks of a small boat are that you have only the cramped deck to sit on when you get out of the water, and your traveling time to the Reef may be longer. If you're a nervous snorkeler, you may feel safer on a boat where you will be swimming with 300 other people.

Great Adventures offers day trips from Cairns to the Great Barrier Reef.

Most day-trip fares include snorkel gear—fins, mask, and snorkel (plus wetsuits in winter, if you want one)—free use of the underwater viewing chambers and glass-bottom-boat rides, a plentiful buffet or barbecue lunch, and morning and afternoon refreshments. Diving is an optional activity for which you pay extra. The big boats post snorkeling scouts to keep a lookout for anyone in trouble and count heads periodically. If you wear glasses, ask whether your boat offers prescription masks—this will make a big difference to the quality of your experience. Don't forget that you can travel as a snorkel-only passenger on most dive boats, too.

Great Adventures ★ (www.greatadventures.com.au; ✆ **07/4044 9944**) does daily cruises from Cairns on fast, air-conditioned catamarans that take you to a three-level pontoon on the Outer Reef. The pontoon has a kids' swimming area, a semisubmersible, and an underwater observatory. The cost for the day is A$242 for adults, A$132 for children 4 to 14, and A$623 for families. You spend at least 3 hours on the Reef. Hotel transfers are available from Cairns, the northern beaches, and Port Douglas for an extra cost. The boat departs the Reef Fleet Terminal at 10:30am.

You can also depart Cairns with Great Adventures at 8:30am and spend 2 hours on Green Island en route. This gives you time to walk nature trails, rent snorkel gear and watersports equipment, or laze on the beach before continuing to the Outer Reef. This cruise costs an extra A$20 per person, or A$50 per family.

Ocean Freedom ★★★ (www.oceanfreedom.com.au; ✆ **07/4052 1111**) offers a more intimate experience, giving you the option of a motor cruise or a sailing tour—in both cases with limited numbers to ensure you don't feel crowded. *Ocean Freedom* is a high-speed launch that gives you 6 hours on the reef with no more than 75 passengers and takes you to two Reef sites including Upolu Cay. The day starts at 7:30am at the Reef Fleet Terminal, returning about 4:30pm. The cost is A$215 adults, A$130 children, and A$629 for a family of four and includes glass-bottom-boat rides, all snorkeling gear, and lunch. You can do an introductory dive for A$105 (and a second one for A$50); if you are certified you can dive for A$70 (and a second one for A$35). This is a great way to see the Reef. On the sailing trip aboard *Ocean Free* (www.oceanfree.com.au) you'll be one of only 25 passengers. *Ocean Free* sails at 7:30am, bound for Pinnacle Reef, an exclusive mooring on the eastern lee of Green Island. Prices are the same as *Ocean Freedom*.

Ocean Spirit Cruises ★★ (www.oceanspirit.com.au; © **07/4044 9944**) operates a 32m (105-ft.) luxury sailing catamaran that takes no more than 150 passengers to Michaelmas Cay, a lovely white-sand cay on the Outer Reef surrounded by rich reefs. This trip includes a 2-hour sail to the cay, snorkeling gear, and a guided beach walk—plus the usual reef ecology talks, semisubmersible rides, lunch, and morning and afternoon tea. You get about 4 hours on the Reef and spend your out-of-water time on a beautiful beach, not on a boat. The cost is A$213 for adults, A$112 for children 4 to 14, and A$543 for families of four. If you'd like a guided snorkeling safari rather than going it alone, add A$64 adults, A$34 children, or A$162 family. Introductory dives cost A$128 with all gear included. The trip departs Reef Fleet Terminal at 8:30am daily and returns around 5pm. Transfers from Cairns hotels are A$28 adults and A$18 kids; from the northern beaches it's A$34 adults, A$19 kids.

Sunlover Reef Cruises ★ (www.sunlover.com.au; © **1800/810 512** in Australia, or 07/4050 1333) motors large, fast catamarans to Moore Reef on the Outer Reef. The trip costs A$229 for adults, A$119 for children 4 to 15, and A$577 for families of four, including 4 hours on the Reef, a glass-bottom-boat ride, and semisubmersible viewing. Moore Reef's new pontoon includes a special children's swimming area and an 8m (26-ft.) waterslide. Introductory dives cost A$149; certified divers pay A$99, including all gear. The cruise includes lunch and leaves from the Reef Fleet Terminal in Cairns at 10am daily.

You can also take a coach transfer from Cairns or Palm Cove to Port Douglas to join the **Quicksilver** *Wavepiercer* (www.quicksilver-cruises.com; © **07/4087 2100**) for a day trip to the Outer Reef; see p. 211 for more details. Transfers from Cairns to Port Douglas cost A$32 per adult or A$16 per child, A$80 for families of four.

Great Adventures, Quicksilver, and Sunlover all offer helicopter flights over the Reef from their pontoons—a spectacular experience! There are fly-and-cruise trips as well.

FOR DIVERS

Tusa Dive ★★ (www.tusadive.com; © **07/4047 9100**) runs a custom-built 24m (72-ft.) dive boat daily to two dive sites from a choice of 15 locations on the Outer Reef. The day costs A$285 for certified divers (two dives included) or A$315 for three dives, and introductory divers pay A$280 for one dive or A$335 for two. Snorkelers pay A$210 adults and A$135 children age 4 to 14, with wetsuits, guided snorkel tours, and lunch provided. If you want to be shown the best spots, you can take a guided dive for an extra A$10. Transfers from your Cairns or northern beaches hotel cost A$15 or A$20, respectively. The boat takes a maximum of 60 people, with a staff-to-passenger ratio of one to five, so you get a good level of personal attention.

Day Trips from Cairns to the Islands

Cairns has several coral cays and reef-fringed islands within the **Great Barrier Reef Marine Park.** Less than an hour from the city wharf, **Fitzroy Island** is a rainforest-covered national park, with a coral beach and great snorkeling right off the shore. **Green Island** is a coral cay with snorkeling equal to that of most other places on the Great Barrier Reef. It is also a popular diving spot. You can visit it in half a day if time is short.

Fitzroy Island ★★★   Scenic Fitzroy Island (www.fitzroyislandcairns. com) is 45 minutes from Cairns by boat. There is a small resort on the island, and day-trippers visit for snorkeling and diving, glass-bottom-boat rides, watersports, rainforest walks, or hikes to the lighthouse at the top of the hill. Three ferry operators offer daily services to the island, costing around A$78 adults, A$39 for kids 4 to 13, or A$205 for a family round-trip; for a little extra you can add glass-bottom-boat rides or snorkel-gear to the package. A kiosk on the beach rents out snorkeling gear, coral viewing boards, paddle skis, and stand-up paddling boards, or you can book a glass-bottom-boat tour. There is also a turtle rehabilitation center on the island that is worth visiting. **Raging Thunder Adventures** (www.ragingthunder.com.au; ⓒ **07/4030 7990**)

Diving the Reef.

Diving Made Easy

Can't swim? Don't want to get your hair wet? Don't worry—you can still get underwater and see the wonders of the Reef. Several companies offer travelers the chance to don a dive helmet and "walk" underwater. Similar to old-style diving helmets, which allow you to breathe underwater, the helmet has air pumped into it by a hose. You walk into the water to a depth of about 4m (13 ft.), accompanied by instructors, and the Reef is right before you. **Quicksilver Cruises** (p. 211) calls it "Ocean Walker"; with **Sunlover Reef Cruises** (p. 199) and at **Green Island Resort** (below) it's called "Sea Walker." You must be at least 12 years old to walk (A\$159–A\$170/20 min.).

runs activities including daily guided sea-kayak expeditions around the island. These include snorkeling gear, lunch, and stinger suits (Nov–May), the return ferry trip, 3 hours of kayaking, and then you can stay on the island for the rest of the day. Tours cost A\$159, but you must be at least 14 years old.

Green Island ★★ This 15-hectare (37-acre) coral cay is just 27km (17 miles) east of Cairns. You can rent snorkel gear, windsurfers, and paddle skis; take glass-bottom-boat trips; go parasailing; take an introductory or certified dive; walk vine-forest trails; or laze on the beach. The beach is coral sand, so it's a little rough underfoot. Day visitors have access to one of the Green Island Resort pools, its main bar, casual or upscale restaurants, and lockers and showers. Ask the beach staff to recommend the best snorkeling spots. The island is home to **Marineland Crocodile Park** (www.greenislandcrocs.com.au; ✆ **07/4051 4032**), where you can see old nautical artifacts, a Melanesian artifacts collection, a turtle and reef aquarium, and live crocodiles, including Cassius, who—at almost 5.5m (18 ft.) in length—is listed by Guinness World Records as the largest croc in captivity in the world. Admission is A\$19 adults, A\$9 kids 5 to 14; croc shows are at 10:30am and 1:30pm. Open daily 9:30am to 4pm.

Great Adventures (www.greatadventures.com.au; ✆ **07/4044 9944**) and **Big Cat Green Island Reef Cruises** (www.greenisland.com.au; ✆ **07/4051 0444**) run to Green Island from Cairns. Both offer a range of half-day and full-day trips with lots of options. Half-day trips with snorkel gear or a glass-bottom-boat cruise cost around A\$96 adults, A\$50 children 4 to 14, or A\$242 for a family of four. Both tours offer pickup from hotels in Cairns, the northern beaches, and Port Douglas for a fee.

Day Trip from Cairns to Kuranda ★★

34km (21 miles) NW of Cairns

Few travelers visit Cairns without making a trip to the mountain village of **Kuranda,** near the Barron Gorge National Park. Although it's undeniably touristy, the cool mountain air and mist-wrapped rainforest refuse to be spoiled, no matter how many tourists clutter the streets. The shopping in Kuranda—for leather goods, Australian-wool sweaters, opals, crafts, and

Kuranda mountain village is known for its local crafts markets.

more—is more unusual than in Cairns, and the handful of cafes and restaurants is much more atmospheric. The town is easy to negotiate on foot; pick up a visitors' guide and map at the Skyrail gondola station or train station. Aside from the village, you can explore the rainforest, the river esplanade, or Barron Falls along a number of easy walking trails.

ESSENTIALS
Getting There

Getting to Kuranda is part of the fun. Some people drive up the winding 25km (16-mile) mountain road, but the most popular approaches are to chuff up the mountainside in a scenic train, or to glide silently over the rainforest canopy in the world's longest gondola cableway, the Skyrail Rainforest Cableway. The most popular round-trip is one-way on the Skyrail and the other way on the train. Mornings are best for photography on Skyrail, but the view is spectacular coming down in the afternoon. Make up your own mind; both are wonderful!

BY SKYRAIL The **Skyrail Rainforest Cableway** (p. 194) takes you up the Kuranda Range in a six-person gondola suspended over the rainforest.

BY TRAIN The 34km (21-mile) **Kuranda Scenic Railway** (www.ksr.com. au; ℗ **1800/577 245** in Australia, or 07/4036 9333) is one of the most scenic rail journeys in the world. The train snakes through the magnificent vistas of the Barron Gorge National Park, past gorges and waterfalls on the 90-minute trip from Cairns to Kuranda. It rises 328m (1,076 ft.) and goes through 15 tunnels before emerging at the pretty Kuranda station, which is smothered in ferns. Built by hand over 5 years in the late 1880s, the railway track is today a monument to the 1,500 men who toiled to link the two towns. The train departs Cairns Central at 8:30 and 9:30am daily (except Christmas Day) and leaves Kuranda at 2 and 3:30pm. The one-way fare is A$50 for adults, A$25 for children 4 to 14, and A$125 for families of four. An upgrade to "Gold Class" (A$99 adults, A$74 children, A$312 for a family) adds snacks, drinks, and waiter service.

BY BUS **Trans North Bus & Coach Service** (www.transnorthbus.com; ℂ 07/4095 8644) operates a bus to Kuranda from Cairns five times a day. The fare is A$6.70 one-way. *Tip:* Buying a return ticket will give you priority if the bus is full at the end of the day. Catch it at Orchid Plaza shopping center (79 Abbott St.), at the railway station, or at the Cairns Central Shopping Centre on Spence Street.

Visitor Information

The **Kuranda Visitor Information Centre** (www.kuranda.org; ℂ **07/4093 9311**) is in Centenary Park, at the top end of Coondoo Street. It is open 10am to 4pm daily, except Christmas Day.

EXPLORING KURANDA

Kuranda is known for its markets. The **Kuranda Original Rainforest Markets,** at 7 Therwine St. (enter through the Kuranda Market Mall; (ℂ **07/4093 9440;** daily 9:30am–3pm), are devoted exclusively to local artisans who vend fashion, jewelry, leather work, and indigenous art, as well as local produce including honey, coffee, fruit, sugarcane juice, coconuts, and macadamias.

The 90-stall **Heritage Market** (www.kurandamarkets.com.au; ℂ **07/4093 8060**) is open daily from 9:30am to 3:30pm on Rob Veivers Drive, with a range of souvenirs, food, produce, and crafts.

A group of about 50 local artisans sell their work in the **Kuranda Arts Co-Operative** gallery on Coondoo Street, opposite the church (www.facebook.com/kurandaartscooperative.kuranda; ℂ **07/4093 9026**). It's open from 10am to 4pm daily. The gallery sells furniture crafted from recycled Australian hardwoods, jewelry, photography, glasswork, and more.

Australian Butterfly Sanctuary ★★ NATURE CENTER   The fluttering array of 1,500 colorful tropical butterflies—including the electric-blue Ulysses and Australia's largest species, the Cairns bird wing—occupies a lush walk-through enclosure here. They may keep you entranced for hours (I was!). Take the free 30-minute guided tour and learn about the butterfly's fascinating life cycle. The butterflies will land on you if you wear pink, red, and other bright colors.

8 Rob Veivers Dr. www.australianbutterflies.com. ℂ **07/4093 7575.** A$20 adults, A$10 children 4–15, A$50 families of 4. Daily 9:45am–4pm. Closed Christmas Day.

Birdworld ★ NATURE CENTER   Behind the markets off Rob Veivers Drive, Birdworld has eye-catching macaws, a pair of cassowaries, and Australia's largest collection of free-flying birds—about 500 of them, representing 75 worldwide species. Two lakes are home to water birds including stilts, herons, and Australia's Black Swan.

Rob Veivers Dr. www.birdworldkuranda.com. ℂ **07/4093 9188.** A$18 adults, A$9 children 4–15. Daily 9am–4pm. Closed Christmas Day.

Kuranda Koala Gardens ★ WILDLIFE VIEWING   You can cuddle a koala and have your photo taken at this small wildlife park next to the Heritage Markets. Other animals include freshwater crocodiles, wombats, lizards, and wallabies. Or take a stroll through the walk-through snake enclosure while they slither at your feet—not for the fainthearted.

Rob Veivers Dr. www.koalagardens.com. © **07/4093 9953.** A$19 adults, A$9.50 kids 4–15. Daily 9am–4pm. Closed Christmas Day.

Kuranda Riverboat Tours ★★ BOAT RIDE   If you want to learn about the rainforest, take one of these informative 45-minute river cruises. The cruises depart five times a day from 10:45am from the riverside landing across the footbridge, near the train station, and are the only ones with rights to operate on the Barron River. A team of local naturalists will answer your questions and point out some of the rainforest secrets. Buy your tickets online or pay onboard (cash only). The last cruise of the day returns in time for the 3:30pm train to Cairns.

Rob Veivers Dr. www.kurandariverboat.com.au. A$20 adults, A$10 children 5–15, A$50 family of 4.

Rainforestation Nature Park ★★ NATURE CENTER/TOUR   At this 40-hectare (99-acre) nature and cultural complex, you can take a 45-minute ride into the rainforest in a World War II amphibious Army Duck. You'll hear commentary on orchids and other rainforest wildlife along the way. You can also see a performance by Aboriginal dancers; learn about Aboriginal legends and throw a boomerang on the Dreamtime Walk; or have your photo taken cuddling a koala or holding a small freshwater crocodile in the wildlife park (photos extra, from A$22). The Army Duck runs on the hour, beginning at 10am; the Aboriginal dancers perform at 10:30am, noon, and 2pm; and the 30-minute Dreamtime Walk leaves at 10, 11, and 11:30am, and 12:30, 1:30, and 2:30pm.

Kennedy Hwy., a 5-min. drive from the center of Kuranda. www.rainforest.com.au. © **07/4085 5008.** A$50 adults, A$25 kids 4–14, A$125 families of 4. Daily 9am–4pm. Closed Christmas Day. Shuttle from the Butterfly Sanctuary, Rob Veivers Dr., every 30 min. 10:45am–2:45pm for A$12 adults, A$6 children.

WHERE TO EAT IN KURANDA

Frogs Restaurant ★★ CAFE   This is a good place to stop for lunch, tucked into the wildlife attractions and Heritage Markets just off the main street. Simple offerings like wraps, pizzas, and salads dominate, but you can also get a hearty steak, seafood, or a bush tasting platter (kangaroo, emu, crocodile). Or try the Curry of the Day, a bargain at only A$9.50. Be on the lookout for the water dragons (they're harmless) on the deck overlooking the rainforest. It also has free Wi-Fi.

2/4 Rob Veivers Dr. www.frogsrestaurant.com.au. © **07/4093 8952.** Main courses A$9.50–A$28. Daily 9:30am–4pm. Closed Christmas Day.

PORT DOUGLAS ★★★

The fishing village of Port Douglas is where the rainforest meets the Reef. Just over an hour's drive from Cairns, through rainforest and along a winding (sometimes treacherously so) road beside the sea, Port Douglas may be small, but stylish shops and seriously trendy restaurants line the main street, and beautiful Four Mile Beach is not to be missed. This is a favorite spot with celebrities big and small. Travelers often base themselves in "Port," as the locals call it, because they like the rural surroundings, the uncrowded beach, and the absence of tacky development (so far, anyway). Many Reef tours originate in Port, and many of the tours in the Cairns section pick up participants here as well.

The waters off Port Douglas boast just as many wonderful reefs and marine life forms as those around Cairns; the reefs are equally close to shore and equally colorful and varied. The closest Reef site off Port Douglas, the **Low Isles,** is only 15km (9 miles) northeast. Coral sand and 22 hectares (55 acres) of coral surround these two cays; the smaller is a sand cay covered in rich vegetation and the larger is a shingle/rubble cay covered in mangroves, home to thousands of nesting Torresian Imperial pigeons. (If you visit the Low Isles, wear shoes that you can get wet, because the coral sand can be rough underfoot.) The coral is not quite as dazzling as the Outer Reef's—which is where you should head if you have only one day to spend on the Great Barrier Reef—but the fish life here is rich, and you may spot sea turtles. Because you can wade out to the coral right from the beach, the Low Isles are a good choice for nervous snorkelers. A half-day or day trip to the Low Isles makes for a more relaxing day than a visit to Outer Reef sites, because in addition to exploring the coral, you can sunbathe on the sand or laze under palm-thatched beach umbrellas.

Essentials
ARRIVING
There is no train to Port Douglas, and no scheduled air service. A small airport handles light aircraft and helicopter charters.

BY CAR Port Douglas is a scenic 65-minute drive from Cairns, in part along a narrow winding road that skirts the coast. Take Sheridan Street north out of the city as it becomes the Captain Cook Highway; follow the signs to Mossman and Mareeba until you reach the Port Douglas turnoff on your right. A **taxi** fare from Cairns to Port Douglas will set you back around A$200; call **Cairns Taxis** (✆ **131 008** in Cairns).

BY BUS A one-way ticket with **Sun Palm Transport** (www.sunpalmtransport.com.au; ✆ **07/4099 1191**) to Port Douglas hotels from Cairns airport is A$39 for adults. One child rides free with a paying adult; additional children pay half price.

The Secret of the Seasons
High season in Port Douglas is roughly June 1 through October 31. Low-season holiday periods run from approximately November to May (excluding Christmas and New Year's).

VISITOR INFORMATION

The biggest and most central information center in town is the privately run **Port Douglas Tourist Information Centre,** 23 Macrossan St. (www.tourismportdouglas. com.au; ℭ **07/4099 5599**), open from 8:30am to 5:30pm daily. There is no official visitor information office in Port Douglas, but the tourism information website of **Tourism Port Douglas and Daintree** (www.visitportdouglasdaintree.com) is a good source.

GETTING AROUND

Avis (ℭ **07/4099 4331**), **Budget** (ℭ **07/4099 5702**), and **Thrifty** (ℭ **07/4099 5555**) have offices in Port Douglas. All rent regular vehicles as well as four-wheel-drives, which you need if you plan to drive to Cape Tribulation. For a taxi, call **Port Douglas Taxis** (ℭ **131 008**).

There is no bus service in Port Douglas, but several companies operate shuttles between the town center and major resorts. Ask your hotel or resort which one services them.

A good way to get around the town's flat streets is by bike. **Port Douglas Bicycle Centre,** 3 Warner St. (www.portdouglasbikehire.com; ℭ **07/4099 5799**), rents bikes from A$16 for 4 hours, A$20 for a full day (or A$16/day for multi-day rental).

Where to Stay in Port Douglas

Port Douglas Accommodation Holiday Rentals (www.portdouglasaccom. com.au; ℭ **07/4099 1340**) rents a wide range of apartments and homes.

EXPENSIVE

By the Sea ★   You won't find a friendlier or more convenient place to stay in Port Douglas than these apartments, 10 seconds from the beach and less than 10 minutes' walk from town. There are also heaps of "extras" such as bikes, iPads, laptops, beach towels, and water sports equipment on loan. Some of the apartments are on the small side (most suit only three people), but all are well cared for and were renovated in 2017. You can opt for a tiny Garden apartment with a patio; Balcony and Seaview apartments are a bit larger and have private balconies. Seaview apartments are quite roomy and have side views of Four Mile Beach. Towels are changed daily and linen weekly, and rooms are serviced every 4 days (or you can pay A$15 per day extra for daily service). It has no elevator and no porter, so be prepared to carry your luggage upstairs.

72 Macrossan St. www.bytheseaportdouglas.com.au. ℭ **07/4099 5387.** 21 units. A$245–A$285 double studio; A$315–A$355 1-bedroom apt; A$455–A$675 2-bedroom apt. or villa. Free parking. **Amenities:** Jacuzzi; outdoor heated pool; bikes; free Wi-Fi.

QT Resort ★★   One of the quirkier resorts in Port Douglas, the QT is a magnet for the hip crowd that jams the bar on weekends, dying to be seen. The rooms are hip and colorful too, with a slightly retro feel (and in case you fall in love with any of the *objets* scattered around, there is—rather strangely, I thought—a price list for everything from the coat hangers to the armchairs). There are also one- and two-bedroom villas to rent. It's too far to walk to town, but you can borrow a bike or take the shuttle (A$6 one-way adults, A$3 kids). From June to October, the QT Moonlight Cinema shows classic and new release films.

87–109 Port Douglas Rd. www.qthotelsandresorts.com/port-douglas. ℗ **07/4099 8900.** 170 units. A$209–A$229 double; A$259–A$279 1-bedroom villa; A$369 2-bedroom villa. Free parking. Shuttle bus to town every 15 min, from 7:30am–11:30pm daily (A$6 one-way adults, A$3 kids). **Amenities:** Restaurant; bar; babysitting; free use of bikes; concierge; health club; 2 outdoor pools; room service; spa; 2 tennis courts; free Wi-Fi.

Thala Beach Nature Reserve ★★   Open to the elements—and the odd curious wallaby—the reception area of this stunning rainforest hideaway makes a striking first impression. From the restaurant upstairs, the impact is even greater, with sweeping views of the coastline and rainforest. Thala (pronounced *Ta*-la) Beach is 16km (10 miles) outside Port Douglas, set on a 58-hectare (145-acre) private peninsula, bordered on three sides by private beaches and coves. Owners Rob and Oonagh Prettejohn took their inspiration from the flora and fauna of the World Heritage area that surrounds it to create secluded treehouse bungalows. I've stayed here twice, and all the rooms are spacious and comfortable, with timber-paneled walls and king-size or twin beds. The Coral Sea bungalows overlook the ocean; the rest have forest and mountain views. Some of the bungalows are a bit of a hike from the public areas, but it's a small price to pay for the privacy and the rainforest setting (and you can call for a golf-buggy pick-up).

Private Rd., Oaks Beach. www.thalabeach.com.au. ℗ **07/4098 5700.** 85 units. A$379–A$769 double; A$935 suite. Free parking. Hotel shuttle to Port Douglas. **Amenities:** Restaurant; bar; 2 outdoor pools; spa; free Wi-Fi (in main lodge only).

MODERATE

Marae ★★   John and Pam Burden's architecturally stunning timber home, on a hillside 15km (9½ miles) north of Port Douglas, is a glamorous and restful bush retreat. The contemporary bedrooms have mosquito nets and smart linens on king-size beds, not to mention elegant bathrooms. The garden room overlooks the valley and the pool. Wallabies and bandicoots (small marsupials) feed in the garden, kingfishers and honeyeaters use the birdbaths, and butterflies are everywhere. A delicious tropical breakfast is served on the deck in the company of a flock of red-browed finches and peaceful doves. Mossman Gorge is just a few minutes' drive. You need a car to stay here.

Ponzo Rd., Shannonvale. www.marae.com.au. ℗ **07/4098 4900.** 2 units. A$180 single; A$245 double. 2-night minimum. Rates include full breakfast. Children 16 and under not accepted. **Amenities:** Outdoor pool; free Wi-Fi.

INEXPENSIVE

Coral Beach Lodge ★★   This modest lodge, popular with backpackers, families, and budget travelers, is on a suburban street that's just a 10-minute walk from town. All rooms were renovated in 2016, building on the Lodge's reputation as an award-wining hostel-style accommodation. You can swap stories with other guests as you cook and eat in the communal kitchen and dining room. The rooms have small patios and are air-conditioned at night (or you can pay A$10 extra for 24-hr. air-conditioning). Dorm-style rooms (male and female) have shared bathrooms.

7 Craven Close. www.coralbeachlodge.com.au. ✆ **07/4099 5422.** 28 units. A$142 double; four- or five-share rooms A$30–A$40 per person. Free parking. Bus: no. 110 (stop at front door). **Amenities:** Outdoor pool; free use of bikes; free Wi-Fi.

Port Douglas Retreat ★   This well-kept two-story studio apartment complex on a quiet street, featuring white-battened balconies in the Queenslander architectural style, is a good value. Even some of the ritzier places in town can't boast its lagoon-like saltwater pool, surrounded by dense jungle and wrapped by an ample, shady sun deck that cries out to be lounged on with a good book and a cool drink. The apartments are not enormous, but they're fashionably furnished with terra cotta tile floors, wrought-iron beds, cane seating, and colorful bedcovers. All have large furnished balconies or patios looking onto tropical gardens; some on the ground floor open onto the common-area boardwalk, so you might want to ask for a first-floor (second-story) unit. The town and beach are a 5-minute walk away.

31–33 Mowbray St., at Mudlo St. www.portdouglasretreat.com.au. ✆ **07/4099 5053.** 36 units. A$114–A$190 double. Minimum 2 or 3-night stay (depending on time of year). Secure covered parking. **Amenities:** Free airport transfers; outdoor saltwater pool; free Wi-Fi.

Where to Eat in Port Douglas

EXPENSIVE

Sassi Cucina e Bar ★★ ITALIAN   Presided over by gregarious Italian owner/chef Tony Sassi—who's something of a local celebrity—this traditional Italian *cucina* offers fresh seasonal flavors done simply and well. Start with some *spuntini* (small plates) of delicacies such as crispy fried small local prawns with garlic and chili, and then move on to a pasta or risotto. There are always specials, depending on what's fresh . . . but make sure you try Tony's special meatballs, or chili mud crab if it's on offer. Sit inside in the air-conditioning, on the pavement outside, or in the garden out the back. Prices are lower at lunch.

4 Macrossan St. (at Wharf St.), Port Douglas. www.sassi.com.au. ✆ **07/4099 6744.** Main courses A$30–A$49. Daily 11am–9:30pm.

MODERATE

Salsa Bar & Grill ★★★ CONTEMPORARY   This trendy restaurant, in a timber Queenslander with wraparound verandas, has seriously good food, great prices, and lively, fun service. Little wonder you need to book well ahead—sometimes up to 2 weeks in advance—and it's the restaurant of choice for everyone from presidents to pop stars. Choose simple fare such as gnocchi or Caesar salad or such mouthwatering delights as a jambalaya with tiger prawns, squid, yabbie, smoked chicken, and crocodile sausage; or kangaroo loin with saltbush, beetroot, and goats' curd marshmallow. Save room for dessert: a chocolate and Cointreau soufflé with double choc ice cream, perhaps? There's a kids' menu, too.

26 Wharf St. (at Warner St.), Port Douglas. www.salsaportdouglas.com.au. © **07/4099 4922.** Main courses A$30–A$42. Daily noon–2:30pm and 5:30-9pm.

Zinc ★★ CONTEMPORARY   If you're like me, you may find yourself coming back more than once to this casual but very smart restaurant during your Port Douglas stay. The food is simple but very good (think coral trout with baby vegetables, herb salad, and beurre noisette, or a succulent steak from the grill). Zinc offers service with a smile, and a bar menu all day. Make sure you check out the restrooms, which have floor-to-ceiling aquariums. Reservations are recommended for dinner.

Macrossan St. (at Davidson St.), Port Douglas. www.zincportdouglas.com. © **07/4099 6260.** Main courses A$29–A$42. Daily noon–late.

Exploring Port Douglas

Some companies in Cairns that offer outdoor activities will pick up from Port Douglas hotels. The best outdoor activity in Port Douglas, however, is to do absolutely nothing on spectacular **Four Mile Beach** ★★★. From May through September, the water is stinger-free. From October through April, swim in the stinger safety net.

Every Sunday from 7:30am to 1pm, a colorful **handicrafts and food market** is held on the lawn under the mango trees by Dickson Inlet, at the end of Macrossan Street. Stalls offer everything from foot massages to fresh coconut milk.

Kuku Yalanji Cultural Habitat Tours ★★★ TOUR/CULTURAL ACTIVITY   Brothers Linc and Brandon Walker will take you on the walk of a lifetime, on the beach opposite their parents' house. This is the traditional fishing ground of the Kubirri Warra people, when the mudflats and mangroves are exposed at low tide; you will spend 2½ hours here learning to throw a spear, hunt and stalk, and use coastal resources wisely. If you are lucky, you may spear a crab (not so lucky for the crab!), and when enough has been foraged to make a small meal, you'll take it back to the house where Linc and Brandon's

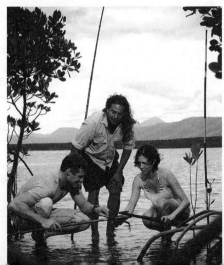
Kuku Yalanji Cultural Habitat Tours.

mother will cook it up for you to eat on the veranda. It's an authentic and unforgettable experience. Don't forget to take insect repellent (just in case), and wear shoes you don't mind getting wet (though bare feet are best). Night fishing tours, either by boat or foot, are run on request. Bookings are essential for all tours.

Bougainvillea St., Cooya Beach (north of Port Douglas; take Bonnie Doon Rd., off the Captain Cook Hwy.). www.kycht.com.au. (✆) **07/4098 3437.** A$90 adults, A$75 kids 4–12; A$150 per person night tours. Daily at 9:30am and 1:30pm; night tours 7:30pm.

Mossman Gorge Centre ★★★ NATURE CENTER/TOUR   This is the gateway to wonderful Mossman Gorge, where the gushing Mossman River tumbles over massive boulders through the rainforest. You can visit the gorge on your own and take the short boardwalks along the river, but I highly recommend joining one of the guided **Ngadiku Dreamtime Walks,** with a member of the local Kuku-Yalanji tribe. You will learn about Aboriginal bush medicines and food, Dreamtime legends, and the sacred sites their families have called home for thousands of years. There are five tours daily (10am, 11am, noon, 1pm, and 3pm) and cost A$75 adults, A$37 children 5 to 15, or A$185 for a family of four. The center has a gift shop, art gallery, and cafe. You can only access the gorge by taking the shuttle bus, which leaves the visitor center every 15 minutes between 8am and 5:30pm daily. The cost is A$9.80 for adults, A$4.85 for children, or A$24 for a family of four. Most tour companies from Cairns and Port Douglas will get you here.

Mossman Gorge Rd., Mossman (20km/12 miles north of Port Douglas). www.mossman gorge.com.au. (✆) **07/4099 7000.** Daily 8am–6pm. Closed Christmas Day.

Wildlife Habitat ★★★ WILDLIFE VIEWING   This is a great place to see animals that are too shy to be spotted in the wild, with 180 animal species from the Wet Tropics all in one place for you to observe up close. You can watch saltwater and freshwater crocodiles, hand-feed kangaroos, and have your photo taken with a koala. The highlight is the walk-through aviary, housing more than 100 Wet Tropics bird species, including cassowaries. Between 9 and 10:30am, the park serves "breakfast with the birds," and between noon and 2pm "lunch with the lorikeets." Breakfast costs A$56 for adults, A$28 for kids, and A$140 families, and includes Habitat admission; lunch costs a few dollars more. Don't miss one of the excellent free, guided tours that run regularly from 9:30am to 4pm. You can also do a "wildnight" tour for A$42 adults, A$31 children, or A$115 families, to see some of Australia's amazing nocturnal creatures. Allow at least 2 hours here.

Port Douglas Rd. (corner Captain Cook Hwy.). www.wildlifehabitat.com.au. (✆) **07/4099 3235.** A$36 adults, A$18 kids 4–14, A$90 families of 4. Daily 8am–5pm. Closed Christmas Day.

Day Trips from Port Douglas to the Reef

The waters off Port Douglas are home to dramatic coral spires and swim-throughs at the Cathedrals; giant clams at Barracuda Pass; a village of parrot fish, anemone fish, unicorn fish, and two moray eels at the pinnacle of Nursery Bommie; fan corals at Split-Bommie; and many other wonderful sites.

Without a doubt, the most popular large vessels visiting the Outer Reef are the **Quicksilver Wavepiercers** (www.quicksilver-cruises.com; ℂ **07/4087 2100**), based out of Port Douglas. These ultrasleek, high-speed, air-conditioned 37m (121-ft.) and 46m (151-ft.) catamarans carry 300 or 440 passengers to Agincourt Reef, a ribbon reef 39 nautical miles (72km/45 miles) from shore on the outer edge of the Reef. After the 90-minute trip to the Reef, you tie up at a two-story pontoon, where you spend 3½ hours.

Quicksilver departs Marina Mirage at 10am daily except on December 25. The cost for the day is A$257 for adults, A$132 for kids 4 to 14, and A$651 for families of four. Guided snorkel safaris cost A$64 per adult, A$32 for kids, A$160 for families; introductory dives cost A$172 per person. Qualified divers can take a dive-tender boat to make one dive for A$124 or two dives for A$174 per person, all gear included. Booking in advance is a good idea.

The dive boat *Poseidon* (www.poseidon-cruises.com.au; ℂ **07/4087 2100**) also welcomes snorkelers. It presents a Reef ecology talk and takes you on a guided snorkel safari. The *Poseidon* is a fast 24m (79-ft.) vessel that visits three Outer Reef sites. The day-trip price of A$247 for adults, and A$177 for kids 4 to 14, includes snorkel gear, a marine-biology talk, snorkel safaris, lunch, and pickups from Port Douglas hotels. You can try an introductory dive for A$69 for one dive or A$134 for two. Certified divers pay an extra A$52 for one dive, A$74 for two dives, or A$90 for three, including all gear. Guides will accompany you, free of charge, to show you great locations. The boat departs the Reef Marina daily at 8:30am, taking about 2 hours to get to the first of three reef sites you will visit during the day at Agincourt Reef. Among the 25-plus dive sites visited by Poseidon's cruises are **Turtle Bay,** where you may meet a friendly Maori wrasse; the **Cathedrals,** a collection of coral pinnacles and swim-throughs; and **Barracuda Pass,** home to coral gardens, giant clams, and schooling barracuda.

The snorkeling specialist boat *Wavelength* (www.wavelength.com.au; ℂ **07/4099 5031**) does a full-day trip to the Outer Reef for A$240 for adults, A$200 for children 8 to 12. *Note:* This trip is not suitable for children age 7 and under. The trip visits three different snorkel sites each day and incorporates a guided snorkel tour and a reef presentation by a marine biologist. It carries only 30 passengers and includes snorkel gear, sunsuits, lunch, and transfers from your Port Douglas hotel. Both beginners and experienced snorkelers will like this trip, which departs daily at 8:30am.

THE LOW ISLES

Another way to spend a pleasant day—closer to shore—on the Great Barrier Reef is to visit the **Low Isles,** 15km (9½ miles) northeast of Port Douglas. The isles are 1.5-hectare (3¾-acre) coral-cay specks of lush vegetation surrounded by white sand and 22 hectares (54 acres) of coral—which is what makes them so appealing. The coral is not quite as good as the Outer Reef's, but the fish life is rich, and the proximity makes for a relaxing day.

The trip aboard the 30m (98-ft.) luxury sailing catamaran *Wavedancer,* operated by Quicksilver (www.wavedancerlowisles.com; ☏ **07/4087 2100**), is A$205 for adults, A$106 for kids 4 to 14, and A$521 for families of 4. You'll leave Port Douglas at 10am, and once there, you can snorkel, take a glass-bottom-boat ride, or do a guided beach walk with a marine biologist. Coach transfers are available through Quicksilver from your Port Douglas accommodations for A$16 adults, A$8 kids, or A$40 for a family.

TOWNSVILLE & MAGNETIC ISLAND ★★

346km (215 miles) S of Cairns; 1,371km (850 miles) N of Brisbane

Australia's largest tropical city (population 140,000), with an economy based on mining, manufacturing, and education as well as tourism, Townsville is sometimes—rather unjustly, I think—overlooked as a holiday destination. The people are friendly, the city is pleasant, and there's plenty to do. The town nestles by the sea below the pink face of Castle Rock, which looms 300m (about 1,000 ft.) directly above. Townsville's popular waterfront parkland, The Strand (p. 215), is complemented by the **Jezzine Barracks,** a A$40-million redevelopment of unused land which now offers a stunning collection of outdoor sculptures and memorials honoring the city's wartime history (with more than a passing nod to the American forces who served here in World War II). It is a wonderful parkland that's well worth exploring.

Cruises depart from Townsville harbor for the Great Barrier Reef, about 2½ hours away, and just 8km (5 miles) offshore is Magnetic Island—"Maggie" to the locals—a popular place for watersports, hiking, and spotting koalas in the wild.

Townsville's waters boast hundreds of large patch reefs, some miles long, with excellent coral and marine life, including mantas, rays, turtles, and sharks, and sometimes canyons and swim-throughs in generally good visibility. One of the best reef complexes is **Flinders Reef,** which is actually in the Coral Sea, beyond the Great Barrier Reef Marine Park boundaries. At 240km (149 miles) offshore, it has 30m (100-ft.) visibility, plenty of coral, and big walls and pinnacles with big fish to match, such as whaler shark and barracuda.

What draws most divers to Townsville, though, is one of Australia's best wreck dives, the **SS** *Yongala.* Still largely intact, the sunken remains of this steamer lie in 15m to 30m (50–98 ft.) of water, with visibility of 9m to 18m (approximately 30–60 ft.). Diving the *Yongala* is not for beginners—most dive companies require their customers to have advanced certification or to have logged a minimum of 15 dives with open-water certification. The boat is usually visited on a live-aboard trip of at least 2 days, but some companies run day trips.

Although Townsville can be hot and humid in the summer—and sometimes in the path of cyclones—it is generally spared the worst of the wet-season rains and boasts 300 days of sunshine a year.

Essentials

ARRIVING

BY PLANE   **Qantas** (www.qantas.com.au; ☎ **131 313** in Australia) flies direct from Brisbane, Cairns, and Darwin. **Jetstar** (www.jetstar.com.au; ☎ **131 538** in Australia) flies direct from Sydney and Melbourne's Tullamarine airport; and **Virgin Australia** (www.virginaustralia.com.au; ☎ **136 789** in Australia) flies direct from Brisbane, Melbourne, and Sydney daily. **Regional Express** (www.rex.com.au; ☎ **131 713** in Australia, or 02/6393 5550) flies from Cairns. **Townsville City Shuttle** (www.shuttletsv.com.au; ☎ **0478/160 036** mobile) operates an airport shuttle service to the city for A$10 adults, A$15 for two or three passengers, and A$20 for a group of four. Bookings essential. A **taxi** from the airport to most central hotels costs about A$25.

BY TRAIN   **Queensland Rail** (www.queenslandrailtravel.com.au; ☎ **1300/131 722** in Queensland, or 07/3606 6630) long-distance trains stop at Townsville on the Brisbane-Cairns route. The 17-hour Spirit of Queensland journey from Brisbane costs A$315 for a premium economy seat.

BY BUS   **Greyhound Australia** (www.greyhound.com.au; ☎ **1300/473 946** in Australia, or 07/4799 3715 in Townsville) coaches stop at Townsville several times a day on their Cairns-Brisbane-Cairns routes. The fare from Cairns is A$66; trip time is around 5 to 6 hours. The fare from Brisbane is A$281; trip time is 24 hours (sometimes longer).

BY CAR   Townsville is on the Bruce Highway, a 3-hour drive north of Airlie Beach and 4½ hours south of Cairns. The Bruce Highway breaks temporarily in the city. From the south, take Bruce Highway Alt. 1 route into the city. From the north, the highway leads into the city. The drive from Cairns to Townsville through sugar-cane fields, cloud-topped hills, and lush bushland is a pretty one—one of the most picturesque stretches in Queensland.

VISITOR INFORMATION

There are two official information centers in town. One is in the heart of the city on Townsville Bulletin Square, just off Flinders Street (www.townsville northqueensland.com.au; ☎ **1800/801 902** in Australia, or 07/4721 3660); it's open Monday through Friday, 9am to 5pm, and weekends from 9am to 1pm. It is closed Good Friday, Christmas Day, and until 1pm on Anzac Day (Apr 25). The **Bruce Highway Visitor Information Centre** (☎ **07/4780 4397**) is at Billabong Sanctuary (p. 216); it's open Monday to Saturday 9am to 4pm and Sunday 10am to 2pm.

GETTING AROUND TOWNSVILLE

Local **Sunbus** (www.sunbus.com.au; ☎ **07/4771 9800**) buses depart from Flinders Street. Car-rental chains include **Avis** (☎ **07/4799 2022**), **Budget** (☎ **07/4762 7433**), **Europcar** (☎ **07/4760 1380**), **Hertz** (☎ **07/4728 9530**), and **Thrifty** (☎ **07/4725 4600**).

For a taxi, call ☎ **131 008.**

Where to Stay in Townsville

EXPENSIVE/MODERATE

Grand Hotel and Apartments Townsville ★★   Just off the bustle of the Palmer Street restaurant strip, all the rooms at this smart hotel, opened in 2014, have private balconies. There's no restaurant—but no need of one. The hotel offers a charge-back service from six nearby restaurants (and room service as well). As well as standard hotel rooms, you have the choice of one- or two-bedroom apartments, which have an open-plan kitchen and living space, separate bedroom(s) and bathroom, and a washing machine and dryer.

8–10 Palmer St. www.grandhoteltownsville.com.au. © **07/4753 2800.** 230 units. A$141–A$314 double; A$185-A$381 1-bedroom apt; A$358–A$378 2-bedroom apt. Free parking. **Amenities:** Gym; Jacuzzi; outdoor pool; room service; Wi-Fi (A$5.50/1 hr.; A$24/24 hr.), free if you book direct.

MODERATE

Hotel Grand Chancellor Townsville ★   Just a stroll from all the city's major attractions and the Magnetic Island ferries, this 20-story hotel is fairly standard but a good choice for its heart-of-the-city location. The locals call it the "Sugar Shaker" because of its distinctive circular shape (which gives every room a view of the city, the bay, or Castle Hill). Suites have kitchenettes. The star attractions are the rooftop pool and sun deck with barbecues. Parking is in a separate building, which can be inconvenient at times.

334 Flinders St. www.grandchancellorhotels.com. © **1800/753 379** in Australia, or 07/4729 2000. 200 units. A$125–A$142 double; A$147–A$173 suite. Parking A$13 per day. **Amenities:** Restaurant; 2 bars; babysitting; bikes; concierge; gym; rooftop pool; room service; free Wi-Fi.

Mercure Townsville ★★   Set in tropical gardens on the shores of a large lake, this resort-style hotel is a pleasant surprise. It's a bit out of town (on the main road north), right next to a big shopping center, but once you're there you may not want to travel far. The free-form swimming pool is Townsville's largest (it also has a Jacuzzi); take a dip or go for a stroll around the lake and watch the birds. Rooms are a good size, and family suites sleep four and have kitchenettes.

Woolcock and Attlee sts. www.mercuretownsville.com.au. © **07/4759 4900.** 162 units. A$159–A$189 double; A$199 family room. Free parking. **Amenities:** Restaurant; bar; babysitting; pool; room service; 2 lit tennis courts; free Wi-Fi.

INEXPENSIVE

Seagulls Seafront Resort ★★   This popular, low-key resort, a 5-minute drive from the city, is built around an inviting free-form saltwater pool in 1.2 hectares (3 acres) of tropical gardens. Despite the Esplanade location, the motel-style rooms do not boast waterfront views, but they are comfortable and a good size. The larger deluxe rooms have painted brick walls, sofas, dining furniture, and kitchen sinks. Studios and family rooms have kitchenettes. Apartments have a main bedroom and a bunk bedroom (sleeps three), a kitchenette, dining area, and a roomy balcony. The resort is wheelchair-friendly, with some ground-floor rooms specially adapted for guests with disabilities. The accommodations wings surround the pool and its pretty open-sided restaurant, which is popular with locals. It's a 10-minute walk to the Strand, and most tour companies pick up at the door.

74 The Esplanade, Belgian Gardens. www.seagulls.com.au. ℭ **07/4721 3111.** 70 units. A$95–A$149 double; A$169 family rooms; A$189 2-bedroom apt. Free parking. Bus: no. 7. **Amenities:** Restaurant; bar; children's playground; 2 large outdoor saltwater pools and children's wading pool; room service; small tennis court; free Wi-Fi.

Where to Eat in Townsville

There are many restaurants and cafes on **Palmer Street,** an easy stroll across the river from Flinders Street, and on the Strand.

C Bar ★★ CONTEMPORARY   Right on the waterfront, C Bar is a great place for casual seaside dining any time of day, offering good, healthy choices for breakfast and an interesting all-day menu (from 11:30am). It's a lovely spot for sundowners or dinner, too. At lunch or dinner, try a prawn and coconut *laksa* with rice noodles and Asian greens, a simple fish 'n' chips, or maybe a roasted sweet potato and haloumi salad. There's also a kids' menu, with all meals A$15. For my money, the view is one of the best in town.

Gregory Street Headland, The Strand. www.cbar.com.au. ℭ **07/4724 0333.** Main courses A$18–A$33. Daily 6am–10pm.

Jam Corner ★★★ CONTEMPORARY   Dishes that will make you groan with pleasure, with flavors designed to delight . . . that's what you will find at this smart, friendly restaurant. It's so good that when visiting Townsville, I usually eat here more than once! At breakfast, try the Asian chicken omelet with snow peas, bean shoots, fried shallots, and chili jam (or the most popular item on the menu, the Queensland avocado on wholegrain sourdough with whipped Danish feta and poached eggs). For dinner, you might find dishes like reef fish with black sesame, lemongrass curry, lotus root, samphire, and prawn fried rice; or for meat-lovers, an eye filet steak with roasted vegetables. The menu changes regularly, but you can be assured that the quality won't. Really, don't miss this restaurant. It's no wonder the awards are rolling in.

1 Palmer St. www.jamcorner.com.au. ℭ **07/4721 4900.** Main courses A$25–A$40; 6-course tasting menu A$75 (or A$120 with matched wine). Tues–Fri 6:30am–2pm and 5:30pm–late; Sat 7am–2pm and 5:30pm–late; Sun 7:30am–11am.

Exploring Townsville

Don't miss the views of the city, Cleveland Bay, and Magnetic Island from **Castle Hill;** it's a 2.5km (1½-mile) drive or a shorter, steep walk up from town (make sure to do it in the cool part of the day). To drive to the top, follow Stanley Street west from Flinders Street to Castle Hill Drive; the walking trails up are posted en route.

The Strand is a 2.5km (1½-mile) strip with safe swimming beaches, a fitness circuit, a great free water park for the kids, and plenty of covered picnic areas and free gas barbecue grills. Stroll along the promenade or relax at one of the many cafes, restaurants, and bars while you gaze across the Coral Sea to Magnetic Island. For the more active, there are areas to in-line skate, cycle, walk, fish, or play half-court basketball. Four rocky headlands and a picturesque jetty adjacent to Strand Park provide good fishing spots, and two surf lifesaving clubs service the three swimming areas along the Strand. Cool off in the Olympic-size Tobruk Memorial Baths (A$5 adults, A$3 kids 2–12) or the seawater Rockpool or at the beach itself. During summer (Nov–Mar), three swimming enclosures operate to keep swimmers safe from marine stingers. If watersports are on your agenda, try jet-skiing, hire a canoe, or take to the latest in pedal skis. A state-of-the-art water park has waterfalls, water slides, and water cannons, plus a huge bucket of water that continually fills until it overturns and drenches laughing children.

Billabong Sanctuary ★★★ WILDLIFE VIEWING You could easily spend 2 or 3 hours here, seeing Aussie wildlife in a natural setting and hand-feeding kangaroos and emus. You can also be photographed (starting at A$24) holding a koala, a (baby) crocodile, a python, or a wombat. Engaging interactive talks and shows run continuously starting at 9:15am; among the most popular are the saltwater-crocodile feeding at 1 and 3:15pm (for an extra A$99, you can also personally feed the croc from a large pole dangled over the fence). The sanctuary also has gas barbecues, a cafe, and a pool.

Bruce Hwy. (17km/11 miles S of Townsville). www.billabongsanctuary.com.au. ⓒ **07/4778 8344.** A$37 adults, A$24 children 4–16, A$105 families of 5. Daily 9am–5pm. Closed Christmas Day.

Museum of Tropical Queensland ★★ MUSEUM If you're lucky enough to be here on the second Tuesday of the month, you'll have the chance to hear a museum expert give an hour-long lunchtime talk as part of the museum's "Discover More" lecture series. Subjects cover everything from underwater robotic research to frogs to the history of Townsville. With its curved roof, shaped like a ship under sail, this interesting museum holds the treasures salvaged from the wreck of the HMS *Pandora,* which sank in 1792 and lies 33m (108 ft.) underwater on the edge of the Great Barrier Reef. This is the highlight of the museum; the exhibit's centerpiece is a full-scale replica of a section of the ship's bow and its 17m-high (56-ft.) foremast, crafted by local shipwrights. The exhibition traces the ship's voyage and the retrieval of the sunken treasure—make sure you watch the film about the salvage. The museum has five other galleries, including a hands-on science center; a natural history display; one dedicated to north Queensland's indigenous heritage, with items from Torres Strait and the South Sea Islands; and stories from people of different cultures about the settlement of north Queensland. Another is devoted to touring exhibitions, which change every 3 months. Allow 2 to 3 hours.

70–102 Flinders St. (next to Reef HQ). www.mtq.qm.qld.gov.au. ⓒ **07/4726 0600.** A$15 adults, A$8.80 children 4–16, A$38 families of 5. Daily 9:30am–5pm. Closed Good Friday, Christmas Day, Boxing Day (Dec 26), and Anzac Day (Apr 25).

Reef HQ Aquarium ★★★ AQUARIUM Reef HQ is the education center for the Great Barrier Reef Marine Park Authority's headquarters and the largest living-coral-reef aquarium in the world. The highlight is walking through a 20m-long (66-ft.) transparent acrylic tunnel, gazing into a giant predator tank where sharks cruise silently. A replica of the wreck of the SS *Yongala* provides an eerie backdrop for blacktip and whitetip reef sharks, leopard sharks, and nurse sharks, sharing their 750,000-liter (195,000-gal.) home with stingrays, giant trevally, and a green turtle. Watching them feed is quite a spectacle. The tunnel also reveals the 2.5-million-liter (650,000-gal.) coral-reef exhibit, with its hard and soft corals providing a home for thousands of fish, giant clams, sea cucumbers, sea stars, and other creatures. During the scuba show, the divers speak to you over an intercom while they swim with the sharks and feed the fish. Other highlights include a touch tank and a wild-sea-turtle rehabilitation center, plus interactive activities for children. Reef HQ is an easy walk from the city center.

2–68 Flinders St. www.reefhq.com.au. ⓒ **07/4750 0800.** A$28 adults, A$14 children 5–16, A$42–A$70 families. Daily 9:30am–5pm. Closed Christmas Day, Anzac Day (Apr 25), and Australia Day (Jan 26). All buses from the City Mall stop nearby.

Day Trips from Townsville to the Reef

Most boats visiting the Reef from Townsville are live-aboard vessels that make trips of 2 or more days, designed for serious divers. **Adrenalin Dive** (www.adrenalindive.com.au; ⓒ **07/4724 0600**) operates day trips on which you can make introductory dives for A$80 for the first one and A$120 for two; certified divers also dive for A$80, all gear included. The cruise costs A$249 for adults and A$199 for children 6 to 12. The price includes lunch, morning and afternoon tea, and snorkel gear. Cruises depart Townsville at 7am, with a pickup at Magnetic Island en route at 7:50am, on Tuesday, Thursday, Friday, and Sunday (and on Mon during high season, June–Sept). They also run day trips to the *Yongala* wreck, in which you will do two dives on the *Yongala*. The cost is A$329, including all gear, and A$10 per dive for a guide, if you have logged fewer than 15 dives.

Day Trip from Townsville to Magnetic Island ★★

Magnetic Island—or just "Maggie"—is a delightful 51-sq.-km (20-sq.-mile) national-park island 20 minutes from Townsville by ferry. About 2,500 people live here, and it's popular with Aussies, who love its holiday atmosphere. Small settlements dot the coastline, offering a good range of restaurants and laid-back cafes. Most people come for the 20 or so pristine and uncrowded bays and white beaches, but hikers, botanists, and birders may want to explore the eucalyptus woods, patches of gully rainforest, and granite tors. The island got its name when Captain Cook thought its "magnetic" rocks were interfering with his compass readings. It is famous for koalas, easily spotted in roadside gum trees; ask a local to point you to the nearest colony. Rock wallabies are often seen in the early morning.

7

CAIRNS & THE GREAT BARRIER REEF | Townsville & Magnetic Island

The island is not on the Great Barrier Reef, but surrounding waters are part of the Great Barrier Reef Marine Park. There is good reef snorkeling at Florence Bay on the southern edge; Arthur Bay on the northern edge; and Geoffrey Bay, where you can even reef-walk at low tide. (Wear sturdy shoes and do not walk directly on coral to avoid damaging it.) First-time snorkelers will have an easy time of it in Maggie's weak currents and softly sloping beaches. Outside the stinger season (Oct–Apr), there is good swimming at any number of bays all around the island. Reef-free Alma Bay, with its shady lawns and playground, is a good choice for families; Rocky Bay is a small, secluded cove.

ESSENTIALS

ARRIVING Sealink (www.sealinkqld.com.au; ℭ **07/4726 0800**) runs 19 round-trip ferry services a day from Townsville's Breakwater terminal on Sir Leslie Thiess Drive. Round-trip tickets are A$33 for adults, A$17 for children 5 to 14, and A$76 for families of five. The trip takes about 20 minutes.

VISITOR INFORMATION There is no information center on Magnetic Island, but you can check **www.magneticinformer.com.au** online. Also, stop off at the **Townsville Bulletin Square Visitor Information Centre** (ℭ **1800/801 902** in Australia, or 07/4721 3660) before you cross to the island. It's open daily (Mon–Fri 9am–5pm, Sat–Sun 9am–1pm).

GETTING AROUND You can take your car on the ferry, or hire a car on the island. For years, the classic way of getting around the island was in an open-sided minimoke (similar to a golf cart) from the many rental outfits on the island. Minimokes are unlikely to go much over 60kmph (36 mph). **Tropical Topless Car Rentals** (www.tropicaltopless.com; ℭ **07/4758 1111**) still rents them—and other vehicles—from around A$65 to A$80 a day. **Magnetic Island Bus Services** (www.sunbus.com.au; ℭ **07/4778 5130**) will get you anywhere on the island for A$3.60 adults and A$1.80 kids age 5 to 15 (or less, depending on where you want to go).

EXPLORING MAGNETIC ISLAND

There is no end to the things you can do on Maggie—snorkeling, swimming in one of a dozen or more bays, catamaran sailing, waterskiing, parasailing, horseback riding on the beach, biking, tennis or golf, scuba diving, sea kayaking, sailing or cruising around the island, taking a Harley-Davidson tour, fishing, and more. Equipment for all these activities is for rent on the island.

One of the best, and most popular, of the island's 20km (13 miles) of hiking trails is the **Nelly Bay–Arcadia trail,** a one-way journey of 5km (3 miles) that takes 2½ hours. The first 45 minutes, starting in rainforest and climbing to a saddle between Nelly Bay and Horseshoe, are the most interesting. Another excellent walk is the 2km (1¼-mile) trail to the **Forts,** remnants of World War II defenses, which, not surprisingly, have great 360-degree sea views. The best koala spotting is on the track up to the Forts off Horseshoe Bay Road. Carry water when walking—some bays and hiking trails are not near shops.

If you feel like splurging, consider a jet-ski circumnavigation of the island with **Magnetic Jet Ski Tours** (www.facebook.com/MagneticJet; ℭ **07/4778 5533**). The 3-hour tour on a two-seat jet ski costs A$395 per ski rental, and a 2-hour tour of the northern side of the island costs A$200 per ski. They'll kit you out with wetsuits, life jackets, and tinted goggles for the ride. Keep your eyes peeled for dolphins, dugongs (manatees), sea turtles, and humpback whales in season. Tours depart from "the Red Shed" on Pacific Drive, Horseshoe Bay. Minimum age is 6 years.

Bungalow Bay Koala Village (www.bungalowbay.com.au; ℭ **07/4778 5577**), on Horseshoe Bay Road, Horseshoe Bay, is a backpacker hostel that has a wildlife sanctuary on its 6.5 hectares (16 acres) of bushland, home to rock wallabies, curlews, lorikeets, and koalas. Two-hour tours of the koala park run at 10am, noon, and 2:30pm, and begin at the reception desk. The first hour is within the wildlife park, where you can wrap yourself in a python, pet a lizard, hold a small saltwater crocodile, and get up close with a koala. The second hour is a guided bush walk to explore nearby habitats of eucalyptus forest, wetlands, mangroves, or coastal dunes, and to learn about the history of the traditional owners, the Wulgurukaba people. Entry to the park costs A$29 adults, A$25 backpackers or students, A$13 children 4 to 16, or A$80 for families of five. Koala holding costs A$18 including a souvenir photo, with proceeds supporting Magnetic Island wildlife care groups.

THE WHITSUNDAYS ★★★

Airlie Beach: 640km (397 miles) S of Cairns; 1,146km (711 miles) N of Brisbane

A day's drive or a 1-hour flight south of Cairns brings you to the dazzling collection of 74 islands known as the Whitsundays. No more than 3 nautical miles (3.4km/2 miles) separate most of the islands, and altogether they represent countless bays, beaches, dazzling coral reefs, and fishing spots that make up one fabulous Great Barrier Reef playground. Sharing the same latitude as Rio de Janeiro and Hawaii, the water is at least 72°F (22°C) year-round, the sun shines most of the year, and in winter you'll require only a light jacket at night.

Most of the islands consist of densely rainforested national-park land. The surrounding waters belong to the Great Barrier Reef Marine Park. But don't expect palm trees and coconuts—these islands are covered with dry-looking pine and eucalyptus forests full of dense undergrowth, and rocky coral coves far outnumber the few sandy beaches. Only a few islands have resorts, but all offer just about every activity you could ever want—snorkeling, scuba diving, sailing, reef fishing, water-skiing, jet-skiing, parasailing, sea kayaking, hiking, rides over the coral in semisubmersibles, fish feeding, putt-putting around in dinghies to secluded beaches, tennis, and more. Accommodations range from small, low-key wilderness retreats to midrange family havens to some of Australia's most luxurious resorts.

The Secret of the Seasons

High season in the Whitsundays coincides with school vacations, which occur in January, in mid-April, from late June to early July, from late September to early October, and in late December. The Aussie winter, June through August, is popular, too. You have to book months ahead to get high-season accommodations, but any other time you can indeed find some good deals: Specials on accommodations, sailing trips, day cruises, and diving excursions fairly leap off the blackboards outside the tour-booking agents in Airlie Beach.

The village of **Airlie Beach** ★★ is the center of the action on the mainland. But the islands themselves are just as good a stepping stone to the outer Great Barrier Reef as Cairns, and some people consider them better, because you don't have to make the 90-minute trip to the Reef before you hit coral. Just about any Whitsunday island has fringing reef around its shores, and there are good snorkeling reefs between the islands, a quick boat ride away from your island or mainland accommodations. The reef here is just as good as off Cairns, with many drop-offs and drift dives, a dazzling range of corals, and a rich array of marine life, including whales, mantas, shark, reef fish, morays, turtles, and pelagics. Visibility is usually around 15m to 23m (49–75 ft.).

A popular reef for both snorkeling and diving is **Blue Pearl Bay** ★★ off Hayman Island, which has loads of corals and some gorgonian fans in its gullies, and heaps of reef fish, including Maori wrasse and sometimes manta rays. It's a good place to make an introductory dive, walking right in off the beach. A little island commonly called **Bali Hai Island** ★★, between Hayman and Hook islands, is a great place to be left to your own devices. You'll see soft-shelf and wall coral, tame Maori wrasse, octopus, turtles, reef shark, various kinds of rays including mantas, eagles, and cow-tails, plus loads of fish.

Note: In early 2017, the Whitsunday region took a direct hit from Cyclone Debbie, which caused extensive damage to some islands and to Airlie Beach. While much of this was quickly rectified, at press time the resorts on Daydream and Hayman islands were still closed for renovations, but expected to be re-opened by the end of 2018.

Essentials
ARRIVING
BY PLANE   There are two air routes into the Whitsundays: Great Barrier Reef Airport on Hamilton Island and Whitsunday Coast Airport at Proserpine on the mainland. **Qantas** (www.qantas.com.au; ✆ **131 313** in Australia) flies direct to Hamilton Island from Cairns, Brisbane, and Sydney. **Virgin Australia** (www.virginaustralia.com; ✆ **136 789** in Australia) flies to Proserpine direct from Brisbane, with connections from other capitals, and direct from Brisbane, Melbourne, and Sydney to Hamilton Island. **Jetstar** (www.jetstar.com.au; ✆ **131 538** in Australia) flies from Brisbane to Proserpine, and from

Melbourne to Hamilton Island. If you stay on an island, the resort may book your launch transfers automatically. These may appear on your airline ticket, in which case your luggage will be checked through to the island. **Whitsunday Transit** (www.whitsundaytransit.com.au; ✆ **07/4946 1800**) provides airport transfers from Proserpine to Airlie Beach for A$22 adults, A$12 children 4 to 14 one-way, or A$36 adults and A$20 children round-trip.

BY TRAIN Several **Queensland Rail** (www.queenslandrailtravel.com.au; ✆ **1300/131 722** in Australia) long-distance trains stop at Proserpine every week. The one-way fare from Brisbane on the Spirit of Queensland is A$289 for a premium economy seat. There is a bus link to Airlie Beach; book through Queensland Rail when booking the train.

BY BUS **Greyhound Australia** (www.greyhound.com.au; ✆ **1300/473 946** in Australia) operates plentiful daily services to Airlie Beach from Brisbane (trip time: around 18 hr.) and Cairns (trip time: 11 hr.). The fare is around A$250 from Brisbane, A$110 from Cairns.

BY CAR The Bruce Highway leads south from Cairns or north from Brisbane to Proserpine, 26km (16 miles) inland from Airlie Beach. Take the Whitsunday turnoff to reach Airlie Beach and Shute Harbour, where most day-trip and charter boats depart. (There are several car-storage facilities at Shute Harbour if you're planning to go to the islands.) Allow a good 8 hours to drive from Cairns.

VISITOR INFORMATION

Contact **Tourism Whitsundays** (www.tourismwhitsundays.com.au; ✆ **07/4945 3967**) for information, or pick up brochures from the many private booking agents lining the main street of Airlie Beach. All stock a vast range of cruise, tour, and hotel information, and make bookings free of charge. All have similar material, but because some represent certain boats exclusively, and because prices can vary a little from one to the next, it pays to shop around.

GETTING AROUND THE WHITSUNDAYS

BY BOAT Airlie Beach has three different harbor areas: **Shute Harbour,** 10km east of Airlie Beach on Shute Harbour Road, where ferries, charter yachts and water taxis depart; **Abell Point Marina,** where you'll find sailing yachts, luxury superyachts and some day tour operators, 15 minutes' walk west from Airlie Beach; and **Port of Airlie,** a marina complex that is also home to the **Cruise Whitsundays** day-tour boats. **Cruise Whitsundays** (www.cruisewhitsundays.com.au; ✆ **07/4846 7000**) operates Resort Connections, providing transfer services between its maritime terminal at Port of Airlie and Hamilton Island Airport, Whitsunday Coast Airport at Proserpine, and Shute Harbour (as well as Daydream Island when the resort re-opens).

Island ferries and Great Barrier Reef cruises leave from the **Port of Airlie,** on The Cove Road, on the edge of Airlie Beach's shopping strip and an easy walk from most hotels in the town center. Some tour-boat operators and bareboat charters anchor at **Abell Point Marina,** a 15-minute walk west from Airlie Beach. Most tour-boat operators pick up guests free from Airlie Beach hotels and at some or all island resorts.

BY BUS   Whitsunday Transit (www.whitsundaytransit.com.au; 𝄐 **07/4946 1800**) meets all flights at Proserpine and provides door-to-door transfers to Proserpine, Airlie Beach, and Shute Harbour. It also runs buses regularly between Proserpine, Airlie Beach, and Shute Harbour.

BY CAR   Avis (𝄐 **07/4967 7188**) and **Hertz** (𝄐 **07/4946 4687**) have outlets in Airlie Beach and Proserpine Airport (telephone numbers serve both locations). **Budget** (𝄐 **07/4945 1024**) has an office at Proserpine Airport and **Europcar** (𝄐 **07/4946 4133**) has an office at Airlie Beach.

Where to Stay in the Whitsundays

The advantages of staying on the mainland are cheaper accommodations, a choice of restaurants, the freedom to visit a different island each day, and a bevy of activities such as jet skiing, kayaking, parasailing, catamaran sailing, and windsurfing.

But if you are here it would be a shame not to spend at least a couple of days soaking up the island life. By staying on an island you get swimming, snorkeling, bushwalking, and a huge range of watersports, many of them free, right outside your door. You won't be isolated if you stay on an island, because most Great Barrier Reef cruise boats, sail-and-snorkel yacht excursions, Whitehaven Beach cruises, dive boats, fishing tour vessels, and so on stop at the island resorts every day or on a frequent basis. Be warned, however, that once you're "captive" on an island, you may be slugged with high food and drink prices. And although most island resorts offer non-motorized watersports (such as windsurfing and sailing) free of charge, you will pay for activities that use fuel, such as parasailing, water-skiing, and dinghy rental.

AIRLIE BEACH

Coral Sea Resort ★★★   In Airlie Beach's best location, on the edge of Paradise Point, this resort is one of the best places to stay on the Whitsunday mainland. It suits everyone from honeymooners to families, and although it's relatively sprawling, the design is such that you can easily feel you're alone. The Coral Sea suites are divine, complete with a Jacuzzi and double hammock on the balcony. There are four styles of suites, plus apartments and family units. Bayview suites have a Jacuzzi inside. There's a nice nautical theme throughout the place, with historic sailing images on the walls, lots of blue, and a scattering of yachting memorabilia and artifacts. It's a 3-minute walk along the waterfront to Airlie Beach village.

25 Oceanview Ave. www.coralsearesort.com. 𝄐 **1800/075 061** in Australia, or 07/4964 1300. 78 units. A$245–A$275 double; A$295–A$345 suite; A$338 family room; A$385 1-bedroom apt; A$395 2-bedroom apt; A$630 3-bedroom apt; A$465–A$875 penthouse. Free parking. **Amenities:** Restaurant; bar; babysitting; bikes; exercise room; 25m (82-ft.) outdoor pool; room service; spa; watersports rental; free Wi-Fi.

Safety in the Water

Deadly **marine stingers** may frequent the shorelines of the Whitsundays from October through April. The best place to swim is in the beachfront Airlie Beach lagoon. The rivers in these parts are home to dangerous **saltwater crocodiles** (which mostly live in fresh water, contrary to their name), so don't swim in streams, rivers, or water holes.

Mantra Boathouse Apartments ★★   Right on the waterfront in the Port of Airlie development that opened in 2015, these smart and spacious two- and three-bedroom apartments have everything you need. Large balconies open out to views over the marina and the Coral Sea. There is no restaurant, but downstairs in the Port of Airlie development are three dining options (at last count) and you are only a 5 minutes' walk from Airlie Beach town center. But you're also not far from nature; I woke to find a row of half a dozen sulphur-crested cockatoos lined up on my balcony rail!

33 Port Drive, Port of Airlie. www.mantra.com.au. © **131 517** in Australia, or 07/4841 4100. 56 units. A$315 2-bedroom apt (sleeps 4); A$440 3-bedroom apt (sleeps 6). Free secure parking. **Amenities:** Outdoor pool; tennis court; kids' playground; Wi-Fi A$23/24 hr.

ISLAND RESORTS

Daydream Island Resort ★★   One of the Whitsundays' oldest and most popular resorts was badly damaged when Cyclone Debbie hit the island in early 2017. A planned major renovation under new owners was brought forward and scheduled for completion in late 2018, when the resort will reopen. Features such as the outdoor cinema and the kids' club have always made a hit with families, while pleasure-seekers head to the 16 therapy rooms at the **Rejuvenation Spa.** Rooms are large, with uninterrupted ocean views. The "village" at the southern end of the island, a short stroll along the boardwalk from the resort, has shops, cafes, a pool and bar, and a tavern. A rainforest walk stretches almost the entire length of the kilometer-long (just over half a mile) island. Check the website for updates.

Daydream Island (40km/25 mi NE of Shute Harbour). www.daydreamisland.com. © **1800/075 040** in Australia, or 07/3259 2350. 296 units. Closed through late 2018; rates for reopening not available at press time. **Amenities:** 3 restaurants, 3 bars; gym; 3 Jacuzzis; kids' club; 3 freshwater outdoor pools (1 heated); sauna; spa; 2 lit tennis courts; watersports; free Wi-Fi.

Hamilton Island ★★   More a vacation village than a single resort, Hamilton has the widest range of activities, accommodations styles, and restaurants of any Great Barrier Reef island resort, and it's ideal for families. Accommodations options include extra-large rooms and suites in the high-rise hotel; high-rise one-bedroom apartments; Polynesian-style bungalows in tropical gardens (ask for one away from the road for real privacy); and

Snorkeling off Hamilton Island.

glamorous rooms in the two-story, adults-only **Beach Club** (with a personal "host" to cater to your every whim, plus a restaurant, lounge, and pool for exclusive use of Beach Club guests); as well as one-, two-, three-, and four-bedroom apartments and villas, including villas at the waterfront Yacht Club. The best sea views are from the second-floor Beach Club rooms, from floors 5 to 18 of the **Reef View Hotel,** and from most apartments and villas. If your budget is huge, the poshest part of the resort is the ultraluxe **qualia,** an exclusive, adults-only retreat on the northern part of the island. It has 60 one-bedroom pavilions, each with a private swimming pool and a guest pavilion. There's a spa and two restaurants reserved just for qualia guests.

Most of the accommodations are set around a large free-form pool and swim-up bar and the curve of Catseye Beach. Nearby is a marina village with cafes, restaurants, shops, and a yacht club. Hamilton offers a huge range of watersports, fishing trips, cruises, speedboat rides, go-karts, a "wire flyer" flying-fox hang glider, a shooting range, mini-golf, an aquatic driving range, beach barbecue safaris, hiking trails, a wildlife sanctuary (you may have seen Oprah here, cuddling a koala), and an extensive daily activities program.

There are no cars on the island, and because a steep hill splits the resort, the best way to get around is on the free bus service, which operates on three loops around the island from 7am to 11pm, or by rented golf buggy (A$49/1 hr.; A$87/24 hr.). The biggest drawback is that just about every activity costs extra, so you are constantly adding to your bill. To get away from the main resort area, hit the beach or the hiking trails—most of the 750-hectare (1,853-acre) island is virgin bushland.

Hamilton Island (16km/10 miles SE of Shute Harbour). www.hamiltonisland.com.au or www.qualia.com.au. © **137 333** in Australia, or 02/9007 0009 (Sydney reservations office), or 866/209 0891 toll-free or 424/206 5274 for North American inquiries. 880 units. A$400 Palm Bungalow; A$370–A$480 double; A$690–A$1,330 suite; A$710 Beach Club double; A$1,250–A$1,900 qualia; A$4,550 qualia house. **Amenities:** 12 restaurants, 7 bars; babysitting; child-care center for kids 6 weeks to 14 years (3 separate age groups); mini-golf and driving range; health club; 7 outdoor pools; room service; tennis courts; free Wi-Fi.

Where to Eat in the Whitsundays

AIRLIE BEACH

Hemingway's ★★ CONTEMPORARY In homage to the literary great Ernest Hemingway, this waterfront dining spot has references to his life and work throughout the decor and the menu. Oysters and seafood feature heavily, and there are Cuban and South African influences as well. For dessert, try the Café Martini—smoked coffee, ricotta, caramel, Frangelico, and biscotti. And, of course, the cocktail list has a Hemingway. A garden bar menu is available from 4pm (just in time for sunset cocktails). This restaurant is deservedly notching up awards; check it out!

60 Shingley Dr. (at Abell Point Marina), Airlie Beach. www.hemingwaysairliebeach.com. au. © **07/4946 4277.** Main courses A$24–A$42. Tues-Sun 4–10pm.

Mangrove Jacks Café/Bar ★★ PIZZA/CAFE FARE Bareboat sailors, local sugar farmers, Sydney yuppies, and European backpackers all flock to this big, open-fronted sports bar and restaurant. The mood is upbeat and pleasantly casual, the surroundings are spick-and-span, and the food passes muster. Wood-fired pizzas with trendy toppings are the specialty. There is no table service; place your order at the bar and collect your food when your number is called.

In the Airlie Beach Hotel, 16 The Esplanade (enter from Shute Harbour Rd.), Airlie Beach. © **07/4964 1888.** Main courses A$17–A$30. Mon–Fri 11:30am–2:30pm and 5:30–9:30pm (to 10pm on Fri); Sat 11:30am–10pm; Sun 11:30am–9:30pm.

Whitsunday Sailing Club ★★ CONTEMPORARY This casual club is a popular hangout for locals, with one of the best views in the Whitsundays, overlooking Pioneer Bay and the islands. The menu includes light meals such as burgers or a Caesar salad; for something heartier go for "reef & beef" (a steak topped with local seafood) or fish 'n' chips. Great for drinks at sunset.

Airlie Point (enter from The Esplanade), Airlie Beach. www.whitsundaysailingclub.com. au. © **07/4946 6138.** Main courses A$17–A$31. Daily 11:30am–2.30pm and 5:30–8:30pm.

Exploring the Whitsundays

The little town of Airlie Beach, perched on the edge of the Coral Sea with views across Pioneer Bay and the Whitsunday Passage, is the focal point of activity on the Whitsunday mainland. Airlie Beach has a massive beachfront artificial lagoon, with sandy beaches and landscaped parkland, which solves the problem of where to swim in stinger season. The lagoon is the size of about six full-size Olympic swimming pools, set in 4 hectares (10 acres) of botanic gardens, with a children's pool, plenty of shade, barbecues, picnic shelters, toilets, showers, and parking. For a bird's-eye view of it all, head to the Lions Lookout.

Getting out on the water is the most important thing here. Countless opportunities are offered, with the focus firmly on sailing, snorkeling, and diving.

Cruises and yachts depart from the Port of Airlie, or from Shute Harbour, a 10-minute drive south on Shute Harbour Road.

REEF CRUISES

Cruise Whitsundays (www.cruisewhitsundays.com.au; ✆ **07/4946 4662**) makes daily trips to Hardy Reef in a high-speed, air-conditioned catamaran. The boat has a bar, and a biologist gives a marine ecology talk en route. You anchor at the massive Reefworld pontoon, which was built to hold up to 600 people, and spend up to 3½ hours on the Reef. The day trip costs A$259 for adults, A$125 for children 4 to 14. Guided snorkel safaris cost A$59 extra for adults and A$35 for children. You can book dives on board for A$139 for first-time divers and A$99 for certified divers (A$59 for a second dive). Cruises depart at 8am from the Port of Airlie, picking up at Hamilton Island at 9am. Passengers from other islands take the ferry to Hamilton to board there.

A unique experience is Cruise Whitsundays' **ReefSleep,** during which you spend the night on the pontoon. You travel with the day-trippers, but when they leave at 3pm you will be with a maximum of nine people. This gives you a fabulous chance to snorkel at night when the coral is luminescent in the moonlight and nocturnal sea creatures get busy. The trip includes 2 full days on the Reef, all meals, and the chance to sleep on the upper deck under the stars in a swag (a type of outdoor sleeping bag). The cost is A$525 for a double swag or A$675 for a single. This is an experience only for those over 12 years old.

In and around the Whitsunday islands, you can visit many excellent dive sites close to shore. **Mantaray Charters** (www.mantaraycharters.com; ✆ **07/4948 1117**), based at Abell Point Marina, runs day tours to Whitehaven Beach and gives you the chance to dive near Hayman Island or Hook Island. Tours are limited to 36 passengers and leave at 8am, returning around 4:30pm. The cost is A$197 adults, A$98 kids age 4 to 12, and A$555 for a family of four. The cost includes lunch, snacks, and all equipment, whether you are diving or snorkeling. You'll pay A$100 for an introductory dive or A$80 if you're certified. Second dives cost A$60.

Hitting the Sand at Whitehaven Beach

The 6km (3¾-mile) stretch of pure-white silica sand on **Whitehaven Beach** ★★ will leave you in rapture. The beach, on uninhabited Whitsunday Island, does not boast a lot of coral, but the swimming is good and the forested shore is beautiful. Take a book and chill out. Some sailboat day trips visit it, as do some motorized vessels. A half-day trip with **Cruise Whitsundays** (www.cruise whitsundays.com; ✆ **07/4946 4662**) costs A$109 for adults and A$55 for children age 4 to 14 and gives you around 2 hours on the beach. You can travel in the morning (leaving the Port of Airlie at 7am) or in the afternoon (departing at noon), with pick-ups at Hamilton Island and Daydream Island on the way. Full-day trips combine Whitehaven Beach with other islands on some tours. **Air Whitsunday** (www.airwhitsun day.com.au; ✆ **07/4946 9111**) offers seaplane flights to Whitehaven Beach for A$295 adults or A$250 children, with a glass of bubbles when you land.

OUTRIGGER sailing

For a different look at the Whitsunday Coast, take a 90-minute tour with **Whitsunday Sailing Outrigger** (www.whitsundaysailingoutrigger.com; ℘ **0402/473 059** mobile) to skim along the water aboard Stephen and Michelle Lynes's lovely craft *Ohana*. With only four guests on board, this is a terrific, personal experience. Tours depart daily at 9 and 11am, and 1pm and cost A$60 per person (age 7 and older). A 2-hour tour to Pigeon Island costs A$90 and sunset champagne tours cost A$80. Bookings are essential.

SAILING & SNORKELING TRIPS

A journey on one of the many yachts offering 3-day, 2-night sailing adventures is a great way to see the islands. You can learn to sail or get involved with sailing the boat as much or as little as you want, snorkel to your heart's content over one dazzling reef after another, beachcomb, explore national-park trails, stop at secluded bays, swim, sunbathe, and generally have a laid-back good time. A few companies offer introductory and qualified scuba diving for an extra cost per dive. Most boats carry a maximum of 12 passengers, so the atmosphere is always friendly and fun. The food is generally good, the showers are usually hot, and you sleep in comfortable but small berths off the galley. Some have small private twin or double cabins.

Prices usually include all meals, Marine Park entrance fees, snorkel gear, and transfers to the departure point (Abell Point Marina or Shute Harbour). In the off season, the boats compete fiercely for passengers; you'll see signboards on the main street in Airlie Beach advertising standby deals.

Prosail (www.prosail.com.au; ℘ **1800/810 116** in Australia, or 07/4946 7533) runs sailing trips through the Great Barrier Reef Marine Park. All trips include sailing, snorkeling, scuba diving, and bushwalking, and you can sail on mega-yachts such as the *Condor, Broomstick,* and *Hammer.* A 2-day overnight trip costs A$349 per person.

These kinds of trips are a cheaper alternative to "bareboating" (skippering your own yacht)—which is a hugely popular thing to do, despite the cost. If you are confident about sailing yourself—and most yacht-charter companies in the islands will want one person on the boat to have a little experience—you do not need a license, and sailing is surprisingly easy in these uncrowded waters, where the channels are deep and the seas are protected from big swells by the Great Barrier Reef. The 74 islands are so close to one another that one is always in sight, and safe anchorages are everywhere. But for extra reassurance, the company may require you to take a skipper along at an extra cost of around A$400 per day (plus meals) if you want them to stay with you. Before departure, the company provides a thorough 2- to 3-hour briefing and easy-to-read maps marking channels, anchorage points, and the very few dangerous reefs. Your charter company will radio in once or twice a day to check that you're still afloat, and you can contact them anytime for advice.

Heart Reef

The iconic image of the Great Barrier Reef is the stunning heart-shaped reef called—yes, **Heart Reef.** But Heart Reef is not a place you can visit; it is protected by law and you can neither swim nor snorkel there. In any case, the best way to see this tiny reef's perfect shape is from the air. There are many helicopter or seaplane options available for that perfect photographic opportunity (or, of course, if you are planning a mid-air proposal). A 1-hour seaplane flight over the Great Barrier Reef costs A$330 adults and A$290 children with **Air Whitsunday** (www.airwhitsunday.com.au; ☏ 07/4946 9111), which offers a large range of tours, including seaplane flights to a Reef pontoon to snorkel for a couple of hours.

You can buy your own provisions or have the charter company stock the boat at an extra cost of about A$30 per person per day. Most operators will load a windsurfer, fishing tackle, and scuba-diving equipment on request, for an extra fee if they are not standard.

In peak season, you may have to charter the boat for a week. At other times, most companies impose a minimum of 5 days, but many will rent for 3 nights if you ask, rather than let a vessel sit idle. In peak season (mid-Sept to mid-Oct, and Christmas to mid-Jan), expect to pay A$750 to A$985 per night for a standard four- to six-berth yacht, more if you want something luxurious. Rates in the off season (mid-Jan to end of Mar), and even in one of the Whitsundays' busiest holiday times, June through August, will be anywhere from A$100 to A$200 less. If you are prepared to book within 14 days of when you want to sail, the deals can be even better; you should be able to find a boat that late in the off season. You may be asked to post a credit card bond of up to A$2,000. Fuel and park fees are extra, and mooring fees apply if you want to stop at one of the island resorts overnight. A number of bareboat-charter companies offer "sail-'n'-stay" packages that combine a few days of sailing with a few days at an island resort.

Most bareboat charter companies will make complete holiday arrangements for you in the islands, including accommodations, transfers, tours, and sporting activities. Most companies operate out of Airlie Beach, Hamilton Island, or both. Well-known operators include **Whitsunday Rent-A-Yacht** (www.rentayacht.com.au; ☏ **1800/075 000** in Australia, or 07/4946 9232); **Queensland Yacht Charters** (www.yachtcharters.com.au; ☏ **1800/075 013** in Australia, or 07/4946 7400); and **Sunsail** (www.sunsail.com.au; ☏ **1800/803 988** in Australia, or 02/8912 7040).

SOUTHERN GREAT BARRIER REEF REGION ★★

Off this stretch of the Queensland coast is the southernmost part of the Great Barrier Reef, where you will find the spectacular **Heron Island,** whose reefs

Page 228

are a source of enchantment for divers and snorkelers. Its waters boast 21 dive sites, and in summer, large turtles lumber ashore to nest on its beaches.

Off the small town of **Bundaberg** is another tiny coral cay, **Lady Elliot Island ★★**, a nesting site for tens of thousands of seabirds and home to a first-rate fringing reef. Bundaberg's major attraction is a mainland loggerhead turtle rookery that draws large crowds in summer.

Gladstone: Gateway to Heron Island

Gladstone: 550km (341 miles) N of Brisbane; 1,162km (720 miles) S of Cairns

The industrial port town of Gladstone is the departure point for beautiful Heron Island. Gladstone is on the coast 21km (13 miles) off the Bruce Highway. Most flights to Gladstone arrive in time to connect with the ferry to Heron Island, but if you need to stay overnight, a couple of good, centrally located options are **Mercure Gladstone** (www.accorhotels.com.au; *℃* **07/4979 8200**) and **Rydges Gladstone** (www.rydges.com; *℃* **07/4970 0000**).

ESSENTIALS
Arriving
BY PLANE   Qantas (www.qantas.com.au; *℃* **131 313** in Australia) and **Virgin Australia** (www.virginaustalia.com.au; *℃* **136 789** in Australia) both have daily flights from Brisbane.

BY TRAIN   Queensland Rail (www.queenslandrailtravel.com.au; *℃* **1800/872 467** in Queensland) operates trains to Gladstone from Brisbane and Cairns most days. The economy fare from Brisbane is A$119 on the high-speed Tilt Train (trip time: 6 hr.).

BY BUS   Greyhound Australia (www.greyhound.com.au; *℃* **1300/473 946** in Australia) operates daily coaches to Gladstone on the Brisbane-Cairns run. The fare is A$154 from Brisbane (trip time: 11½ hr.), around A$208 from Cairns (trip time: 20 hr.).

GETTING AROUND
Avis (*℃* **07/4978 2633**), **Budget** (*℃* **07/4972 8488**), **Europcar** (*℃* **07/4978 7787**), and **Hertz** (*℃* **07/4978 6899**) have offices in Gladstone.

VISITOR INFORMATION
The **Gladstone Visitor Information Centre** is in the ferry terminal at Gladstone Marina, 72 Bryan Jordan Dr., (www.gladstoneregion.info; *℃* **07/4972 9000**). It's open 8:30am to 4:30pm Monday through Friday and 9am to 1pm Saturday and Sunday. Closed Christmas Day.

Heron Island ★★★

72km (45 miles) NE of Gladstone

Heron Island is often referred to as "the jewel of the Reef." And rightly so. The difference between Heron and other islands is that once there, you are right on the Reef. Step off the beach and you enter magnificent fields of coral that seem to stretch for miles. And the myriad life forms that abound here are accessible to everyone through diving, snorkeling, or reef walks at low tide.

COAST VILLAGES: 1770 and agnes water

About 50km (31½ miles) from Gladstone, on the coast, are the lovely coastal hamlets of **Agnes Water ★★** and **1770 ★** (so named by British explorer Captain James Cook the year he mapped the coastline of Australia). These tiny places are well worth the detour. Stop in at the **Agnes Water/1770 Visitor Information Centre,** 71 Springs Rd., Agnes Water (② **07/4902 1533**), to get the low-down on things to do in the region. The info center is open Monday through Friday 9am to 5pm and weekends from 10am to 2pm; it's closed Christmas Day and Good Friday.

I highly recommend two tours in this area. The **1770 LARC! Tours** (www.1770 larctours.com.au; ② **07/4974 9422**) will see you ride high on a bright pink amphibious craft that gives access to land and sea to explore the waterways and coast of 1770. Owner Neil Mergard and his team provide fascinating and entertaining commentary about the land and environment and you'll come away with a new appreciation of this part of Australia. One-hour afternoon tours cost A$40 adults, A$18 kids 5 to 16; a full-day tour costs A$160 adults, A$99 children.

Another way of getting out on the water is on a kayak tour with Simon and Janina of **1770 Liquid Adventures** (www.1770liquidadventures.com.au; ② **0428/956 630** mobile). A 2-hour tour costs A$50 per person; 2½-hour sunset tours cost A$55. You might spot dolphins, and may also have the company of Bailey, their golden Labrador, who rides in the lead kayak.

There has been a resort on Heron since 1932, and in 1943 the island became a national park. An experience of a lifetime is almost guaranteed at any time of year, particularly if you love turtles—Heron is a haven for giant green and loggerhead turtles. Resort guests gather on the beach from late November to February to watch the female turtles lay eggs, and from February to mid-April to see the hatched babies scuttle down the sand to the water. Every night during the season, volunteer guides from the island's University of Queensland research station tag and measure the turtles before they return to the water. Only 1 in 5,000 hatchlings will live to return in about 50 years to lay its own eggs. Humpback whales also pass through from June through September.

Three days on Heron will give you plenty of time. The island is so small that you can walk around it at a leisurely pace in about half an hour. One of the first things to do is to take advantage of the organized activities that the resort offers several times a day, to give guests flexibility in planning their time. Book your activities at the resort information center. Snorkeling and reef walking are major occupations for visitors—if they're not diving, that is. The island is home to 21 of the world's most stunning dive sites.

Guided walks provide another way to explore the island. Walks include a visit to the island's research station. As for the reef walk, just borrow a pair of sand shoes, a balance pole, and a viewing bucket, and head off with a guide at low tide. The walk can take up to 90 minutes.

Heron is also home to colonies of mutton birds; be warned, they can be particularly noisy during their breeding and mating season, from November to

January. They also create a fairly . . . shall I say . . . distinctive smell (you get used to it, but some people find it highly offensive). That's nature for you.

ARRIVING

A **170-seater launch** currently departs Gladstone Marina, Bryan Jordan Drive, at 2pm, 5 days a week (no service on Tues or Thurs). After March 31, 2019, the service will run at 10am. Transfers cost A$64 one-way for adults, half-price for kids 2 to 12. Trip time is around 2 hours. Return transfers leave Heron Island at 10am (until March 31, 2019, when the return time will be 2pm). Seaplane transfers can also be arranged for A$349 per person.

WHERE TO STAY ON HERON ISLAND

Heron Island Resort ★★★ This is a lovely, low-key resort, with no day-trippers and a focus very much on the outdoors. The colors of the island's surrounding water and Reef are reflected in the interiors, and everything is light-filled and breezy. Heron's central complex is equal parts grand Queenslander home and sophisticated beach house, with bar and lounge areas open to ocean views and sunsets. Duplex-style Turtle rooms are designed for couples or families, or you can go for greater luxury in the Wistari or Point suites or the private Beach House (the only rooms with air-conditioning). Rooms are TV-free, but there is a lounge with TVs and public phones (only the four Point suites and the Beach House have private phones). There is no mobile phone coverage, but there are pay phones and you can get Wi-Fi in the bar. The **Aqua Soul Spa** offers double treatment rooms and all the usual spa treatments and pampering.

Heron Island, off Gladstone. www.heronisland.com. ℂ **1800/875 343** in Australia, or 855/251 8261 in the U.S., or 07/4972 9055 (resort). 109 units. A$330 Turtle Room double or A$346 for families; A$428 Reef Room double or A$459 families; A$572–A$1,350 suites; A$840 Beach House. Rates include breakfast and some activities. **Amenities:** Restaurant; bar; children's program (ages 7–12) during Australian school vacations; Jacuzzi; outdoor pool; spa; 2 lit tennis courts; limited watersports equipment rental.

Bundaberg ★: Gateway to Lady Elliot Island

384km (238 miles) N of Brisbane; 1,439km (892 miles) S of Cairns

The small sugar town of Bundaberg is the closest to the southernmost point of the Great Barrier Reef. If you visit the area between November and March, allow an evening to visit the Mon Repos Turtle Rookery (p. 233). Divers may want to take in some of Australia's best shore diving right off Bundaberg's beaches. The southern reefs of the Great Barrier Reef are just as prolific, varied, and colorful as the reefs farther north off Cairns, with the added advantage that, because this part of the coast is less accessible, fewer snorkel and dive boats visit them.

There are two islands to visit in this area: **Lady Musgrave Island** (p. 234) and **Lady Elliot Island** (p. 234), both part of the Bunker Group, which are around 80km (50 miles) due north of Bundaberg. While the islands are due east of Gladstone and closer to that town, only live-aboard boats visit them from there.

ESSENTIALS
Arriving
BY PLANE Qantas (www.qantas.com.au; ℭ **131 313** in Australia) and **Virgin Australia** (www.virginaustralia.com.au; ℭ **136 789** in Australia) both fly from Brisbane daily. Flight time is about 55 minutes.

BY TRAIN **Queensland Rail** (www.queenslandrail.com.au; ℭ **1800/872 467** in Queensland) trains stop in Bundaberg every day en route between Brisbane and Cairns. The fare is A$89 from Brisbane in economy class or A$115 business class on the Tilt Train; the trip takes about 4½ hours.

BY BUS **Greyhound Australia** (www.greyhound.com.au; ℭ **1300/473 946** in Australia) stops here many times a day on runs between Brisbane and Cairns. The 8-hour trip from Brisbane costs A$95.

BY CAR Bundaberg is on the Isis Highway, about 50km (31 miles) off the Bruce Highway from Gin Gin in the north and 53km (33 miles) off the Bruce Highway from just north of Childers in the south.

Getting Around
BY CAR **Avis** (ℭ **07/4131 4533**), **Budget** (ℭ **07/4155 0095**), **Hertz** (ℭ **07/4154 1030**), and **Thrifty** (ℭ **07/4151 6222**) all have offices in Bundaberg.

BY BUS **Duffy's City Buses** (www.duffysbuses.com.au; ℭ **1300/383 397** in Australia, or 07/4151 4226) operates the town bus service. There are no public buses on Sundays.

VISITOR INFORMATION
The **Bundaberg Visitor Information Centre** (www.bundabergregion.org; ℭ **1300/722 099** in Australia, or 07/4143 8888), at 271 Bourbong St. (next to the hospital), is open daily 9am to 5pm, public holidays 9am to 2pm. Closed Good Friday, Anzac Day (Apr 25), and Christmas Day.

WHERE TO STAY IN BUNDABERG
Zen Beach Retreat ★★★ Hosts Shane and Pascaline Emms transformed an old beachfront motel into some of the best accommodations in the Bundaberg region. Four themed two-story villas sit behind the main building (no sea views, unfortunately), opening out onto a Balinese-style pavilion and the pool. The exotic and colorful Oriental villa is my favorite, with design touches from Morocco, Turkey, and the Middle East, but you might prefer the French villa, adorned with some of Pascaline's personal treasures. The Asian villa and a more subdued Executive villa round out the villa options. You can also book the main house, which has three bedrooms, plus entertaining areas, as well as access to the expansive upstairs open-plan living area and gourmet kitchen.

54 Miller St., Bargara. www.zenbeachretreat.com. ℭ **07/4154 7757.** 5 units. A$500 double; A$1,500 whole house (sleeps 6). Free parking. **Amenities:** Outdoor pool; spa; free Wi-Fi.

WHERE TO EAT IN BUNDABERG

Café 1928 ★ CAFE   Set in the leafy surrounds of the Bundaberg Botanic Gardens, this casual cafe is a nice spot for brunch or lunch. Apart from good coffee, it offers quite an extensive menu, everything from muffins and sandwiches to home-cooked lasagna, quiche, salads, chicken schnitzel, and a range of burgers and pizzas. There's also an A$8 kids' menu.

Bundaberg Botanic Gardens, Young St. www.bundabergcafe.com.au. ℗ **07/4153 1928.** Main courses A$8–A$18. Daily 9am–3pm (kitchen closes 2:30pm); public holidays 10am–3pm.

EXPLORING BUNDABERG

By far the most popular attraction in Bundaberg is the annual turtle nesting season on Mon Repos Beach, about 14km (8¾ miles) from the city center. **Mon Repos Regional Park** is one of the two largest loggerhead-turtle rookeries in the South Pacific. The visitor center by the beach has a great display on the turtle life cycle and shows films at 7:30pm daily in summer. There is a strict booking system for turtle-watching tours, to help cope with the crowds. Access to the beach is by ticket only, and you must book your visit to Mon Repos during the turtle season. Tickets are sold through the **Bundaberg Visitor Information Centre** at 271 Bourbong St. (℗ **1300/722 099** in Australia, or 07/4143 8888), or online at www.bundabergregion.org/turtles. The website has a lot of very useful information on how to get to the rookery and what to expect from your turtle-watching experience. Tours start at 7pm, but you may have to wait up to 2 hours or more, depending on when the turtles appear. Nesting happens around high tide; hatching usually occurs between 8pm and midnight. Take a sweater, as it can get quite cool.

The **Mon Repos Turtle Centre** (www.nprsr.qld.gov.au/parks/mon-repos; ℗ **07/4159 1652**) at 141 Mon Repos Rd. is well signposted. During turtle-nesting season (Nov to late Mar), the park and information center are open daily 8am to 5pm (closed Christmas Eve, Christmas Day, and New Year's Eve). Public access to the beach is closed from 6pm to 6am, unless you are on a tour. Turtle-viewing tours run from 7pm until midnight daily (except for Dec 24, 25, and 31). From April to early November (when no turtles are around), the information center is open Monday to Friday (except public holidays) from 8am to 3:30pm, and the park is open 24 hours. Admission to the visitor center is free from April through November; but when the turtles start nesting, you pay A$12 for adults, A$6.45 for children age 5 to 14 and seniors, and A$30 for families of four, including your tour. It's the best value anywhere!

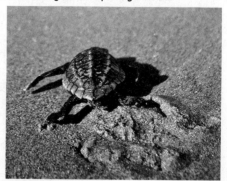

Turtle nesting at Mon Repos Regional Park.

Lady Musgrave Island

Snorkelers and divers also head out from Bundaberg on a daily basis to pretty **Lady Musgrave Island** (www.ladymusgraveexperience.co.au; ℭ **07/4151 5225**), a vegetated 14-hectare (35-acre) national-park coral cay, 52 nautical miles off the coast. It is surrounded by a lagoon 8km (5 miles) in circumference, filled with hundreds of corals and some 1,200 of the 1,500 species of fish and other marine creatures found on the Great Barrier Reef.

Lady Elliot Island ★★

80km (50 miles) NE of Bundaberg

Reef walking, snorkeling, and diving are the main reasons people come to this 42-hectare (104-acre) coral cay ringed by a wide, shallow lagoon filled with dazzling coral life. Divers will see a good range of marine life, including brilliantly colored fish, clams, sponges, urchins, and anemones. Green and loggerhead turtles nest on the beach November through March; whales pass by from June through September. You may snorkel and reef walk only during the 2 to 3 hours before and after high tide, so plan your day accordingly.

Lady Elliot is a sparse, grassy island rookery, not a sandy tropical paradise—it's so small you can walk across it in 15 minutes. Some find it too spartan; others relish chilling out in a beautiful, peaceful spot with reef all around. Just be prepared for the smell and constant noise of the birds.

ARRIVING

The 30-minute flight with **Seair** (www.seairpacific.com.au; ℭ **07/5599 4509**) from Bundaberg runs twice daily at 8:40am and 1:30pm; it costs A$349 adults, A$220 kids 3 to 12, round-trip. You can make it a day trip by returning on the 4pm flight back to Bundaberg. (You can also do a day-trip flight from Brisbane—see p. 176). Day trips include a welcome drink and orientation tour, glass-bottom-boat ride or guided snorkel tour, lunch, and use of the resort facilities (including towels, reef-walking shoes, sunscreen, and snorkel equipment). If you plan to stay longer than a day, book your flights with your accommodation, and remember there is a 10-kilogram (22 lb.) luggage limit.

WHERE TO STAY ON LADY ELLIOT ISLAND

Lady Elliot Island Eco Resort ★★★ Accommodations here are fairly basic, but visitors come for the Reef, not the room. The top-of-the-range rooms, the Island suites (the only rooms with air-conditioning), have one or two separate bedrooms and great sea views from the deck. Most Reef rooms sleep four and have decks with views through the trees to the sea. The cool, spacious safari-tent "eco-cabins" have four bunks, electric lighting, fans, and timber floors, but share toilets and showers. The limited facilities include a boutique, an education center, and a dive shop, which runs shore and boat dives, introductory dives, and rents equipment. There are also two "glamping" tents, which have private bathrooms. There are no TVs, radio, mobile phone reception, or phones in the rooms (but there is a public telephone). A program of mostly free activities includes glass-bottom-boat rides, table tennis, guided walks, and beach volleyball.

Great Barrier Reef, off Bundaberg, Runaway Bay. www.ladyelliot.com.au. © **1800/072 200** in Australia, or 07/4156 4444. 43 units. A$370–A$410 eco-cabin double; A$570–A$690 double; A$650-A$690 glamping tent; A$770–A$810 suite. A$99–A$130 children 3–12 years. 3-night minimum Christmas/New Year; 2-night minimum for suites. Rates include breakfast, dinner, and some guided tours. **Amenities:** Restaurant; bar; children's program (ages 5–12) during school holidays; saltwater pool; Wi-fi hotspot available (in public areas) for a fee (from $4.95 for 3 days).

THE NORTHERN TERRITORY

Though there's no border between them, the Northern Territory is really two distinctly different regions. The "Top End" is a last frontier, a place of wild, rugged beauty and sometimes hardship, with its major center the capital, Darwin. The "Red Centre" is a landscape of endless horizons, vast red deserts, cloudless blue skies, and the Outback town of Alice Springs. At its heart lies the magnificent monolith Uluru (Ayers Rock), the main reason visitors are drawn to this arid land.

Darwin is a small, modern city, wealthy, tropical, and ever-changing. To the east, the wetlands of Kakadu National Park teem with crocs and birds; a third of the country's bird species are here. Here, you'll find a wealth of experiences: Visit an Aboriginal community, canoe along remote rivers, and soak in thermal pools.

Life in the Top End is different from life elsewhere in Australia. Locals relish its slightly lawless image, but in Darwin you'll also get a sense of a city on the move. Isolation, Wet season monsoons, crocodiles, and other dangers make 'em tough up here, but you don't have to do without the comforts you're used to.

The Red Centre is home to sprawling cattle ranches, ancient mountain ranges, palm trees that survived the Ice Age, cockatoos and kangaroos, ochre gorges, lush water holes, and desert tracks leading to heart-stopping landscapes. Aboriginal people have lived here for tens of thousands of years.

There's one important fact to get straight from the start: Alice Springs is a gateway to Uluru, but the two destinations are *not* side by side. Indeed, they are 462km (286 miles) apart. You can get to Uluru from Alice Springs and see it in a day, but in doing so you will miss much of the experience: Visiting Uluru is much more than just a quick photo opportunity—it may well be the most meaningful and memorable part of your trip to Australia. You can also fly direct to Ayers Rock Airport, which takes its name from the European name given to Uluru by early explorers but seldom used today.

One highway connects "The Alice" to Darwin; beyond that, a few roads and four-wheel-drive tracks make a lonely spider web across the Northern Territory. There are still many areas where non-Aborigines have never set foot.

A four-wheel-drive vehicle is best for traversing the long distances from point to point in the Northern Territory, often on unpaved roads.

Allow yourself a few days to experience all there is in both the Top End and the Centre—to do otherwise will deprive yourself of experiencing the essence of Australia.

TERRITORY ESSENTIALS

Visitor Information

Tourism NT has a great website (www.northernterritory.com) with special sections tailored for international travelers (choose your country). It details many hotels, tour operators, car-rental companies, and attractions, and offers information on local Aboriginal culture and Aboriginal tours. Tourism NT's **Territory Discoveries division** (www.territorydiscoveries.com; ✆ **1300/738 111** in Australia, or 08/8968 3200) offers package deals.

When to Go

The main factor to consider when visiting Darwin and Kakadu National Park is the difference between dry and wet seasons. The Dry (May–Oct) is the most popular time to go, with temperatures around 86°F (30°C) and sunny days. Many tours, hotels, and even campsites are booked a year in advance, so make sure you have reservations. In the Wet season (Nov–Apr), heat and humidity are extreme, and floodwaters may cover much of the Kakadu park, cutting off some attractions entirely. Some tour companies do not operate during the Wet, and park ranger talks, walks, and slide shows are not offered. The upside is that the crowds vanish, the brownish vegetation bursts into green, waterfalls swell from a trickle to a roar, and lightning storms are spectacular, especially in the hot "buildup" to the season in October and November. The landscape can change dramatically from one day to the next as floodwaters rise and fall, so be prepared for surprises—nice ones (such as giant flocks of geese) and unwelcome ones (such as blocked roads). Although it can pour down all day, it's more common for the rain to fall in late-afternoon storms and at night. Take it easy in the humidity, and make sure you are staying in air-conditioned accommodations.

For the Red Centre and Alice Springs, April, May, September, and October offer the best weather, with sunny days (coolish in May, hot in Oct). Winter (June–Aug) means mild temperatures with cold nights. Summer (Nov–Mar) is ferociously hot and best avoided. In summer, limit exertions to early morning and late afternoon, and choose air-conditioned accommodations. Rain is rare but can come at any time of year.

Driving Tips

The **Automobile Association of the Northern Territory,** 14 Knuckey St., Darwin, NT 0800 (www.aant.com.au; ✆ **08/8925 5901**), dispenses maps and advice and also offers emergency-breakdown service (✆ **131 111**) to members of affiliated overseas automobile associations. It has no office in the Red Centre. For **road condition reports,** call ✆ **1800/246 199** in Australia or check out www.roadreport.nt.gov.au.

Only a handful of highways and arterial roads in the Northern Territory are sealed (paved) roads. A conventional two-wheel-drive car will get you to most of what you want to see, but consider renting a **four-wheel-drive** (4WD) for complete freedom. All the big car-rental chains have them. Some attractions are on unpaved roads good enough for a two-wheel-drive car, but your car-rental company will not insure a two-wheel-drive for driving on them.

Normal restricted speed limits apply in all urban areas, but speed limits on Northern Territory highways (introduced in 2006) are considerably higher than in other states. The speed limit is set at 130kmph (81 mph) on the Stuart, Arnhem, Barkly, and Victoria highways, while rural roads are designated 110kmph (68 mph) speed limits unless otherwise signposted. The road fatality toll in the Northern Territory is high: an average of 40 fatalities each year.

Another considerable risk while driving is that of hitting wildlife: camels, kangaroos, and other protected native species. Avoid driving at night, early morning, and late afternoon, when 'roos are more active; beware of cattle lying down on the warm bitumen at night. Road trains (trucks hauling more than one container) and fatigue caused by driving long distances are two other major threats.

OTHER TRAVEL TIPS

Always carry drinking water. When hiking, carry 4 liters (about a gallon) per person per day in winter and a liter (1 quart) per person per hour in summer. Wear a broad-brimmed hat, high-factor sunscreen, and insect repellant.

Bring warm clothing for chilly winter evenings. Make sure you have a full tank of gas before setting out and check distances between places you can fill up.

The Northern Territory

Kakadu National Park (see p. 255)

Arafura Sea

Tiwi Islands
Melville Island
Cobourg Peninsula
Gurig Nat'l Park
C. Wessel
Wessel Is.
Bathurst Island
Nhulunbuy (Gove)

Darwin
Kakadu Nat'l Park
Arnhem Hwy.
Jabiru
ARNHEMLAND

Litchfield Nat'l Park
Adelaide River
Groote Eylandt

Timor Sea
Daly R.
Daly River
Pine Creek
Katherine
Nitmiluk National Park (Katherine Gorge)
Roper R.

Gulf of Carpentaria

Mataranka

Wyndham
Timber Creek
1
Larrimah
Sir Edward Pellew Group

Kununurra
Victoria Hwy.
Victoria R.
1
Daly Waters

Elliot
Newcastle Waters
Renner Springs

Darwin
NORTHERN TERRITORY
AUSTRALIA
Perth
Sydney
Canberra
Melbourne

Tennant Creek
66
Barkly
Barkly Hwy.

Stuart Hwy.
87
Devil's Marbles Conservation Reserve
Wauchope

Barrow Creek

WESTERN AUSTRALIA
QUEENSLAND

West MacDonnell National Park
MACDONNELL RANGES
Arltunga
Glen Helen
Ross River Homestead
Mereenie Loop Rd.
Hermannsburg
Alice Springs
Kings Canyon
Finke Gorge National Park
87
Simpson Desert
Ayers Rock Resort
Luritja Rd.
Lasseter Hwy.
Mt. Olga
Erldunda
Uluru–Kata Tjuta Uluru (Ayers Rock) National Park

Tropic of Capricorn

SOUTH AUSTRALIA

0   100 mi
0   100 km

Unpaved Road

Package Tour Operators

Given the great distances between destinations in the Red Centre, you may want to consider opting for a package tour. Numerous coach, minicoach, and 4WD tour operators run tours that take in Alice Springs, Kings Canyon, and Uluru. These depart from Alice Springs or Uluru, offering accommodations ranging from spiffy resorts, comfortable motels, and basic cabins to shared bunkhouses, tents, or swags (sleeping bags) under the stars. Most pack the highlights into a 2- or 3-day trip, though leisurely trips of 6 days or more are available. Many offer one-way itineraries between Alice and the Rock (via Kings Canyon if you like), or vice versa, which will allow you to avoid backtracking.

Among the reputable companies are **AAT Kings** (www.aatkings.com; ✆ **1300/228 546** in Australia), which specializes in coach tours but also has 4WD camping itineraries, and **Intrepid** (www.intrepidtravel.com; ✆ **1300/468 693** in Australia), which conducts camping safaris (or if you prefer, hotel, motel, or lodge accommodations) in small groups for all ages. **Tailormade Tours** (www.tailormadetours.com.au; ✆ **08/8952 1731**) offers general tours as well as customized luxury charters. **Mulga's Adventures** (www.mulgas adventures.com.au; ✆ **1800/359 089** in Australia, or 08/8952 1545), operates a 3-day tour of the area, including Uluru and Kata-Tjuta (A$399).

DARWIN

1,489km (923 miles) N of Alice Springs

Australia's proximity to Asia is never clearer than when you are in Darwin. Named after the naturalist and biologist Charles Darwin (who visited Australia in 1836), the city is an exotic blend of frontier town, Asian village, and modern life. With a population of about 140,000, Darwin has had a turbulent history—and it shows. This city has battled just about everything that man and nature could throw at it. Most of its buildings date from the mid-1970s; Cyclone Tracy wiped out the city on Christmas Eve 1974. Despite all this destruction, some of Darwin's historic buildings—or at least parts of them—have survived, and you can see them around the city center.

The vibe here is relaxed and very casual. Don't bother bringing a jacket and tie; shorts and sandals will be acceptable most places—even the swankiest

Where Can I Swim?

Crocodiles and stingers render Darwin's beaches a no-swim zone year-round. The man-made lagoon at **Stokes Hill Wharf** solves the problem. Locals also sunbathe on Casuarina Beach and swim within view of the sea in **Lake Alexander** in East Point Reserve. About an hour's drive from the city, on the way to the Territory Wildlife Park, **Berry Springs Nature Park** has swimming holes with steps for easy access, and small waterfalls that create natural whirlpool action. They may be closed in the Wet season.

Darwin

ACCOMMODATIONS ■
Adina Apartment Hotel
  Darwin Waterfront **25**
Mandalay **18**
Mantra on the Esplanade **16**
Skycity Darwin **7**
Travelodge Resort Darwin **13**
Value Inn **17**
Vibe Hotel Darwin Waterfront **26**
Villa La Vue **19**

RESTAURANTS ◆
Darwin Sailing Club **3**
Darwin Ski Club **2**
Hanuman **20**
Il Piatto **8**
Pee Wee's at The Point **5**
Shenanigan's **14**
The Roma Bar **22**
Tim's Surf 'n' Turf **21**

ATTRACTIONS ●
Crocodylus Park & Zoo **11**
Crocosaurus Cove **15**
Darwin Aviation Museum **12**
Deckchair Cinema **23**
Defence of Darwin Experience **4**
Mindil Beach Sunset Market **6**
Museum & Art Gallery
  of the Northern Territory **1**
Parap Markets **10**
RFDS Darwin Tourist Facility **27**
Territory Wildlife Park **9**
World War II
  Oil Storage Tunnels **24**

Tours of Darwin

The double-decker **Big Bus Darwin** (www.theaustralianexplorer.com.au; ☎ **0416/140 903**) offers 1- or 2-day tickets for tours that take in 11 stops around town, including the major attractions. One-day tickets cost A$40 for adults, A$25 for children 5 to 15, or A$110 for a family of four. A 2-day pass is A$60 adults, A$40 children, and A$170 for families. Tours start from the Visitor Information Centre at the Bennett Street end of Smith Street Mall at regular intervals each morning (times vary seasonally). **Darwin Day Tours,** operated by AATKings (www.aatkings. com.au; ☎ **1300/228 546** in Australia), also has a range of sightseeing tours, including a half-day City Sights tour that costs A$99 adults and A$50 children age 2 to 15.

invitations stipulate "Territory Rig" dress, meaning long pants and a short-sleeved open-neck shirt for men.

Darwin is most commonly used as a gateway to Kakadu National Park (p. 255), and many Australians have never visited it—or at least not for long. And that's a shame, because it is an attractive and interesting place. Give yourself a day or two to wander the pleasant streets and parklands, see the wildlife attractions, or shop for Aboriginal art and South Sea pearls. An easy day trip is **Litchfield National Park** ★★ (p. 252), one of the Territory's best-kept secrets, boasting waterfalls that you'd usually only see in vacation brochures.

Essentials

ARRIVING

BY PLANE   Qantas (www.qantas.com) serves Darwin daily from Alice Springs, Adelaide, Brisbane, Cairns, Melbourne, Perth, Sydney, and Townsville, either direct or connecting through Alice Springs. **Virgin Australia** (www.virginaustralia.com) flies direct to Darwin from Sydney, Brisbane, Melbourne, Alice Springs, and Perth. **Jetstar** (www.jetstar.com.au) flies from Melbourne, Cairns, Brisbane, Sydney, and Adelaide. **Tigerair** (www.tigerair. com.au; ☎ **1300/174 266** in Australia, or 07/3295 2104) flies from Brisbane.

From the Airport to the City Center

Darwin Airport Shuttle Services (www.darwincityairportshuttleservice. com.au; ☎ **08/8947 3979**) meets every flight and delivers to any hotel between the airport and city for A$18 one-way or A$36 round-trip per person. A cab to the city is around A$35. For car rentals, **Avis** (www.avis.com.au; ☎ **08/8936 0600**), **Budget** (www.budget.com.au; ☎ **08/8981 9800**), **Europcar** (www. europcar.com.au; ☎ **08/8941 0300**), **Hertz** (www.hertz.com.au; ☎ **08/8941 0944**), or **Thrifty** (www.thrifty.com.au; ☎ **08/8924 0000**) have airport desks, as does **Redspot** (www.redspot.com.au; ☎ **08/8945 3909**).

BY BUS   **Greyhound Australia** (www.greyhound.com.au; ☎ **1300/473 946** in Australia) makes a daily coach run from Alice Springs. The trip takes around 22 hours, and the fare is A$277. Greyhound also has a daily service from Broome that takes around 24 hours and costs A$297.

BY TRAIN   The Adelaide–Alice Springs–Darwin railway line is the Top End's only rail link. Great Southern Railway's *Ghan* (www.greatsouthernrail.com.au; ✆ 132 147 in Australia) leaves Adelaide on Sundays at 12:15pm and Alice Springs on Mondays at 6:15pm, arriving in Darwin at 5:30pm on Tuesdays (with a stop at Katherine for a morning excursion). The return trip leaves Darwin on Wednesdays at 10am. The adult one-way fare starts at A$1,119 from Alice Springs or A$2,069 from Adelaide for a twin cabin, more for Platinum Class, which has cabins around twice the size of standard Gold Twin Cabins.

BY CAR   Darwin is at the end of the Stuart Highway. Allow at least 2 long days, 3 to be comfortable, to drive from Alice Springs. The nearest road from the east is the long and dull Barkly Highway, which connects with the Stuart Highway at Tennant Creek, 922km (572 miles) south. The nearest road from the west is Victoria Highway, which joins the Stuart Highway at Katherine, 314km (195 miles) to the south.

VISITOR INFORMATION

Tourism Top End runs the official visitor center at 6 Bennett St. (at Smith St.) (www.tourismtopend.com.au; ✆ 1300/138 886 in Australia, or 08/8980 6000). They can make bookings and provide you with maps, national park notes, and information on Darwin and other regions throughout the Northern Territory, including Kakadu and Litchfield national parks.

GETTING AROUND

For car rental options, see above.

BY BUS   Buslink (www.buslink.com.au; ✆ 08/8944 0821) is the local bus company. A A$3 bus fare gives unlimited travel for 3 hours. A daily ticket costs A$7, or you can buy a 10-trip ticket (each trip valid for 3 hours), or a weekly ticket for unlimited travel for A$20. Buy tickets on the bus (cash only) or at a bus interchange. The city terminus is on Harry Chan Avenue (off Smith St., near Civic Square; ✆ 08/8924 7666). The information desk, where you can pick up a timetable, is open Monday to Friday 8am to noon and 1 to 4pm.

BY TAXI   Darwin Radio Taxis (✆ 131 008) is the main cab company. Taxi stands are at the Knuckey Street and Bennett Street ends of Smith Street Mall.

CITY LAYOUT

The city heart is the **Smith Street pedestrian mall.** The other main street, one street over, is **Mitchell Street,** with backpacker lodges, cheap eateries, and souvenir stores. Two streets away is the harborfront **Esplanade.** But the hot new hub of Darwin life is the **Wharf Precinct,** looking out to the Arafura Sea, with its parklands, restaurants, boutiques, swimming lagoon and wave pool, and some of the city's swishest hotels and residential apartment blocks. **Cullen Bay Marina** is another hub for restaurants, cafes, and expensive boats; it's about a 25-minute walk northwest of the city center. Also northwest is **Fannie Bay,** where you'll find the Botanic Gardens, the sailing club, a golf course, museum and art gallery, and the casino.

Where to Stay in Darwin

April through October is the peak Dry season; hotels usually drop their rates from November through March (the Wet).

EXPENSIVE

Adina Apartment Hotel Darwin Waterfront ★★　This apartment hotel has a prime location overlooking the city's swimming lagoon and wave pool at Stokes Hill Wharf. From the top floor of the hotel, you can take a covered walkway right into the heart of the city, just minutes away. All one-bedroom apartments have balconies (studios do not), while all rooms have kitchens with microwaves. Apartments also have laundry facilities. Most apartments connect with a studio to make a two-bedroom apartment, if needed. There are also limited numbers of two-bedroom apartments.

7 Kitchener Drive. www.adinahotels.com. ☎ **1300/633 462** in Australia, or 08/8982 999. 121 units. A$169–A$203 studio double; A$199–A$254 1-bedroom apt; A$424–A$589 2-bedroom apt. Parking A$15. **Amenities:** Restaurant; bar; babysitting; exercise room; outdoor pool; room service; spa; free Wi-Fi.

Mantra on the Esplanade ★★　Right on the Esplanade overlooking Darwin Harbour and the Arafura Sea, and just a block from Smith Street Mall, this eight-floor apartment hotel is one of Darwin's most comfortable, elegant lodgings. Bright sofas and striking artwork in the lobby set a welcoming tone. Besides regular hotel rooms, two-thirds of the accommodations here are spacious contemporary-style one-, two-, and three-bedroom apartments with private balconies. Apartment kitchens feature granite countertops and stainless-steel appliances, including dishwashers, and all have laundry facilities. All rooms and apartments have city or harbor views.

88 The Esplanade (at Peel St.). www.mantra.com.au. ☎ **131 517** in Australia, or 08/8943 4333. 204 units. A$189 double; A$209 1-bedroom apt; A$289 2-bedroom apt; A$379 3-bedroom apt; A$479 penthouse. Parking A$15. **Amenities:** Restaurant; bar; concierge; executive-level rooms; Jacuzzi; outdoor pool; spa; free Wi-Fi.

Skycity Darwin ★　Attached to Darwin's casino on Fannie Bay, this five-star complex resembles a tropical palace, with a private white-sand beach, infinity pool, and 12 hectares (30 acres) of gardens on Mindil Beach, next to the Botanic Gardens. The rooms are a cocktail of contemporary furniture and tropical elegance. All have balconies. It's worth paying a little extra for an ocean-facing room so you can watch Darwin's great Dry season sunsets and spectacular Wet-season lightning storms. Superior rooms feature luxurious Japanese-inspired spa tubs and cool marble in the bathrooms. Full-length glass windows provide views over a private balcony terrace to lush tropical gardens and Mindil beach. "Resort rooms" have greater privacy, with views of the lagoon. A free shuttle runs four times a day to and from the city.

Gilruth Ave., The Gardens. www.skycitydarwin.com.au. ☎ **1800/891 118** in Australia, or 08/8943 8888. 152 units. A$279–A$329 double; A$349–A$369 suite. Free valet and self-parking. Bus: 4 or 6. **Amenities:** 5 restaurants; 7 bars; babysitting; exercise room; Jacuzzi; heated outdoor pool; room service; spa; sauna; free Wi-Fi.

If you're looking for a bit more space and privacy than a hotel room gives you, or perhaps are traveling as a family, a "home away from home" option is provided by **More Than a Room Darwin Accommodation** (www.morethanaroom.com.au; ☎ **08/8942 3012,** or 0418/616 888 mobile). The company has a portfolio of around 30 properties, from one-bedroom waterfront apartments to luxurious villas. The stylish **Mandalay,** built in 1988 by Lord McAlpine, is on the Esplanade, close to the city center. It has three bedrooms, free Wi-Fi, a pool, barbecue area, off-street parking, and bikes for your use. Next door is **Villa La Vue,** which is equally spacious but has a different style. Rates range from A$99 to A$595 per night.

MODERATE

Travelodge Resort Darwin ★ You're just a stone's throw from the city center at this modern hotel complex, where the tempting swimming pools and the Treetops restaurant, all shaded by the leaves of a sprawling strangler fig, have a castaway-island feel. Each room is a decent size and has a garden or pool view. As well as a range of hotel rooms, the complex has 32 self-contained one-bedroom town houses, which are a good option for families.

64 Cavenagh St. www.travelodge.com.au. ☎ **138 642** in Australia, or 08/8946 0111. 224 units. A$127–A$269 double; A$237–A$279 town house. Free off-street parking. **Amenities:** Restaurant; poolside cafe; 2 bars; babysitting; exercise room; 2 Jacuzzis; 2 outdoor pools; room service; free Wi-Fi.

Vibe Hotel Darwin Waterfront ★ This is a lovely casual place to stay and relax. The rooms are spacious and fresh, with a cheery white-and-aqua color scheme, but no balconies. Each has a small desk, and all have bathtubs as well as showers. Location is everything here, right in the heart of the waterfront precinct, within easy walking distance of the city center and major attractions. It's just 200m (660 ft.) from the wave pool and lagoon. The ground-level Curve Restaurant & Bar overlooks the parkland.

7 Kitchener Dr. www.vibehotels.com.au. ☎ **138 423** in Australia, 02/9356 5063 (Sydney reservations center), or 08/8982 9998. 121 units. A$299–A$339 double. Parking A$15. **Amenities:** Restaurant; bar; babysitting; exercise room; outdoor pool; room service; spa; free Wi-Fi.

INEXPENSIVE

Value Inn ★ The rooms at this neat little hotel in the Mitchell Street tourist precinct are tiny but tidy. Each room is just big enough to hold a queen-size and a single bed, a bar fridge, and a small writing table. The views aren't much, but you'll probably spend your time in the nearby cafes. Smith Street Mall and the Esplanade walking path are 2 blocks away. There is a pay phone (no phones in the rooms), cold drink and coffee vending machines, an iron on each floor, microwave ovens on the first and second floors, and a very small

Cheap Eats & More!

If it's Thursday or Sunday, join the entire city and hundreds of other visitors at the **Mindil Beach Sunset Market** ★★ to feast at the 60 terrific (and cheap—most dishes are less than A$10 a serving) Asian, Greek, Italian, African, Mexican, and Aussie food stalls. Listen to live music; wander among almost 200 arts-and-crafts stalls; and mix and mingle with masseurs, tarot-card readers, and street performers as the sun sets into the sea. The action runs from 4 to 9pm in the Dry (approximately May–Oct). The market's season changes from year to year, so if you're visiting on the seasonal cusp, in April or October, check whether it's on by calling the organizers (✆ **08/8981 3454**) or visiting

www.mindil.com.au. The beach is about a 20-minute walk or a A$10 cab ride from town, or take bus no. 15. Some hotels provide a shuttle bus.

On Saturdays (8am–2pm), head to suburban **Parap Markets** ★, which transform a small street into a corner of Asia. The focus is on food, with a sprinkling of arts and crafts, and it's a favorite place for locals to have breakfast or brunch, choosing from the Southeast Asian soups, noodle dishes, and satays, washed down with fresh-squeezed tropical fruit drinks. The market stalls cover only about a block, on Parap Road in Parap (www.parapvillagemarkets.com.au; ✆ **08/8942 0805**, or 0438/882 373 mobile).

garden swimming pool off the parking lot. It's definitely 2.5-star and doesn't pretend to be otherwise.

50 Mitchell St. www.valueinn.com.au. ✆ **08/8981 4733**. 91 units. A$67 double. Free parking. **Amenities:** Bikes; outdoor pool; tennis courts; free Wi-Fi.

Where to Eat in Darwin

Cullen Bay Marina, a 25-minute walk or a short cab ride from town, is packed with trendy restaurants and cafes. If it's Thursday, don't even think about eating anywhere other than the **Mindil Beach Sunset Market ★★**. And on Saturday, head to the suburban Parap Markets for Asian goodies (see "Cheap Eats & More!" above).

EXPENSIVE

Il Piatto ★★ ITALIAN Classic Italian food in a beautiful airy restaurant—what could be better? Simple food, very well done is the key to this place. As well as the pizza and pasta dishes, there are treats such as Northern Territory barramundi (fish) with cauliflower cream, vegetables, and crisp garlic wafers; or char-grilled butterflied chicken with grilled zucchini and a kipfler potato salad, with lemon sauce and salsa verde. Pizzas cost A$20 to A$26, and there's a design-your-own option too.

Skycity Darwin, Gilruth Ave., Mindil Beach. www.skycitydarwin.com.au/restaurants/il-piatto. ✆ **08/8943 8940**. Main courses A$26–A$61. Mon–Fri noon–2:30pm and 6–10pm; Sat-Sun noon–10pm.

Pee Wee's at The Point ★★ CONTEMPORARY Surrounded on three sides by forest, this steel-and-glass venue affords views of Fannie Bay from just about every table, inside, out on the deck, or down on the lawn. The food emphasizes fresh local produce and employs local ingredients as much as possible. An example: oven-baked saltwater barramundi crusted with macadamia nuts and lemon myrtle, with steamed greens and white bean puree. A tasting plate for two costs A$42. It's all complemented by an extensive wine list. Get there in time to watch the sunset.

Alec Fong Lim Dr., East Point Reserve (4km/2½ miles from town). www.peewees.com. au. ℰ **08/8981 6868.** Main courses A$41–A$55. Mon–Sat 4pm–late; Sun 3pm–late. Free parking.

Tim's Surf 'n' Turf ★ STEAK/SEAFOOD This Darwin favorite is housed in a classic elevated Darwin home that has been transformed into a modern restaurant. Diners can choose between the air-conditioned open-plan dining and bar area, its walls hung with Top End Aboriginal artworks, or head outside to sit under the shady trees and palms. Open for dinner only, the menu includes steaks, seafood platters, oysters, and vegetarian dishes, along with a range of salads, chicken, and pasta dishes. There's a kids' menu too, and children eat free Tuesday through Thursday before 6:30pm.

10 Litchfield St. www.timssurfandturf.com. ℰ **08/8981 1024.** Main courses A$20–A$55. Tues–Sun 5:30–9pm.

MODERATE

Hanuman ★★ CONTEMPORARY ASIAN One of the most exotic places in Darwin to eat, Hanuman features "Nonya"-style cuisine, a fusion of Chinese- and Malaysian-style cooking. You can rely on dishes such as red duck curry with coconut, litchis, kaffir lime, Thai basil, and fresh pineapple; or wok-tossed prawns in a coconut, wild ginger, and curry sauce. There is also a tandoori menu. A tasting plate for two takes the agony out of choosing and costs A$36. This is a large restaurant, with seating for 90 diners inside and the same number outside. There's also a stylish cocktail bar. Service is prompt and friendly.

93 Mitchell St. (in the Doubletree Hilton complex). www.hanuman.com.au. ℰ **08/8941 3500.** Main courses A$16–A$39. Mon–Fri noon–2:30pm; daily 6–10:30pm.

Shenannigan's ★ IRISH PUB FARE Hearty pub food—pork and sage sausages with mash and gravy, or slow-cooked pork belly—along with a good smattering of local produce (smoked kangaroo and spiced crocodile skewers, anyone?) is what you'll find at this convivial bar and restaurant. A friendly mix of solo travelers, families, seniors, and backpackers converge here. There's also lighter fare, including vegetarian dishes, salads, burgers and wraps, and daily chef's specials.

69 Mitchell St. (at Peel St.). www.shenannigans.com.au. ℰ **08/8981 2100.** Main courses A$18–A$28. Daily 11:30am–5pm and 6–9.30pm.

INEXPENSIVE

The Roma Bar ★ CAFE At this Darwin stalwart, you're likely to see media types rubbing shoulders with politicians, musicians, artists, and lobbyists. The coffee's good, and the food is tasty and well-priced. It's a great spot for breakfast and the menu is slanted to an all-day breakfast, with omelets,

Join the Club!

Two great places to catch Darwin's technicolor sunsets over a casual meal are the **Darwin Sailing Club** and the **Darwin Ski Club** (we're talking water-ski, of course). These are super-casual places to dine, with good food at good prices (mains around A$20–A$40). Ask a staff member to sign you in as a visitor, then grab a table, preferably outside.

The **Darwin Ski Club** (Conacher St., Fannie Bay, opposite the museum and art gallery; ✆ **08/8981 6630**) is a favorite for families, with its huge lawn and two saltwater pools. The outdoor Bali Bar is open from noon each day (except Good Friday and Christmas Day) and is a great place for a bistro meal (bucket of fresh prawns, anyone?). There's live music on Friday and Saturday nights.

The **Darwin Sailing Club** (Atkins Dr., Fannie Bay; www.dwnsail.com.au; ✆ **08/8981 1700**) waterfront bistro is open daily from noon to 2pm for lunch and 5:30 to 9pm for dinner (the bar stays open later), offering everything from paninis and burgers to a A$99 seafood platter.

banana pancakes, and avocado on sourdough. At lunch, burgers and sandwiches take over.

9 Cavenagh St. www.romabar.com.au. ✆ **08/8981 6729.** Main courses A$11–A$18. Mon–Fri 7am–3pm; Sat 8am–2pm; Sun 8am–1pm.

Exploring Darwin

Darwin's parks, harbor, and tropical clime make it lovely for strolling during the Dry. The **Esplanade** makes for a pleasantly short and shady saunter, and the 42-hectare (104-acre) **George Brown Darwin Botanic Gardens** (✆ **08/8999 4418**), on Gardens Road 2km (1¼ miles) from town, has paths through palms, orchids, every species of baobab in the world, and mangroves. Entry is free. The visitor center (daily 8am–4pm), near the Geranium Street entrance, has self-guiding maps to the Aboriginal plant-use trails.

Crocodylus Park & Zoo ★ ZOO   In addition to housing a small crocodile museum, this wildlife park, a 15-minute drive from town, holds croc-feeding sessions and free hour-long guided tours at 10am, noon, and 2pm. It doubles as Darwin's zoo, with exotic species including lions, Bengal tigers, leopards, and monkeys on display.

815 McMillans Rd., Berrimah. www.territorywildlifepark.com.au. ✆ **08/8922 4500.** A$40 adults, A$20 children 3–15, A$105 families. Daily 9am–5pm. Closed Christmas Day.

Crocosaurus Cove ★ WILDLIFE VIEWING   Strong men have known to pale in the face of an attack by Chopper, a 790kg (1,742-lb.) crocodile with no front feet. At Crocosaurus Cove, the very brave can get into a plexiglass "cage" and be lowered into Chopper's enclosure, which also houses several huge crocs who have survived into their 70s and 80s, as well as large numbers of juveniles. These territorial beasts aren't usually happy with the intrusion—and the scratch marks on the 145mm (6-in.) thick walls of the cage tell the rest of the story. You spend about 15 minutes in the water. I confess: I have not done this and will not—not even in the interests of research! Less scary is the chance to swim in a pool next door to the younger crocs, with just a plexiglass wall between you and them. Crocosaurus Cove also has Australia's largest collection of reptiles, about 70 species, all from the Top End.

58 Mitchell St. www.crocosauruscove.com © **08/8947 2145.** A$35 adults, A$23 children 4–15, A$77–A$132 families. Cage of Death A$170 for one person, A$260 for two. Daily 9am–6pm. Closed Christmas Day.

Darwin Aviation Museum ★★★ MUSEUM   Even if you are not a military or aircraft buff, you may enjoy this excellent museum, about 10 minutes' drive from town. A B-52 bomber on loan from the United States is the prized exhibit, but the center also boasts a B-25 Mitchell bomber; Mirage and Sabre jet fighters; rare Japanese Zero fighter wreckage; funny, sad, and heartwarming (and heart-wrenching) displays on World War II and Vietnam; and displays about female aviators.

557 Stuart Hwy., Winnellie. www.darwinaviationmuseum.com.au. © **08/8947 2145.** A$15 adults, A$7 children 11 and under, A$35 families. Daily 9am–5pm. Closed New Year's Day, Good Friday, Christmas Day, and Boxing Day (Dec 26).

Defence of Darwin Experience ★★ MUSEUM   Housed in a World War II gun command post, this small museum is another tribute to Darwin's wartime history. It has small but fine displays of photos, memorabilia, artillery, armored vehicles, weaponry old and new, and gun emplacements outside. Take time to watch the video of the 1942 and 1943 Japanese bombings.

5434 Alec Fong Lim Dr., East Point. www.defenceofdarwin.nt.gov.au © **08/8981 9702.** A$18 adults, A$8 children 5–15, A$40 families of 5. Daily 9:30am–5pm. Closed Good Friday and Christmas Day.

The man-made lagoon at Stokes Hill Wharf adds watersports to the mix along Darwin's smartly redeveloped waterfront.

Movies Under the Stars

Lie back in a canvas deck chair under the stars at the **Deckchair Cinema** (www.deckchaircinema.com; ☏ **08/8981 0700**) to watch Aussie hits, foreign films, and cult classics. Located on the edge of Darwin Harbour (at the end of Jervois Rd., opposite Parliament House on the Esplanade), this Darwin institution is run by the Darwin Film Society. Take a picnic dinner and get there early to soak up the scene: the twinkling lights from boats anchored in the Arafura Sea and the fabulous sunsets. A kiosk sells wine, beer, soft drinks, and snacks, and there's a hot buffet every night (or you can bring your own food, but no alcohol). There are 250 deck chairs as well as about 100 straight-backed seats; cushions and even insect repellent are available if you need them. Entry is by a walkway from the Esplanade, or by car off Kitchener Drive (there's a parking lot). The box office and kiosk open at 6pm and movies start at 7:30pm daily in the Dry (mid-Apr–mid-Nov), with double features on Fridays, Saturdays, and some Sundays. Tickets are A$16 adults, A$8 children 5 to 15, and A$35 for families of four; for double features, it's A$24 adults, A$12 children, and A$55 families.

Museum and Art Gallery of the Northern Territory ★★★

MUSEUM There's another attraction here for crocodile fans—the preserved body of **Sweetheart,** a 5m (16-ft.) man-eating saltwater croc captured in Kakadu National Park. Beyond that, this museum and gallery is a great place to learn about Darwin's place in Australia's modern history. It has sections on Aboriginal, Southeast Asian, and Pacific art and culture, and a maritime gallery with a pearling lugger and other boats that have sailed into Darwin from Indonesia and other northern parts. A highlight is the Cyclone Tracy gallery, where you can stand in a small, dark room as the sound of the cyclone rages around you.

19 Conacher St., Bullocky Point. www.magnt.nt.gov.au. ☏ **08/8999 8364.** Admission free. Daily 10am–5pm. Closed New Year's Day, Good Friday, Christmas Day, and Boxing Day (Dec 26).

RFDS Darwin Tourist Facility ★★★ MUSEUM

Despite its less-than-catchy name, this is one of the best attractions in Darwin—don't miss it. In a building shaped something like an old aircraft hangar, two attractions tell two different Darwin stories. One is that of the Royal Flying Doctor Service, founded in the Northern Territory in 1939 and affectionately known throughout Australia as the RFDS. The museum relates the experiences of the pilots, engineers, doctors and nurses, and patients of the RFDS. But it is the second story—the Bombing of Darwin on February 19, 1942—that will grip you. Darwin was bombed 64 times during World War II, and 12 ships were sunk in its harbor. As an Allied supply base, Darwin had many American airmen based here. The bombing of the harbor brought destruction to the city, and many of the experiences of that day are brought to life using holograms and virtual reality—making you feel that you are actually *there*! There is another RFDS visitor center in Alice Springs (p. 273).

45 Stokes Hill Rd., Stokes Hill Wharf. www.rfdsdarwin.com.au. © **08/8983 5700.** A$28 adults, A$16 children, A$70 families. Daily 9:30am–6pm, public holidays 10am–3pm. Closed Good Friday and Christmas Day.

Territory Wildlife Park ★★ ZOO   Walk the many tracks, or take a free shuttle along bush trails to see native Northern Territory wildlife in re-created natural habitats, including monsoon rainforest boardwalks, lagoons with hides (shelters for watching birds), a walk-through aviary, a walk-through aquarium housing sting rays and sawfish, and a nocturnal house with marsupials such as the bilby. Bats, birds, spiders, crocs, frill-neck lizards, kangaroos, and other creatures also make their homes here (but not koalas, because they don't live in the Territory). A program of animal talks runs throughout the day. The best is the birds of prey show, at 11am. Go first thing to see the animals at their liveliest, and allow 4 hours to see everything, plus 45 minutes traveling time.

Cox Peninsula Rd., Berry Springs, 61km (38 miles) S of Darwin. www.territorywild lifepark.com.au. © **08/8988 7200.** A$32 adults, A$16 children 5–16, A$55–A$87 families. Daily 9am–5pm. Closed Christmas Day.

World War II Oil Storage Tunnels ★★ MUSEUM   Under the city's cliffs, this warren of empty World War II oil storage tunnels houses a collection of black-and-white photographs of the war in Darwin, each lit up in the dark. It's a simple but haunting attraction, offering an interesting window on yet another aspect of Darwin's war history. A gatekeeper has brochures, will answer questions, and sells history books.

Kitchener Dr., Wharf Precinct. www.ww2tunnelsdarwin.com.au. © **08/8985 6322.** A$8 adults, A$5 children 4–16. May–Sept daily 9am–4pm; Oct–Apr daily 9am–1pm. Closed December 7–25.

Shopping in Darwin

Darwin's best buys are Aboriginal art and crafts, pearls, opals, and diamonds. You will find many shops and galleries selling authentic Aboriginal artworks and artifacts at reasonable prices. To make a heavyweight investment in works by internationally sought-after artists, visit the Aboriginal-owned **Aboriginal Fine Arts Gallery,** on the second floor at 44 Mitchell St. (www.aaia.com.au; © **08/8981 1315**).

Cruising Darwin Harbour

If you have an evening free, get out on the harbor to see the sunset, and the city lights. **Darwin Harbour Cruises** (www.darwinharbourcruises.com.au; © **08/8942 3131**) operates a sunset cruise aboard the 25m (82-ft.) catamaran Charles Darwin. Tickets cost A$58 per adult and A$43 for children 4 to 14, or a 3-course buffet dinner cruise for A$102 adults and A$68 children. Cruises leave from Stokes Hill Wharf at 6pm, returning around 8:30pm.

The world's best South Sea pearls are farmed in the Top End seas. Buy, or just drool in the window at **Paspaley Pearls,** in the Charles Darwin Centre at 19 Smith St. (www.paspaleypearls.com; *✆* **1300/888 080** in Australia, or 08/8930 4500). If you fancy a pink diamond (the world's rarest) from the Argyle Diamond Mine in Kununurra, you can get them at **Creative Jewellers,** 32 Smith Street Mall (www.creativejewellers.com; *✆* **08/8941 1233**), an Argyle-appointed supplier that buys direct from the mine. It also stocks champagne diamonds, for which Argyle is renowned, and other Argyle diamonds, as well as opals and South Sea pearls.

Jokes about "snapping handbags" abound in croc country. For your own croc-skin fashion statement, head to **di Croco,** 27 Smith Street Mall (www.dicroco.com, *✆* **08/8941 4470**). You'll find bags, purses, wallets, belts, pens, and other accessories, all made from saltwater croc skins farmed locally.

Day Trip to Litchfield National Park ★★★

120km (74 miles) S of Darwin

An easy 90-minute drive south of Darwin is a miniature Garden of Eden full of forests, waterfalls, rocky sandstone escarpments, glorious swimming holes, and prehistoric cycads that look as if they belong on the set of *Jurassic Park.* Litchfield National Park is much smaller (a mere 146,000 hectares/360,620 acres) and much less famous than its big sister, Kakadu (p. 255), but it is no less stunning.

The park's main attractions are spring-fed swimming holes, like the magical plunge pool at **Florence Falls ★★★**, 29km (18 miles) from the forest. At Florence Falls, it's a 15-minute hike down stairs to the water, so the easily accessible pool at **Wangi Falls ★**, 49km (30 miles) from the eastern entrance, gets more crowds. (That's also a beautiful spot, surrounded by cliffs and forests with a lookout from the top.) More idyllic grottoes are 4km (2½ miles) from Florence Falls at **Buley Rockhole,** a series of tiered rock pools and waterfalls. You can't swim at **Tolmer Falls,** but during the Wet when they're flowing, take the boardwalk about 400m (1,312 ft.) to the lookout and see the cascade against a backdrop of red cliffs. Roads to most swimming holes are paved, although a few are accessible only by four-wheel-drive.

There are a number of short **walking trails** through the park, such as the half-hour Shady Creek Circuit from Florence Falls up to the parking lot.

Parts of the park are also home to thousands of 2m-high (6½-ft.) **"magnetic" termite mounds,** so called because they run north-south to escape the fierce midday heat. A display hut and a viewing point are 17km (11 miles) from the park's eastern entrance.

To get there from Darwin, head south for 86km (53 miles) on the Stuart Highway and follow the park turnoff on the right through the town of Batchelor for another 34km (21 miles). A number of day-trip tours run from Darwin. Crowds of locals can shatter the peace in Litchfield on weekends, especially in the Dry season, but the park is worth visiting, crowds or no crowds. Entry is free.

Cooling off in rocky swimming holes is a prime pleasure in Litchfield National Park.

Tip: In the Wet (approximately Nov–Apr), some roads—usually the four-wheel-drive ones—may be closed, and the Wangi water hole may be off-limits due to turbulence and strong currents. Check with the **Parks & Wildlife Commission** (© **08/8999 4555**) before you leave Darwin during this time.

Day Trip to Nitmiluk National Park (Katherine Gorge) ★★★

In 1989, after a 10-year campaign, the indigenous Jawoyn people regained legal ownership of the land they had inhabited for tens of thousands of years before Europeans arrived, land that included the gorge formerly named Katherine after the daughter of explorer John McDouall Stuart's sponsor, pastoralist James Chambers. The gorge now takes its name from *nitmiluk*, the Jawoyn word derived from the "nit-nit" sound of the cicadas you may hear. Nitmiluk Gorge is actually a series of 13 gorges, and cruising the Katherine River in an **open-sided boat** is the most popular way to appreciate its beauty. Most cruises ply only the first two or three, but you can go further by canoe.

Nitmiluk Tours (www.nitmiluktours.com.au; © **1300/146 743** in Australia) operates all cruises. Most people take a 2-hour Aboriginal cultural cruise, available three times a day at 9 and 11am, and 2pm. The cost is A$92 for adults and A$46 for children 6 to 15. There is also a 4-hour cruise once daily, although you will probably be satisfied with 2 hours. They also run dawn cruises and sunset dinner cruises. Wear sturdy shoes; because each gorge is cut off from the next by rapids, all cruises involve some walking along the bank.

Cruising is nice, but in a **canoe** you can discover sandy banks and waterfalls and get up close to the gorge walls, the birds, and those crocs. (Don't worry—they're the freshwater kind and not typically regarded as dangerous to humans.) Rocks separate the gorges, so be prepared to carry your canoe quite often. You may even want to camp out on the banks overnight. A half-day canoe rental is A$70 for a single and A$81 double, with a A$50 cash deposit. Canoeing the gorge is popular, so book canoes ahead, especially in the Dry season. (Canoe rentals are not available Dec–May.)

Some 100km (62 miles) of **hiking trails** crisscross Nitmiluk National Park, ranging in duration from a 1-hour walk to the lookout to a 5-day trek to Leliyn (Edith Falls; see below). Trails—through rocky terrain and forests, past water holes, and along the gorge—start from the Nitmiluk Visitor Centre, where you can pick up trail maps. Overnight walks require a permit, and a A$3.30 per-person camping permit, payable at the Nitmiluk Visitor Centre.

One of the nicest spots in the park is 42km (26 miles) north of Katherine, 20km (13 miles) off the Stuart Highway: **Leliyn** (also known as Edith Falls) ★ is a wonderland of natural, croc-free swimming holes bordered by red cliffs, monsoonal forest, and pandanus palms. Among the bushwalks leading from Edith Falls is a 2.6km (1.5-mile) round-trip trail, which takes about 2 hours and incorporates a dip at the upper pool en route.

For a vaster perspective, it's also fascinating to get aerial views of the entire ravine-ridden Arnhem Plateau, which stretches uninhabited to the horizon. **Nitmiluk Scenic Flights** (www.nitmilluktours.com.au; ✆ **08/8971 0877**) operates from a helipad near the Nitmiluk Gorge Visitor Centre and runs a range of scenic flights, starting from A$105 per person for a 10-minute flight over the first three gorges.

Canoes are the perfect way to explore the scenic gorges of Nitmiluk National Park.

If you want to stay overnight, the lovely **Cicada Lodge** (www.cicadalodge. com.au; © **1300/146743** in Australia, or 08/8971 0877) is close to the park visitor center. Owned by the Jawoyn people, it is only 10 minutes' walk from the base of the first gorge on the Katherine River. The lodge has 18 rooms, an outdoor swimming pool with lounges and sun umbrellas, and a smart restaurant. There is also a **camping ground** with permanent tents (with beds, from A\$120 per tent per night double) and camping sites (A\$50 double powered; A\$20 per person unpowered).

KAKADU NATIONAL PARK ★★★

257km (159 miles) E of Darwin

The ecological gem that is Kakadu National Park covers 1.7 million hectares (4.2 million acres), making this World Heritage area Australia's largest national park. You'll see only a fraction of it, but will remember it forever.

Cruising the lily-clad wetlands to spot crocodiles, plunging into exquisite natural swimming holes, hiking through spear grass and cycads, fishing for barramundi, soaring in a helicopter over torrential waterfalls during the Wet season, photographing thousands of birds flying over the eerie red sandstone escarpment that juts 200m (650 ft.) above the flood plain, and admiring some of Australia's ancient Aboriginal rock-art sites—these are the activities that draw people to Kakadu. It is also one of the richest wildlife habitats in Australia, home to 275 species of birds and 75 species of reptiles. Wildlife viewing here is not quite as breathtaking as in an African game park, where herds roam the plains—even Australians get excited when they spot a kangaroo in the wild—but with patience, you may have some rewarding sightings.

Kakadu is a big place—about 200km (124 miles) long by 100km (62 miles) wide—so plan to spend at least a night. Day trips are available from Darwin, but it's too far and too big to see much in a day. It is best in the late Dry, around September and October, when crocs and birds gather around shrinking water holes. Note that facilities are limited: The only town of any size is Jabiru (population 1,100), a mining community where you can find banking facilities and a few shops.

Essentials

ARRIVING

Follow the Stuart Highway 34km (21 miles) south of Darwin, and turn left onto the Arnhem Highway to the park's northern entrance station. The trip takes 2½ to 3 hours. If you're coming from the south, turn off the Stuart Highway at Pine Creek onto the Kakadu Highway, and follow the Kakadu Highway for 79km (49 miles) to the park's southern entrance.

A big range of coach, minibus, and four-wheel-drive tours and camping safaris, usually lasting 1, 2, or 3 days, depart from Darwin daily. These are a good idea, because many of Kakadu's geological, ecological, and Aboriginal attractions come to life only with a guide. The best water holes, lookouts, and

Kakadu's Heritage

The name Kakadu comes from Gagudju, the group of languages spoken by Aborigines in the northern part of the park, where they and their ancestors have lived for at least 50,000 years.

Today, these traditional owners manage the park in conjunction with the Australian government. Their culture is on display at a cultural center and at rock painting sites.

wildlife-viewing spots change dramatically from month to month, even from day to day.

VISITOR INFORMATION

Before you arrive, you can find information on Kakadu, and book tours at the Tourism Top End information center in Darwin. You can also contact the rangers at the park directly (© **08/8938 1120**).

Both the park entrances—the northern station on the Arnhem Highway used by visitors from Darwin and the southern station on the Kakadu Highway for visitors from Katherine—hand out free visitor guides with maps. In the Dry they also issue a timetable of free ranger-guided bushwalks, art-site talks, and slide shows taking place that week. Park entry costs A$40 adults and A$20 children 5 to 15. Park permits can be purchased online (**www.parks australia.gov.au/kakadu**), or at the **Bowali Visitor Centre** (© **08/8938 1120**), on the Kakadu Highway, 5km (3 miles) from Jabiru, 100km (62 miles) from the northern entry station, and 131km (81 miles) from the southern entry station. Passes are also available through other outlets (check the website) and are valid for 7 days.

The Bowali Visitor Centre, an attractive, environmentally friendly Outback-style building, shows a program of 1-hour videos on the park's natural history and Aboriginal culture; it also has a library, displays, a gift shop, and a cafe. You may want to spend a good hour or so here, more to see a video. It is open daily from 8am to 5pm.

You can also book tours and get information at **Kakadu Tours and Travel,** Shop 6, Tasman Plaza, Jabiru (www.kakadutoursand travel.com.au; © **08/8979 2548**).

GETTING AROUND

Most major attractions are accessible in a two-wheel-drive vehicle on sealed (paved) roads, but a four-wheel-drive vehicle allows you to get to more falls, water holes, and campsites. Car-rental companies will not permit you to take two-wheel-drive vehicles on unpaved roads. **Territory Thrifty** (© **08/8979 2552**) rents cars at the Mercure Kakadu Crocodile Hotel, Flinders Street, Jabiru; otherwise, rent a car in Darwin. If you rent a four-wheel-drive in the Wet season (Nov–Apr), always check floodwater levels on all roads at the **Bowali Visitor Centre** (© **08/8938 1120**). The Bowali Visitor Centre, many attractions such as Nourlangie and Yellow Water Billabong, and the towns of Jabiru and Cooinda usually stay above the floodwaters year-round.

Where to Stay & Eat Around Kakadu NP

Garnamarr Campground (named for the red-tailed black cockatoo commonly found in Kakadu) is near Jim Jim Falls and Twin Falls. It has sites for 200 people but doesn't accept reservations, so check at the Bowali Visitor Centre (📞 **08/8938 1120**) before driving there, to see whether it is full. High season is April to late October or early November. The campground manager collects the fee of A$15 adults, A$7.50 children, and A$38 families (cash only). For information on other campgrounds, check **www.parksaustralia. gov.au/kakadu/stay/camping**.

Aurora Kakadu ★ This property's location—near the northern entrance to the park—might seem handy, but that makes it the farthest accommodation from such major attractions as Yellow Waters and Nourlangie (many tour operators do pick up here). However, the resort's green lawns and tropical gardens adorned with wandering peacocks and goannas and chattering native birds are a wonderfully restful haven from the harsh surroundings of Kakadu outside. A 3.6km (2-mile) nature trail winds from the hotel through monsoon forest and past a billabong. Don't yield to the temptation to dive into the lily-filled lagoon down the back—like every other waterway in Kakadu, it is home to saltwater crocs! But you can safely walk out on the fenced-off viewing platform for a close-up look at the wildlife. All rooms have a balcony or patio, and there are family rooms that sleep four.

Arnhem Hwy., South Alligator (41km/25 miles W of Bowali Visitor Centre). www.aurora resorts.com.au. 📞 **1800/818 845** in Australia, or 08/8979 0166. 138 units. A$174–A$238 double; A$194–A$204 family rooms. Free parking. **Amenities:** Restaurant; bar; Jacuzzi; shaded outdoor pool; day/night tennis court; free Wi-Fi.

Bamurru Plains ★★★ There can be few experiences to beat waking up to the sight of buffalo roaming the green, lush floodplains of Kakadu in the Wet. This stylish luxury lodge on the edge of the Mary River flood plains, between the coast and the western boundary of Kakadu National Park, offers a rich array of wildlife encounters and an eco-friendly environment in which to base yourself. Your luxury tent has a timber floor, fine linens on the bed, and a high-pressure shower in the bathroom, but no phone, TV, or other distractions. Three tents have air-conditioning—at a price: To discourage the use of generator power, Bamurru Plains charges an extra A$120 for using the air-conditioning (it must be requested when booking). On three sides, the tents' walls are one-way screens that give stupendous views and total privacy. For the adventurous, a tree-house "sleep-out" called The Hide is available for two to four guests, a bit away from the main lodge, where you sleep on the floor surrounded by the sounds of the bush. I have only visited in the Wet, but other guests were repeat visitors, determined to see both seasons . . . a sure indication their first visit—in the Dry—was memorable. Meals are served at the main lodge building around a communal table. Activities include guided walks, airboat safaris on the wetlands, river cruises, fishing, 4WD safaris to view wildlife (*Bamurru* is the Aboriginal name for the magpie geese you will see in the thousands), and day tours to Kakadu or Arnhemland. *Tip:* The best way to get to Bamurru Plains is by light plane, a 30-minute flight from Darwin. If you drive to this working buffalo station, you will have to leave your car at the gate, and a staff member will pick you up for the 20-minute drive to the lodge. It is about a 3-hour drive from Darwin and 2½ hours from Jabiru.

Swim Creek Station, Harold Knowles Rd. (P.O. Box 1020), Humpty Doo. www.bamurru plains.com. ℂ **1300/790 561** in Australia, or 02/9571 6399. 10 units. A$1,300 double; A$325 children 17 and under sharing with adults; A$585 children sharing a separate room. Minimum 2-night stay. Rates include all meals, drinks, and activities. Closed Nov–Apr. **Amenities:** Restaurant; bar; swimming pool; no Wi-Fi.

Mercure Kakadu Crocodile Hotel ★★ Some people think this hotel is kitsch; others declare it an architectural masterpiece. I like it. It was built to the specifications of its Aboriginal owners, the Gagudju people, in the form of their spirit ancestor, a giant crocodile called Ginga. The building's entrance is the "jaws," the two floors of rooms are in the "belly," the circular parking lot clusters are "eggs," and so on. From the ground, it's hard to see, but from the air, the shape is quite distinct. Love it or hate it, it is one of the best places to stay in Kakadu, a stylish modern hotel with basic but comfortable rooms. The lobby doubles as a gallery selling the works of local Aboriginal artists, and a trail leads to the Bowali Visitor Centre. There is a 9-hole golf course, tennis courts, and Olympic-size swimming pool a few blocks away.

1 Flinders St. (5km/3 miles E of Bowali Visitor Centre), Jabiru. www.accorhotels.com. ℂ **1800/007 697** in Australia, or 08/8979 9000. 110 units. A$289–A$309 double, A$329 family room (sleeps 4). **Amenities:** Restaurant; 2 bars; babysitting; small outdoor pool; room service; free Wi-Fi.

Cooinda Lodge ★ These modest but pleasant accommodations are set among tropical gardens at the departure point for Yellow Water Billabong cruises. The simply furnished tile-floor bungalows are big, comfortable, and air-conditioned, and there are 22 family rooms that sleep up to four. The lodge is something of a town center, with a general store, gift shop, currency exchange, post office, fuel, camping sites, and other facilities. Eat at the rustic **Barra Bistro and Bar,** which serves an all-day snack menu, with live entertainment in the Dry season. Dining options can be limited between November and March in the Wet. Scenic flights take off from the lodge's airstrip, and the Warradjan Aboriginal Cultural Centre is a 15-minute walk.

Kakadu Hwy. (50km/31 miles S of Bowali Visitor Centre), Jabiru. www.accorhotels.com. ℂ **08/8979 1500.** 48 units. A$294 double; A$329 family room (sleeps 4). **Amenities:** Restaurant; bar; outdoor pool; no Wi-Fi.

Highlights En Route to Kakadu NP

En route to the park, stop in at the **Fogg Dam Conservation Reserve** (ℂ **08/8988 8009**), 25km (16 miles) down the Arnhem Highway and 7km (4⅓ miles) off the highway. You'll get a close-up look at geese, finches, ibis, brolgas, and other wetland birds from lookouts over ponds of giant lilies, or by walking through monsoon forests to viewing "hides." There are two lookouts

NEVER smile AT A YOU-KNOW-WHAT!

The Aboriginal Gagudju people of the Top End have long worshiped a giant crocodile called Ginga, but the way white Australians go on about these reptilian relics of a primeval age, you'd think they worshiped them, too. There is scarcely a soul in the Northern Territory who will not regale you with his or her personal croc story, and each one will be more outrageous than the last.

Aussies may be good at pulling your leg with tall tales, but when they warn you not to swim in crocodile country, they're deadly serious. After all, crocodiles are good at pulling your leg, too—literally. Here are some tips:

- There are two kinds of crocodile in Australia: the highly dangerous and enormously powerful saltwater or "estuarine" croc; and the "harmless" freshwater croc, which will attack only if threatened or accidentally stood on. **Note:** Saltwater crocs can and do swim in the ocean, but they live in fresh water.
- Don't swim in *any* waterway, swimming hole, or waterfall unless you have been specifically told it

is safe. Take advice only from someone such as a recognized tour operator or a park ranger. You can never be sure where crocodiles lurk from year to year, because during every Wet season crocs head upriver to breed, and they spread out over a wide flooded area. As the floodwaters subside, they are trapped in whatever water they happen to be in at the time—so what was a safe swimming hole last Dry season might not be croc-free this year.

- Never stand on or walk along a riverbank, and stand well back when fishing. A 6m (20-ft.) croc can be 2½ centimeters (1 in.) beneath the surface of that muddy water yet remain invisible. It moves fast, so you won't see it until you're in its jaws.
- Make your campsite and clean your fish at least 25m (82 ft.) from the bank.

And if you do come face to face with a crocodile? There is little you can do. Just don't get into this situation in the first place!

on the road and three walks, two that are 2.2km (1.5 miles) round-trip and one that is 3.6km (2.3 miles) round-trip. Entry is free. Crocs live here, so don't swim, and keep away from the water's edge.

Four kilometers (2½ miles) further down the Arnhem Highway at Beatrice Hill, you can stop at the **Window on the Wetlands Visitor Centre** (*©* **08/8988 8188**), which offers views across the Adelaide River flood plain, as well as displays and touch-screen information on the wetlands' ecology. It's free and open daily from 8am to 5:30pm (except Christmas Day).

Just past Beatrice Hill on the highway at the Adelaide River Bridge (look out for the statue of a grinning croc), **Adelaide River Queen Cruises** (www. jumpingcrocodilecruises.com.au; *©* **08/8988 8144**) runs the **jumping crocodiles cruise.** From the relative safety of a restored paddle steamer (or a smaller boat in the Wet), you can watch wild crocodiles leap out of the water for hunks of meat dangled over the edge by the boat crew—but don't lean out too far! It's an unabashed tourist trap, with a souvenir shop that sells all things croc, including crocodile toilet-seat covers. It may not be to my taste—or yours—but because crocs typically move fast only when they attack, it may be your only chance to witness their immense power and speed. The cruises depart at 9 and 11am, and 1 and 3pm daily year-round (except on Dec 24–25 and Sun from Nov–Feb). The cost is A$50 adults and A$30 for children 4 to 14 for all cruises. If you need transport, Adelaide River Transfers (www.adelaiderivertransfers.com; ☏ **0438/946 444** mobile) provides a return shuttle for A$90 adults and A$70 children 1 to 14 (including cruise fare).

Top Attractions in Kakadu National Park

WETLANDS CRUISES

One of Kakadu's most popular attractions is **Yellow Water Billabong,** 50km (31 miles) south of the Bowali Visitor Centre at Cooinda. It's rich with freshwater mangroves, paperbark trees, pandanus palms, water lilies, and masses of birds gathering to drink—sea eagles, honking magpie geese, kites, chinablue kingfishers, and jaçanas (called "Jesus birds" because they seem to walk on water as they step across the lily pads). This is one of the best places in the park to spot saltwater crocs. Cruises in canopied boats with commentary depart near Cooinda Lodge six times a day starting at 6:45am in the Dry (Apr–Oct) and four times a day in the Wet (Nov–Mar). A 90-minute cruise is A$72 for adults and A$50 for children 4 to 15. A 2-hour cruise is A$90 for adults, A$62 for children (or A$99 adults and A$70 children for the early morning cruise, including breakfast). Book online (www.kakadutourism.com) or through **Cooinda Lodge** (☏ **08/8979 1500**).

Fair warning: In the Wet, when the Billabong floods and joins up with Jim Jim Creek and the South Alligator River, the bird life spreads far and wide over the park and the crocs head upriver to breed, so don't expect wildlife viewing to be spectacular.

Another worthwhile cruise is the Aboriginal-owned and -operated **Guluyambi Cultural Cruise** on the East Alligator River (www.kakaduculturaltours.com.au; ☏ **1800/525 238** in Australia). The East Alligator River forms the border between Kakadu and isolated Arnhemland. Unlike the Yellow Water cruise, which focuses on crocs, birds, and plants, this excursion teaches you about Aboriginal myths, bush tucker, and hunting techniques. The cruise lasts about 1 hour and 45 minutes, starting at 9 and 11am, and 1 and 3pm daily May through November. It costs A$79 for adults, A$52 for children 4 to 14. Cruises are limited to 25 passengers, so book ahead.

ABORIGINAL ART & CULTURE

There are as many as 5,000 rock painting sites—some of them believed to be 50,000 years old—throughout the park, though for cultural reasons the indigenous owners make only a few accessible to visitors. The best are Nourlangie Rock and Ubirr Rock. Access to the sites is free (once you have your park permit, available from the Bowali Visitor Centre; see p. 256).

Nourlangie, 31km (19 miles) southeast of the Bowali Visitor Centre, features "X-ray"-style paintings of animals; a vivid, energetic striped Dreamtime figure of Namarrgon, the "Lightning Man"; and modern depictions of a white man in boots, a rifle, and a sailing ship. You'll also find rock paintings at **Nanguluwur,** on the other side of Nourlangie Rock. There is a 1.5km (1-mile) signposted trail past Nourlangie's paintings (short trails to the art sites shoot off it) and an easy 1.7km (1-mile) trail from the parking lot into Nanguluwur.

There are a variety of excellent sites at **Ubirr Rock,** which is more remote, around 43km (27 miles, or an hour's drive) from the Bowali Visitor Centre, and around 3km north of the Border Store at the East Alligator River. A 1km (.5-mile) signposted trail leads past the sites at Ubirr, and while you can see paintings at lower levels, it is worth the effort to hike to the top of the 250m (820-ft.) outlook for the additional art sites higher up, and for spectacular views of the flood plain. Unlike most sites in Kakadu, Ubirr is not open 24 hours—it opens at 8:30am April through November and at 2pm December through March, and closes at sunset year-round. Ubirr Rock can be cut off in the Wet, but the views of afternoon lightning storms from the top at that time are breathtaking.

Displays and videos about bush tucker, Dreamtime creation myths, and lifestyles of the Bininj Aborigines can be found at the **Warradjan Aboriginal Cultural Centre** at Cooinda (© **08/8979 0525**). At the direction of the Aboriginal owners, the center was built in the shape of a pig-nose turtle; its quality gift shop sells such items as didgeridoos, bark paintings by local artists, and baskets woven from pandanus fronds. The center is open daily from 9am to 5pm, and admission is free. A 1km-long (.5-mile) trail connects it to Cooinda Lodge (p. 258) and the Yellow Water Billabong (see above).

Yellow Water Billabong cruises often encounter Kakadu's most intriguing denizen: the powerful (and dangerous) saltwater crocodile.

Aboriginal Art at Injalak

If you are taking a tour to Arnhemland, make sure it goes to **Injalak Arts** (www.injalak.com; © **08/8979 0190**) at Gunbalanya (Oenpelli), a small Aboriginal township about 300km (186 miles) east of Darwin.

Injalak draws its inspiration from Injalak Hill, a site rich in rock paintings. Since it opened in 1989, the center has gained a reputation for producing fine indigenous contemporary art, carvings, and weavings. This is the place to buy them at their source and to meet the artists, some of whom are likely to be working on the veranda when you visit. Injalak is a nonprofit, community enterprise, and you can be sure that all artists are paid upfront in full for their work.

Tours of Injalak Hill, taking about 3 hours, run from the arts center during the Dry season (May–Nov) at 9am daily (except Sun and public holidays). The cost is A$110 adults and A$33 children 17 and under. Injalak is open Monday through Friday 8:30am to 5pm and Saturdays from 9am to 2pm, but it is advisable to check first.

Note: Visitors to Injalak need a permit from the **Northern Land Council** (© **08/8920 5100** in Darwin, or 08/8938 3000 in Jabiru). It is only possible to drive to Gunbalanya in the Dry, May to November. Unless you have a 4WD, ensure you check road conditions with the NLC before setting out. You will need to drive across a flooded causeway on the East Alligator River, so check tide times. Between December and April, in the Wet, access is by air only. Permits are required whether driving or flying. The permit is to visit Injalak only—once you cross the East Alligator River you may not stop anywhere until you arrive at Injalak. It may sound difficult, but if you are fascinated by Aboriginal art and culture you will find it very rewarding.

SCENIC FLIGHTS

Scenic flights over the flood plains and the rainforest-filled ravines of the escarpment are worth taking if the strain is not too great on your wallet. They're much more interesting in the Wet than in the Dry, because the flood plains spread and Jim Jim Falls and Twin Falls swell from their Dry season trickle to a flood. Viewing it from the air is also the best way to appreciate the clever crocodile shape of the Crocodile Hotel. **Kakadu Air Services** (www.kakaduair.com.au; © **1800/089 113** in Australia, or 08/8941 9611) runs 30-minute fixed-wing flights from Jabiru for A$150 adults and A$120 children, as well as helicopter flights from A$230 per person for 20 minutes. **Airborne Solutions** (www.airbornesolutions.com.au; © **1300/435 486** in Australia, or 08/8972 2345) runs a Kakadu helicopter day trip from Darwin for A$2,095 per person (minimum 2 people), in which you will cover nearly 700km (435 miles) and see places inaccessible to most people. The tour includes a lunch stop at Cooinda Lodge and isolated rock painting sites. It's expensive, but worth every cent in my book!

FISHING

Kakadu's wetlands are brimming with barramundi, and Territorians like nothing more than to hop in a tin dinghy barely big enough to resist a croc attack and go looking for them. **Kakadu Fishing Tours** (www.kakadufishingtours.

com.au; © **08/8979 2025**) takes you fishing in a 5.7m (19-ft.) sportfishing boat. Tours depart from Jabiru, 5km (3 miles) east of the Bowali Visitor Centre, and cost A\$240 per person for 5½ hours and A\$380 per person for a full day (10½ hours).

BUSHWALKING

Wide-ranging **bush and wetlands walking trails,** including many short walks and six half- to full-day treks, lead throughout the park. The Bowali Visitor Centre sells hiking-trail maps. Typical trails include a less than 1km (less than .5-mile) amble through the Manngarre Monsoon Forest near Ubirr Rock; an easy 3.8km (2.5-mile) circular walk at the Iligadjar Wetlands near the Bowali Visitor Centre; and a tough 12km (7.5-mile) round-trip trek through rugged sandstone country at Nourlangie Rock.

One of the best wetlands walks is at **Mamukala wetlands,** 29km (18 miles) from Jabiru. Thousands of magpie geese feed here, especially in the late Dry season around October. An observation platform gives you a good view, and a sign explains the dramatic seasonal changes the wetlands undergo. Choose from a 1km (.5-mile) or 3km (1.8-mile) round-trip meander.

SWIMMING

In the eastern section of the park rises a massive red-sandstone escarpment that sets the stage for two waterfalls, **Jim Jim Falls** and **Twin Falls.** In the Dry, the volume of water may not be all that impressive, but the settings are magical. Both are accessible by four-wheel-drive only, and neither is open in the Wet.

A 1km (.5-mile) walk over rocks and through rainforest leads to a deep green plunge pool at **Jim Jim Falls,** 103km (64 miles) from the Bowali Visitor Centre. An almost perfectly circular 150m (492-ft.) cliff surrounds the water. Allow 2 hours to drive the final unpaved 60km (37 miles) off the highway. Due to floodwaters, Jim Jim Falls may not open until as late as June. At **Twin Falls,** the waterfalls descend into a natural pool edged by a sandy beach, surrounded by bush and high cliffs. Note that you must swim or float the last 500m (1,640 ft.) to the base of the falls—and be warned that saltwater crocodiles have been found in this area.

Some people swim at spots that are generally regarded as croc-free, such as Jim Jim Falls; however, you do so at your own risk. Although rangers survey the swimming holes at the start of the season, and crocodiles are territorial

A Swim in the Falls

Remember the idyllic pool that Paul Hogan and Linda Koslowski plunged into in *Crocodile Dundee*? That was **Gunlom Falls,** 170km (105 miles) south of the Bowali Visitor Centre. A climb to the top rewards you with great views of southern Kakadu. It is generally regarded as croc-free and safe for swimming. Access is by four-wheel-drive; it is cut off in the Wet.

creatures, no one can guarantee that a saltwater crocodile has not moved into a swimming hole. Ask at the Bowali Visitor Centre which pools are croc-free (it can change from year to year) before setting off. If you are unsure about a water hole's safety, the only place rangers recommend you swim is your hotel pool.

ALICE SPRINGS

462km (286 miles) NE of Uluru; 1,491km (924 miles) S of Darwin; 1,544km (957 miles) N of Adelaide; 2,954km (1,831 miles) NW of Sydney

"Alice" or "the Alice," as Australians fondly call it, is the unofficial capital of the Red Centre and a gateway to Uluru.

Many tourists visit Alice only to get to Uluru, but you might like to spend a few days here exploring its indigenous culture and outlying natural attractions. Home to about 29,800 people, it's a rambling, unsophisticated place that is the heart of the Aboriginal Arrernte people's country. Alice is a rich source of tours, shops, and galleries for those interested in Aboriginal culture, art, or souvenirs. However, parts of this region are also evidence that ancient Aboriginal civilization has not always meshed well with the 21st century, which has resulted in fractured riverbed communities plagued by alcohol and other social problems. And it is likely that you will see evidence of this on the streets.

No matter what direction you come from to get here, you will fly for hours over a vast, flat landscape. On arrival, you will see that in fact it is close to a low, dramatic range of rippling red mountains, the **MacDonnell Ranges.** Many visitors excitedly expect to see Uluru, but that marvel is about 462km (286 miles) down the road.

The red folds of the MacDonnell Ranges hide lovely gorges with shady picnic grounds. The area has an old gold-rush town to poke around in, quirky little museums, wildlife parks, a couple of cattle stations (ranches) that welcome visitors, hiking trails to put red dust on your boots, and one of the world's top 10 desert golf courses.

Essentials

ARRIVING

BY PLANE   **Qantas** (www.qantas.com) flies direct from Sydney, Adelaide, Darwin, Perth, Melbourne, Brisbane, Cairns, and Uluru. **Virgin Australia** (www.virginaustralia.com) flies direct from Adelaide, Brisbane, Melbourne, and Darwin.

Alice Springs Airport (www.alicespringsairport.com.au) is about 15km (9⅓ miles) out of town. The airport shuttle operated by **Alice Wanderer Airport Transfers** (www.alicewanderer.com.au; ✆ **1800/722 111** in Australia, or 08/8952 2111) meets all flights and transfers you to your Alice hotel door for A$17 adults, A$8.50 children, or A$40 for a family of four. A taxi from the airport to town is around A$35.

Alice Springs

Downtown Area

ATTRACTIONS ●
Alice Springs Desert Park **3**
Alice Springs Reptile Centre **14**
Alice Springs Telegraph Station
   Historical Reserve **2**
Araluen Cultural Precinct **4**
Central Australian Aviation
   Museum **5**
Royal Flying Doctor Service **15**
School of the Air **1**

0   1/4 mi
0   0.25 km

see inset above

RESTAURANTS ◆
Barra on Todd **6**
Hanuman **8**
Overlanders Steakhouse **11**
Red Ochre Grill **13**

HOTELS ■
Alice on Todd Apartments **9**
Aurora Alice Springs **10**
Desert Palms Resort **7**
Elkira Court Motel **12**
Mercure Alice Springs Resort **6**

Who was Alice?

Alice Springs was named after Alice Todd, wife of astronomer and engineer Charles Todd, who won the tender to construct the Overland Telegraph line. In 1871, surveyor William Mills was charged with finding a suitable location for a repeater station as part of the Overland Telegraph line, and discovered a massive inland river system. He named it for his boss, Charles Todd—not knowing that the Todd River would almost always be dry. He found what he believed to be a natural spring in the river system, and named it for Mrs. Todd. In fact, there was no spring, just a water hole left when the rest of the river had dried up. Alice Todd died in Adelaide in 1898, aged 52.

BY TRAIN   If you are a train buff, you may want to plan a trip from Sydney to Alice Springs that takes in two of Australia's great train journeys. First take the 24-hour journey on the **Indian Pacific** (which travels across the continent from Sydney to Perth) from Sydney to Adelaide, then change direction (and trains) to head north to Alice on **The Ghan** (so named after Afghan camel-train drivers who carried supplies in the Red Centre during the 19th century). The Ghan makes the trip from Adelaide to Alice every week—it's another 24-hour ride—before continuing to Darwin. It promises to be a very long—but memorable—journey. For information, contact **Great Southern Railway** (www.greatsouthernrail.com.au; ℂ **1800/703 357** in Australia, or 08/8213 4401).

BY BUS   Greyhound (www.greyhound.com.au; ℂ **1300/473 946** in Australia, or 08/8952 7888 in Alice Springs) runs from Darwin. The trip takes about 22 hours, and the fare is A$277.

BY CAR   Alice Springs is on the Stuart Highway linking Adelaide and Darwin. Allow a very long 2 days or a more comfortable 3 days to drive from Adelaide, the same from Darwin. From Sydney, connect to the Stuart Highway via Broken Hill and Port Augusta north of Adelaide; from Cairns, head south to Townsville, then west via the town of Mount Isa to join the Stuart Highway at Tennant Creek. Both routes are long and dull. From Perth, it is even longer; drive across the Nullarbor Plain to connect with the Stuart Highway at Port Augusta. If you fancy a driving holiday of the area, check out **www.northernterritory.com** for advice on routes, accommodations, and other important details, such as locations of fuel stops.

VISITOR INFORMATION

The **Alice Springs Visitor Information Centre,** Todd Mall (www.discover centralaustralia.com; ℂ **1800/645 199** in Australia, or 08/8952 5800), is the official one-stop shop for bookings and touring information for the Red Centre, including Alice Springs, Kings Canyon, and Uluru–Kata Tjuta National Park. It also acts as the visitor center for the Parks & Wildlife Commission of the Northern Territory. It's open Monday through Friday from 8:30am to 5pm and weekends and public holidays (except Christmas Day, New Year's Day, and Good Friday) from 9:30am to 4pm.

GETTING AROUND ALICE SPRINGS

Virtually all tours pick you up at your hotel. If your itinerary traverses unpaved roads, as it may in outlying areas, you will need to rent a 4WD vehicle, because regular cars will not be insured on an unpaved surface. However, a regular car will get you to most attractions. **Budget,** 113 Todd Mall (www.budget.com.au; © **08/8952 8899**); **Hertz,** 34 Stott Terrace (www.hertz. com.au; © **08/8953 6257**); and **Thrifty,** 71 Hartley St. (www.thrifty.com.au; © **08/8952 9999**), all rent conventional and 4WD vehicles. **Avis** (www.avis. com.au; © **08/8952 3694**) and **Europcar** (www.europcar.com.au; © **08/8953 3799**) have desks at the airport, as do all the other companies.

Many rental outfits for motor homes (camper vans) have Alice offices. They include **Apollo Campers,** 40 Stuart Hwy. (www.apollocamper.com; © **08/8955 5305**, or 1800/777 779 in Australia), and **Britz Campervan Rental,** corner of Stuart Highway and Power Street (www.britz.com; © **08/8952 8814**). Renting a camper van can be significantly cheaper than staying in hotels and going on tours, but do the math first.

The best way to get around town without your own transport is aboard the **Alice Wanderer** bus (see "Organized Tours," p. 274). **Public buses** (© **08/8924 7666**) run around town; the main bus stop is at the corner of Gregory Terrace and Railway Terrace. The A$3 fare gives you unlimited bus travel for 3 hours. A daily ticket costs A$7 and provides unlimited bus travel on that day. For A$20 you can buy a weekly ticket, valid for 7 days from the date of purchase, or a 10-trip flexi-trip ticket (each valid for 3 hours). Both A$20 tickets are electronic "tap-and-ride" cards. Tickets can be bought on the bus. There are no public bus services on Sundays or public holidays.

For a taxi, call **Alice Springs Taxis** (© **131 008,** or 08/8952 1877) or find one at the rank (stand) on the corner of Todd Street and Gregory Terrace. Taxi fares here are high.

CITY LAYOUT

Todd Mall is the heart of town. Most shops, businesses, and restaurants are here or within a few blocks' walk. Most hotels, the casino, the golf course, and many of the town's attractions are a few kilometers outside of town. The dry Todd River "flows" through the city east of Todd Mall.

Behold the Bizarre

Alice Springs hosts a couple of bizarre events. The **Camel Cup** camel race (www.camelcup.com.au) takes place on the second Saturday in July. On the third Saturday in August, people from hundreds of miles around come out to cheer the **Henley-on-Todd Regatta** (www.henleyontodd.com.au), during which gaudily decorated, homemade bottomless "boats" race down the dry Todd River bed. Well, what else do you do on a river that rarely flows? See "Australia Calendar of Events" in chapter 2 (p. 31) for more details.

The Henley-on-Todd Regatta of bottomless boats racing on the dry Todd River bed.

Where to Stay in Alice Springs

Alice's hotel stock is not grand. Many properties have dated rooms and modest facilities; they're no match for the gleaming **Ayers Rock Resort** (p. 283). You may pay lower rates than those listed in the summer off-season (Dec–Mar) and even as late as June. Peak season typically runs from July through October or November.

If you've rented a camper van, the **Alice Springs Tourist Park,** Larapinta Drive, Alice Springs (www.alicespringstouristpark.com.au; ℭ **1300/823 404** in Australia, or 08/8952 2547), has powered sites costing A$40 a night. Cabins here cost between A$90 and A$175 per night, depending on the cabin and the season.

MODERATE/EXPENSIVE

Aurora Alice Springs ★★ This pleasant hotel is smack in the center of town. Rooms all have a fresh, contemporary decor. Executive rooms have a king-size bed and private balconies facing the Todd River; deluxe and standard rooms have either a double or queen bed and one single bed. Family rooms have a queen-size bed and two single beds. The small pool and Jacuzzi are tucked away in a corner, so this is not the place for chilling out poolside; stay here to be within walking distance of shops and restaurants. The hotel's Red Ochre Grill (p. 270) is recommended for gourmet "bush tucker" dining.

11 Leichhardt Terrace (backing onto Todd Mall). www.auroraresorts.com.au. ℭ **1800/089 644** in Australia, or 08/8950 6666. 109 units. A$145–A$245 double; A$158 family room. **Amenities:** Restaurant; barbecue in courtyard; airport shuttle; babysitting; Jacuzzi; small outdoor pool; room service; free Wi-Fi.

MODERATE

Alice on Todd Apartments ★★ Overlooking the Todd River, this contemporary complex has nice studios and one- and two-bedroom apartments. The one-bedroom "deluxe" apartments are a good option, particularly if you have kids. The apartments are very large, and some have two bathrooms. All but the studios have balconies, and some two-bedroom apartments have sofa beds. There is a washing machine in each unit and other amenities such as free storage lockers. The hotel is a short stroll from town.

Strehlow St. and South Terrace. www.aliceontodd.com.au. ℗ **08/8953 8033.** 57 units. A$135 studio apt; A$165–A$180 1-bedroom apt; A$210–A$245 2-bedroom apt. Covered parking. **Amenities:** Babysitting; bikes; children's playground; Jacuzzi; pool; free Wi-Fi.

Desert Palms Resort ★★ A large swimming pool with its own palm-studded island is the focal point at this complex of bright cabins, where privacy from your neighbors is ensured by trailing pink bougainvillea and palm trees. Don't be deterred by the prefab appearance; inside, the cabins are surprisingly large, well kept, and inviting, with pine-pitched ceilings, kitchenettes, a tiny bathroom, and furnished front decks. Four rooms are suitable for travelers with disabilities. The pleasant staff at the front desk sells basic grocery and liquor supplies, and can also book tours. You are also right next door to Lasseter's Casino (a debatable advantage) and the Alice Springs Golf Club. This is one of the nicest places to stay in Alice.

74 Barrett Dr. www.desertpalms.com.au. ℗ **1800/678 037** in Australia, or 08/8952 5977. 80 units. A$150 double; A$185 family. **Amenities:** Pool; half-size tennis court; free Wi-Fi.

Mercure Alice Springs Resort ★★ This low-rise property, a 3-minute walk from town over the Todd River, underwent a A$2-million upgrade in mid-2017, with all new fittings in the standard bedrooms and bathrooms, along with the installation of artworks that reflect the history of the Alice Springs region in all rooms. Deluxe rooms have bathtubs and bathrobes, a coffee machine, and a balcony or veranda overlooking the Todd River or the gardens. In summer, it's nice to repair to the pool under a couple of desert palms for a drink at the poolside bar. A new outdoor amphitheater will be a hub for Aboriginal workshops and cultural sessions. It's also a 5-minute walk along the boardwalk to the Olive Pink Botanic Garden.

34 Stott Terrace. www.accorhotels.com. ℗ **08/8951 4545.** 139 units. A$149–A$189 double. **Amenities:** Restaurant; 2 bars; free airport shuttle; babysitting; bikes; concierge; solar-heated outdoor pool; room service; free Wi-Fi.

MODERATE/INEXPENSIVE

Elkira Court Motel ★ The cheapest rooms in the heart of town—decent ones, that is—are at this clean, comfortable, unpretentious motel. The rooms are basic, but you won't get better value and all are air-conditioned. Deluxe rooms have kitchenettes, and some have king-size beds. Deluxe Spa rooms have two-person Jacuzzis. Ask for a room away from the road; the traffic is noisy during the day.

65 Bath St. (opposite Kmart). www.elkiracourtmotel.com.au. ℂ **08/8952 1222.** 58 units. A$110–A$180 double. **Amenities:** Restaurant; airport shuttle; nearby golf course; Jacuzzi; outdoor pool; free Wi-Fi.

Where to Eat in Alice Springs

Barra on Todd ★★ CONTEMPORARY   Part of the Mercure Alice Springs Resort, this restaurant serves up barramundi 10 ways. You can try this freshwater fish simply chargrilled with lemon and dill risotto, topped with asparagus, green beans, beurre blanc, and king prawns, or served in a variety of ways with nods to Chinese, Indian, Thai, and Greek tastes. If you're not a fan of fish, the menu offers plenty of other dishes including chicken, steaks, lamb, and duck. Barra on Todd does a buffet breakfast and has all-day (well, 11:30am–9pm) dining by the pool. It's popular for dinner, so book ahead.

In the Mercure Alice Springs Resort, 34 Stott Terrace. www.accorhotels.com. ℂ **08/8952 3523.** Main courses A$29–A$42. Daily 6–10am breakfast; 11:30am–5:30pm lunch; 6–11pm dinner.

Hanuman ★★★ CONTEMPORARY ASIAN   This is one of the most exotic restaurants in Alice Springs. The cuisine is a fusion of Thai and Indian cooking, and the decor is created with use of Asian artifacts and moody lighting. You are very unlikely to be disappointed by dishes such as red duck curry with coconut, lychees, kaffir lime, Thai basil, and fresh pineapple; or black pepper prawns with garlic, onion, and fresh curry leaf. There are plenty of vegetarian options too. There is another branch of Hanuman in Darwin (p. 247).

In the DoubleTree by Hilton, 82 Barrett Dr. www.hanuman.com.au. ℂ **08/8953 7188.** Main courses A$15–A$38. Mon–Fri noon–2:30pm; daily 6–10:30pm.

Overlanders Steakhouse ★★ STEAK/BUSH TUCKER   A landmark on the Alice dining scene, Overlanders is famous for its "Drover's Blowout" menu, which assaults the mega-hungry with soup and *damper* (a traditional Australian campfire bread), then a tasting platter of crocodile, camel, kangaroo fillets, and wild buffalo—these are just the appetizers—followed by rump steak or barramundi and dessert (apple pie or Pavlova). There's a regular menu with a 500-gram (1.1-lb.) steak, plus some lighter fare. From the rustic bar to the saddlebags and buffalo horns hanging from the roof and walls, it's Outback style throughout. Vegetarians, take heart: There's actually a reasonable menu for you too. It sounds over-the-top, but it's not; it's fun and interesting.

72 Hartley St. www.overlanders.com.au. ℂ **08/8952 2159.** Reservations required in peak season. Main courses A$19–A$43. Daily 6–10pm.

Red Ochre Grill ★★ GOURMET BUSH TUCKER   The chef at this upscale restaurant fuses native Aussie ingredients with dishes from around the world. If you've never tried crocodile ribs (served with a mint pea and corn fritter) or chargrilled kangaroo fillet with a red wine glaze, then this is your chance. Although it might seem a touristy formula, the food is delicious. Dine in the contemporary interior fronting Todd Mall or outside in the attractive courtyard. Reservations recommended at dinner, when the menu offers the best "bush tucker" options.

Todd Mall. www.redochrealice.com.au. ⓒ **08/8952 9614.** Main courses A$19–A$36. Daily 6:30-10am, noon–2:30pm, and 5–9pm (closed Christmas Day).

Exploring Alice Springs

All the major attractions in Alice Springs are within easy reach of the city center.

Alice Springs Desert Park ★★★ WILDLIFE VIEWING   By means of an easy 1.6km (1-mile) trail through three reconstructed natural habitats, this impressive wildlife and flora park shows you 120 or so of the animal species that live in the desert around Alice but that you won't spot too easily in the wild (including kangaroos you can walk among). Most of the creatures are small mammals (like the rare bilby), reptiles (cute thorny devil lizards), and birds. Don't miss the excellent free-flying bird presentation at 10am and 3:30pm daily. For a close-up meeting with Australia's largest bird of prey, the wedge-tailed eagle, another A$30 will give entry (and a photo session) to the **Eagle Encounter** show at 1:30pm weekdays. There's a cafe on premises. Allow 2 to 3 hours to see it all. **Tailormade Tours** (www.tailormadetours. com.au; ⓒ **08/8952 1731**) and **Alice Wanderer** (www.alicewanderer.com.au; ⓒ **1800/722 111** in Australia, or 08/8952 2111) both offer transfers from accommodations several times a day in each direction.

Larapinta Dr., 6km (3¾ miles) W of Alice Springs. www.alicespringsdesertpark.com.au. ⓒ **08/8951 8788.** A$32 adults, A$16 children 5–15, A$55–A$87 families. Daily 7:30am–6pm (last entry 4:30pm). Closed Christmas Day.

Alice Springs Reptile Centre ★★ WILDLIFE VIEWING   Kids love this place, where they can drape a python around their neck or have a bearded dragon (lizard) perch on their shoulder. Rex, the easygoing proprietor, helps you get the best photos and lets kids hand-feed bugs to the animals at feeding time. More than 50 species are on display, including the world's deadliest land snake (the taipan) and big goannas. Also here are brown snakes, death adders, and mulga, otherwise known as king brown snakes. Don't miss the saltwater

8

THE NORTHERN TERRITORY | Alice Springs

croc exhibit, with underwater viewing. The best time to visit is between 11am and 3pm, when the reptiles are at their most active. There are talks at 11am and 1 and 3:30pm. Allow an hour or so.

9 Stuart Terrace (opposite the Royal Flying Doctor Service). www.reptilecentre.com.au. *©* **08/8952 8900.** A$17 adults, A$9 children 4–16, A$44 families of 4. Daily 9:30am–5pm. Closed Christmas Day and New Year's Day.

Alice Springs Telegraph Station Historical Reserve ★★ HISTORIC SITE

This oasis marks the first European settlement of Alice Springs, which takes its name from the water hole nearby. Alice Springs began life here in 1872 as a telegraph repeater station, against a backdrop of red hills and sprawling gum trees. Arm yourself with the free map or join a free 45-minute tour at 9:30 and 11:30am, and 1:30 and 3:30pm. You can wander around the old stationmaster's residence; the telegraph office, with its Morse-code machine tap-tapping away; the shoeing yard, packed with blacksmithing equipment; and the stables, housing vintage buggies and saddlery. From the on-site computer, you can "telegraph" e-mail messages to your friends or be really old-fashioned and send mail through the Telegraph/Post Office, which will be stamped with a special franking stamp. It's a charming and much-underrated place. Allow an hour—more to walk one of the several hiking trails—or bring a picnic and stay longer. You are also likely to see kangaroos and rock wallabies. It has a gift shop and a kiosk where you can buy coffee and snacks. A pleasant way of getting there is to take the 4km (2.5-mile) riverside pedestrian/bike track that starts in town near the corner of Wills Terrace and Undoolya Road.

Stuart Hwy., 4km (2½ miles) N of Alice Springs (past the School of the Air turnoff). www.alicespringstelegraphstation.com.au. *©* **08/8952 3993.** Free admission to picnic grounds and trails; station A$15 adults, A$9.30 children 12–16, A$5.50 children 6–11, A$35 families of 4. Daily 9am–5pm (picnic grounds and trails 8am–9pm). Station closed Christmas Day.

Araluen Cultural Precinct ★★ GALLERIES/MUSEUMS

Take several hours to explore the many facets of this interesting complex of attractions. Impressive Aboriginal and contemporary Aussie art is on display at the **Araluen Arts Centre,** the town's performing-arts hub, which incorporates the **Araluen Art Collection,** focusing on works by Aboriginal artists from Central Australia from the early 1930s onwards, including Albert Namatjira and artists from the Papunya community in the early 1970s. Check out the "Honey Ant Dreaming" stained-glass window in the foyer. You can buy stylish crafts, and sometimes catch artists at work, in the **Central Craft** gallery. You may also want to amble among the fabulous outdoor sculptures, including the 15m (49-ft.) Yeperenye caterpillar, or among the gravestones in the cemetery next door, where "Afghani" camel herders (from what is now Pakistan) are buried facing Mecca. The **Museum of Central Australia** mostly shows local fossils, natural history displays, and meteorites, and the **Central Australian Aviation**

The gigantic Yeperenye caterpillar is among the outdoor sculptures featured in the Araluen Cultural Precinct.

Museum has a collection of old aircraft, radios, and wreckage that preserves the territory's aerial history. Located on the site of the 1939 Alice Springs "aerodrome," the museum includes the original hangar; among its highlights are a Beech 18 and a Wackett Trainer aircraft.

61 Larapinta Dr., at Memorial Ave., 2km (1¼ miles) W of Alice Springs. www.araluenarts centre.nt.gov.au. ✆ **08/8951 1122.** A$15 adults, A$10 children 5–16, A$40 families of 4. Daily 10am–4pm. Closed Good Friday and 2 weeks from Christmas Day.

Royal Flying Doctor Service Tourist Facility ★★ MUSEUM Alice is a major base for this airborne medical service that treats people living and traveling in the vast Outback. The visitor center provides a great insight into the work the RFDS does. Guided tours run every half-hour from 9am (last tour at 4pm); allow another 30 minutes or so to browse the museum and listen to some of the recorded conversations between doctors and patients. You can explore a replica fuselage of a Pilatus PC12, test your hand at the throttle in a flight simulator, and "meet" the life-size hologram of RFDS founder Reverend John Flynn. It also has a cafe, gift shop, and art gallery.

8–10 Stuart Terrace (at end of Hartley St.). www.rfdsalicesprings.com.au. ✆ **08/8958 8411.** A$17 adults, A$10 children 6–15, A$52 families of 5. Mon–Sat 9am–5pm; Sun and public holidays 1–5pm. Closed New Year's Day, Good Friday, and Christmas Day.

School of the Air ★★★ BEHIND-THE-SCENES TOUR Sitting in on school lessons may not be your idea of a vacation, but this school is different—it broadcasts by radio to a 1.3-million-sq.-km (502,000-sq.-mile) "schoolroom" of about 140 children on Outback stations. That area is as big as Germany, Great Britain, Ireland, New Zealand, and Japan combined—or twice the size of Texas. Visitors watch and listen in when classes are in session; outside class hours, you may hear taped classes. You can browse the kids' artwork, photos, video, and other displays in the well-organized visitor center. Allow about an hour.

80 Head St. (2.5km/1½ miles NW from Alice Springs). www.assoa.nt.edu.au. ✆ **08/8951 6834.** A$11 adults, A$8.50 children 5–16, A$25–A$30 families. Mon–Sat 8:30am–4:30pm; Sun and public holidays 1:30–4:30pm. Closed Good Friday and usually Dec 21–Jan 5. Bus: nos. 100 or 101 (except Sun and public holidays).

Organized Tours of Alice Springs

AROUND TOWN & OUT IN THE DESERT

Alice Wanderer Centre Sightseeing (www.alicewanderer.com.au; © **1800/722 111** in Australia, or 08/8952 2111) offers a large range of half- and full-day tours. It's well worth checking out their website to help you plan your time before you visit. The company also runs full- and half-day tours to outlying areas, including to Palm Valley in the West MacDonnell Ranges (p. 276), costing A$155 for adults and A$116 for kids age 2 to 15.

Many Alice-based companies offer minicoach or 4WD day trips and extended tours of Alice and of outlying areas including the East and West Macs, Hermannsburg, and Finke Gorge National Park.

CAMEL SAFARIS

The camel's ability to get by without water was key to opening the arid inland parts of Australia to European settlement in the 1800s. With the advent of cars, the camels were released into the wild, and today more than 200,000 roam Central Australia. Australia even exports them to the Middle East! **Pyndan Camel Tracks** (www.cameltracks.com; © **0416/170 164**) runs camel rides daily, with pickup from your hotel. A 1-hour tour, at noon, 2:30pm, or sunset, costs A$79 adults and A$39 for kids 14 and under (A$10 more at sunset). Kids 2 and under must ride with an adult. Make sure you wear comfortable, casual clothes, and sensible shoes—you are likely to get a bit dirty.

HOT-AIR BALLOON FLIGHTS

Dawn balloon flights above the desert are popular in Central Australia. (You do have to get up 90 minutes before dawn, though.) **Outback Ballooning** (www. outbackballooning.com.au; © **1800/809 790** in Australia, or 08/8952 8723) offers a 1-hour flight followed by champagne breakfast in the bush for A$390 adults, A$318 for kids 6 to 16. A 30-minute breakfast flight costs A$295 adults, A$242 for children. Kids 5 and under are discouraged from participating because they cannot see over the basket. Don't make any other morning plans—you probably won't get back to your hotel until close to noon.

Outback Ballooning offers dawn flights over the desert.

Outdoor Activities

The **Alice Springs Golf Club,** 1km (.6 mile) from town on Cromwell Drive (www.alicespringsgolfclub.com.au;

(⊘ **08/8952 1921**), boasts a Thomson-Wolveridge course rated among the world's top desert courses by touring pros. The course is open from sunup to sundown. Nine holes cost A$27; 18 holes, A$48. Club rental is A$29, and a motorized cart, which many locals don't bother with, goes for A$35 for 18 holes. There's also a driving range (A$9 for a small bucket of balls). If lawn bowling is more your style, the golf club also has a bowling green (A$10 for a lane for 2 hr. for up to 8 people).

For those interested in a bit of bushwalking, the 223km (138-mile) **Larapinta Trail** begins in Alice Springs and winds west through the picturesque semi-desert scenery of the **Tjoritja/West MacDonnell National Park.** For more details, see "Hiking the West MacDonnells," p. 277.

Shopping for Aboriginal Art

Alice Springs is one of the best places in Australia to buy Aboriginal art and crafts. You will find no shortage of paintings, didgeridoos, spears, clapping sticks, *coolamons* (dishes used by women to carry anything from water to babies), animal carvings, baskets, and jewelry, as well as books, CDs, and all kinds of merchandise printed with Aboriginal designs. Prices can soar to many thousands for large canvases by world-renowned painters, but you'll also find plenty of smaller, more affordable works. Most galleries arrange shipment. Store hours can vary with the seasons and the crowds, so it pays to check ahead.

Mbantua Fine Art Gallery and Cultural Museum, 64 Todd Mall (www.mbantua.com.au; ⊘ **08/8952 5571**), is a highly respected and reliable source of authentic Aboriginal art, with a dazzling selection to choose from. The art comes from a harsh desert region called Utopia, home to several Aboriginal communities. Mbantua owner Tim Jennings began supplying locals with paints and canvas in the late 1980s during food deliveries to Utopia, first as sheriff, then as the general-store owner. Some of the 200 Utopia residents who paint have been recognized internationally, including Barbara Weir, Gloria Petyarre, the late Emily Kame Kngwarreye, and Minnie Pwerle. Jennings authenticates every piece of art; he and his team photograph the artist with the work and record the traditional meaning behind it. Works by established artists can be priced up to tens of thousands of dollars, but a much smaller investment can get you work by lesser-known but talented painters. Mbantua Gallery is a member of Art Trade, an organization that promotes the ethical trade of indigenous art. The gallery is open Monday to Friday 9am to 5pm, Saturday 9am to 3pm, and (May–Oct only) Sunday 10am to 2pm.

Papunya Tula Artists, 63 Todd Mall (www.papunyatula.com.au; ⊘ **08/8952 4731**), sells paintings on canvas and linen from Papunya, a settlement 240km (150 miles) northwest of Alice Springs, and work by other artists living in the Western Desert, as far as 700km (434 miles) from Alice Springs.

Day Trip to the MacDonnell Ranges ★★★

The key attraction of a day trip to the MacDonnell Ranges is unspoiled natural scenery and few crowds. Many Alice Springs companies run coach or 4WD tours—half- or full-day, sometimes overnight—to the West and East Macs; one of our favorites is **Alice Wanderer Centre Sightseeing** (www.alice wanderer.com.au; ✆ **1800/722 111** in Australia, or 08/8952 2111).

ARRIVING

If you are not driving yourself, you can arrange to be dropped off by **Larapinta Transfers** (www.larapintatransfers.com.au; ✆ **1800/722 111** in Australia, or 08/8952 2111) at several stops in the Ranges. It costs A$95 per person (minimum of two) for the return trip to Simpson's Gap or Standley Chasm; A$170 to Ellery Creek, Serpentine Gorge, Ormiston Gorge, Glen Helen Gorge, or the ochre pits. The **Alice Wanderer** (see above) also does group tours.

THE WEST MACDONNELL RANGES

The 300km (186-mile) round-trip drive west from Alice Springs into **Tjoritja/ West MacDonnell National Park ★★** (https://nt.gov.au/leisure/parks-reserves/find-a-park-to-visit/tjoritja-west-macdonnell-national-park) is a stark but picturesque expedition to a series of red gorges, semi-desert country, and the occasional peaceful swimming hole.

From Alice, take Larapinta Drive west for 18km (11 miles) to the 8km (5-mile) turnoff to **Simpson's Gap,** a water hole lined with ghost gums. Black-footed rock wallabies hop out on the cliffs in the late afternoon (so you may want to time a visit here on your way back to Alice). There are a couple of short trails here, including a .5km (.3-mile) Ghost Gum circuit and a 17km (11-mile) round-trip trail to Bond Gap. Swimming is not permitted. There is an information center/ranger station and free use of barbecues.

Twenty-three kilometers (14 miles) farther down Larapinta Road, 9km (5½ miles) down a turnoff, is **Standley Chasm** (www.standleychasm.com.au; ✆ **08/8956 7440**). This rock cleft is only a few meters wide but 80m (262 ft.) high, reached by a 10-minute creekside trail. Aim to be here at midday, when the walls glow orange in the overhead sun. A kiosk sells snacks and drinks. Admission is A$12 for adults, A$7 for children 5 to 14, and A$30 for a family of 4. The chasm is open daily from 8am to 5pm (last entry at 4:30pm; closed Christmas Day). This is a private reserve, owned by local Aboriginal people. Half-day indigenous tours are offered daily at 9am (bookings required) for A$85 adults and A$60 children.

Six kilometers (3¾ miles) past Standley Chasm, you can branch right onto Namatjira Drive or continue to Hermannsburg Historic Precinct (see below). If you take Namatjira Drive, you'll go 42km (26 miles) to picturesque **Ellery Creek Big Hole.** *Fair warning:* The spring-fed water is icy cold. A 3km (2-mile) walking trail explains the area's geological history.

hiking THE WEST MACDONNELLS

The 223km (138-mile) Larapinta Trail winds west from Alice through some of the most unique and isolated country in the world: the Tjoritja/West MacDonnell National Park (see above). The hills, colors, birds, water holes, gorges, and the never-ending diversity of this trail will leave you spellbound by the beauty of Central Australia.

This long-distance walking track is divided into 12 sections, each a 1- to 2-day walk. Sections range from easy to hard. The shortest is 8km (5 miles), and they go up to 29km (18 miles). The trail begins at the old Alice Springs Telegraph Station and meanders through many gaps and sheltered gorges and climbs steeply over rugged ranges. Each section is accessible to vehicles (some by high-clearance 4WD only), so you can join or leave the trail at any of the trail heads.

Camping out under a sea of stars in the Outback is a highlight of the experience. Although they vary, most campsites offer picnic tables and hardened tent sites—all trail heads have a water supply and some have free gas barbecues.

Tips: The Parks & Wildlife Commission of the Northern Territory strongly recommends any individual or group walking the Larapinta Trail to carry a satellite phone or a location device such as a PLB/EPIRBS or Spot Messenger. Don't attempt this walk in the height of summer unless you are very well prepared. **Warning:** Always carry drinking water. The trail may close in extremely hot summer periods.

Detailed track notes are at the Visitor Information Centre in Alice Springs and online at www.nt.gov.au/leisure/recreation/bushwalking-hiking/larapinta-trail. The website also lists companies that provide transfers to access points along the way, food drops, camping equipment, or fully guided and supported treks.

Eleven kilometers (7 miles) farther along Namatjira Drive is **Serpentine Gorge,** where a trail leads up to a lookout for a lovely view of the ranges through the gorge walls. Another 12km (7½ miles) on are **ochre pits,** which Aboriginal people quarried for body paint and for decorating objects used in ceremonial performances. Twenty-six kilometers (16 miles) farther west, 8km (5 miles) from the main road, **Ormiston Gorge and Pound** (© **08/8956 7799** for the ranger station/visitor center) is a good spot to picnic, swim in the wide, deep pool below red cliffs, and walk a choice of trails, such as the 30-minute Ghost Gum Lookout trail or the easy 7km (4⅓-mile) scenic loop (allow 3–4 hr.). The water is warm enough for swimming in the summer.

Farther on is **Glen Helen Gorge,** where the Finke River cuts through the ranges, with more gorge swimming, a walking trail, guided hikes, and helicopter flights. **Glen Helen Lodge** (www.glenhelenlodge.com.au; © **1300/269 822** in Australia, or 08/8956 7489) has a restaurant and offers 4WD tours from A$190 per person for a half day and scenic helicopter flights from March through November (two-person minimum) from A$89 per person.

ROAD trips TO THE EAST & WEST MACS

Facilities are scarce outside Alice, so bring food, drinking water, and a full gas tank. Leaded, unleaded, and diesel fuel are for sale at Glen Helen Resort and Hermannsburg. Wear walking shoes.

Many of the water holes dry up too much to be good for swimming—those at Ellery Creek (p. 276), Ormiston Gorge (see above), and Glen Helen (see above) are the most permanent. They can be intensely cold, so take only short dips to avoid cramping and hypothermia, don't swim alone, and be careful of underwater snags. Don't wear sunscreen, because it pollutes drinking water for native animals.

Two-wheel-drive rental cars will not be insured on unsealed (unpaved) roads, which includes the last few miles into Trephina Gorge Nature Park and the 11km (7-mile) road into N'Dhala Gorge Nature Park, both in the East Macs. If you are prepared to risk it, you can probably get into Trephina in a two-wheel-drive car, but you will definitely need a 4WD vehicle for N'Dhala and Arltunga. The West MacDonnell road is paved to Glen Helen Gorge; a few points of interest may require driving for short lengths on unpaved road. Before setting off, drop into the **Alice Springs Visitor Information Centre** (p. 266) for tips on road conditions and details on the free ranger talks, walks, and slideshows that take place in the West and East Macs from April through October. Entry to all sights, parks, and reserves (except Standley Chasm) is free.

HERMANNSBURG HISTORIC PRECINCT ★★ An alternative to visiting the West Mac gorges is to stay on Larapinta Drive all 128km (79 miles) from Alice Springs to the old **Lutheran Mission** at the **Hermannsburg Historic Precinct** (www.hermannsburg.com.au; © **08/8956 7402**). Some maps show this route as an unpaved road, but it is paved. Settled by German missionaries in the 1870s, this is a cluster of 16 National Trust–listed farmhouse-style mission buildings and a historic cemetery. There is a museum, a gallery housing landscapes by Aboriginal artist Albert Namatjira, and tearooms serving light snacks and apple strudel from an old German recipe. The precinct is open daily 9am to 5pm; closed Good Friday and Christmas Day. Admission to the precinct is A$12 for adults, free for children.

FINKE GORGE NATIONAL PARK ★★ Just west of Hermannsburg, turn south off Larapinta Drive to reach the 46,000-hectare (113,620-acre) **Finke Gorge National Park** (about a 2-hr. drive west of Alice Springs). You will need to have a four-wheel-drive vehicle or take a tour to explore this park; access along the last 16km (10 miles) of unpaved road, which follows the sandy bed of the Finke River, is limited to four-wheel-drive vehicles only. Heavy rains may cause this section of the road to be impassable. The park is most famous for **Palm Valley,** where groves of rare *Livistona mariae* cabbage palms have survived since Central Australia was a jungle millions of years ago. Four walking trails between 1.5km (1 mile) and 5km (3 miles) take you among the palms or up to a lookout over cliffs; one is a signposted trail exploring Aboriginal culture. For information, call the Visitor Information Centre in Alice Springs before you leave; there is no visitor center in the park.

THE EAST MACDONNELL RANGES ★★★

Not as many tourists tread the path on the Ross Highway into the East Macs, but if you do, you'll be rewarded with lush walking trails, fewer crowds, traces of Aboriginal history, and possibly even the sight of wild camels.

The first points of interest are **Emily Gap,** 10km (6 miles) southeast from Alice, and **Jessie Gap,** an additional 7km (4⅓ miles), a pretty picnic spot. You can cool off in the Emily Gap swimming hole if there is any water. Don't miss the *Caterpillar Dreaming* Aboriginal painting art on the wall, on your right as you walk through.

At **Corroboree Rock,** 37km (23 miles) farther along Hwy. 8, you can make a short climb up the outcrop, which was important to local Aborigines. The polished rock "seat" high up in the hole means Aboriginal people used this rock for eons.

Twenty-two kilometers (14 miles) farther is the turnoff to **Trephina Gorge Nature Park,** an 18-sq.-km (7-sq.-mile) beauty spot with peaceful walking trails that can take from 45 minutes to 4½ hours. The last 5km (3 miles) of the road into the park are unpaved, but you can make it in a two-wheel-drive car.

N'Dhala Gorge Nature Park, 10km (6 miles) past Trephina Gorge Nature Park, houses an "open-air art gallery" of rock carvings, or petroglyphs, left by the Eastern Arrernte Aboriginal people. An interesting 1.5km (1-mile) signposted trail explains the Dreamtime meanings of a few of the 6,000 rock carvings, hundreds or thousands of years old, that are thought to be in this eerily quiet gorge. A 4WD vehicle is a must to traverse the 11km (7-mile) access road.

Caterpillar Dreaming Aboriginal painting at Emily Gap swimming hole.

ULURU–KATA TJUTA NATIONAL PARK ★★★

462km (286 miles) SW of Alice Springs; 1,934km (1,199 miles) S of Darwin; 1,571km (974 miles) N of Adelaide; 2,841km (1,761 miles) NW of Sydney

Why travel so far to look at a large red rock? Because it will send a shiver up your spine. Because it may move you to tears. Because there is something indefinable and indescribable but definitely spiritual about this place. Up close, Uluru is more magnificent than you can imagine. It is immense and overwhelming and mysterious. Photographs never do it justice. There is what is described as a "spirit of place" here. It is unforgettable and irresistible (and you may well want to come back again, just for another look). It will not disappoint you. On my first visit—yes, I am one who will keep coming back—a stranger whispered to me: "Even when you are not looking at it, it is always just *there,* waiting to tap you on the shoulder." A rock with a presence.

"The Rock" has a circumference of 10.6km (6½ miles), and two-thirds of it is thought to be underground. In photos, it looks smooth and even, but the reality is much more interesting—dappled with holes and overhangs, with curtains of stone draping its sides, creating little coves that hide water holes and Aboriginal rock art. It also changes color from pink to a deep wine red depending on the angle and intensity of the sun. And if you are lucky enough to be visiting when it rains, you will see a sight like no other. Here, rain brings everyone outside to see the spectacle of the waterfalls created off the massive rock, which was formed by sediments laid down 600 to 700 million years ago in an inland sea and thrust up aboveground 348m (1,141 ft.) by geological forces.

In 1985, **Uluru–Kata Tjuta National Park** was returned to its Aboriginal owners, the Pitjantjatjara and Yankunytjatjara people, known as the Anangu, who manage the property jointly with the Australian government. A visit to Uluru isn't just about snapping a few photos and going home. There are many ways of exploring it, and one of the best is to join Aboriginal people on guided walks. You can walk around the Rock, fly over it, ride a camel to it, circle it on a Harley-Davidson or a bicycle, trek through the nearby Olgas, and dine under the stars while you learn about them.

The Rock in a Day?

It's a *loooong* day to visit Uluru in a day from Alice Springs by road. Many organized coach tours pack a lot—perhaps a Rock-base walk or climb, Kata Tjuta (the Olgas), the Uluru–Kata Tjuta Cultural Centre, and a champagne sunset at the Rock—into a busy trip that leaves Alice around 5:30 or 6am and gets you back late at night. You should consider a day trip only between May and September. At other times, it's too hot to do much from early morning to late afternoon.

The massive monolith known as Uluru.

Just do yourself one favor: Plan to spend at least 2 days here, if not 3.

Isolation (and a lack of competition) makes such things as accommodations, meals, and transfers relatively expensive. A coach tour or 4WD camping safari is often the cheapest way to see the place (see "Package Tour Operators," p. 240).

Essentials

ARRIVING

BY PLANE   Qantas (www.qantas.com) flies to Ayers Rock (Connellan) Airport direct from Alice Springs and Cairns. Flights from other airports go via Alice Springs. **Jetstar** (www.jetstar.com.au) flies from Sydney, Brisbane, and Melbourne, and **Virgin Australia** (www.virginaustralia.com) from Sydney. The airport is 6km (3¾ miles) from Ayers Rock Resort. A free shuttle ferries all resort guests, including campers, to their door.

BY CAR   Take the Stuart Highway south from Alice Springs 199km (123 miles), turn right onto the Lasseter Highway, and go 244km (151 miles) to Ayers Rock Resort. The Rock is 18km (11 miles) farther on. It is about a 4½-hour drive in total.

If you are renting a car in Alice Springs and want to drop it at Uluru and fly out from there, be prepared for a one-way penalty. Only Avis, Hertz, and Thrifty have Uluru depots (see "Getting Around," below).

VISITOR INFORMATION

For online information before you arrive, check out the Uluru–Kata Tjuta National Park website, **www.parksaustralia.gov.au/uluru**. Another good source of online information is Ayers Rock Resort's site (www.ayers

Cultural Etiquette
The Anangu ask you not to photograph sacred sites or Aboriginal people without permission and to approach quietly and respectfully. For information on climbing Uluru, see p. 288.

rockresort.com.au). The visitor information center in Alice Springs (p. 266) also can provide you with information before you head to Uluru.

One kilometer (.6 mile) from the base of the Rock, the **Uluru–Kata Tjuta Cultural Centre** (www.parksaustralia.gov.au/uluru/do/cultural-centre.html; © **08/8956 1128**), owned and run by the Anangu, the Aboriginal owners of Uluru, uses eye-catching wall displays, frescoes, interactive recordings, and videos to tell about Aboriginal Dreamtime myths and laws. It's worth spending some time here to understand a little about Aboriginal culture. A National Park desk has information on ranger-guided activities and animal, plant, and bird-watching checklists. The center also has a cafe, a souvenir shop, and two Aboriginal arts and crafts galleries. It's open daily 7am to 6pm.

You can book tours at the **tour desk** in every hotel at Ayers Rock Resort, or visit the **Tour & Information Centre** (© **08/8957 7324**) in the resort's Town Square. It's open daily 8am to 7pm.

PARK ENTRANCE FEES

Entry to the Uluru–Kata Tjuta National Park is A$25 per adult, A$13 for children 5 to 15, or A$65 for a family, and valid for 3 days. Some tours include this fee but others do not, so it pays to check. National Park tickets can only be purchased from the National Park Entry Station. The park opens between 5 and 6:30am (depending on the time of year) and closes between 7:30 and 9pm.

GETTING AROUND

Ayers Rock Resort runs a **free shuttle** every 20 minutes or so around the resort complex from 10:30am to after midnight, but to get to the Rock or Kata Tjuta (the Olgas), you will need to take transfers, join a tour, or have your own wheels. The shuttle also meets all flights. There are no taxis at Yulara.

BY SHUTTLE **Uluru Hop On Hop Off** (www.uluruhoponhopoff.com.au; © **08/8956 2019**) provides a shuttle from Ayers Rock Resort to and from the Rock several times a day from before sunrise to sundown, and twice a day to Kata Tjuta. The basic round-trip fare is A$49 for adults and A$15 for kids 1 to 14. To Kata Tjuta, it costs A$95 for adults and A$40 for children. A 2-day pass that enables you to explore Uluru and Kata Tjuta costs A$160 adults and A$60 children; a 3-day pass costs A$210 for adults and A$100 for kids. A National Park entry pass, if you don't already have one, is A$25 extra.

BY CAR If there are two of you, the easiest and cheapest way to get around is likely to be a rental car. All roads in the area are paved, so 4WD is unnecessary. Expect to pay around A$120 to A$140 per day for a medium-size car. Rates drop a little in low season. Most car-rental companies give you unlimited kilometers on all vehicles, but take the cost of your fuel into account because the round-trip from the resort to the Olgas is just over 100km (63 miles), and it's about 20km (13 miles) to the Rock and back. Rental periods of less than 3 days incur a one-way fee up to A$385. **Avis** (www.avis.com.au; ⓒ **08/8956 2266**), **Hertz** (www.hertz.com.au; ⓒ **08/8956 2244**), and **Thrifty** (www.thrifty.com.au; ⓒ **08/8956 2030**) all rent regular cars and four-wheel-drives.

ORGANIZED TOURS

Several tour companies run a range of daily-experiences: sunrise and sunset viewings, circumnavigations of the Rock by coach or on foot, guided walks at the Rock or the Olgas, camel rides, observatory evenings, visits to the Uluru–Kata Tjuta Cultural Centre, and innumerable combinations of all of these. Some offer "passes" containing the most popular activities. Virtually every company picks you up at your hotel. Among the most reputable are AAT Kings and Tailormade Tours (p. 240).

WHERE TO STAY & EAT NEAR ULURU

Ayers Rock Resort is not only in the township of Yulara—it *is* the township. Located about 30km (19 miles) from Uluru, outside the national park boundary, it is the only place to stay. It is an impressive contemporary complex, built to a high standard, efficiently run, and attractive—all things (along with its remoteness) that don't come cheaply. Because everyone either is a tourist, or lives and works here, it has a village atmosphere—with a supermarket, bank, post office, newsstand, medical center, beauty salon, gas station, and several gift, clothing, and souvenir shops.

You have a choice of seven places to stay, from luxury hotel rooms and apartments to campsites. No matter where you stay, even in the campground, you are free to use all the pools, restaurants, and other facilities of every hostelry, except the exclusive Sails in the Desert pool, which is reserved for Sails guests, and Longitude 131°.

You can book any of the accommodations through a central reservations office (www.ayersrockresort.com.au; ⓒ **1300/134 044** in Australia, or 02/8296 8010). High season is July through November. Book well ahead, and shop around for special deals on the Internet and with travel agencies. Ask about special packages for 2- or 3-night stays, as these will be considerably cheaper rates than the 1-night rate quoted below. All stays include a free indigenous activities program, including guided walks, dance shows, and access to the Mani Mani Indigenous Cultural Theatre.

In addition to the resort dining options, the small shopping center has the pleasant **Gecko's Café,** which offers gourmet pizzas, pastas, and burgers (as well as takeout); **Kulata Academy Cafe,** where the staff are part of an

Water, Water . . .

Water taps are scarce and kiosks nonexistent in Uluru–Kata Tjuta National Park. Always carry plenty of your own drinking water when sightseeing.

indigenous trainee program; and the **Ayers Wok Noodle Bar** (yes, really!). Several of the resort restaurants offer kids' menus.

Ayers Rock Campground ★   Instead of red dust, you get green lawns at this campground, which has barbecues, a playground, swimming pool, a small general store, clean communal bathrooms and kitchen, and an Internet kiosk. If you don't want to camp but want to travel cheap, consider the modern two-bedroom cabins. They're a great value; each has air-conditioning, a TV, a kitchenette, dining furniture, a double bed, and four bunks (but no phone). They book up quickly in winter.

Yulara Dr. www.ayersrockresort.com.au/accommodation/ayers-rock-campground. ℘ **08/8957 7001.** 220 tent sites, 198 powered sites, 14 cabins with shared bathroom. A$179–A$184 cabin for up to 6; A$39–A$43 tent site; A$48–A$53 motor-home site. **Amenities:** Free airport shuttle; children's playground; outdoor pool.

Desert Gardens Hotel ★★   This is the only hotel in the resort complex that has views of Uluru (albeit rather distant ones) from some of the rooms. It is set amid wonderful ghost gum trees and the flowering native shrubs that give it its name. The accommodations are not as lavish as Sails in the Desert (below), but they're equally comfortable and were completely refurbished in mid-2016. The **Arnguli Grill** serves a la carte flame-grilled meals at dinner.

Yulara Dr. www.ayersrockresort.com.au/accommodation/desert-gardens-hotel. ℘ **08/8957 7714.** 218 units. A$520–A$650 double. **Amenities:** Restaurant, bar; free airport shuttle; outdoor pool; room service; free Wi-Fi.

Emu Walk Apartments ★★   Completely renovated and refurbished in 2015, these bright, contemporary apartments have full kitchens, separate bedrooms, and roomy living areas. They have daily maid service, and sleep four or six people, so they're great for families or groups of friends. There's no restaurant or pool, but the Town Square cafes and supermarket are close, and you can cool off in the Desert Gardens Hotel pool.

Yulara Dr. www.ayersrockresort.com.au/accommodation/emu-walk-apartments. ℘ **08/8957 7799.** 63 apts. A$550 double 1-bedroom apt; A$730 double 2-bedroom apt. **Amenities:** Free airport shuttle; free Wi-Fi

Longitude 131° ★★★   When you wake in your luxury "tent" here, you can reach out from your king-size bed and press a button to raise the blinds on your window for a view unmatched anywhere in the world: Uluru as dawn strikes its ochre walls. Your bed, under a softly draped romantic white canopy, is in one of 16 five-star eco-sensitive "tents" set among isolated sand dunes a mile or two from the main resort complex. Each room's decor combines tributes to the European explorers and pioneers of this region and fabulous indigenous art. There's a music system, but no TV (and who needs one?). The ultra-luxe **Dune Pavilion** is the only accommodation in Australia with views of both Uluru and Kata-Tjuta—and you pay more for the privilege. It also has a private plunge pool. The central area, the **Dune House,** has a restaurant with superb food, a 24-hour open bar, and a library. Settle in for some after-dinner

DINNER IN THE desert

Why sit in a restaurant when you can eat outside and soak up the desert air? Ayers Rock Resort offers two fine-dining-under-the-stars experiences in the dunes outside the resort. The **Sounds of Silence** dinner is hugely popular (book well ahead, even up to three months ahead in peak season). In an outdoor clearing, you sip champagne and nibble canapés as the sun sets over the Rock to the strains of a didgeridoo. Then head to communal white-clothed, candlelit tables and a buffet meal that will include kangaroo, emu, crocodile, and barramundi. The food is not exceptional, but you're really here for the atmosphere. After dinner, the lanterns fade and you're left with stillness. For some city folk, it's the first time they have ever heard complete silence. Look up into the usually clear skies, and (if it's a clear night) an astronomer will point out the constellations of the Southern Hemisphere. You can also look at the stars through telescopes. Sounds of Silence is held nightly, weather permitting, and costs A$210 adults and A$105 children, including transfers from Ayers Rock Resort. Surcharges apply for Christmas Day. A more intimate desert dinner is **Tali Wiru,** limited to only 20 people, where you can sit at a table for two or your own party of up to six people. This is a more upmarket experience, offering four courses, champagne, and waiter service. It costs A$360 per person, and runs April to October only. Book through the Ayers Rock Resort office in Sydney (🕿 **1300/134 044** in Australia, or 02/8296 8010) or online (www.ayersrock resort.com.au).

Uluru–Kata Tjuta National Park

chess or chat. For a special dining experience, book your place at **Table 131°,** where dinner is set up in style under the stars among gently rolling sand dunes. No children 9 and under.

Yulara Dr. www.longitude131.com.au. 🕿 **08/8957 7131** (lodge), or 02/9918 4355 (bookings). 15 units. A$3,000 double; A$5,800 double Dune House. Rates include walking and bus tours, entry to the national park, meals, selected drinks. 2-night minimum. **Amenities:** Restaurant; bar; free airport shuttle; outdoor pool; free Wi-Fi.

The Lost Camel Hotel ★   Set to reopen in 2018, this boutique-style hotel returns to the Ayers Rock Resort accommodation mix after 5 years as staff accommodation. Originally built in 2002, it offers refurbished studio rooms, each with a king-size bed (that can separate into twins) and open-plan bathroom. The hotel has a central swimming pool and is adjacent to the Town Square.

Yulara Dr. www.ayersrockresort.com.au/accommodation. 🕿 **02/8296 8010.** 99 units. A$450 double. **Amenities:** Free airport shuttle; outdoor pool; free Wi-Fi.

Outback Pioneer Hotel and Lodge ★   An all-ages crowd congregates at this midrange collection of hotel rooms, budget rooms, shared bunkrooms, and dorms. Standard hotel rooms offer clean, simple accommodations with private bathrooms, a queen-size bed, and a single; these have TVs with pay movies, a fridge, a minibar, and a phone. Budget rooms have access to a common room with a TV, as well as a communal kitchen and laundry. Quad bunkrooms are coed and share bathrooms. The single-sex dorms sleep 20.

FIELD OF light

The incredible Field of Light art installation, created by internationally acclaimed artist Bruce Munro, will run at Uluru until December 31, 2020. As darkness falls in the desert, a field of more than 50,000 stems of light, covering an area the size of seven football fields, comes to life. Thousands of visitors have walked through the pathways of light, aptly named **Tili Wiru Tjuta Nyakutjaku** or "looking at lots of beautiful lights" in local Pitjantjatja language, which was created in 2016. Entry passes cost from A$42 adults and A$30 children, including transfers from all hotels. You can also take a camel ride or helicopter tour there or spend the whole evening. Field of Light is also packaged with the Sounds of Silence dinner (see above), at A$250 adults and A$125 children (10–15 years), including transfers from Ayers Rock Resort. Sunrise tours cost from A$75 adults and A$38 children age 2 to 15. Book through the Ayers Rock Resort office in Sydney (✆ **1300/134 044** in Australia, or 02/8296 8010) or online at www.ayersrockresort.com.au.

Plenty of lounge chairs sit by the pool. The **Bough House Restaurant** offers buffet meals, or settle in at the **Outback Pioneer Bar,** where what seems like the entire resort gathers nightly. This barn with big tables, lots of beer, and live music is the place to join the throngs throwing a steak or sausage on the cook-it-yourself barbie (buy your meat at the bar).

Yulara Dr. www.ayersrockresort.com.au/accommodation. ✆ **08/8957 7605.** 125 units. A$380 double hotel room; A$265 budget room with bathroom; A$225 budget room without bathroom; A$184 budget quad room; A$92 bed in coed quad; A$76 dorm bed. **Amenities:** 2 restaurants; bar; free airport shuttle; outdoor pool; free Wi-Fi.

Sails in the Desert ★★★   This top-of-the-range hotel offers expensive, contemporary-style rooms with private balconies, many overlooking the pool, and some with Jacuzzis. You can't see the Rock from your room, but most guests are too busy sipping cocktails by the pool to care. The pool area is shaded by white shade "sails" and surrounded by sun lounges. The lobby art gallery has artists in residence. **Ilkari** is a smart brasserie with a sumptuous buffet, with some dishes incorporating bush-tucker ingredients. The hotel's **Red Ochre Spa** is the only day spa at Yulara. It has four therapy rooms, with two rooms offering "dry" massage therapies and two "wet" rooms with tubs on the veranda.

Yulara Dr. www.ayersrockresort.com.au/accommodation/sails-in-the-desert. ✆ **08/ 8957 7888.** 228 units. A$660–A$780 double; A$1,080 suite. **Amenities:** Restaurant, 2 bars; free airport shuttle; heated outdoor pool; room service; 2 lighted tennis courts; free Wi-Fi.

Exploring Uluru

AT SUNRISE & SUNSET   The peak time to catch the Rock's beauty is sunset, when oranges, peaches, pinks, reds, and then indigo and deep violet creep across its face. Some days it's fiery; on others, the colors are muted. A sunset-viewing car park is on the Rock's western side. Plenty of sunset and sunrise tours operate from the resort, and many throw in a glass of wine to toast the end of the day as you watch. At sunrise, the colors are less dramatic, but the bonus is seeing Uluru unveiled by the dawn to birdsong. It's an early start—most tours leave about 90 minutes before sunup. A typical sunrise tour is offered by **AAT Kings** (www.aatkings.com; ✆ **08/8956 2171**). It includes morning tea and costs A$75 for adults, A$38 for children 2 to 15. AAT Kings offers several other tours around the area, so if large-group touring is what you want, check out its website.

BASE WALKS   A paved road runs around the Rock. The easy 10.6km (6.5-mile) **Base Walk** circumnavigating Uluru takes about 2 hours (the best time is early morning), but allow extra time to linger around the water holes, caves, folds, and overhangs that make up its walls. A shorter walk is the easy 1km (.6-mile) round-trip trail from the **Mutitjulu** parking lot to the pretty water hole near the Rock's base, where there is some rock art. The **Liru Track** is another easy trail; it runs 2km (1.2 miles) from the Cultural Centre to Uluru, where it links with the Base Walk.

Before setting off, it's a good idea to pick up the self-guided walking notes available from the Cultural Centre (see "Visitor Information," p. 266).

CYCLING   Hire a bike to cycle the flat and easy paths around the base of the Rock. **Outback Cycling** (www.outbackcycling.com) has a trailer based at the Cultural Centre, where you can hire a basic bike (and a helmet) for 3 hours, beginning at 7:30 and 10:30am, and 1:30pm. The cost is A$50 adults, A$35 kids age 6 and up. Toddler seats to attach to your bike are A$20. This is a really fun and easy way to see the Rock.

The Base Walk around Uluru reveals water holes, caves, folds, and overhangs.

THE END OF THE climb

In 1979 the Australian government recognized the existence of the traditional Aboriginal owners and created a national park to protect Uluru and Kata Tjuta. In 1983, the traditional owners were granted ownership of the land and the park was leased to the Australian National Parks and Wildlife Service for 99 years. Under that agreement, the climb would close permanently when climber numbers dropped below 20 percent of all visitors to Uluru. That time has now come.

From September 2019 on, climbing Uluru will be banned by law. Climbing Uluru is against the wishes of the traditional owners, the Anangu ("the people," a term used by Aboriginal people from the Western Desert to refer to themselves), because of its deep spiritual significance to them. The Anangu feel a duty to safeguard visitors to their land, and feel great sorrow and responsibility when visitors are killed or injured.

For more than 50 years, climbs have followed the trail the ancestral Dreamtime Mala (rufous hare-wallaby) men took when they first came to Uluru. If you visit before September, tourists are still allowed to climb, but please consider that the traditional owners strongly prefer that they don't—and there are several good practical reasons for not doing so. The 348m (1,142-ft.) hike up the face of "The Rock" is dangerously steep and rutted with ravines about 2.5m (8¼ ft.) deep; 37 people have died while climbing—either from heart attacks or falls—in the past 5 decades. In 2016, three men who went off the regular path to the top got stuck and it took 11 hours for a rescue team to get them safely down. In mid-2018, a tourist died after falling while climbing. There are sometimes strong winds, the walls are almost vertical in places (you have to hold onto a chain), and it can be freezing cold or maddeningly hot. The climb takes at least 1 hour up for the fit, and 1 hour down. The less sure-footed should allow 3 to 4 hours.

The Rock is closed to climbers during bad weather; when the forecasted temperature is expected to exceed 97°F (36°C), which it often does from November to March; and when wind speed exceeds 25 knots. It is always closed overnight, and at 8am daily in December, January, and February because of the extreme heat.

FLYOVERS   Several companies do scenic flights by light aircraft or helicopter over Uluru, Kata Tjuta (the Olgas), nearby Mount Conner, the vast white saltpan of Lake Amadeus, and as far as Kings Canyon. **Professional Helicopter Services** (www.phs.com.au; © **08/8956 2003**), for example, does a 15-minute flight over Uluru for A$150 per person, and a 25-minute flight, which includes Kata Tjuta, for A$245, among others. Helicopters don't land on top of the Rock.

MOTORCYCLING   Harley-Davidson tours are available as sunrise or sunset rides, laps of the Rock, and various other Uluru and Kata Tjuta tours with time for walks. A blast out to the Rock at sunset with **Uluru Motorcycle Tours** will set you back A$229; it includes a glass of champagne. The guide drives the bike, and you sit behind and hang on. Book through Ayers Rock Resort (www.ayersrockresort.com.au/experiences/detail/uluru-motorcycle-tours).

Most tourists visit Uluru in the mornings and Kata Tjuta (the Olgas) in the afternoon. Reverse the order (do the Valley of the Winds walk in the morning and Uluru in the afternoon), and you'll likely find both spots a little more silent and spiritual.

CAMEL RIDES Legend has it that a soul travels at the same pace as a camel; it's certainly a peaceful way to see the Rock. **Uluru Camel Tours** (www.ulurucameltours. com.au; ✆ **08/8956 3333**) makes daily forays aboard "ships of the desert" to view Uluru. Amble through red-sand dunes with great views of the Rock, dismount to watch the sun rise or sink over it, and ride back to the depot for billy tea and beer bread in the morning, or champagne in the evening. The 1-hour rides depart Ayers Rock Resort 1 hour before sunrise or 1½ hours before sunset and cost A$132 per person, including transfers from your hotel. All tours leave from the Camel Depot at the Ayers Rock Resort. Shorter rides are available.

Exploring Kata Tjuta ★★★

While it would be worth coming all the way to Central Australia just to see Uluru, there is a second unique natural wonder to see, just a 50km (31-mile) drive away. Kata Tjuta, or the Olgas, consists of 36 immense ochre rock domes rising from the desert, rivaling Uluru for spectacular beauty. Some visitors find it lovelier and more mysterious than Uluru. With its tallest dome 200m (656 ft.) higher than Uluru, Kata Tjuta ("many heads") figures more prominently in Aboriginal legend than Uluru.

A camelback tour is a peaceful way to see Uluru.

8

THE NORTHERN TERRITORY

Uluru–Kata Tjuta National Park

Buzz Off!

Uluru is notorious for plagues of flies in summer. Don't be embarrassed to cover your head with the fly nets sold in souvenir stores—there will be "no flies on you, mate," an Aussie way of saying you are clever.

English explorers first came upon this part of Australia's red heart in the 1870s. Ernest Giles named part of Kata Tjuta "Mount Olga" after the reigning Queen Olga of Wurttemberg, while William Gosse gave Uluru the name "Ayers Rock" after Sir Henry Ayers, the Chief Secretary of South Australia.

Two walking trails wind among the domes: the 7.4km (4.6-mile) **Valley of the Winds ★★** walk, which is fairly challenging and takes 3 to 5 hours, and the easy 1-hour, 2.6km (1.6-mile) **Gorge** walk. The Valley of the Winds trail is the more rewarding in terms of scenery. Both have lookout points and shady stretches. The trail closes when temperatures hit 97°F (36°C).

TASMANIA

A place of wild beauty colored by a tragic past, the Australian island of Tasmania stands separated from the rest of Australia by Bass Strait. For centuries, this island state has forged its own, not always smooth, path. While geographical isolation has preserved much of its unique wilderness, it has still had to contend with the worst efforts of man to spoil it at times.

Tasmanians have always been at the forefront of Australia's environmental movement, and some of Australia's fiercest battles over development have been waged in Tasmania. Among the issues Tasmania is grappling with right now are the possible extinction of Tasmanian devils due to a spreading facial-tumor disease (p. 306), reports that foxes have been introduced to this predator-free environment, and ongoing resistance against proposals for pulp mills that may hasten the destruction of forestlands. You will not, despite local legend, run into any Tasmanian tigers here—the last known one died in 1936 (despite more recent "sightings").

Tasmania's history has been a violent one. In the 19th century, the island was used as a dumping ground for convicts from Great Britain, often transported for petty crimes. The brutal system of control, still evident in the ruins at Port Arthur and elsewhere, spilled over into persecution of the native population. The last full-blooded Tasmanian Aborigine died in 1876, some 15 years after the last convict transportation.

Despite its dark history, Tasmania is a tranquil and largely unspoiled place to visit—more than 20 percent of it has been declared a World Heritage area, and nearly a third of the island is protected by national parks. The locals are friendly and hospitable—and they have a reputation for producing some of Australia's best food. Remnants of the Aboriginal people who lived here for thousands of years are evident in rock paintings, engravings, and storytelling, as well as a pervasive aura of spirituality that still holds in places that modern civilization has not yet reached.

TASMANIA ESSENTIALS

Arriving

BY PLANE

Qantas (www.qantas.com), **Virgin Australia** (www.virginaustralia.com), **Jetstar** (www.jetstar.com.au), and **Tigerair** (www.tigerair.com) fly into Hobart and Launceston.

BY FERRY

Two high-speed ships connect Melbourne and Tasmania. *Spirit of Tasmania I* and *II* can each carry up to 1,400 passengers and up to 500 vehicles. They make the crossing from Melbourne's Station Pier to Tasmania's Devonport (on the north coast) in 9 to 11 hours. The twin ships leave both Melbourne and Devonport at 7:30pm and arrive around 6am the next day. During busy times, a day service is added leaving both ports at 9am and arriving at 6pm.

Facilities on the ships include a la carte and buffet restaurants, bars, two cinemas, and children's play areas. Accommodations range from reclining seats to comfortable air-conditioned cabins with queen-size beds and en suite bathrooms, and four-berth cabins suited to families. Day tickets with no seat allocation start at A$89. Reclining seats cost from A$99 adults, or you can upgrade to a twin cabin from A$180 per cabin. Fares for an inside four-berth cabin start from A$132 (or A$33 if you are willing to share a single-sex cabin, backpacker style). Top of the range is a deluxe cabin with queen-size bed, from A$460. Transporting a standard car costs A$89.

Prices vary depending on demand and availability, but specials and discounts are regularly available. For reservations, call 🕾 **132 010** in Australia, or 03/6421 7209, or book online at www.spiritoftasmania.com.au.

Tasmanian Redline Coaches (www.tasredline.com.au; 🕾 **1300/360 000** in Australia) connect with each ferry for transfers to Hobart and Launceston. Driving a car from Devonport on the north coast to Hobart on the south coast takes less than 4 hours.

Visitor Information

Tourism Tasmania (www.discovertasmania.com.au) is the official tourism body and operates visitor centers in more than 20 towns throughout the state.

Driving Tips

Driving in Tasmania can be dangerous; there are more accidents involving tourists on Tasmania's roads than anywhere else in Australia. Many roads are narrow and bends can be tight, especially in the mountainous inland regions, where you may also come across black ice early in the morning or any time in winter.

Marsupials are common around dusk, and swerving to avoid them has caused countless crashes. In fact, you may be shocked by the amount of road-kill you will see here.

Tasmania

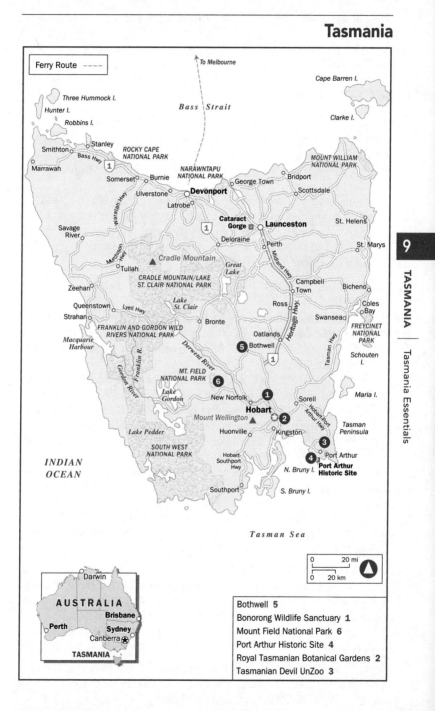

Ferry Route ----

To Melbourne

Bass Strait

Cape Barren I.

Three Hummock I.

Hunter I.

Robbins I.

Clarke I.

Stanley

Smithton

ROCKY CAPE NATIONAL PARK

MOUNT WILLIAM NATIONAL PARK

Marrawah

Bass Hwy

Somerset   Burnie

NARAWNTAPU NATIONAL PARK

George Town   Bridport

Scottsdale

Ulverstone   **Devonport**

Latrobe

Savage River

Cataract Gorge   **Launceston**

St. Helens

Deloraine   Perth

St. Marys

Cradle Mountain

Great Lake

CRADLE MOUNTAIN/LAKE ST. CLAIR NATIONAL PARK

Tullah

Zeehan

Campbell Town   Bicheno

Queenstown   Lyell Hwy

Lake St. Clair

Ross

Coles Bay

Strahan

Bronte

Swansea

FREYCINET NATIONAL PARK

Macquarie Harbour

FRANKLIN AND GORDON WILD RIVERS NATIONAL PARK

Oatlands

Schouten I.

5 Bothwell

MT. FIELD NATIONAL PARK

6

Lake Gordon

New Norfolk

1

Sorell

Maria I.

Lake Pedder

Mount Wellington

Hobart

2

Kingston

Tasman Peninsula

SOUTH WEST NATIONAL PARK

Huonville

Hobart-Southport Hwy

3 Port Arthur

4 **Port Arthur Historic Site**

N. Bruny I.

INDIAN OCEAN

Southport

S. Bruny I.

Tasman Sea

0   20 mi
0   20 km

Darwin

AUSTRALIA

Brisbane

Perth   Sydney

Canberra

TASMANIA

Bothwell **5**
Bonorong Wildlife Sanctuary **1**
Mount Field National Park **6**
Port Arthur Historic Site **4**
Royal Tasmanian Botanical Gardens **2**
Tasmanian Devil UnZoo **3**

9

TASMANIA | Tasmania Essentials

The Royal **Automobile Club of Tasmania** 179-191 Murray St., Hobart, (www.ract.com.au; ℭ **132 722** in Australia), offers emergency-breakdown service (ℭ **131 111**) to members of affiliated overseas automobile associations and dispenses maps and advice.

HOBART

281km (175 miles) S of Devonport; 200 km (124 miles) S of Launceston

Hobart (population 222,500), set on the Derwent River, is Tasmania's capital. Europeans settled in Hobart in 1804, a year after Tasmania's first colony was set up at Risdon (10km/6¼ miles up the Derwent), making it Australia's second-oldest city after Sydney.

The southernmost Australian state capital, Hobart is closer to the Antarctic coast than it is to Perth in Western Australia; navigators, whalers, and explorers have long regarded it as the gateway to the south. Hobart's main features are its wonderful harbor (the city's focal point) and the colonial cottages that line the narrow lanes of Battery Point.

Essentials

ARRIVING

BY PLANE **Qantas** (www.qantas.com.au) flies from Melbourne and Sydney, and **Virgin Australia** (www.virginaustralia.com.au) flies to Hobart from Sydney, Melbourne, Brisbane, and Perth. **Tigerair** (www.tigerair.com) flies to Hobart from Melbourne.

The trip from the airport (www.hobartairport.com.au) to the city center takes about 20 minutes and costs about A$50 by taxi. The **Redline Airporter** shuttle bus (www.tasredline.com.au; ℭ **1300/360 000** in Australia) meets all flights and delivers passengers to hotels in the city for A$20 one-way or A$35 round-trip, A$18/A$25 for kids. Book 24 hours ahead for departures; note that the booking line operates from 8am to 6pm daily.

Car- and camper-rental offices at the airport include **Avis** (www.avis.com.au; ℭ **03/6214 8777**), **Budget** (www.budget.com.au; ℭ **03/6248 5333**), **Europcar** (www.europcar.com.au; ℭ **03/6248 5849**), **Hertz** (www.hertz.com.au; ℭ **03/6335 1111**), and **Thrifty** (www.thrifty.com.au; ℭ **03/6248 5678**). You might find better bargains at some of the local rental companies such as **Redspot** (www.redspot.com.au; ℭ **03/6248 4043**).

VISITOR INFORMATION

The city of Hobart's **Tasmanian Travel and Information Centre,** at 20 Davey St. (www.hobarttravelcentre.com.au; ℭ **03/6238 4222**), can arrange travel passes, ferry and bus tickets, car rentals, cruises, and accommodations. It is open daily 9am to 5pm and public holidays 9am to 2pm (closed Christmas Day).

CITY LAYOUT

Hobart straddles the Derwent River on the south coast of Tasmania. The open ocean is about 50km (31 miles) down the river, though the Derwent empties into Storm Bay just 20km (12 miles) downstream.

Hobart

To New Town

Brisbane St.
Argyle St.
Melville St.
Bathurst St.
Elizabeth St. Mall
Liverpool St.
Criterion St.
Murray St.
Collins St.
Macquarie St.
Harrington St.
Campbell St.
Sackville St.
Sun St.
Market Pl.

Theatre Royal

Victoria Dock

Wharf

Constitution Dock

Franklin Square

Despard St.
Morrison St.
Franklin

Elizabeth St. Pier

Sullivans Cove

Brooke St. Pier

Murray St. Pier

Parliament Square

Salamanca Place

St. David's Park

Castray Esplanade

Salamanca Market

Davey St.
Wilmot St.
Barrack St.
Gladstone St.
Montpelier Retreat
Kirksway
Battery Point
McGregor St.
Runnymede St.
Princes Park
Battery Sq.

Hampden Rd.
James St.
Stowell Ave.
Kelly St.
South St.

Ellerslie Rd.
Bay Rd.
Newcastle St.
Logan St.
DeWitt St.
Cromwell St.
Waterloo Cres.
Francis St.
Colville St.
Sloane St.
Findlay St.
Secheron Rd.
Clarke Ave.
Mona St.
Trumpeter St.
Marine Terr.
River Derwent

Albuera St.
Byron St.
Crelin St.
St. Georges Terrace

A3
A6
A6
A6

0   100 yds
0   100 m

AUSTRALIA
Darwin
Brisbane
Perth
Sydney
Canberra
Melbourne
Hobart
Evans St.
Hunter St.

HOTELS ◼
Customs House Hotel **18**
The Henry Jones Art Hotel **10**
Hobart Central YHA **6**
The Islington **17**
The Lodge on Elizabeth **4**
Macquarie Manor **14**
MONA Pavilions **1**
Salamanca Inn **21**
Wrest Point **25**
Zero Davey **8**

RESTAURANTS ◆
Drunken Admiral Restaurant **9**
Machine Laundry Café **20**
Peacock & Jones **11**
Peppermint Bay **23**
The Point Revolving Restaurant **24**
The Source **2**

ATTRACTIONS ●
Cascade Brewery **15**
Cascades Female Factory Historic Site **16**
Maritime Museum of Tasmania **13**
Mawsons Hut Replica Museum **12**
Museum of Old and New Art (MONA) **3**
Narryna Heritage Museum **22**
Salamanca Market **19**
Tasmanian Museum and Art Gallery **7**
Theatre Royal **5**

Hobart, viewed from the top of Mount Wellington.

Along the waterfront, the popular areas of Salamanca Place and nearby Battery Point overlook **Sullivan's Cove,** home to hundreds of yachts. The row of sandstone warehouses that dominates **Salamanca Place** dates to the city's heyday as a whaling base in the 1830s. Behind Princes Wharf, **Battery Point** is the city's historic district, which in colonial times was the home of sailors, fishermen, whalers, coopers, merchants, shipwrights, and master mariners. The **central business district** is on the west side of the water, with the main thoroughfares—Campbell, Argyle, Elizabeth, Murray, and Harrington streets—sloping down to the busy harbor.

The Tasman Bridge and regular passenger ferries cross the Derwent River. Set back from and overlooking the city is 1,270m-tall (4,166-ft.) **Mount Wellington,** a popular day-trip destination.

GETTING AROUND

Central Hobart is very small, and most of the attractions are in easy walking distance. **Metro Tasmania** (www.metrotas.com.au; ℂ **132 201** in Australia) operates public buses throughout the city and suburbs. The buses operate on an electronic Green Card system, or you can just buy a ticket on board. Single tickets cost from A$3.40, and the most you'll pay is A$7.

For a taxi, call **Yellow Cabs** (ℂ **131 924** in Australia) or **Taxis Combined** (ℂ **133 227** in Australia).

Where to Stay in Hobart

EXPENSIVE

The Henry Jones Art Hotel ★★★   One of Australia's most unique and interesting hotels, the Henry Jones takes its name from one of Hobart's most successful pioneering entrepreneurs. Henry Jones's name, and that of his IXL brand of jam, is still on the factory building that became Australia's first dedicated art hotel. The walls of this luxurious hotel are hung with more than 400 works, in changing exhibitions, often by young, emerging Tasmanian artists, many from the Tasmanian School of Arts (next door). Guest rooms are works of art in themselves, reflecting Australia's early trade with China and India in an eclectic mix of modern and historic. Sandstone walls abut ultra-modern glass and stainless steel bathrooms. (All but standard rooms have double spa tubs.) Every room has a view, either of the harbor or the hotel's magnificent glass atrium. I've stayed here several times, and so far my favorite is the spacious Art Installation Suite, which has a small balcony.

22 Hunter St. www.thehenryjones.com. ℂ **03/6210 7700.** 56 units. A$180–A$390 double; A$760–A$1,020 suite. Free parking. **Amenities:** Restaurant; bar; room service; free Wi-Fi.

The Islington ★★★   This luxury boutique hotel, just 10 minutes' walk from the city center, may make you feel as if you are staying in someone's home. Someone wealthy. The Islington is lavishly but tastefully decorated with fine artworks and antiques, its contemporary extension (with soaring glass walls and ceilings, and views of Mount Wellington) blending beautifully with the original 1847 Regency-style building (one of the first in Hobart's "dress circle" area). At the end of a busy day's sightseeing there's nothing better than a long soak in the generous bathtub, and sinking into an "Islington Angel," a king-size bed custom-made in Tasmania, for a fabulous night's sleep. No kids 14 and under.

321 Davey St. www.islingtonhotel.com. ℂ **03/6220 2123.** 11 units. A$385–A$580 double. Rates include breakfast. **Amenities:** Restaurant; bar; free Wi-Fi.

The MONA Pavilions ★★★   Located upriver in the town of Berriedale, next to the Museum of Old and New Art (p. 303), eight state-of-the-art pavilions (all equipped with wireless touch panels to control temperature, audiovisual components, lighting, blinds, and more) are named for either noted architects or Australian modernist painters (these pavilions are decorated with the artists' works). All sit high above the banks of the Derwent Estuary, with large balconies overlooking the water. Antiquities and artworks from owner David Walsh's private collection are included in the decor of each pavilion. Each of the one- or two-bedroom pavilions also has a private cellar stocked with Moorilla wines and Moo Brew beer from the estate. Guests can arrive by private boat or on the fast catamaran from Hobart. A MONA bus from Brooke Street Pier costs A$22 per person (kids 3 and under free) for either one-way or round-trip. MONA is about 15 minutes' drive from the city center, but the river is an even more appealing way to get there.

655 Main Rd., Berriedale. www.mona.net.au/stay/mona-pavilions. ℂ **03/6277 9900.** 8 units. A$700–A$1,100 double. Rates include breakfast. Bus: 510, 520, 521, 522, or X20. **Amenities:** Restaurant; bar; gym; heated indoor pool; room service; sauna; free Wi-Fi.

Zero Davey ★   With a great waterfront location, and fresh, contemporary studios and apartments, Zero Davey is a good choice for those who want a bit of space. The three-bedroom Zero Penthouse, with its pink, orange, and red decor, will fulfill those rock-star fantasies; the Davey Penthouse has harbor views, and some studios have balconies and Jacuzzis. All are very functional as well as being bright, fun, and a little bit funky.

15 Hunter St. www.zerodavey.com.au. © **1300/733 422** in Australia, or 03/6270 1444. 31 units. A$280 studio double; A$340–A$600 apt. **Amenities:** Restaurant; exercise room; sauna; free Wi-Fi.

MODERATE

Customs House Hotel ★★   You won't find a better value than the rooms above this historic sandstone pub overlooking the waterfront. Built in 1846, the Heritage-listed property offers large, clean, and comfortable colonial-style rooms, seven of which look across at the water. Some of the other rooms look across Parliament House and its gardens, and the rest are toward the back of the hotel with no views to speak of. Downstairs, the restaurant and public bar overlook the water. Live music plays downstairs (Wed–Sat nights). During the summer period, when the Sydney Hobart Yacht Race comes to town, it can get noisy but is central to all the action.

1 Murray St. www.customshousehotel.com. © **03/6234 6645.** 22 units. A$145–A$205 double. Rates include breakfast. **Amenities:** Restaurant; bar; free Wi-Fi.

The Lodge on Elizabeth ★   The convict-built Lodge on Elizabeth is among the oldest buildings in Tasmania, completed in 1829 and now listed by the National Trust. Originally a gentleman's residence (including, at one time, a Tasmanian premier), it later became the first private boys' school in Tasmania. It's well situated, just a 12-minute walk from Salamanca Place, and is surrounded by restaurants. All rooms are decorated with antiques; many are quite romantic, with four-poster beds and some with Jacuzzis. Complimentary drinks are served in the communal living room in the evening. The Convict Cottage is a cute, self-contained spa cottage, just for two, on the grounds. No children 13 and under.

249 Elizabeth St. www.thelodge.com.au. © **03/6231 3830.** 13 units. A$155–A$185 double; A$225 Convict Cottage (2-night minimum). Rates include breakfast. **Amenities:** Bar; free Wi-Fi.

Macquarie Manor ★★   As soon as you walk into this classic colonial-style manor, you'll know you want to stay. Macquarie Manor was built in 1875 as a surgeon's operating office and residence. Extra rooms were added in 1950. Thick carpets and double-glazed windows keep the place very quiet, even though it's on the main road, 2 blocks from the central bus terminal. Rooms, which vary enormously and include single rooms, are comfortable and elegantly furnished. One room is suitable for people with disabilities. Check out the delightful dining room and the drawing room, complete with old couches and a grand piano.

172 Macquarie St. www.macmanor.com.au. © **03/6224 4999.** 16 units. A$208–A$268 double; A$308–A$328 suite. Parking A$15. **Amenities:** Free Wi-Fi.

Salamanca Inn ★★ Conveniently located on the edge of the central business district and toward the waterfront near Battery Point, Salamanca Inn features modern and pleasant suites and apartments, all of which benefitted from a multimillion-dollar refurbishment in 2015. Rooms have queen- or king-size beds, leather couches, Tasmanian oak and leather furniture, galley-style kitchens, and spacious living areas. The pricier suites are a bit plusher, and have personal computers as well as iPhone/iPod docking stations. There's also a heated indoor pool on the rooftop.

10 Gladstone St. www.salamancainn.com.au. ☏ **1800/030 944** in Australia, or 03/6223 3300. 60 units. A$259–A$345 double; A$330–A$410 2-bedroom apt. Bus: 54B. **Amenities:** Restaurant; bar; babysitting; Jacuzzi; indoor pool; room service; free Wi-Fi.

Wrest Point ★ This Hobart landmark, built in 1973, launched Australia's annual A$2-billion casino industry. Beside the Derwent River, 3km (almost 2 miles) from the city center, the casino-hotel complex looks out across the harbor and the city and up to nearby Mount Wellington. All rooms feature Tasmanian oak furniture and plush carpets, and more expensive units have exceptional views. While it may be a little out of the city center (though it's certainly a walkable distance from downtown), the views make it a worthwhile choice. The hotel's signature restaurant, the **Point Revolving Restaurant,** is another city icon. It's open for dinner from 6:30 to 10:30pm Tuesday to Sunday, on Fridays for lunch from noon, and for high tea from 2:30 to 4:30pm Wednesday to Sunday.

410 Sandy Bay Rd., Sandy Bay. www.wrestpoint.com.au. ☏ **03/6111 4628.** 197 units. A$149–A$279 double; A$299–A$319 suite. Bus: 54 or 55 from Franklin Square, Macquarie St., to stop 15. **Amenities:** 5 restaurants; 4 bars; babysitting; concierge; 9-hole putting course; health club; indoor pool; room service; tennis court; free Wi-Fi.

INEXPENSIVE

Hobart Central YHA ★ With a great location just 2 blocks from the waterfront and close to both the city center and Salamanca precinct, this is a great value-for-money location. Rooms are clean, comfortable, and basic. Double rooms (some with en suite bathrooms) and family rooms are available, along with dorms, and there is a small, plainly furnished lounge area, as well as a laundry and small kitchen.

9 Argyle St.. www.yha.org.au. ☏ **03/6231 2660.** 22 units. A$76–A$105 double; A$22–A$29 dorms; A$139 family room (sleeps 4). **Amenities:** Bar; free Wi-Fi.

Where to Eat in Hobart

Tasmania is known for its fresh seafood, including oysters, crab, crayfish, salmon, and trout. Although the seafood here was once cheap, in recent years prices have crept up to match or even surpass those on the mainland. Generally, the food in Tasmania is of very good quality.

EXPENSIVE

The Source ★★★ TASMANIAN/AUSTRALIAN As you climb the stairs to this amazing restaurant, your eyes will be drawn to the painting from

For magnificent views over Hobart and across a fair-size chunk of Tasmania, drive inland to the Pinnacle lookout on top of **Mount Wellington,** about a 40-minute drive from the city center. Take a warm coat; the wind in this alpine area can really bite. An extensive network of walking trails offers good hiking. You can order a copy of the Wellington Park Recreation Map, as well as other day-walk maps, for A$12 online from Tasmap (www.tasmap.tas.gov.au). The website also has other free maps for download, including street maps of Hobart and Launceston.

which it takes its name: *The Source,* by Australian artist John Olsen, is a stunning 6m-tall (20-ft.) work set into the ceiling directly above the central staircase. It will take your breath away. So too will the entire experience of dining here, which promises delivery "with a MONA twist" (the restaurant is part of the Museum of Old and New Art; see p. 303). The menu changes daily, but you can be assured that seasonal and local produce (with an eye toward "food miles") is important here. Offerings might include dishes such as ocean trout with borlotti beans, mussels, and kimchi, or pork belly with almond-and-raisin mole, green apples, tamarind, and cauliflower. Huge windows afford stunning views of the Derwent River.

Moorilla Estate, 655 Main Rd., Berriedale. www.mona.net.au/eat-drink/the-source-restaurant. *℘* **03/6277 9904.** Main courses A$32–A$40. Wed–Mon 7:30–10am and noon–3pm; Fri–Sat 6pm–late. Free parking. Bus: 510, 520, 521, 522, or X20. A MONA bus operates from Brooke Street Pier and costs A$22 per person (kids 3 and under free) for either one-way or round-trip.

MODERATE

Drunken Admiral Restaurant ★ SEAFOOD The Drunken Admiral, on the waterfront, is an extremely popular spot with tourists and can get raucous on busy evenings. The main attraction to start the meal is the famous seafood chowder, swimming with anything that was on sale at the docks that morning. The seafood platter for two (A$69.50 per person; minimum 2) is a huge plate of squid, oysters, fish, mussels, and prawns, but there are plenty of simpler dishes on the menu, too. Try the crunchy fried prawns or the steamed mussels in a tomato, garlic, and white wine sauce.

17–19 Hunter St.. www.drunkenadmiral.com.au. *℘* **03/6234 1903.** Main courses A$30–A$45. Daily 6–10:30pm.

Peacock & Jones ★★ CONTEMPORARY A fireplace in the atrium of the Henry Jones factory building might lure you in to this smart and buzzing addition to the Hobart dining scene, but it's the cozy atmosphere and fine food inside that will keep you here. The open kitchen produces unique combinations, with a focus on local produce. The snack menu—charcuterie, beef tartare, and other tapas-style dishes—is available from 4 to 6pm. Heartier fare such as steaks, a wallaby fillet with beetroot and rhubarb, or a locally sourced pork chop are on the dinner menu, starting at 6pm.

33 Hunter St. www.peacockandjones.com.au. (C) **1800/375 692.** Snacks A$12–A$25; main courses A$36–A$39. Daily 4–10pm.

Peppermint Bay ★★ CONTEMPORARY You'd be hard pressed to find a lovelier setting for lunch. A 150-year-old oak tree dominates the gardens, and the relaxed Terrace Bar has water's-edge views of Bruny Island and the D'Entrecasteaux Channel. The menu includes Tasmanian oysters, steamed mussels, lamb, and fish dishes, and always an interesting vegetarian dish too, such as roasted pumpkin with Georgian spice butter, pepitas, and pear chutney. For something special, try the porchetta with walnut sauce (A$70 for two). Hobart Cruises (© **1300/137 919** in Australia) runs 90-minute scenic cruises, priced from A$118 adults and A$88 children, which include a three-course lunch at Peppermint Bay.

3435 Channel Hwy., Woodbridge (35km/22 miles S from Hobart). www.peppermintbay. com.au. (C) **03/6267 4088.** Main courses A$13–A$32. Daily noon–3pm; Thurs–Sat 5:30–8:30pm.

INEXPENSIVE

Machine Laundry Cafe ★★ CAFE Here's a colorful and cute retro-style cafe that's popular with all demographics. There are bright tables and chairs outside on Salamanca Square if you prefer, or a cozy interior that is separated by the line of washing machines in the laundromat next to a large window. Yes, wash your clothes while you eat! Great for breakfast or brunch, with offerings such as scrambled eggs in roti, eggs Benedict, or ricotta hotcakes.

12 Salamanca Square. (C) **03/6224 9922.** Main courses A$15–A$20. Mon–Sat 7:30am–5pm; Sun 8:30am–5pm.

Exploring Hobart

Simply strolling around the harbor and popping into the shops at **Salamanca Place** can keep you nicely occupied, but don't miss the lovely colonial stone cottages of **Battery Point.** This area got its name from a battery of guns set up on the promontory in 1818 to defend the town against potential invaders (particularly the French). Today, there are tearooms, antiques shops, restaurants, and atmospheric pubs interspersed between grand dwellings.

Bonorong Wildlife Sanctuary ★★★ WILDLIFE VIEWING Tasmanian devils and wallabies are the main attractions at Bonorong (it means "native companion"). Most of the animals have been rescued after injury; owner Greg Irons is passionate about saving and conserving indigenous creatures. You'll also find snakes, koalas, echidnas, kangaroos, and wombats here. Everyone gets a free bag of kangaroo food on entry. Koala cuddling isn't allowed in Tasmania, but you may get to stroke one. Tour times are 11:30am, and 2 and 3:30pm daily, with a special Tasmanian devil tour at 10am. Night tours (A$160 adults, A$85 children 3–15) allow you to see the animals when they are most active, and are highly recommended. Feeding Frenzy tours (A$160 adults, A$85 children) and 10-minute Animal Encounters (with sugar gliders, wombats, or tawny frogmouth owls; A$20 per person) are also on offer.

593 Briggs Rd., Brighton (25 min. N of Hobart on Rte. 1). www.bonorong.com.au. ✆ **03/6268 1184.** A$29 adults, A$15 children 3–15, A$80 families of 4. Daily 9am–5pm.

Cascade Brewery ★ FACTORY TOUR   Cascade Premium is one of Australia's most popular beers. To see how this heady amber nectar is produced, head to Australia's oldest brewery and tag along on a 90-minute tour, which includes a stroll through the grand old Woodstock Gardens behind the factory. Ghost tours also run several times a week (check the website) for 45 minutes and cost A$20 per person. Wear flat shoes and long trousers for all tours. Tours include tastings for participants age 18 and over.

140 Cascade Rd., South Hobart. www.cascadebreweryco.com.au. ✆ **03/6212 7800.** Tours A$30 adults, A$15 students and seniors. No children 15 and under. Tours daily at 11am, and 12:30 and 2:15pm. Closed Christmas Day and Good Friday. Reservations required. Bus: 446 or 449 (stop 18).

Cascades Female Factory Historic Site ★ HISTORIC SITE   Unless you are really into convict history, you may wish to save yourself for Port Arthur (p. 307). All that is left here are the stone walls of this prison and a memorial garden, but recent improvements to the interpretation of the site—including the stories of 57 women incarcerated here—help tell its important history. The "factory" prison, where women worked at spinning, washing, and sewing, operated from 1828 to 1856, housing up to 1,200 women and children. After it ceased operation as a female factory, the institution continued as a jail until 1877. Taking a guided tour ensures you get the most from your visit. Another option besides a tour is "Her Story," a 45-minute dramatized tour by two actors, performed daily at noon. It costs A$25 adults, A$15 children, or A$70 families.

16 Degraves St., South Hobart. www.femalefactory.org.au. ✆ **1800/139 478.** A$8 adults, A$5 children 7–17, A$20 families of 8. Tours A$18 adults, A$12 children, A$45 families. Daily 9:30am–4pm. Tours daily 10 and 11am, and 1, 2, and 3pm. Closed Christmas Day. Bus: 446, 447, or 449 from Franklin Square (stop 13).

Maritime Museum of Tasmania ★★★ MUSEUM Renowned as one of the best of its type in Australia, this museum explores the influence of the sea on the lives of Tasmanians and the island's strong maritime heritage. It has displays about Aboriginal watercraft, early European explorers and whalers, and how ships helped develop Tasmania's industries. Collections include ship models, artifacts, paintings, boat builder's tools, historic dinghies, and navigation instruments. There's also a section on shipwrecks. Free 1-hour talks are held on the first Tuesday of each month (except Jan) at noon.

16 Argyle St. (at Davey St.). www.maritimetas.org. ☏ **03/6234 1427.** A$10 adults, A$5 children 13–18, free for children 12 and under, A$20 for families. Daily 9am–5pm. Closed Christmas Day.

Mawson's Hut Replica Museum ★★ MUSEUM Designed to raise funds for the conservation and maintenance of the originals, these wooden huts on the Hobart waterfront, just opposite Mawson Place, are exact replicas of the shelter afforded to the explorer Douglas Mawson and his expedition team in 1912 to 1914. One of Hobart's newest attractions, they are also fast becoming one of the city's most popular. Inside, there are tributes to the men and 50 huskie dogs that traveled with them to the frozen south.

Corner Argyle and Morrison sts. www.mawsons-huts-replica.org.au. ☏ **03/6231 1518,** or 1300/551 422. A$12 adults, A$4 kids 15 and under, A$28 family. Oct–Apr daily 9am–6pm; May–Sept daily 10am–5pm. Closed Good Friday, Anzac Day (Apr 25), and Christmas Day.

Museum of Old and New Art (MONA) ★★★ MUSEUM Australia's largest privately owned art gallery promises to "shock and offend." Owner David Walsh wants his art museum to be daring and provocative—and

The Maritime Museum explores the island's strong maritime heritage.

so it is. But more often, it delights and amazes. This museum of old and new art challenges, informs, and entertains, with a collection that ranges from antiquities from Egypt, Greece, Italy, Africa, and Mesoamerica to contemporary art, including Australian modernism and contemporary Australian, British, European, and American art. For the sensitive (or those bringing children with them), there's a map that shows how to avoid works that are sexually explicit or "potentially confronting." The museum is part of Walsh's Moorilla Estate, which is also home to a winery, a microbrewery, a restaurant (**The Source ★★★**; p. 299), and stunning accommodations (**The MONA Pavilions ★★★**; p. 297). It's almost worth going to Tasmania just for this.

655 Main Rd., Berriedale. www.mona.net.au. © **03/6277 9900.** A$28 adults, free for kids 17 and under. Wed–Mon 10am–5pm; daily (same hours) in Jan. Closed Christmas Day. Bus: 510, 520, 521, 522, or X20. A MONA bus from Brooke Street Pier costs A$22 per person (kids 3 and under free) for either one-way or round-trip.

Narryna Heritage Museum ★ HISTORIC HOME   One of the houses worth looking into at Battery Point is Narryna, which depicts the life of upper-class pioneers. Built by Captain Andrew Haig in 1837 to 1840, it was later the home of several Hobart businessmen and -women, lawyers, politicians, and bankers.

103 Hampden Rd. www.tmag.tas.gov.au/visitor_information/house_museums/narryna_heritage_museum. © **03/6234 2791.** A$10 adults, A$8 students, A$4 children 5 and under. Tues–Sat 10am–4:30pm (closes 12:30–1pm Tues–Fri); closed Sun–Mon. Closed Good Friday, Hobart Show Day (late Oct), Christmas Day, Boxing Day (Dec 26), New Year's Day, and any other Tasmanian public holidays.

Royal Tasmanian Botanical Gardens ★ GARDENS   Established in 1818, these gardens are known for English-style plant and tree layouts—including a great conifer collection—a superb Japanese garden, and seasonal blooming plants. A restaurant serves lunch and teas. To walk here from the city center, partly along a pleasant country lane known as Soldier's Walk, takes around 40 minutes, or you can use the cycle track or arrive by ferry. There are maps of the gardens at each entrance, or visitor guides and self-guided tour brochures are available at the Visitor Centre, which is near the entrance on Lower Domain Road.

Queens Domain, near Government House. www.rtbg.tas.gov.au. © **03/6166 0451.** Free. Oct–Apr daily 8am–6:30pm; May–Sept daily 8am–5pm.

Salamanca Market ★★ OPEN-AIR MARKET   If you are in Hobart on a Saturday, don't miss this—it's one of the best markets in Australia. Some 300 stalls offer everything from fruit and vegetables to crafts made from pottery, glass, and native woods. Salamanca Place has plenty of crafts shops that are worth exploring, though the prices sometimes reflect the fashionable area.

Salamanca Place. www.salamanca.com.au. Sat 8am–3pm.

Tasmanian Museum and Art Gallery ★ MUSEUM   Come here to find out more about Tasmania's Aboriginal heritage, its history since

Hobart's famed Salamanca Market offers everything from produce to crafts.

settlement, and the island's wildlife. This wonderful museum has undergone a major redevelopment—with more to come—to open up new areas and transform it, while still telling Tasmania's story. Traveling exhibitions are mounted from time to time, but always on display are colonial-era paintings, including an impressive collection of works by Tom Roberts and several convict artists. The pride of the collection is the historically significant *The Conciliation,* by Benjamin Duterreau. You can also find out about the fate of the Tasmanian tiger and see archival film of this lost treasure. Free 40-minute guided tours are run Wednesday to Sunday at 11am and 1:30pm. One-hour theatrical tours called "Settlement Secrets" run through the museum buildings at 11:30am and 2pm Wednesday to Friday and cost A\$20 adults, A\$15 children 15 and under, or A\$60 families of six (visit www.antipodeanentertainment.com.au for details and bookings).

Dunn Place (via Macquarie and Davey sts.). www.tmag.tas.gov.au. ℂ **03/6165 7000.** Free. Daily 10am–4pm (closed Mon Apr–Dec 24). Closed Good Friday, Christmas Day, and Anzac Day (Apr 25).

Theatre Royal ★ THEATER Built in 1837, this 747-seat venue is the oldest theater in Australia. It's known for its excellent acoustics and its classical Victorian decor, and is the centerpiece of a A\$96-million performing arts development taking place around it, expected for completion by the end of April 2019. As Hobart's major stage venue, the theater will be upgraded and a modern extension added. Once the upgrade is finished, 1-hour tours led by Friends of the Theatre Royal will be available, telling the theater's fascinating history on Mondays, Wednesdays, and Fridays at 11am (A\$15 adults, A\$10 kids). Otherwise, check out what's on and have a night out in this grand old theater.

29 Campbell St. www.theatreroyal.com.au. ℂ **1800/650 277** in Australia, or 03/6233 2299.

TASMANIAN DEVIL disaster

Tasmania's unique carnivorous mammal, the handsomely sleek Tasmanian devil, is much more interesting than his namesake, the manic character from Bugs Bunny cartoons. Whereas dingoes wiped out the devil's cousin on the Australian mainland, dingoes never crossed Bass Strait, and so Tasmania's devils flourished, becoming one of the island's iconic mascots. But now, the Tasmanian devil population is in desperate trouble.

Since 1996, the animals have been afflicted by a deadly cancer known as Devil Facial Tumour Disease (DFTD). This malady has decimated the wild population—in some areas by an estimated 90 percent—and the disease is spreading rapidly. It's believed that around half of the state's approximately 150,000 Tasmanian devils have already died, and some scientists fear that it may soon wipe out the wild population entirely. Healthy specimens are being captured and relocated in an urgent campaign to try to preserve the species from extinction.

There are several places where you can see captive Tasmanian devils and learn more about this one-of-a-kind animal. About 88km (55 miles) from Hobart, on the Port Arthur Highway, Taranna, is the **Tasmanian Devil UnZoo** (www.tasmaniandevilunzoo.com.au; ✆ **1800/641 641** in Australia), which is currently working to breed devils with genes that could make them resistant to the disease. The park is open daily from 9am to 5pm (except Christmas Day). Devil feeding is at 10 and 11am, and 12:15, 1:30, 3, and 5pm (4:30pm May–Sept) daily. Entry is A\$36 adults, A\$20 children 4 to 16, and A\$89 for a family of six.

Another great place to see devils near Hobart is **Bonorong Wildlife Sanctuary** (p. 301).

For more information on devil conservation efforts, visit www.tassiedevil.com.au.

Cute yet fierce, Tasmanian devils are an endangered species found only on the island.

Organized Tours
WALKING TOURS

Hobart Historic Tours (www.hobarthistorictours.com.au; ✆ **03/6234 5550**) runs fascinating 90-minute walking tours of Hobart. The Historic Walk departs from outside the **Tasmanian Travel and Information Centre** (p. 294) at 2pm Wednesday to Sunday. The Old Hobart Pub Tour (not recommended for children), departing at 5pm on Thursdays, Fridays, and Saturdays, takes you to two waterfront pubs and will enthrall you with stories of alcohol-fueled shenanigans. Tours cost A\$33 per person. A 3-hour Grand Hobart Walk costs A\$50 per person and runs Wednesday to Sunday at 2pm.

CRUISES

Bruny Island Cruises (www.brunycruises.com.au; ✆ **03/6293 1465**) offers a range of tours including a full-day jaunt from Hobart to Bruny Island, leaving Franklin Wharf at 8am and returning around 5:30pm daily. A bus and ferry take you to Bruny Island, where (after morning tea) you take a 3-hour boat trip along the coastline to a seal colony and a memorable (but sometimes wet; warm, shower-proof coats are provided) foray onto the wild Southern Ocean. On returning, lunch includes a much-needed hot soup to warm you up, before you get back on the bus for the trip back to Hobart. It's a pleasant day out, although considering the hours spent, serious wildlife fans might be disappointed. The trip costs A$225 adults, A$165 children ages 3 to 16.

BUS TOURS

Grayline (www.grayline.com.au; ✆ **1300/858 687** in Australia) offers a range of sightseeing tours of Hobart and Mount Wellington by coach. A 3-hour tour costs A$55 for adults, A$28 for kids. Grayline also runs tours to other Tasmanian destinations including Russell Falls, Bruny Island, Port Arthur, Cradle Mountain, Richmond, and the Bay of Fires.

DAY TRIPS FROM HOBART

Port Arthur ★★★

96 km (60 miles) southeast of Hobart

Port Arthur, on the Tasman Peninsula, is an incredibly picturesque yet haunting place. Set on one of Australia's prettiest harbors, it shelters the remains of Tasmania's largest penal colony. It's the state's number-one tourist destination, and you really should plan to spend at least a day here.

From 1830 to 1877, Port Arthur was one of the harshest institutions of its type anywhere in the world. It was built to house the most notorious prisoners transported from Great Britain, many of whom had escaped from lesser institutions elsewhere in Australia. Nearly 13,000 convicts found their way here, and nearly 2,000 died while incarcerated.

A strip of land called Eaglehawk Neck connects Port Arthur to the rest of Tasmania. Guards and dogs kept watch over this narrow path, while the authorities perpetuated rumors that the waters around the peninsula were shark-infested. Only a few convicts ever managed to escape, and most of them either eventually perished in the bush or were tracked down and hanged. As you pass through Eaglehawk Neck, look out for the blowhole and other weird coastal formations, including Tasman's Arch, Devil's Kitchen, and the Tessellated Pavement.

The **Port Arthur Historic Site ★★** (www.portarthur.org.au; ✆ **1800/659 101** in Australia, or 03/6251 2310) is large and scattered, with around 30 19th-century buildings. You can tour the remains of the church, the guard tower, a prison, and several other buildings. Don't miss the fascinating museum in the old lunatic asylum, which has a scale model of the prison complex, as well as leg irons and chains. The main feature of the visitor center is an interesting **Interpretive Gallery,** which takes visitors through the process of sentencing in England to transportation to Van Diemen's Land (Tasmania's original name). The gallery contains a courtroom, a section of a transport ship's hull, a blacksmith's shop, a lunatic asylum, and more.

Port Arthur's tragic history did not finish at the end of the convict era. In 1996, the Port Arthur Historic Site became the scene of one of Australia's worst mass murders, when a lone gunman killed 35 people and injured dozens more, including tourists and staff. The devastating events of that day led to new gun-control laws for Australia that are among the strictest in the world. The gunman was sentenced to life imprisonment with no eligibility for parole. Many of the staff at Port Arthur lost friends, colleagues, and family members, and they still find it difficult and painful to talk about that tragic day. Visitors are requested not to question their guide about these events, but to instead read the plaque at the Memorial Garden.

The site is open daily from 9am to dusk; buildings are open 10am to 5pm. (On Christmas Day, the site closes at 3pm.) Admission is A$39 for adults, A$17 for children 4 to 17, and A$99 for families of two adults and up to six children. The admission price includes a guided walking tour and a boat cruise around the harbor.

Passes that combine different experiences and tours are also available. You can get off the harbor cruise for a 45-minute guided walk on the **Isle of the Dead,** where 1,769 convicts and 180 free settlers were buried, mostly in mass graves with no headstones, or at **Point Puer,** which was once home to 800 boys shipped to Tasmania for a "better life" or for petty crimes. The tour costs

At the historic Port Arthur penal colony, the lunatic asylum is a particularly poignant site.

A DAY TRIP TO bothwell

A charming little town an hour's drive north of Hobart (take Highway 1 and then A5), **Bothwell** ★★ sits on the picturesque Clyde River at the foothills of the central Tasmanian highlands. The town was settled by Scottish colonists in 1822, with convict labor building many of the sandstone establishments still lining the streets today.

Bothwell's major claim to fame is as the home of **Ratho,** Australia's oldest golf course (www.rathofarm.com; ☎ **03/6259 5553**), which was also established in 1822, as soon as the Scottish settlers arrived. **Ratho Farm,** on which the 18-hole course sits, is also home to new luxury accommodations in the form of 16 converted convict cottages and stables, priced from A$175 double. Ratho is a public course, and greens fees are only A$40.

After a round of golf, drop into the **Australasian Golf Museum** (www.ausgolfmuseum.com; ☎ **03/6259 4033**), which doubles as the local information center, on Market Place. It's open daily 10am to 4pm September to May and 11am to 3pm June to August. While you're there, pick up a brochure that gives you a self-guided tour of Bothwell's many historic buildings.

Another spot worth ducking into is the historic **Castle Hotel** (www.facebook.com/CastleHotelBothwell; ☎ **03/6259 5502**) in Bothwell's main street. The sandstone pub, built in 1829, is one of Australia's oldest, and like much of the town, is Heritage-listed. There are three guest rooms upstairs, but the action is mostly in the bar, where locals gather to swap stories of trout fishing.

an extra A$20 for adults, A$10 for kids, and A$45 for families. Lantern-lit **Ghost Tours** of Port Arthur leave nightly at 6 and 8pm and cost A$27 for adults, A$15 for kids, or A$75 for a family. Reservations are essential. Tours last about 90 minutes. There are various other passes and tours available; check the website.

Port Arthur Historic Site is a 90-minute drive from Hobart. Take the Tasman Highway (A3) past the airport to Sorell, then turn south on the Arthur Highway (A9) and continue until you reach Port Arthur. The Historic Site is well signposted along the way.

Mount Field National Park ★★

80 km (50 miles) northwest of Hobart

Mount Field National Park is one of the prettiest landscapes in Tasmania. It was proclaimed a national park in 1916 to protect a plateau dominated by dolerite-capped mountains (**Mount Field West** is the highest point at 1,417m/4,647 ft.) and dramatic glaciated valleys (some of the lakes and tarns were formed as much as 30,000 years ago). Since 2013, it has been included as part of the Tasmanian Wilderness World Heritage Area.

The most mountainous regions support alpine moorlands of cushion plants, pineapple and sword grass, waratahs, and giant pandani. You can get a look at these various ecosystems on a 16km (10-mile) drive from the park entrance to Lake Dobson. Note that this drive is along an unpaved and often badly rutted road, which is not suitable for conventional vehicles in winter or after heavy rains. As you follow the drive, you'll notice that wallabies, wombats, bandicoots, Tasmanian devils, and quolls are prolific, as is the birdlife: You may spot such bird species as black cockatoos, green rosellas, honeyeaters, currawongs, wedge-tailed eagles, and lyrebirds.

There are many walking trails running through the park, including one to the spectacular 45m-high (148-ft.) **Russell Falls,** near the park's entrance. The walk to the falls along a paved, wheelchair-accessible track takes 15 minutes and passes ferns and forests, with some of Tasmania's tallest trees, swamp gums that stand up to 85m (279 ft.) high.

Mount Field National Park is just over an hour's drive from Hobart via the town of New Norfolk. From Hobart, take the Brooker Highway (A10) northwest to New Norfolk. After New Norfolk, you can follow the road on either side of the Derwent River (the A10 or B62) until you reach Westerway. From there, it is a short drive to the clearly marked entrance to Mount Field National Park. There is an entrance fee of A$12 per person or A$24 per car (up to eight people).

The park's visitor center (www.parks.tas.gov.au; ✆ **03/6288 1149**) on Lake Dobson Road has a cafe and information on walks. It's open daily from 8:30am to 5pm between November and April and 9am to 4pm in winter.

LAUNCESTON

198km (123 miles) N of Hobart; 92 km (57 miles) SE of Devonport

Tasmania's second-largest city is Australia's third oldest, after Sydney and Hobart. Situated at the head of the Tamar River, 50km (31 miles) inland from the state's north coast, and surrounded by delightful undulating farmland, Launceston is crammed with elegant Victorian and Georgian architecture and plenty of remnants of convict days. Launceston (pop. 86,000) is one of Australia's most beautiful cities and has delightful parks and churches. It's also the gateway to the wineries of the Tamar Valley, the highlands and alpine lakes of the north, and the stunning beaches to the east.

Essentials

ARRIVING

BY PLANE **Qantas** (www.qantas.com) flies to Launceston from Melbourne, and **Jetstar** (www.jetstar.com.au) flies from Sydney and Brisbane. **Virgin Australia** (www.virginaustralia.com.au) flies from Melbourne, Brisbane, Sydney and the Gold Coast. The **Airporter Shuttle** (✆ **1300/385 522** in Australia, or 0488/200 700 mobile) meets all flights and runs between city hotels and the airport for A$15 one-way. **Avis** (www.avis.com.au; ✆ **136 333** in Australia), **Budget** (www.budget.com.au; ✆ **03/6391 8566**), **Europcar** (www.europcar.com.au; ✆ **03/6391 9161**), **Hertz** (www.hertz.com.au; ✆ **1300/030 222**), **Thrifty** (www.thrifty.com.au; ✆ **03/6391 8105**), and **Redspot** (www.redspot.com.au; ✆ **03/6391 9060**) all have airport rental desks.

THE heritage HIGHWAY

The **Heritage Highway** links Launceston in the north with Hobart in the south, cutting through the middle of Tasmania. By the 1820s, several garrison towns had been built between the two towns, and by the middle of the 19th century convict labor had produced what was considered to be the finest highway of its time in Australia. Today, many of the towns along the road retain magnificent examples of Georgian and Victorian architecture. It takes about 2 hours to drive between Launceston and Hobart on this route (also known as the A1, or the Midland Highway), but you could easily spend a couple of days exploring.

Picturesque **Ross** (121km/75 miles north of Hobart or 78km/48 miles south of Launceston) is one of Tasmania's best-preserved historic villages. Ross was established in 1812 on a strategically important crossing point on the Macquarie River. **Ross Bridge,** the third oldest in Australia, was built in 1836. The bridge is decorated with Celtic symbols, animals, and faces of notable people of the time. It is lit up at night, and there are good views of it from the river's north bank. The town's **main crossroads** is the site of four historic buildings, humorously known as "Temptation" (the Man-o'-Ross Hotel), "Salvation" (the Catholic church), "Recreation" (the town hall), and "Damnation" (the old jail). The **Tasmanian Wool Centre,** 48 Church St., details the growth of the region and the wool industry since settlement. It also houses the **Ross Visitor Information Centre** (www.visitross.com.au; (℡) **03/6381 5466**); both are open from 9:30am to 5pm Monday through Friday, and 10am to 5pm Saturday and Sunday. If you are so charmed you want to stay overnight, try the historic **Colonial Cottages of Ross** (www.rossaccommodation.com.au; (℡) **03/6381 5354**) on Church Street.

The town post office, in the historic village of Ross.

BY BUS **Tasmania's Redline Coaches** (www.tasredline.com.au; ℂ **1300/360 000** in Australia) departs Hobart for Launceston several times daily (trip time: around 2½ hr.). The one-way fare is A$42. If you're arriving on the ferry from Melbourne, Launceston is around 1½ hours from Devonport, and the bus ride will cost A$18.

BY CAR Driving from Hobart to Launceston takes just over 2 hours on Hwy. 1.

VISITOR INFORMATION

The **Launceston Visitor Information Centre** is located in the historic GPO building, 68–72 Cameron St. (www.destinationlaunceston.com.au; ℂ **1800/651 827** in Australia); it's open Monday through Friday from 9am to 5pm, and Saturday, Sunday, and public holidays from 9am to 3pm (9am–1pm May–Nov).

CITY LAYOUT

The main pedestrian shopping mall, **Brisbane Street,** along with St. John and Charles streets on either side, forms the heart of the central area. The Victorian-Italianate Town Hall is 2 blocks north on **Civic Square,** opposite the red-brick post-office building dating from 1889. The **Tamar River** slips quietly past the city's northern edge and is crossed at two points by **Charles Bridge** and **Tamar Street. City Park,** to the northeast of the central business district, is a nice place for a stroll.

GETTING AROUND

BY BUS **Metro Tasmania** (www.metrotas.com.au; ℂ **132 201** in Australia) operates public buses throughout the city and suburbs. The buses operate on an electronic Green Card system, or you can just buy a ticket on board. Single tickets cost from A$3.40, and the most you'll pay is A$7. The free **Tiger Bus**—painted with the distinctive black stripes of the extinct Tasmanian Tiger—loops around the city every 30 minutes from 10am to 3:30pm on two different routes. It is also run by Metro Tasmania; check the website for details.

BY CAR Launceston has a few one-way street systems that can make driving tricky for visitors.

Where to Stay in Launceston

EXPENSIVE

Country Club Tasmania & Villas ★ Wallabies grazed outside my window when I stayed at this resort-style hotel located between Launceston city and the airport. This is a place that will appeal to those who want space, entertainment, and activities. There is an 18-hole golf course, a small casino, and lots of things to do, from fly-fishing on the private lake to horse riding and more. All rooms have everything you'd expect; Manor suites have a separate bedroom, lounge, private balcony, and spa tub. There are also one-, two-, and three-bedroom villas with full kitchens and car parking right outside. Villas are set apart from the main complex, but there is a free shuttle bus to take you there.

Country Club Ave., Prospect Vale. www.countryclubtasmania.com.au. ℭ **1800/635 344** in Australia, or 03/6335 5777. 182 units. A$189–A$219 double; A$319–A$329 suite; A$179–A$359 villa. Free valet parking. **Amenities:** 5 restaurants; 4 bars; babysitting; concierge; golf course; exercise room; Jacuzzi; indoor heated pool; room service; sauna; 2 lit tennis courts; free Wi-Fi.

Peppers Seaport Hotel ★★ Built in 2004 on the site of an old dry dock and designed in the shape of a ship, this hotel is part of a major redevelopment of the Seaport Dock area—just 5 minutes by car from downtown—which also includes new restaurants, entertainment venues, and shopping facilities. The decor is smart contemporary nautical in style, using soft, light colors, natural timbers, and chromes. Rooms are spacious, and most have balconies either looking out over the Tamar River and marina or over the town center to the mountains beyond. Each has a good kitchenette and an extra fold-out sofa bed.

28 Seaport Blvd. www.peppers.com.au/seaport. ℭ **1300/987 600** in Australia, 07/5665 4426 (central reservations), or 03/6345 3333 (hotel). 60 units. A$199–A$219 double; A$234–A$393 suite. Parking A$10. **Amenities:** Restaurant; bar; babysitting; concierge; room service; free Wi-Fi.

Peppers Silo ★★ You'll be greeted at reception by a black Labrador called Archie, who is available for walks and may later bring your newspaper to your door. And that's not the only notable thing about this terrific hotel. One of Tasmania's—and maybe Australia's—most innovative new hotels, it is built in and between four former grain silos, massive circular structures that have been transformed into a nine-level hotel. Opened in mid-2018, the rooms have views of the Tamar River and Cataract Gorge. Adjacent to the silos, the North Tower is a contemporary addition with more rooms and suites (some with private balconies) furnished with natural tones and interesting artwork reflecting the hotel construction project. It's a 10-minute walk to the city center.

89-91 Lindsay St. www.peppers.com.au/silo. ℭ **1300/987 600** in Australia, 07/5665 4426 (central reservations), or 03/6700 0600 (hotel). 108 units. A$209–A$269 double; A$339–A$449 suite. Rates include breakfast. **Amenities:** Restaurant; bar; babysitting; gymnasium; room service; spa; free Wi-Fi.

Quamby Estate ★★ This gorgeous historic house, built in 1848, is about a 20-minute drive from Launceston. Rooms are large and beautifully appointed, with massive bathtubs (some are spa tubs). Each room is different from the others, with original art, antique furniture, and gleaming hardwood floors. Some rooms have doors opening onto the wrap-around veranda. Some of the layout is a little odd, but that adds to the historic feel. There are bikes available for exploring, or you can hit the 9-hole golf course (watch out for Sir Richard Branson, he holds the No.1 membership here!).

1145 Westwood Rd., Hagley. www.quambyestate.com.au. ⓒ **03/6392 2135.** 10 units. A$169–A$349 double. Breakfast A$25. Free parking. Free airport shuttle. **Amenities:** Restaurant; babysitting; CD, DVD, and book library; 9-hole golf course; tennis court; free Wi-Fi.

York Mansions ★★★   Within the walls of the National Trust–classified York Mansions, built in 1840, are five spacious two-bedroom apartments and one three-bedroom apartment, each with a distinct character. The Lodge apartment is fashioned after a gentleman's drawing room, complete with rich leather sofa, antiques, and an extensive collection of historical books. The light and airy Duchess and Countess apartments are more feminine. Each apartment has its own kitchen, dining room, living room, bedrooms, bathroom, and laundry. There's also a delightful cottage garden with a massive Heritage-listed oak tree—just the spot for sundowners.

9–11 York St. www.yorkmansions.com.au. ⓒ **03/6334 2933.** 6 units. A$248–A$262 double. Free parking. **Amenities:** Free Wi-Fi.

MODERATE

Alice's Cottages & Spa Hideaways ★★   Tucked down a romantic lane and known collectively as the Shambles, these themed cottages are designed to bring out the romantic in you. Four of the six cottages, which sleep only two, are named for the places the "colonials" came from: England, Wales, Ireland, and Scotland. The other two are the Camelot and Boudoir "spa hideaways." Four-poster beds, soft drapes, roaring log fires . . . you get the picture.

121–129 Balfour St. www.alicescottages.com.au. ⓒ **0498/525 716** mobile. 6 units. A$190–A$210 double including breakfast basket. Free parking. **Amenities:** Free Wi-Fi.

Quality Hotel Colonial Launceston ★   Those who are looking for tried-and-true above-standard motel lodging will feel at home at the Colonial, a place that combines old-world ambience with modern facilities. Beautiful gardens surround the property; rooms are fairly standard but they are large, with attractive furnishings. There are also family rooms and apartments. The clientele tends to be mostly corporate.

31 Elizabeth St. www.coloniallaunceston.com.au. ⓒ **03/6331 6588.** 70 units. A$180–A$350 double; A$290 family room; A$295–A$500 apartments. Free parking. **Amenities:** Restaurant; exercise room; room service; free Wi-Fi.

Waratah on York ★   This Victorian mansion was built in 1862 for Alexander Webster, an ironmonger who was mayor of Launceston in the 1860s and 1870s. Some original features—pressed brass ceiling roses and a staircase with a cast-iron balustrade—remain, while others have been faithfully recreated. Six rooms come with a Jacuzzi, one with a balcony, and another with a sunroom. All have high ceilings and ornate (but nonfunctional) fireplaces.

The executive rooms have four-poster beds and sweeping views of the Tamar River.

12 York St. www.waratahonyork.com.au. © **03/6331 2081.** 10 units. A$110–A$175 double. Rates include breakfast. Free parking. **Amenities:** Bar; free Wi-Fi.

INEXPENSIVE
Hillview House Bed & Breakfast ★ The rooms at this restored farmhouse are cozy and quite comfortable. Each comes with a double bed and a shower. The family room has an extra single bed; it's the nicest unit and has the best views. The hotel overlooks the city (the hill is a bit steep to walk up), and the large veranda and colonial dining room have extensive views over the city and the Tamar River. No children age 4 and under.

193 George St. www.hillviewhouse.net.au. © **03/6331 7388.** 9 units. A$89–A$109 double; A$200 2-bedroom apt. Rates include breakfast. Free parking. **Amenities:** Free Wi-Fi.

Where to Eat in Launceston

Inside Cafe ★ CAFE Set in an 1880s warehouse building, this open and airy cafe shares its space with a homewares shop. It's a great spot for breakfast—your eggs might come with truffle mushrooms or smashed avocado—and the lunch menu is equally tasty with offerings such as duck salad, halloumi and sweetcorn fritters, or crab tacos. There's a kids' menu too.

10–14 Patterson St. www.insidecafe.com.au. © **03/6331 7348.** Main courses A$14–A$24. Mon–Fri 7:30am–4pm; Sat 8am–3:30pm.

Me Wah Restaurant ★★★ CHINESE The name of this restaurant means "exquisite setting" and exquisite food is what you will find here. Old-style courtesy and service, coupled with wonderful flavors, will have you coming back for more. The Peking duck is divine, and there's a host of Cantonese dishes that will leave you drooling, including the Greenlip abalone found off the shores of Tasmania's King and Flinders islands. It's expensive, but the elegant Chinese decor, and wonderful service make it memorable and worthwhile.

39-41 Invermay Rd. www.mewah.com.au/launceston. © **03/6331 1308.** Main courses A$28–A$42. Tue–Thurs 11:30am–2:20pm and 5–9:30pm; Fri–Sat 11:30am–2:20pm and 5–10:30pm.

Mudbar ★★ CONTEMPORARY One of Launceston's best restaurants, Mudbar has a lovely setting overlooking the marina and river. Locals flock here, and there's a terrific relaxed vibe, helped along by excellent staff. Take a table in the dining area, or a bar table or couch in the lounge area. The menu has an Asian twist to it, with dishes like soy-roasted duckling with Thai basil or Chinese slow-braised lamb chili, and there's also grass-fed local beef on the char grill. A vegetarian menu is available.

28 Seaport Blvd. www.mudbar.com.au. © **03/6334 5066.** Main courses A$29–A$30; dinner fixed price menus A$60 for 2 courses, A$78 for 3 courses. Daily 11am–late.

Stillwater ★★ CONTEMPORARY   This fabulous and popular eatery is located inside an old mill beside the Tamar River. Come here for a good breakfast, a casual lunch at one of the tables outside overlooking the river, or an atmospheric dinner. Menus change seasonally and sometimes at short notice, but the food is always fascinating, with all sorts of delicacies on offer. Maybe something like this: whole roasted snapper with lemongrass-and-turmeric paste, roasted lime, and herbs, or small plates that include whiskey-cured Tasmanian salmon with a dill and honey vinaigrette, salmon pearls, and puffed wild rice. The wine cellar brings up a good selection of Tasmanian wines. If you just can't decide, go for the five-course tasting menu at A$125, or A$195 including matching wines. Reservations are recommended.

Ritchies Mill (bottom of Paterson St.). www.stillwater.net.au. © **03/6331 4153.** Main courses A$21–A$65. Daily from 8:30am for breakfast and noon for lunch; Tues–Sat (Sept–Mar) and Wed–Sat (Apr–Aug) 6-10pm. Closed Good Friday and Christmas Day.

Exploring Launceston

Cataract Gorge ★★ NATURAL WONDER   The result of violent earth-quakes that rattled Tasmania some 40 million years ago, this natural attraction is a must-see. It's a wonderfully scenic area, and you can walk there along the riverbank from the city in about 15 minutes. The South Esk River flows through the gorge and collects in a small lake called the Basin, traversed by a striking suspension bridge and the longest single-span chairlift in the world (308m/1,010 ft.). The **chairlift** operates daily from 9am to 4:30pm (later in summer) and costs A$15 for adults and A$10 for children 15 and under, round-trip. A funicular cable car also runs to higher parts of the gorge. The hike to the **Duck Reach Power Station,** now an interpretive center, takes about 45 minutes. Other walks in the area are shorter and easier. The **Gorge Restaurant** (© **03/6331 3330;** closed Mon) and the cafe next door are open daily from 8am, with glorious views from the outdoor tables.

Cataract Gorge Reserve, Basin Rd. www.launcestoncataractgorge.com.au. © **03/6331 5915** (chairlift office). Free admission.

Design Tasmania ★ MUSEUM   Inspiring and innovative contemporary design is the focus here, from the building itself—a light-filled structure added on to a Heritage-listed church hall—to its contents. The permanent display is the Tasmanian Wood Design Collection, but you will also find changing exhibitions of ceramics, textiles, works on paper, and mixed media.

Cruise the Tamar

Tamar River Cruises (www.tamarrivercruises.com.au; © **03/6334 9900**) offers regular 50-minute cruises to Cataract Gorge up the Tamar River from Home Point Wharf in Launceston. The cost is A$33 adults, A$15 children 5 to 17, and A$80 for families of four. Longer cruises are also available.

Just outside Launceston, the suspension bridge over Cataract Gorge is a scenic highlight.

There is a new exhibition every month, from the industrial to the aesthetic. There's a shop as well.

City Park, Brisbane St. (at Tamar St.). www.designtasmania.com.au. ℂ **03/6331 5506.** Free admission. Mon–Fri 9:30am–5:30pm; Sat–Sun 10am–4pm.

Launceston Historic Walks ★ WALKING TOUR A must for any visitor is a 90-minute stroll with Launceston Historic Walks, for a fascinating insight into Launceston's history. Your enthusiastic guide Robyn is full of stories of the characters who built this city, delivered with theatrical flair.

1842 Gallery, corner of St. John and Cimitiere sts. www.1842gallery.com.au/launceston-historic-walks. ℂ **03/6331 2213.** A$15 adults. Mon 4pm; Tues–Sat 10am.

The Old Umbrella Shop ★ HISTORIC SITE Built in the 1860s, this unique shop is the last genuine period store in Tasmania. Run by three generations of the umbrella-making Shott family since the turn of the 20th century until a few years ago, it is now operated by the National Trust. Umbrellas spanning the last 100 years are on display, and modern "brollies" and souvenirs are for sale.

60 George St. www.nationaltrust.org.au/places/old-umbrella-shop. ℂ **03/6331 9248.** Free admission. Mon–Fri 9am–5pm; Sat 9am–noon. Closed Christmas Day, Boxing Day (Dec 26), New Year's Day, and Good Friday.

The Queen Victoria Museum & Art Gallery ★★ MUSEUM This museum, opened in honor of Queen Victoria's Golden Jubilee in 1891, is in two parts: the art gallery on Wellington Street, Royal Park, in the heart of Launceston, and the other in the inner suburb of Inveresk, just a few minutes' drive away (or catch the Tiger Bus). The Inveresk complex, a smart redevelopment of old railyards, is home to the Launceston Planetarium and focuses on science, which kids will find fun. Free tours are run on Sundays, at the art gallery at 11:30am and the museum at 1pm.

2 Invermay Rd., Inveresk, and 2 Wellington St., Royal Park. www.qvmag.tas.gov.au. ℂ **03/6323 3777.** Free admission. Planetarium admission A$6 adults, A$4 children, A$16 family of 4 (no children 4 and under). Daily 10am–4pm (5pm in Jan). Closed Good Friday and Christmas Day. Planetarium closed Sun–Mon and public holidays; show times Tues–Fri 1 and 3pm, Sat 2 and 3pm.

Woolmers Estate ★★ HISTORIC HOME   The grand estate of pioneer Thomas Archer is an extraordinary time capsule. It is inscribed on the World Heritage List of Australian Convict Sites. Once the most powerful family in Tasmania's north, the Archers settled at this homestead near Longford, about 25km (16 miles) from Launceston, in 1817. The six generations who lived here until 1994 have left an unrivaled legacy in the almost-untouched Woolmers Estate. There are 20 buildings, from the grand mansion to the servants' quarters, shearing sheds, a blacksmith's shop, and seven free settler's cottages. (You can stay in some of them, for A$150 per night.) Entry to the homestead is by guided tour only, or you can take a self-guided tour of the gardens and outbuildings. There's also a restaurant serving Devonshire teas, lunches, and snacks. Take time to smell the roses next door at the **National Rose Garden of Australia** (free entry), where more than 2 hectares (5 acres) are planted with around 4,000 bushes.

658 Woolmers Lane, Longford. www.woolmers.com.au. ℂ **03/6391 2230.** Entry to grounds A$16 adults, A$7 children, A$35 family; guided tour A$22 adults, A$9 children 15 and under. Daily 9:30am–4pm. Closed Good Friday, Anzac Day (Apr 25), Queen's Birthday (second Mon of June), Christmas Day, and Boxing Day (Dec 26). Tours at 10 (except in winter) and 11:15am, and 12:30 and 2pm.

PLANNING YOUR TRIP TO AUSTRALIA

A little preparation is essential before you start your journey to Australia, especially if you plan to do any special-interest activities, such as diving the Great Barrier Reef or visiting the Aboriginal landmarks in the Red Centre. This chapter provides a variety of planning tools, including information on how to get there and on-the-ground resources.

ARRIVING

By Plane

Australia is a very long haul from just about anywhere except New Zealand. Sydney is a nearly 15-hour nonstop flight from Los Angeles, and even longer if you come via Honolulu, Hawaii. If you're flying from the East Coast of the United States, add 5½ hours. If you're coming from the U.S. via Auckland, add transit time in New Zealand plus 3 hours for the Auckland-Sydney leg.

If you are coming from the United Kingdom, brace yourself for a flight of 12 hours, more or less, from London to Asia, followed possibly by a long day in transit, because flights to Australia have a habit of arriving in Asia early in the morning and then not departing until around midnight, after which you still have an 8- to 9-hour flight to Australia.

Sydney (SYD), Cairns (CNS), Melbourne (MEL), and Brisbane (BNE) are all international gateways. Sydney is the major entry point into Australia, but you may also fly through another airport first, depending on where you're departing from. Major airlines flying to Australia from North America are **Qantas** (www.qantas.com.au), **Virgin Australia** (www.virginaustralia.com.au), **Air Canada** (www.aircanada.com), **American Airlines** (www.americanairlines.com.au), **Delta** (www.delta.com), **Hawaiian Airlines** (www.hawaiianairlines.com.au), and **United** (www.united.com). In 2017, **Qantas** also inaugurated a direct London-Sydney route; several other airlines connect the U.K. with Australia but make one or two stops en route, traveling either east or west.

By Boat

Sydney Harbour is Australia's main port for cruise ships and the only port in Australia with two dedicated cruise-passenger terminals—the Overseas Passenger Terminal at Circular Quay (in the heart of the city, close to major tourist attractions) and the White Bay Cruise Terminal in the suburb of Rozelle, about 5km (3 miles) from the city center. Melbourne and Brisbane are also major cruise ports, and some cruises also stop off at Hobart. Cruise lines offer hundreds of itineraries that include Australia; most also include New Zealand and the South Pacific. Major cruise companies to check out include **Carnival Cruises** (www.carnival.com.au), **Cunard** (www.cunardline.com.au), **Holland America** (www.hollandamerica.com), **P&O Cruises** (www.pocruises.com.au), Princess Cruises (www.princess.com), **Royal Caribbean** (www.royalcaribbean.com), **Seabourn Cruises** (www.seabourn.com), and **Silversea Cruises** (www.silversea.com).

GETTING AROUND

By Plane

Australia is a big country with a small population to support its air routes, so airfares may be higher than you are used to paying. Don't assume there is a direct flight to your chosen destination, or that there is a flight every hour or even every day.

Most domestic air travel is operated by **Qantas** (www.qantas.com.au; © **800/227-4500** in the U.S. and Canada, 131 313 in Australia, 0800/964 432 in the U.K., 0800/808 767 in New Zealand), **Virgin Australia** (www.virginaustralia.com; © **1855/253-8021** in the U.S., 136 789 or 07/3295 2296 in Australia, 0800/051 1281 in the U.K., 0800/670 000 in New Zealand), or Qantas-owned **Jetstar** (www.jetstar.com.au; © **1866/397-8170** in the U.S., 131 538 or 03/9645 5999 in Australia, 0800/800 995 in New Zealand). **Regional Express** (www.rex.com.au; © **131 713** in Australia) serves some regional ports in New South Wales, Victoria, South Australia, Tasmania, and Queensland.

Between them, Virgin Australia and Qantas and its subsidiaries, QantasLink and Jetstar, service every capital city, as well as most major regional towns on the east coast. Note that Melbourne has two airports: the main international and domestic terminals at Tullamarine, and Avalon Airport, about 50km (31 miles) from the city, which is used by some Jetstar flights. Make sure you check which one your flight leaves from before you book.

Low-cost carrier **Scoot** (www.flyscoot.com; © **02/9009 0860** in Australia) flies to all capital cities (except Hobart) as well as the Queensland ports of Cairns and Gold Coast.

Competition is hot and the airline industry constantly changing, so it's possible that all airlines will have changed their route networks by the time you read this.

DISCOUNTED FARES FOR INTERNATIONAL TRAVELERS

Qantas offers international travelers discounts off the full fares that Australians pay for domestic flights bought within Australia. To qualify, quote your passport number and international ticket number when reserving. Don't assume the fare for international travelers is the best deal, though—the latest deal in the market that day (or even better, perhaps, a package deal with accommodations thrown in) may be cheaper still.

AIR PASSES

If you are visiting from the U.S. and plan on visiting more than one city, purchasing a **Qantas Explorer pass** is much cheaper than buying regular fares. The pass is for economy-class travel only and must be purchased along with your Qantas or American Airlines fare from the U.S. to Australia. Prices vary according to which "zone" you are traveling to, and there are more than 30 Australian destinations to choose from, but the deals will get you to all major destinations covered in this book.

By Car

Australia's roads sometimes leave a bit to be desired. The taxes of 24 million people get spread pretty thin when it comes to maintaining roads across a continent. Some "highways" are two-lane affairs with the occasional rut and pothole, often no outside line markings, and sometimes no shoulders to speak of. You will strike these if you plan to drive in the Red Centre.

If you plan long-distance driving, get a road map (see "Maps," p. 324, for sources) that distinguishes between paved and unpaved roads.

You can use your current driver's license or an international driver's permit in every state of Australia. By law, you must carry your license with you when driving. The minimum driving age is 16 or 17, depending on which state you visit, but some car-rental companies require you to be 21, or sometimes 26, if you want to rent a four-wheel-drive (4WD) vehicle.

CAR RENTALS

Think twice about renting a car in tourist hot spots such as Cairns. In these areas most tour operators pick you up and drop you back at your hotel door, so having a car may not be worth the expense.

The "big four" car-rental companies—**Avis** (www.avis.com.au), **Budget** (www.budget.com.au), **Hertz** (www.hertz.com.au), and **Thrifty** (www.thrifty.com.au)—all have networks across Australia. Other major car-rental companies are **Europcar** (www.europcar.com.au), which has the third largest fleet in Australia, and **Red Spot Car Rentals** (www.redspot.com.au), which has depots in all state capital cities as well as other major centers such as Cairns, Townsville, and Rockhampton.

A small sedan for zipping around a city will cost about A$45 to A$80 a day. A feistier vehicle with enough grunt to get you from state to state will cost around A$70 to A$100 a day. Rentals of a week or longer usually reduce the price by A$5 a day or so.

Damage to a rental car caused by an animal (hitting a kangaroo, for instance) may not be covered by your car-rental company's insurance policies. Different car-rental companies have very different rules and restrictions, so make sure you check each one's coverage. For example, some will not cover animal damage incurred at night, while others don't have such limits. The same applies to the rules about driving on unpaved roads, of which Australia has many. Avis and Budget say you may only drive on roads "properly formed and constructed as a sealed, metalled, or gravel road," while the others limit you largely to sealed roads. Check the fine print.

A regular car will get you to most places in this book, except for some parts of the Red Centre, where you will need a 4WD vehicle. All the major car-rental companies rent them. Four-wheel-drives are more expensive than a regular car, but you can get them for as little as A$75 per day if you shop around (cheaper for rentals of a week or longer).

The rates quoted here are only a guide. Many smaller local companies— and the big guys, too—offer competitive specials, especially in tourist areas with distinct off-seasons. Advance purchase rates, usually 7 to 21 days ahead, can offer significant savings.

If you are concerned about reducing your carbon emissions, consider hiring a hybrid car. In Australia, the major car-hire companies have the hybrid Toyota Prius available. Ask when making your bookings.

INSURANCE

Insurance for loss of or damage to the car and third-party property insurance are usually included, but read the agreement carefully because the fine print contains information the front-desk staff may not tell you. For example, damage to the car body may be covered, but not damage to the windshield or tires, or damage caused by water or driving too close to a bushfire.

The deductible, known as **"excess"** in Australia, on insurance may be as high as A$2,000 for regular cars and up to A$5,500 on 4WDs and motor homes. You can reduce it, or avoid it altogether, by paying a premium of between about A$20 to A$50 per day on a car or four-wheel-drive, and around A$25 to A$50 per day on a motor home. The amount of the excess reduction premium depends on the vehicle type and the extent of reduction you choose. Your rental company may bundle personal accident insurance and baggage insurance into this premium. And again, check the conditions; some excess reduction payments do not reduce excesses on single-vehicle accidents, for example.

ONE-WAY RENTALS

Australia's long distances often make one-way rentals a necessity, for which car-rental companies can charge a hefty penalty amounting to hundreds of dollars. A one-way fee usually applies to motor-home rentals, too—usually around A$260 to A$360. An extra A$650 remote-location fee can apply for Outback areas such as Alice Springs. And there are minimum rental periods of between 7 and 21 days.

MOTOR HOMES

Motor homes (Aussies call them camper vans) are popular in Australia. Generally smaller than the RVs in the United States, they come in two- to six-berth versions and usually have everything you need, such as a minifridge and/or freezer (icebox in the smaller versions), microwave, gas stove, cooking and cleaning utensils, linens, and touring information, including maps and campground guides. All have showers and toilets, except some two-berthers.

Most of these camper vans have air-conditioned driver's cabins, but note that not all have air-conditioned living quarters, which is more or less a necessity to have in most parts of the country from November through March. Ask to make sure that the vehicle you're renting is fully air-conditioned if you're traveling this time of year. Four-wheel-drive campers are available, but while they offer an advantage in traversing wilderness roads, they tend to be small, and some lack hot water, toilet, and shower, not to mention air-conditioning.

Australia's biggest national motor-home-rental companies are **Apollo Motorhome Holidays** (www.apollocamper.com; ℂ **1800/777 779** in Australia, or 07/3265 9200), **Britz Campervan Rentals** (www.britz.com; ℂ **1800/331 454** in Australia, or 800/2008 0801 from outside Australia), and **Maui** (www.maui.com.au; ℂ **800/2008 0801** from anywhere in the world, or 1800/827 821 within Australia, or 02/9316 9071).

Rates vary with the seasons and your choice of vehicle. May and June are the slowest months; December and January are the busiest. It's sometimes possible to get better rates by booking in your home country before departure. Renting for longer than 3 weeks knocks a few dollars off the daily rate. Most companies will require a minimum 4- or 5-day rental. Give the company your itinerary before booking, because some routes may need the company's permission. Note that the minimum driver age for renting motor homes is usually 21.

Most local councils take a dim view of "free camping," the practice of pulling over by the roadside to camp for the night. Instead, in most places you will have to stay in a campground—and pay for it.

ON THE ROAD

GAS   Prices go up and down, but at press time you were looking at around A$1.33 a liter (about ¼ gal.) for unleaded petrol in Sydney, and slightly more in the Outback. Most rental cars take unleaded gas, and motor homes run on diesel.

DRIVING RULES   Australians drive on the left, which means you give way to the right. Left turns on a red light are not permitted unless a sign says so.

Roundabouts (traffic circles) are common at intersections; approach these slowly enough to stop if you have to, and give way to all traffic on the roundabout. Flash your indicator (turn signal) as you leave the roundabout (even if you're going straight, because technically that's a left turn).

It's a sad fact, but kangaroos are a road hazard. Avoid driving in country areas between dusk and dawn, when 'roos are most active. If you hit one, always stop and check its pouch for live joeys (baby kangaroos), because females usually have one in the pouch. Wrap the joey tightly in a towel or old sweater, don't feed or over-handle it, and take it to a vet in the nearest town or call one of the following wildlife care groups: **Wildlife Information & Rescue Service (WIRES)** in New South Wales (℗ **1300/094 737**); **Wildlife Victoria** (℗ **1300/094 535**); **Wildcare Australia** in Queensland (℗ **07/5527 2444**); or **Wildcare NT** in Darwin (℗ 08/8988 6121. In Tasmania,

Bonorong Wildlife Sanctuary (℗ **03/ 6268 1184**) has the state's only 24-hour wildlife rescue service. Most vets will treat native wildlife for free.

Some highways run through unfenced stations (ranches), where sheep and cattle pose a threat. Cattle like to rest on the warm bitumen road at night, so put your lights on high to spot them. If an animal does loom up, slow down—but never swerve, or you may roll. If you have to, hit it. Tell farmers within 24 hours if you have hit their livestock.

Car-rental companies will not insure for animal damage to the car, which should give you an inkling of how common an occurrence this is.

The maximum permitted blood alcohol level when driving is .05 percent, which equals approximately two 200-milliliter (6.6-oz.) drinks in the first hour for men, one for women, and one drink per hour for both sexes after that. The police set up random breath-testing units (RBTs) in cunningly disguised and unlikely places all the time, so getting caught is easy. You will face a court appearance if you do.

The speed limit is 50kmph (31 mph) or 60kmph (37 mph) in urban areas, 100kmph (62 mph) in most country areas, and sometimes 110kmph (68 mph) on freeways. In the Northern Territory, the speed limit is set at 130kmph (81 mph) on the Stuart, Arnhem, Barkly, and Victoria highways, while rural roads are designated 110kmph (68 mph) unless otherwise signposted. *Be warned:* The Territory has a high death toll. Speed-limit signs show black numbers circled in red on a white background.

Drivers and passengers, including taxi passengers, must wear a seatbelt at all times when the vehicle is moving forward, if the car is equipped with a belt. Young children are required to sit in the rear seat in a child-safety seat or harness; car-rental companies will rent these to you, but be sure to request them in advance. Tell the taxi company you have a child when you book a cab so that it can send a car with the right restraints.

MAPS   The maps published by the state automobile clubs listed below in "Auto Clubs" will likely be free if you are a member of an affiliated auto club in your home country. None will mail them to you overseas; pick them up on arrival. Remember to bring your auto-club membership card to qualify for discounts or free maps.

Two of the biggest map publishers in Australia are **HEMA Maps** (www.hemamaps.com) and **UBD Gregory's** (www.hardigrant.com/au/travel). Both publish an extensive range of national (including road atlases), state, regional, and city maps. HEMA has a strong list of regional maps, while UBD Gregory's produces a complete range of street directories by city, region, or state. HEMA produces 4WD and motorbike road atlases and many regional 4WD maps—good if you plan to go off the trails. Many of its maps are also available as smartphone apps.

TOLL ROADS   Electronic "beeper" or e-tags are used on all major Australian toll roads, including Melbourne's City Link motorways, Brisbane's tunnels and Logan and Gateway motorways, the Sydney Harbour Bridge and tunnel, and all Sydney's major tunnels and motorways. The tag is a small device attached to the vehicle's front windshield, which transmits signals to toll points on the road. This deducts the toll amount from your toll account. The same e-tag can be used on all Australian toll roads. While some toll roads still have physical collection points where you can pay the toll, others—such as Melbourne's freeways—don't. If you are likely to need an e-tag, your car-rental company can arrange one for you.

ROAD SIGNS   Australians navigate by road name, not road number. The easiest way to get where you're going is to familiarize yourself with the major towns along your route and follow the signs toward them.

AUTO CLUBS   Every state and territory in Australia has its own auto club. Your auto association back home probably has a reciprocal agreement with Australian clubs, which may entitle you to free maps, accommodations guides, and roadside assistance. Don't forget to bring your membership card.

Even if you're not a member, the clubs are a good source of advice on local traffic regulations, touring advice, road conditions, traveling in remote areas, and any other motoring questions you may have. The clubs sell maps, accommodations guides, and camping guides to nonmembers at reasonable prices. They even share a website: **www.aaa.asn.au**.

ROAD CONDITIONS & SAFETY

Here are some common motoring dangers and ways to avoid them:

FATIGUE   Fatigue is a killer on Australia's roads. The rule is to take a 20-minute break every 2 hours, even if you don't feel tired. In some states, "driver reviver" stations operate on major roads during holiday periods. Serving free tea, coffee, and cookies, they are often found at roadside picnic areas with restrooms.

ROAD TRAINS   Road trains consist of as many as three big truck carriages (tractor trailers) linked together to make a "train" up to 54m (177 ft.) long. If you're in front of one, give the driver plenty of warning when you brake, because the trains need a lot of distance to slow down. Allow at least 1 clear kilometer (.6 miles) before you pass one, but don't expect the driver to make it easy—"truckies" are notorious for their lack of concern for motorists.

UNPAVED ROADS   Many country roads are unsealed (unpaved). They are usually bone-dry, which makes them more slippery than they look, so travel at a moderate speed—35kmph (22 mph) is not too cautious, and anything over 60kmph (37 mph) is dangerous. That said, when you are on a heavily corrugated or rutted road (which many are), you may need to keep to a higher speed (60kmph/37 mph) just to stay on top of them. Don't overcorrect if you veer to one side. Keep well behind any vehicles, because the dust they throw up can block your vision.

FLOODS   Floods are common north of Cairns from November or December through March or April (the "Wet" season). Never cross a flooded road unless you are sure of its depth. Crocodiles may be in the water, so do not wade in to test it! Fast-flowing water is dangerous, even if it's very shallow. When in doubt, stay where you are and wait for the water to drop; most flash floods subside in 24 hours. Check the road conditions ahead at least once a day in the Wet season.

RUNNING OUT OF GAS   Gas stations (also called "roadhouses" in rural areas) can be few and far between in the Outback, so fill up at every opportunity.

TIPS FOR FOUR-WHEEL DRIVERS   Always keep to the four-wheel-drive track. Going off-road causes soil erosion, a significant environmental problem in Australia. Leave gates as you found them. Obtain permission from the owners before venturing onto private station (ranch) roads. On an extended trip or in remote areas, carry 5 liters (1⅓ gal.) of drinking water per person per day (dehydration occurs fast in the Australian heat); enough food to last 3 or 4 days more than you think you will need; a first-aid kit; spare fuel; a jack and two spare tires; spare fan belts, radiator hoses, and air-conditioner hoses; a tow rope; and a good map that marks all gas stations. In seriously remote areas outside the scope of this book, carry a high-frequency and a CB radio (a mobile phone may not work in the Outback). Advise a friend, your hotel

---

What If Your Vehicle Breaks Down?

Warning: If you break down or get lost, **never leave your vehicle.** Many motorist—often an Aussie who should have known better—has died wandering off on a crazy quest for help or water, knowing full well that neither is to be found for maybe hundreds of miles. Most people who get lost do so in Outback spots; if that happens to you, conserve your body moisture by doing as little as possible and staying in the shade of your car.

The **emergency breakdown assistance** telephone number for every Australian auto club is ℂ **131 111** from anywhere in Australia. It is billed as a local call. If you are not a member of an auto club at home that has a reciprocal agreement with the Australian clubs, you'll have to join the Australian club on the spot before the club will tow or repair your car. This usually costs around A$80, not a big price to pay when you're stranded—although in the Outback, the charge may be considerably higher. Most car-rental companies also have emergency assistance numbers.

manager, the local tourist bureau, or a police station of your route and your expected time of return or arrival at your destination.

By Train

Australia's trains are clean, comfortable, and safe, and for the most part service standards and facilities are perfectly adequate. The rail network in Australia links Perth to Adelaide and on to Melbourne, and north to Sydney, Brisbane, and Cairns. There's also a line into the interior from Adelaide to Alice Springs and Darwin. Trains generally cost more than buses but are still reasonably priced.

Most long-distance trains have sleepers with big windows, air-conditioning, electric outlets, wardrobes, sinks, and fresh sheets and blankets. First-class sleepers have en suite bathrooms, and fares often include meals. Second-class sleepers use shared shower facilities, and meals are not included. Some second-class sleepers are private cabins; on other trains, you share with strangers. Single cabins are usually of broom-closet dimensions but surprisingly comfy, with their own toilet and basin. The onboard food ranges from mediocre to pretty good. Note that smoking is banned on all Australian rail networks.

Different entities manage Australia's rail routes. They include the government-owned **Queensland Rail** (www.queenslandrailtravel.com.au; ✆ 1300/131 722 in Australia, or 07/3606 6630), which handles rail within that state, and **NSW TrainLink** (www.transportnsw.info/regional; ✆ 132 232 in Australia), which manages travel within New South Wales and from Sydney south to Melbourne and north to Brisbane. **Great Southern Rail** (www.great southernrail.com.au; ✆ 1800/703 357 in Australia, or 08/8213 4401) has a range of fabulous Outback train journeys, including *The Ghan* (p. 266), which links Adelaide, Alice Springs, and Darwin, *The Indian Pacific* (p. 266), which travels between Sydney and Perth, and *The Overland*, between Melbourne and Adelaide.

Queensland Rail operates the high-speed *Spirit of Queensland* five times a week on the Brisbane-Cairns route with business-class-style seating and "railbeds" (similar to business class lie-flat airline beds). The trip takes around 24 hours. The *Tilt Train* runs between Brisbane and the coastal towns of Bundaberg and Rockhampton. All Queensland and New South Wales long-distance trains stop at most towns en route, so they're useful for exploring the eastern states.

RAIL PASSES NSW TrainLink's **Discovery Pass** gives you unlimited economy-class trips anywhere on its network, including to Melbourne and Brisbane, for up to 6 months. A 14-day pass costs A$232, a 1-month pass A$275, a 3-month pass A$298, and a 6-month pass A$420.

The **Queensland Explorer** pass offers unlimited economy seat travel for 1 or 2 months across the Queensland Rail network, from Cairns in the north to Brisbane in the south, and in the Queensland Outback. It costs A$299 for 1 month or A$389 for 2 months. If you only fancy the coast, the **Queensland Coastal Pass** allows travel between Brisbane and Cairns for A$209 for 1 month, A$289 for 2 months. *Note:* These passes are only available to international travelers.

By Bus

Bus travel in Australia is as comfortable as it can be, given the nature of long-distance coach travel. Terminals are centrally located and well lit, the buses—called "coaches" Down Under—are clean and air-conditioned, you sit in adjustable seats, videos play onboard, and drivers are polite and sometimes even point out places of interest along the way. Buses are all nonsmoking, and some have restrooms. The country's extensive bus network will take you almost everywhere.

Australia has one national coach operator: **Greyhound Australia** (www.greyhound.com.au; ✆ **1300/473 946** in Australia, or 07/4690 9850; no relation to Greyhound in the U.S.). In addition to point-to-point services, Greyhound Australia offers a limited range of tours at popular locations on its networks, including Uluru in the Northern Territory and the Whitsunday islands in Queensland.

Fares and some passes are considerably cheaper for students, backpacker cardholders, and Hostelling International/YHA members.

BUS PASSES   Bus passes are a great value. Note that during school vacation periods, which are always busy, booking as much as a week ahead is smart. Greyhound Australia's **Whimit Passes** let you travel any route, in any direction. There are seven passes to choose from: 7, 21, 45, 60, 90, 120, or 365 days. You'll pay A$249 for 7 days, and A$1,499 for the whole year. **Hop-on-hop-off Passes** are valid for 90 days and link most of the popular destinations: from Sydney, Brisbane or Melbourne to Cairns; Melbourne or Sydney to Brisbane. Travel from Melbourne to Cairns costs A$549.

[FastFACTS] AUSTRALIA

ATMs/Banks   The easiest and best way to get cash away from home is from an **ATM (automated teller machine),** sometimes referred to as a "cash machine" or "cashpoint."

The **Cirrus** (www.mastercard.com) and **PLUS** (www.visa.com) networks span the globe. Be sure you know your daily withdrawal limit before you depart.

Note that Australian ATMs use a four-digit code, so check with your bank and make sure you change yours before you leave. **Note:** Some banks impose a fee every time you use a card at another bank's ATM, and that fee can be higher for international transactions (A$5 or more). In addition, the bank from which you withdraw cash may charge its own fee. For international withdrawal fees, ask your bank.

Customs   The duty-free allowance in Australia is A$900 or, for those 17 and under, A$450. Anyone 18 and over can bring in up to 25 cigarettes or 25 grams of cigars or other tobacco products, 2.25 liters (41 fluid oz.) of alcohol, and "dutiable goods" to the value of A$900 (A$450 if you are 17 or under). "Dutiable goods" are luxury items such as perfume, watches, jewelry, furs, plus gifts of any kind. Keep this in mind if you intend to bring presents for family and friends in Australia; gifts given to you also count toward the dutiable limit.

Personal goods that you're taking with you are usually exempt from duty, but if you are returning with valuable goods that you already own, file form B263. Customs officers do not collect duty—less than A$50—as long as you declared the goods in the first place.

For more information, contact the **Department of Home Affairs** (⏾ **131 881** in Australia), or check out **www.homeaffairs.gov.au**.

You need not declare cash in any currency, and other currency instruments, such as traveler's checks, under a value of A$10,000.

Australia is a signatory to the **Convention on International Trade in Endangered Species (CITES)**, which restricts or bans the import of products made from protected wildlife. Banned items include ivory, tortoise (marine turtle) shell, rhinoceros, or tiger products, and sturgeon caviar. Bear this in mind if you stop in other countries en route to Australia, where souvenirs made from items like these may be sold. Australian authorities may seize these items.

Because Australia is an island, it is free of many agricultural and livestock diseases. To keep it that way, *strict* **quarantine** applies to importing plants, animals, and their products, including food. "Sniffer" dogs at airports detect these products (as well as drugs). Some items may be confiscated, and others may

be held over for you to take with you when you leave the country. Heavy fines apply to breaches of the laws. Amnesty trash bins are available before you reach the immigration counters in airport arrivals halls for items such as fruit. Don't be alarmed if, just before landing, the flight attendants spray the aircraft cabin (with products approved by the World Health Organization) to kill potentially disease-bearing insects. For more information on what is and is not allowed, contact the nearest Australian embassy or consulate, or Australia's Department of Agriculture and Water Resources (www.agriculture.gov.au/travelling; ⏾ **1800/900 090** in Australia).

For information on what you're allowed to bring home, contact one of the following agencies:

U.S. Citizens: U.S. Customs & Border Protection (CBP), 1300 Pennsylvania Ave. NW, Washington, DC 20229 (www.cbp.gov; ⏾ **877/CBP-5511** [227-5511]).

Canadian Citizens: Canada Border Services Agency, Ottawa, Ontario, K1A 0L8 (www.cbsa-asfc.gc.ca).

U.K. Citizens: Check with HM Revenue & Customs (www.gov.uk/duty-free-goods).

New Zealand Citizens: The Customhouse, 1 Hinemoa St., Harbour Quays, Wellington, 6011 (www.customs.govt.nz; ⏾ **09/927-8036,** or 0800/428-786 in New Zealand).

Doctors & Hospitals

Doctors are listed under "M," for "Medical Practitioners," in the Yellow Pages in Australia, and most large towns and cities have 24-hour clinics. Your hotel may be able to help you find a local doctor. Failing that, go to the local emergency room. See "Fast Facts" in other chapters of this book for local details.

Drinking Laws   Hours vary from pub to pub, but most are open daily from 10am or noon to 10pm or midnight. The minimum drinking age is 18.

Random breath tests to catch drunk drivers are common, and drunk-driving laws are strictly enforced. Getting caught drunk behind the wheel will mean a court appearance, not just a fine. The maximum permitted blood-alcohol level is .05 percent.

Alcohol is sold in liquor stores, in the "bottle shops" attached to every pub, and in some states in supermarkets.

Electricity   The current is 240 volts AC, 50 hertz. Sockets take two or three flat, not rounded, prongs. Bring a connection kit of the right power and phone adapters, a spare phone cord, and a spare Ethernet network cable—or find out whether your hotel supplies them to guests. North Americans and Europeans will need to buy a converter before they leave home. (Don't wait until you get to Australia, because Australian stores are likely to stock only converters for Aussie appliances to fit American and European outlets.) Some large hotels have 110V outlets for electric shavers (or dual voltage), and some will lend converters, but don't count on it in smaller, less expensive hotels, motels, or B&Bs. **Note:** Power does not start automatically when you plug in an appliance; you need to flick the switch beside the socket to the "on" position.

Embassies & Consulates Most diplomatic posts are in Canberra. **United States:** United States Embassy, 21 Moonah Place, Yarralumla, Canberra, ACT 2600 (http:// au.usembassy.gov; © **02/6214 5600**), the United States Consulate General, 553 St Kilda Rd., Melbourne (© **03/9526 5900**); or the United States Consulate General in Sydney, Level 10, 19-29 Martin Place (© **1300/139 399**). **Canada:** High Commission of Canada, Commonwealth Avenue, Yarralumla, Canberra, ACT 2600 (www. canadainternational.gc.ca/ australia-australie; © **02/6270 4000**). **Ireland:** Consulate General of Ireland, Level 26, 1 Market St., Sydney, NSW 2000 (www.irishconsulatesydney. net; © **02/9264 9635**). **New Zealand:** New Zealand High Commission, 140 Commonwealth Ave., Yarralumla, Canberra, ACT 2600 (www.mfat.govt.nz; © **02/6270 4211**). **United Kingdom:** British High Commission, Commonwealth Avenue, Yarralumla, Canberra, ACT 2600 (www.gov.uk/world/ australia; © **02/6270 6666**).

Emergencies Dial © **000** anywhere in Australia for police, ambulance, or the fire department. This is a free call from public and private telephones and needs no coins. The TTY emergency number is © **106.**

Family Travel Australians travel widely with their own kids, so facilities for families, including family passes to attractions, are common.

Many hotels will offer connecting units or "family rooms." Ask when booking. Most Australian hotels will arrange babysitting when given a day's notice.

Many Australian resorts have "kids' clubs" with extensive programs designed for children 11 and under and, in some cases, teenagers. Other resorts have "kids stay, eat, and play free" offers, particularly during holiday periods.

A great accommodations option for families is Australia's huge stock of holiday apartments (with or without daily maid service). Often less expensive than a hotel room, they offer a living room, a kitchen, a bathroom or two, and the privacy of a separate bedroom for adults.

International airlines and domestic airlines in Australia charge 75 percent of the adult fare for kids 11 and under. Most charge 10 percent for infants under 2 years not occupying a seat. Australian transport companies, attractions, and tour operators typically charge half-price for kids under 12 or 14 years.

Don't forget that children entering Australia on their parent's passport still need their own visa.

Resources for Family Travel: There are two terrific Australian travel magazines devoted to traveling with children. *Holidays with Kids* (www.holidayswithkids. com.au) and *Out & About With Kids* (www.outand aboutwithkids.com.au) both have comprehensive websites listing great options for family travel in Australia. **Family Travel Forum** is also a good resource; see **www. myfamilytravels.com** for destinations, ideas, and more.

Health No vaccinations are needed to enter Australia unless you have been in a yellow fever danger zone—that is, South America or Africa—in the 6 days prior to entering.

Australian pharmacists may only fill prescriptions written by Australian doctors, so carry enough medication with you for your trip. Doctors are listed under "M," for "Medical Practitioners," in the Yellow Pages, and most large towns and cities have 24-hour clinics. Failing that, go to the local hospital emergency room.

Generally, you don't have to worry much about health issues on a trip to Australia.

KNOW BEFORE YOU GO: health hazards

Tropical Illnesses Some parts of tropical far-north Queensland have sporadic outbreaks of the mosquito-borne dengue fever. The areas affected include Cairns, Port Douglas, and Townsville. But as dengue-fever mosquitoes breed in urban environments, tourist activities in north Queensland such as reef and rainforest trips carry a modest risk as well. The risk can be minimized by staying in screened or air-conditioned accommodations, using insect repellent at all times, and wearing long, loose, light-colored clothing that covers arms and legs.

Bugs, Bites & Other Wildlife Concerns Snake and spider bites may not be as common as the hair-raising stories you will hear would suggest, but it pays to be wary. Your other concerns should be marine life, including jellyfish, and saltwater crocodiles. For more information and background on the fauna of Australia, and how to avoid dangerous encounters with them, see p. 25.

Sun/Elements Australians have the world's highest death rate from skin cancer because of the country's intense sunlight. Limit your exposure to the sun, especially during the first few days of your trip, and from 11am to 3pm in summer and 10am to 2pm in winter.

Remember that UV rays reflected off walls, water, and the ground can burn you even when you're not in direct sunlight. Use a broad-spectrum sunscreen with a high protection factor (SPF 30 or higher). Wear a broad-brimmed hat that covers the back of your neck, ears, and face (a baseball cap won't do it), and a long-sleeved shirt.

Remember that children need more protection than adults do. Don't even think about traveling without sunglasses, or you'll spend your entire vacation squinting against Australia's "diamond light."

Extreme Weather Exposure Cyclones sometimes affect tropical areas, such as Queensland's coastal regions, from about Gladstone north, during January and February. Serious damage is normally rare.

Hygiene standards are high, hospitals are modern, and doctors and dentists are well qualified. Because of the continent's size, however, you can sometimes be a long way from a hospital or a doctor. Remote areas are served by the Royal Flying Doctor Service. But it may be advisable to purchase standard medical travel insurance.

Insurance Standard medical and travel insurance is advisable for travel to Australia. Divers should also ensure they have the appropriate insurance. For information on traveler's insurance, trip cancelation insurance, and medical insurance while traveling, please visit www.frommers.com/tips.

Internet Access Most hotels throughout Australia offer dataports for laptop modems, high-speed Internet access, and free Wi-Fi. Check the list of hotel amenities in each hotel listing to see what kind of Internet service your hotel offers, and at what cost.

Most **youth hostels** and **public libraries** have Internet access. Avoid **hotel business centers** unless you're willing to pay exorbitant rates. Cybercafes (called **Internet cafes** in Australia) can be found almost everywhere.

Most major cities also have free Wi-Fi hubs that you can hook into in public places. Most major airports have **Internet kiosks** that provide basic Web access for a per-minute fee that's usually higher than cyber-cafe prices.

Legal Aid If you find yourself in trouble with the long arm of the law while visiting Australia, the first thing you should do is contact your country's embassy or nearest consulate in

Australia. See contact details for Canberra diplomatic posts under "Embassies & Consulates" above. Embassies or consulates with posts in state capitals are listed in "Fast Facts" in chapters 4, 5, and 6.

The U.S. Embassy considers an "emergency" to be either your arrest or the loss of your passport. If arrested in Australia, you will have to go through the Australian legal process for being charged, prosecuted, possibly convicted and sentenced, and for any appeals process. U.S. consular officers (and those of other countries) provide a wide variety of services to their citizens arrested abroad and to their families. These may include providing a list of local attorneys, providing info about judicial procedures, and notifying your family and/or friends, if you wish. However, they cannot demand your release, represent you at your trial, give you legal advice, or pay your fees or fines.

LGBTQ Travelers Sydney is one of the most gay-friendly cities in the world, and across most of Australia the gay community has a high profile and lots of support services. Same-sex marriage was legalized in Australia in 2017.

There are plenty of gay and lesbian bars, and most Saturday nights see a privately operated gay dance party taking place in an inner-city warehouse somewhere. The cafes and pubs of Oxford Street in

Darlinghurst, a short cab ride or long stroll from Sydney's downtown area, are the liveliest gay spots in that city. The annual **Sydney Gay & Lesbian Mardi Gras,** culminating in a huge street parade and party in late February or early March, is a high point on the city's calendar.

In rural areas of Australia, you may still encounter a little conservative resistance to gays and lesbians, but Australians everywhere are generally open-minded. Noosa, on Queensland's Sunshine Coast, is a favored destination for gay revelers after Mardi Gras, and a couple of resorts in north Queensland cater to gay and lesbian travelers. One of the best known is **Turtle Cove Beach Resort** (www.turtlecove.com; ✆ **1300/ 727 979** in Australia, or 07/4059 1800), located on a private beach between Cairns and Port Douglas.

LGBTQ Resources: A service you may find useful is **Twenty10** (incorporating the Gay & Lesbian Counselling Service of NSW), which runs a national hotline (✆ **1800/184 527** in Australia) from 3pm to midnight daily. Its website, **www.twenty10.org.au,** has lots of useful information. In Sydney, the **Albion Street Centre** (www.thealbioncentre.org.au; ✆ **1800/451 600** in Australia, or 02/9332 9600) is a clinic and information service for gay men's health. **The International Gay and Lesbian Travel Association (IGLTA;** www.

iglta.org; ✆ **954/630-1637** in the U.S.) offers an online directory of gay- and lesbian-friendly travel businesses and tour operators. **Visit Gay Australia** (www.galta.com.au) has listings of businesses in each state.

Mail & Postage A postcard or letter (up to 50g/1.7 oz. in weight) will cost A$2.10 to send from Australia to New Zealand, or A$3 from Australia to the U.S., Canada, or U.K. Mail will take up to 8 business days to reach North America or Europe from Australia.

A parcel of up to 2kg (4.4lb.) will cost A$15.85 to send to the United States by airmail.

Mobile Phones The three letters that define much of the world's wireless capabilities are **GSM** (Global System for Mobile Communications), a big, seamless network that makes for easy cross-border cellphone use throughout Europe and dozens of other countries worldwide.

In the U.S., T-Mobile and AT&T Wireless use this quasi-universal system; in Canada, Microcell and some Rogers customers are GSM; and all Europeans and most Australians use GSM.

GSM phones function with a removable plastic SIM card, encoded with your phone number and account information. If your cellphone is on a GSM system, and you have a world-capable multiband phone, you can make and receive calls around much of the globe.

Just call your wireless operator and ask for "international roaming" to be activated on your account. But be sure to check the cost of "data roaming" on smart phones, because the cost can be astronomical, and you do not want a nasty (and I mean *really* nasty!) surprise on your return home when you get the bill. Unless you turn off your data roaming, it will activate automatically.

For many, **renting** a phone is a good idea. While you can rent a phone from any number of overseas sites, including kiosks at airports and at car-rental agencies, we suggest renting the phone before you leave home. North Americans can rent one before leaving home from **RoadPost** (www. roadpost.com; ☎ **888/290-1616,** or 416/253-4539) or **InTouch U.S.A.** (www. intouchglobal.com). InTouch will also give free advice on whether your existing phone will work overseas; simply call ☎ **703/222-7161** between 9am and 4pm EST, or go to **http:// intouchglobal.com/travel. htm**.

In Australia—reputed to have one of the world's highest per-capita rates of ownership of "mobile" telephones, as they are known here—the cell network is

digital, not analog. Calls to or from a mobile telephone are generally more expensive than calls to or from a land line. The price varies depending on the telephone company, the time of day, the distance between caller and recipient, and the telephone's pricing plan.

Buying a prepaid phone can be economically attractive. Once you arrive in Australia, stop by a local cellphone shop and get the cheapest package; you'll probably pay less than A$100 for a phone and a starter calling card with a significant amount of free credit.

In Australia, the mobile phone company **Vodafone** (www.vodafone.com.au; ☎ **1300/650 410** in Australia, or +61/426 320 000) has outlets at Brisbane international airport and at both international and domestic terminals in Sydney selling SIMs, handsets, and mobile broadband. **Optus** (www. optus.com.au; ☎ **1300/727 414** in Australia) has stores at Sydney and Melbourne airports.

Charges vary depending on the kind of phone and coverage you want, but some of the benefits include one low call rate throughout Australia, free incoming calls, international direct-dialing access, text

messaging, and voicemail. Alternatively, you should be able to rent a mobile phone or SIM card for your existing mobile phone to stay in touch while you're traveling.

Money & Costs The Australian dollar is divided into A100¢. Coins are A5¢, A10¢, A20¢, and A50¢ pieces (silver) and A$1 and A$2 pieces (gold).

Bank notes come in denominations of A$5, A$10, A$20, A$50, and A$100.

Note that Australian prices often end in a variant of A1¢ and A2¢ (for example, A78¢ or A$2.71), a relic from the days before 1-cent and 2-cent pieces were phased out. In these cases, prices are rounded to the nearest A5¢—so A77¢ rounds down to A75¢, and A78¢ rounds up to A80¢.

Frommer's lists exact prices in the local currency. However, exchange rates always fluctuate, so before departing consult a currency exchange website such as **www.oanda.com/currency/ converter** to check up-to-the-minute rates.

You should consider changing a small amount of money into Australian currency before you leave (though don't expect the exchange rate to be ideal), so that you can avoid long lines at airport ATMs or

THE VALUE OF THE AUSTRALIAN DOLLAR VS. OTHER POPULAR CURRENCIES

Aus$	US$	€	Can$	NZ$	UK£
1	0.74	0.64	0.96	1.09	0.56

exchange desks. You can exchange money at your local American Express or Thomas Cook office or your bank.

If you're using a **credit card,** note that Visa and MasterCard are universally accepted in Australia; American Express and Diners Club are less common; and Discover is not used. Always carry a little cash, especially in outback regions.

Beware of hidden credit-card **fees** while traveling. Check with your credit-or debit-card issuer to see what fees, if any, will be charged for overseas transactions. Fees can amount to 3 percent or more of the purchase price. Check with your bank before your departure to avoid any surprise charges on your credit card statement.

For help with currency conversions, tip calculations, and more, download Frommer's convenient **Travel Tools app** for your mobile device. Go to www.frommers.com/go/mobile and click on the Travel Tools icon.

Newspapers & Magazines

The national daily newspaper is *The Australian,* which publishes an expanded edition with a color magazine on Saturday. All capital cities also have their own daily papers. Newspapers and magazines can be bought at a wide range of retail outlets including newsagents, supermarkets, gas stations, and convenience stores.

Packing Tips Dressing in layers (and packing layers) is the best way of kitting yourself out for Australia.

Depending on where you are going in Australia—and the season—you will need different gear. For example, if you are visiting Queensland or central Australia in the summer, pack only light clothing (but always throw in a little something warm just in case!). But if you're heading for Victoria in winter you'll need full cold-weather outfits.

Wherever and whenever you go, take a light rain jacket: Summer in the tropics can often be quite wet!

Most restaurants in Australia accept "smart casual" dress; in the cities, you will need proper shoes (no flip-flops) and often (for men) a shirt with a collar to dine in most places.

For more helpful information on packing for your trip, download our convenient Travel Tools app. Go to **www.frommers.com/go/mobile** and click on the Travel Tools icon.

Police Dial ⓒ **000** anywhere in Australia. This is a free call from public and private telephones and requires no coins.

Safety Travelers to Australia should follow the same precautions against petty theft and potential identity theft as they would at home or in any other country. Violent crime is, of course, not uncommon, but you are not likely to

become a target in the normal course of your travels.

Driving probably poses one of the greatest safety risks to visitors to Australia. Australians drive on the left, something that North American and European visitors often have difficulty remembering. Drivers and passengers, including taxi passengers, must wear a seatbelt at all times, by law.

Senior Travel Seniors—often called "pensioners" in Australia—from other countries don't always qualify for the discounted entry prices to tours, attractions, and events that Australian seniors enjoy, but it is always worth asking. Inquire about discounts when booking hotels, flights, and train or bus tickets. The best ID to bring is something that shows your date of birth or that marks you as an "official" senior, such as a membership card from AARP.

Senior Resources: Many reliable agencies and organizations target the 50-plus market. **Road Scholar** (www.roadscholar.org; ⓒ **800/454-5768** in the U.S.) arranges worldwide study programs—including to Australia—for those ages 55 and over.

Smoking Smoking is banned in most indoor public places throughout the country, including government buildings, museums, cinemas, theaters, restaurants, and airports (and on all aircraft).

In Queensland, you are not allowed to smoke on a patrolled beach or near

GETTING YOUR GST refund

Through the **Tourist Refund Scheme** (TRS), Australians and international visitors can claim a refund of the 10 percent Goods and Services Tax (and of a 14.5 percent wine tax called the Wine Equalisation Tax, or WET) paid on a purchase of more than A$300 from a single outlet, within the last 60 days before you leave. More than one item may be included in that A$300. For example, you can claim the GST you paid on 10 T-shirts, each worth A$30, as long as they were bought from a single store. Do this as you leave by presenting your receipt or "tax invoice" to the Australian Customs Service's TRS booths, in the International Terminal departure areas at most airports.

Items must be taken as carry-on baggage, because you must show them to Customs. You can use the goods before you leave Australia and still claim the refund, but you cannot claim a refund on things you have consumed (say, perfume or food). You cannot claim a refund on alcohol other than wine.

Claims at airports are available up to 30 minutes before your flight's scheduled departure.

You can also claim a refund if you leave Australia as a cruise passenger from Sydney, Melbourne, Brisbane, Cairns, Darwin, Hobart, or Fremantle (Perth). Claims at seaports should be made no later than 1 hour before the scheduled departure time of the ship. If your cruise departs from elsewhere in Australia, or if you are flying out from an airport other than Sydney, Melbourne, Brisbane, Adelaide, Cairns, Perth, Darwin, or the Gold Coast, telephone the Department of Home Affairs (📞 **1300/555 043** in Australia, or 02/6245 5499) to see if you can still claim the refund.

children's playgrounds; in Victoria, you may find that some pubs have outdoor (or rooftop) smoking areas. Laws vary from state to state, so the safest thing is to ask before you light up.

Student Travel Australia has agreements with many countries, including the U.S., Canada and the U.K., that give students between 18 and 30 years old the right to apply for a "working holiday" visa to stay in Australia for up to 12 months. You must apply for your visa outside of Australia, show evidence of your student or recent graduate status, and hold a return ticket as well as sufficient funds for the first part of your stay. For more information, check the website **www.border.gov.au**.

Check out the **ISIC Association** (www.isic.org) website for comprehensive travel-services information and details on how to get an **International Student Identity Card (ISIC),** which qualifies students for substantial savings on rail passes, plane tickets, entrance fees, and more. It also provides students with basic health and life insurance and a 24-hour helpline. The card is valid for a maximum of 16 months. You can apply for the card online or in person at your university or a host of other outlets (check the website). If you're no longer a student but are still under 30, you can get an **International Youth Travel Card (IYTC),** which entitles you to some discounts.

Travel CUTS (www.travelcuts.com; 📞 **800/667-2887**) offers similar services for Canadians and U.S. residents. Irish students may prefer to turn to **USIT** (www.usit.ie; 📞 **01/602-1906**), an Ireland-based specialist in student, youth, and independent travel.

Taxes Australia applies a 10 percent Goods and Services Tax (GST) on most products and services. Your international airline tickets to Australia are not taxed, nor are domestic airline tickets for travel within Australia *if you bought them outside Australia*. If you buy Australian airline tickets once you arrive in Australia, you will pay GST on them.

There are other exceptions. Items bought in duty-free stores will not be charged GST. Nor will items you export—such as an Aboriginal painting that you buy in a gallery in Alice Springs and have shipped straight to your home outside Australia. Basic groceries are not GST-taxed, although restaurant meals are.

Other taxes include a "reef tax," officially dubbed the **Environmental Management Charge,** of A$6.50 per day (or A$3.25 for a half day) for every person over the age of 4 every time he or she enters the Great Barrier Reef Marine Park on a commercial tour. This charge goes toward park upkeep, and is sometimes (but not always) included in the ticket price.

Most airlines and an increasing number of tour operators, such as cruise

companies and long-distance trains, also impose a "fuel surcharge" to help them combat rising fuel costs. This is usually added to the price of your ticket.

Tipping   Tipping is not expected in Australia, but it is always appreciated. It is usual to tip around 10 percent or round up to the nearest A$10 for a substantial meal in a family restaurant.

Some passengers round up to the nearest dollar in a taxicab, but it's quite okay to insist on every bit of change back. Tipping bellboys and porters is sometimes done, but no one tips bar staff, barbers, or hairdressers.

Toilets   Public toilets are easy to find—and free—in most Australian cities and towns. If you are driving, most towns have "restrooms" on the main street (although the cleanliness may vary wildly).

In some remote areas, public toilets are "composting," meaning there is no flush, just a drop into a pit beneath you.

If you really want to plan ahead, consult the **National Public Toilet Map** (www. toiletmap.gov.au).

Travelers with Disabilities   Most disabilities shouldn't stop anyone from traveling to Australia. There are more options and resources than ever before. Most hotels, major stores, attractions, and public restrooms in Australia have wheelchair access. Many smaller lodges and even B&Bs are starting to cater to guests with disabilities, and some diving companies cater to scuba divers with disabilities. National parks make an effort to include wheelchair-friendly pathways. Taxi companies in bigger cities can usually supply a cab equipped for wheelchairs. TTY facilities are still limited largely to government services. A good Australian website for accessible travel options is **www.cango everywhere.com.au**, which has listings for accommodations, restaurants, and tourist attractions.

Index

See also Accommodations and Restaurant indexes, below.

General Index

A
Aboriginal art, shopping for, 275
Aboriginal Cultural Cruises, 84
Aboriginal cultural tours, 5
  in Kakadu National Park,
    260–262
  in Port Douglas, 209–210
  of Sydney Harbour, 84
  Tjapukai, 196
Aboriginal Fine Arts Gallery, 251
Aborigines
  food of, 24
  last "first contact," 19
  stolen generations, 16–17
Accessibility, 336
Accommodations. See also
  Accommodations index
  in Alice Springs, 268–270
  best of, 8–9
  in Brisbane, 163–165
  in Bundaberg, 232
  in Cairns, 188–191
  in Darwin, 244–246
  on Heron Island, 231
  in Hobart, 296–299
  in Kakadu National Park,
    257–258
  on Lady Elliot Island, 234–235
  in Launceston, 312–315
  in Melbourne, 113–118
  near Uluru, 283–286
  in Port Douglas, 206–208
  in Sydney, 59–70
  in Townsville, 214–215
  in Whitsunday Islands, 222–224
Adelaide River Queen Cruises,
  259
The Adventures of Priscilla,
  Queen of the Desert, 19
Agnes Water, 230
Air travel
  to Alice Springs, 264
  to Australia, 319
  in Australia, 320–321
  to Brisbane, 154–155, 158
  to Bundaberg, 232
  to Cairns, 185–186
  to Darwin, 242
  to Gladstone, 229
  to Hobart, 294
  to Launceston, 310
  to Melbourne, 105–107
  in Queensland, 179
  to Sydney, 48–50
  to Tasmania, 292
  to Townsville, 213
  to Uluru–Kata Tjuta National
    Park, 281
  to Whitsunday Islands, 220–221

Air Whitsunday, 226, 228
Airborne Solutions, 262
Airlie Beach, 220, 222–223, 225
Airport accommodations in
  Sydney, 70
Alice Springs, 264–279
  accommodations, 268–270
  arrival information, 264–266
  attractions, 271–273
  city layout, 267
  day trip to MacDonnell Ranges,
    276–279
  origin of name, 266
  outdoor activities, 274–275
  restaurants, 270–271
  shopping, 275
  tours, 274
  transportation in, 267
  two-week itinerary, 42–43
  visitor information, 266
Alice Springs Desert Park, 271
Alice Springs Golf Club, 274–275
Alice Springs Reptile Centre,
  271–272
Alice Springs Telegraph Station
  Historical Reserve, 272
Alice Wanderer Centre
  Sightseeing, 274
Andrew (Boy) Charlton Swimming
  Pool, 98
Animal Kingdom, 20
Antarctic Journey, 142
Anzac Day, 31, 32
Araluen Cultural Precinct,
  272–273
Art
  Field of Light, 286
  rock paintings, 14, 260–262,
    279
  shopping for, 275
  street art in Melbourne, 129
Art Gallery of Ballarat, 151
Art Gallery of New South Wales,
  87–88
Art hotels in Melbourne, 116
Arthurs Seat State Park, 145
The Arts Centre, 126
Ashcombe Maze & Lavender
  Gardens, 145
ATMs, 328
  in Brisbane, 162
  in Melbourne, 112
  in Sydney, 58
Australasian Golf Museum, 309
Australia
  arrival information, 319–320
  authentic experiences, best of,
    4–5
  calendar of events, 31–33
  current demographics, 12–13
  family itinerary, 43–47
  fast facts, 328–336
  geography of, 24–25
  history of, 13–18
  literature of, 21–22
  movies about, 18–20
  music in, 20–21
  one-week itinerary, 34–40
  threats to landscape, 28

  transportation in, 320–328
  two-week itinerary, 40–43
  when to go, 30–33
  wildlife, types of, 25–28
Australia, 20
Australia Day, 31, 31–32
Australian Butterfly Sanctuary, 10,
  203
Australian Museum, 88
Australian National Maritime
  Museum, 86–87
Australian Open, 31
Authentic experiences, best of,
  4–5
Auto clubs, 325
Auto insurance, 322
Ayers Rock. See Uluru

B
Bali Hai Island, 220
Ballarat, 150–153
Ballarat Botanical Gardens, 151
Ballooning, 274
Balmain, 53
Balmain Market, 100
Balmoral, 95
Banks, 328
  in Brisbane, 162
  in Melbourne, 112
  in Sydney, 58
Barangaroo Reserve, 97
Bareboat sailing, 5, 227–228
Base Walk, 287
Beaches
  in Cairns, 193
  in Sydney, 93–95
Beer, 23–24
Big Bus Darwin, 242
Bikescape, 93
Biking
  in Brisbane, 162
  in Melbourne, 139
  in Sydney, 97
  Uluru, 287
Billabong Sanctuary, 216
Birdworld, 203
Birrarung Marr, 139
Blood on the Southern Cross,
  151–152
Blue bottles, 94
Blue Mountains, 5, 100–104
  arrival information, 101–102
  attractions, 103–104
  family itinerary, 45
  one-week itinerary, 38–39
  restaurants, 104
  tours, 102–103
  transportation in, 102
  visitor information, 102
Blue Mountains Botanic Garden,
  104
Blue Mountains Walkabout,
  102–103
Blue Pearl Bay, 220
Bondi Beach, 53, 93–94
  accommodations, 69
  restaurants, 77–78
  two-week itinerary, 43

Bondi Icebergs Club, 98
Bondi Markets, 100
Bonorong Wildlife Sanctuary, 301–302
Bonza Bike Tours, 97
Books about Australia, 21–22
Bothwell, 309
Boxing Day, 31
Breath, 20
BridgeClimb, 83–84
Brisbane, 154–177
    accommodations, 163–165
    arrival information, 154–158
    attractions, 168–173
    city layout, 159
    fast facts, 162–163
    Great Barrier Reef day trip, 176–177
    neighborhoods in brief, 160
    restaurants, 165–168
    tours, 173–176
    transportation in, 160–162
    visitor information, 158
Brisbane City Gardens, 175
Brisbane City Hall, 168
Brisbane Festival, 33
Brisbane Greeters, 174
Brisbane Powerhouse Arts, 168
Brisbane Whale Watching, 175
Bronte Beach, 94
Bruny Island Cruises, 307
Bundaberg, 231–234
Bus passes, 328
Buses
    to Alice Springs, 266
    in Australia, 328
    to Brisbane, 158
    in Brisbane, 161
    to Bundaberg, 232
    to Cairns, 186–187
    in Cairns, 187
    to Darwin, 242
    in Darwin, 243
    to Gladstone, 229
    in Hobart, 307
    to Kuranda, 203
    to Launceston, 312
    in Launceston, 312
    to Melbourne, 107
    in Melbourne, 111
    to Port Douglas, 205
    to Sydney, 50
    in Sydney, 54–55
    to Townsville, 213
    to Whitsunday Islands, 221
    in Whitsunday Islands, 222
Bushwalking in Kakadu National Park, 263
Business hours
    in Brisbane, 162
    in Melbourne, 112
    in Sydney, 58

C

Cafes in Melbourne, 121
Cairns, 184–204
    accommodations, 188–191
    arrival information, 185–187

attractions, 193–197
city layout, 187
day trip to Kuranda, 201–204
day trips to Great Barrier Reef, 197–200
day trips to islands, 200–201
diving/snorkeling, 11
one-week itinerary, 39
restaurants, 191–193
transportation in, 187–188
visitor information, 187
Cairns Aquarium, 193–194
Cairns ZOOM and Wildlife Dome, 194
Calendar of events, 31–33
Camel Cup, 267
Camel safaris, 274, 289
Camper vans, 323
Cape Schanck, 145
Captain Cook Cruises, 91–92
Car rental, 321–322
Carlton, 110
    restaurants, 123–124
Cascade Brewery, 302
Cascades Female Factory Historic Site, 302
Castle Hill, 215
Castle Hotel, 309
Cataract Gorge, 316
Cellphones, 332–333
Centennial Park, 97
Centennial Park Cycles, 97
Chemist shops. *See* pharmacies
Chinatown, 109, 160
Christmas Day, 31
Churchill Island Heritage Farm, 142–143
Circular Quay, 52
    accommodations, 62–64
    restaurants, 71–75
City Center (Brisbane), 160
City Center (Melbourne), 109
    accommodations, 113–117
    restaurants, 119–123
City Center (Sydney), 53
    accommodations, 64–66
    restaurants, 71–75
CityCycle, 162
Climate of Australia, 25
Climbing Uluru, 288
Clovelly Beach, 94
Conservation Volunteers Australia, 29
Consulates. *See* embassies and consulates
The Convent, 149
Coogee, 94
Cooks' Cottage, 128
Creative Jewellers, 252
Crocodile Dundee, 19
Crocodiles, 259
Crocodylus Park & Zoo, 248
Crocosaurus Cove, 248–249
Crown Casino, 128
Cruise Whitsundays, 226
Cruises
    Aboriginal Cultural Cruises, 84
    to Australia, 320
    in Brisbane, 169, 173–174

in Darwin, 251
of Hobart, 307
in Kakadu National Park, 260
to Sydney, 50
in Sydney Harbour, 91–92
Tamar River Cruises, 316
from Whitsunday Islands, 226
Cultural tours. *See* Aboriginal cultural tours
Culture Scouts, 92
Currency exchange, 333–334
Customs, 328–329
Cycling. *See* biking
Cyclones, 331

D

Darling Harbour, 52
    accommodations, 66–67
    attractions, 86–87
    restaurants, 75–76
Darlinghurst, 52–53
    accommodations, 68–69
    restaurants, 77
Darwin, 240–255
    accommodations, 244–246
    arrival information, 242–243
    attractions, 248–251
    city layout, 243
    day trip to Litchfield National Park, 252–253
    day trip to Nitmiluk National Park (Katherine Gorge), 253–255
    restaurants, 246–248
    shopping, 251–252
    tours, 242
    transportation in, 243
    visitor information, 243
Darwin Aviation Museum, 249
Darwin Day Tours, 242
Darwin Harbour Cruises, 251
Daylesford, 148–150
Deckchair Cinema, 250
Defence of Darwin Experience, 249
Dentists
    in Brisbane, 162
    in Melbourne, 112
    in Sydney, 58
Design Tasmania, 316–317
Di Croco, 252
Didgeridoo, 20
Dining. *See* restaurants
The Dish, 19
Dive Queensland, 182
Divers Den, 182
Diving
    best of, 11
    Great Barrier Reef, 182, 199–200, 211, 217
    islands near Cairns, 200–201
    Whitsunday Islands, 226
Docklands, 110
Doctors, 329
    in Brisbane, 162
    in Melbourne, 112–113
    in Sydney, 58

Dreamtime, 13, 16
Drinking laws, 329
Driving
    to Alice Springs, 266
    in Australia, 321–327
    to Brisbane, 158
    in Brisbane, 162
    to Bundaberg, 232
    to Cairns, 187
    in Cairns, 187–188
    to Darwin, 243
    to Launceston, 312
    in Launceston, 312
    to MacDonnell Ranges, 278
    to Melbourne, 108
    in Melbourne, 112
    in Northern Territory, 238
    to Port Douglas, 205
    in Queensland, 179–180
    rules of, 323–324
    safety, 325–327
    to Sydney, 50
    in Sydney, 57–58
    in Tasmania, 292–294
    to Townsville, 213
    to Uluru–Kata Tjuta National
        Park, 281
    in Uluru–Kata Tjuta National
        Park, 282–283
    to Whitsunday Islands, 221
    in Whitsunday Islands, 222
Drugstores. See pharmacies

E

East MacDonnell Ranges, 279
East Melbourne accommodations,
    117
Easter Monday, 31
Ecotourism, 28–30
Electricity, 329–330
Elizabeth Bay House, 88
Embassies and consulates, 330
    in Brisbane, 163
    in Melbourne, 113
    in Sydney, 58
Emergencies, 330
    in Brisbane, 163
    in Melbourne, 113
    in Sydney, 58
    vehicle break downs, 326
Environmental Management
    Charge (EMC), 180, 336
Esplanade, 248
Eureka Centre – Home of the
    Eureka Flag, 152
Eureka Skydeck, 128–129
Eureka Uprising, 151

F

Families
    Melbourne attractions, 137
    suggested itinerary, 43–47
    Sydney attractions, 93
    travel tips, 330
Featherdale Wildlife Park, 90
Federation Square, 129

Ferries
    in Brisbane, 161–162
    in Sydney, 55–56, 79
    to Tasmania, 292
Field of Light art installation, 286
Finke Gorge National Park, 278
"First contact," last of, 19
Fishing in Kakadu National Park,
    262–263
Fitzroy, 110
    accommodations, 117
    restaurants, 124
Fitzroy Island, 200–201
Flinders Reef, 212
Floods, 326
Fogg Dam Conservation Reserve,
    258–259
Food and drink, 22–24. See also
    restaurants
Formula 1 Australian Grand Prix,
    32
Fortitude Valley, 160
Four Mile Beach, 5, 46, 209
Four Park Pass, 197

G

Gallipoli, 19
Gardens
    in Macedon Ranges, 147
    in Melbourne, 134, 139
    in Sydney, 96–97
Gasoline, 323
Gateways to Great Barrier Reef,
    183–184
Geography of Australia, 24–25
George Brown Darwin Botanic
    Gardens, 248
Ghost Tours, 176
Gladstone, 229
Glebe, 53
The Gold Museum, 152
Golf, 309
Good Friday, 31
Government House (Melbourne),
    134
Great Adventures, 198
Great Barrier Reef, 4, 25, 178–184
    diving, 182, 199–200
    family itinerary, 45–47
    gateways to, 183–184
    one-week itinerary, 40
    overnighting on, 189
    reef tax, 180
    safety in, 184
    snorkeling, 183
    southern region, 228–235
    threats to, 28, 179
    transportation in Queensland,
        179–180
    types of reef, 180
    visitor information, 178–179
    when to go, 179
Great Barrier Reef day trips
    from Brisbane, 176–177
    from Cairns, 197–200
    from Port Douglas, 210–212
    from Townsville, 217
Green Island, 201

GST refund, 335–336
Guluyambi Cultural Cruise, 260

H

HalfTix, 108
Hanging Rock Recreation Reserve,
    147
Harbour Jet, 86
Hartley's Crocodile Adventures,
    10, 46, 196–197
Harvest Market, 318
Healesville Sanctuary, 135
Health. See safety
Heart Reef, 228
Henley-on-Todd Regatta, 33, 267
Hepburn Bathhouse & Spa, 149
Heritage Highway, 311
Heritage Market, 203
Hermannsburg Historic Precinct,
    278
Heron Island, 10, 11, 229–231
High season, 30
Hiking
    in Kakadu National Park, 263
    Kata Tjuta (the Olgas), 290
    Larapinta Trail, 275
    in Magnetic Island, 218
    Nitmiluk National Park, 254
    West MacDonnell Ranges, 277
History of Australia, 13–18
    British arrival, 14–16
    Dreamtime, 13
    early European explorers, 14
    immigration, 18
    independence, 17
    last "first contact," 19
    stolen generations, 16–17
    World Wars I and II, 16–17
Hobart, 294–307
    accommodations, 296–299
    arrival information, 294
    attractions, 301–305
    city layout, 294–296
    day trips from, 307–310
    restaurants, 299–301
    tours, 306–307
    transportation in, 296
    visitor information, 294
Holgate Brewhouse, 147
Holidays, 31
Hospitals, 329
    in Brisbane, 162
    in Melbourne, 112–113
    in Sydney, 58
Hot-air ballooning, 274
Hotels. See accommodations
Hyde Park, 96
Hyde Park Barracks Museum, 88

I

The Ian Potter Centre, 130
Injalak Arts, 262
Insurance
    auto, 322
    travel, 331
Internet access. See Wi-Fi access
Itineraries. See suggested
    itineraries

J

Jet boats on Sydney Harbour, 86

K

Kakadu Air Services, 262
Kakadu Fishing Tours, 262–263
Kakadu National Park, 255–264
  accommodations, 257–258
  arrival information, 255–256
  attractions, 258–264
  tours, 260–264
  transportation in, 256
  visitor information, 256
Kata Tjuta (the Olgas), 5
  exploring, 289–290
  two-week itinerary, 41
Katherine Gorge, 253–255
Kayaking in Sydney, 97–98
Kings Canyon, 42
Kings Cross, 52
  accommodations, 67–68
  restaurants, 77
King's Domain, 134
Koala Conservation Centre, 143
Koala Park Sanctuary, 90–91
Kookaburra River Queen, 174
Kuku Yalanji Cultural Habitat
  Tours, 209–210
Kuranda, 201–204
  arrival information, 202–203
  attractions, 203–204
  one-week itinerary, 40
  restaurants, 204
  visitor information, 203
Kuranda Arts Co-Operative, 203
Kuranda Koala Gardens, 204
Kuranda Original Rainforest
  Markets, 203
Kuranda Riverboat Tours, 204
Kuranda Scenic Railway, 202–203
Kuranda Wildlife Experience pass,
  197

L

La Boite Theatre, 169
La Trobe's Cottage, 134
Lady Elliot Island, 11, 176,
  234–235
Lady Musgrave Island, 234
Larapinta Trail, 5, 275
Last Cab to Darwin, 20
Launceston, 310–318
  accommodations, 312–315
  arrival information, 310–312
  attractions, 316–318
  city layout, 312
  restaurants, 315–316
  transportation in, 312
  visitor information, 312
Launceston Historic Walks, 317
Lavandula, 149
Legal aid, 331–332
LGBTQ travelers, 332
Light rail in Sydney, 56–57
Lion, 20
Litchfield National Park, 252–253
Literature of Australia, 21–22

Lone Pine Koala Sanctuary, 10,
  169
Low Isles, 211–212
Low season, 30
Luna Park, 47, 93

M

MacDonnell Ranges, 6, 276–279
Macedon Ranges, 146–148
Mad Max, 19
Magazines. See newspapers and
  magazines
Magnetic Island, 217–219
Magnetic Jet Ski Tours, 219
Mail and postage, 332
  in Brisbane, 163
  in Melbourne, 113
  in Sydney, 58–59
Malmsbury Botanic Gardens,
  147–148
The Man from Snowy River, 19
Manly, 53
  accommodations, 69–70
  beaches, 94
Mantaray Charters, 226
Maps, 324–325
Marineland Crocodile Park, 201
Maritime Museum of Tasmania,
  303
Market City, 100
Markets. See street markets
Mawson's Hut Replica Museum,
  303
Mbantua Fine Art Gallery and
  Cultural Museum, 275
Medical needs, 330–331
Melbourne, 105–153
  accommodations, 113–118
  arrival information, 105–108
  attractions, 126–137
  Ballarat day trip, 150–153
  city layout, 108–109
  Daylesford day trip, 148–150
  fast facts, 112–113
  Macedon Ranges day trip,
    146–148
  Mornington Peninsula day trip,
    144–146
  neighborhoods in brief,
    109–110
  outdoor activities, 139
  Phillip Island day trip, 141–144
  restaurants, 118–126
  shopping, 140–141
  tours, 137–139
  transportation in, 110–112
  visitor information, 108
Melbourne Bike Share, 139
Melbourne City Sightseeing
  Tours, 137
Melbourne Cup, 33
Melbourne Fringe, 33
Melbourne International Comedy
  Festival, 32
Melbourne International Film
  Festival, 33
Melbourne Museum, 130
Melbourne River Cruises, 138

Melbourne Shopping Experiences,
  140
Melbourne Street Art Tours, 129
Melbourne Zoo, 130
Metro light rail in Sydney, 56–57
Milton, 160
Mobile phones, 332–333
Mon Repos Regional Park, 10,
  233
Mon Repos Turtle Centre, 233
Money, 333–334
Moonlit Sanctuary, 10, 145
Mornington Peninsula, 144–146
Mornington Peninsula Regional
  Gallery, 145
Mossman Gorge, 46
Mossman Gorge Centre, 210
Motor home rentals, 323
Motorcycle tours
  of Sydney, 92–93
  of Uluru, 288
Mount Coot-tha, 166
Mount Field National Park,
  309–310
Mount Wellington, 300
Movies about Australia, 18–20
Muriel's Wedding, 19
Museum and Art Gallery of the
  Northern Territory, 250
Museum of Contemporary Art
  (MCA), 79, 82
Museum of Old and New Art
  (MONA), 303–304
Museum of Sydney, 88–89
Museum of Tropical Queensland,
  216
Music, 20–21
MV Mirimar, 169

N

Nanguluwur, 261
Narryna Heritage Museum, 304
National Gallery of Victoria
  International, 131
National public holidays, 31
National Rose Garden of
  Australia, 318
National Sports Museum,
  131–132
National Vietnam Veterans
  Museum, 143
Natural Wanders, 97–98
N'Dhala Gorge Nature Park, 279
Neighborhoods in brief
  Brisbane, 160
  Melbourne, 109–110
  Sydney, 52–53
New Farm, 160
New Year's Day, 31
New Year's Eve, 33
Newspapers and magazines, 334
  in Brisbane, 163
  in Melbourne, 113
  in Sydney, 59
Ngadiku Dreamtime Walks, 46,
  210
Nitmiluk National Park, 253–255
Nitmiluk Scenic Flights, 254

Nitmiluk Tours, 253
North Shore, 53
North Sydney, 53
Northern Land Council, 262
Northern Territory, 236–290
  Alice Springs, 264–279
  Darwin, 240–255
  driving in, 238
  Kakadu National Park, 255–264
  tour operators, 240
  Uluru–Kata Tjuta National Park,
    280–290
  visitor information, 237
  when to go, 237–238
Nourlangie, 260–261

O

Ocean Freedom, 198–199
Ocean Spirit Cruises, 199
Old Melbourne Gaol, 132
The Old Umbrella Shop, 317
Olgas. See Kata Tjuta (the Olgas)
One-way rentals, 322–323
One-week itinerary, 34–40
Opal Cards, 54
Opera Queensland, 170
Outback Ballooning, 274
Outback Cycling, 287
Outdoor activities. See also
  specific activities and places
  in Alice Springs, 274–275
  best of, 5–6
  in Melbourne, 139
  in Sydney, 93–99
Outrigger sailing, 227
Oxford Street, 52, 68–69
Oz Jet Boat, 86

P

Packing tips, 334
Paddington, 160
Paddington Markets, 100
Paddington/Oxford Street, 52,
  68–69
Paddy's Markets, 100
Palm Cove, 193
Papunya Tula Artists, 275
Parks in Sydney, 96–97
Parliament House Victoria, 133
Paspaley Pearls, 252
Penguin parade, 141, 143–144
Pharmacies
  in Brisbane, 163
  in Melbourne, 113
  in Sydney, 59
Phillip Island, 141–144
Phillip Island Penguin Reserve,
  143–144
Picnic at Hanging Rock, 18
Police, 334
  in Brisbane, 163
  in Sydney, 59
Polly Woodside, 133–134
Popular culture, Australia in
  literature, 21–22
  movies, 18–20
  music, 20–21

Port Arthur, 307–309
Port Arthur Historic Site, 307–309
Port Douglas, 45, 205–212
  accommodations, 206–208
  arrival information, 205
  attractions, 209–210
  day trips to Great Barrier Reef,
    210–212
  diving/snorkeling, 11
  restaurants, 208–209
  transportation in, 206
  visitor information, 206
Poseidon, 211
Postage. See mail and postage
Powerhouse Museum, 87
Professional Helicopter Services,
  288
Prosail, 227
Public transportation. See
  transportation
Pubs in Sydney, 74
Puffing Billy Railway, 136
Pylon Lookout, 83
Pyndan Camel Tracks, 274

Q

Queen Street Mall, 169–170
Queen Victoria Market, 134
The Queen Victoria Museum &
  Art Gallery, 317–318
Queensland, transportation in,
  179–180
Queensland Art Gallery, 170
Queensland Cultural Centre,
  170–171
Queensland Gallery of Modern
  Art (GOMA), 170
Queensland Museum, 171
Queensland Performing Arts
  Centre, 170
Queensland Symphony Orchestra,
  170
Queensland Theatre, 170
Quicksilver Wavepiercer, 199, 211

R

Rabbit Proof Fence, 19
Rail passes, 327–328
Rainforestation Nature Park, 204
Ratho Farm, 309
Ratho golf course, 309
Real Gap Experience, 30
Real Melbourne Bike Tours, 138
Red Dog, 20
Reef cruises from Whitsunday
  Islands, 226
Reef HQ Aquarium, 217
Reef tax, 180, 336
Reef walking, 201
Refunds on taxes, 335
Responsible travel, 28–30
Restaurants. See also Restaurants
  index
  in Alice Springs, 270–271
  in Ballarat, 153
  best of, 7–8
  in Blue Mountains, 104

  in Brisbane, 165–168
  in Bundaberg, 233
  in Cairns, 191–193
  in Darwin, 246–248
  in Daylesford, 150
  in Hobart, 299–301
  in Kuranda, 204
  in Launceston, 315–316
  in Macedon Ranges, 148
  in Melbourne, 118–126
  on Mornington Peninsula, 146
  near Uluru, 283–286
  in Port Douglas, 208–209
  in Sydney, 70–78
  in Townsville, 215
  in Whitsunday Islands, 225
RFDS Darwin Tourist Facility,
  250–251
Richmond, 110
Rip tides, 93, 96
River cruises, 316
The River District, 109
Road trains, 325
Rock paintings, 14, 260–262, 279
The Rocks, 52
  accommodations, 62–64
  attractions, 79–86
  restaurants, 71–75
The Rocks Discovery Museum, 82
The Rocks Market, 100
The Rocks Walking Tours, 92
Rosalie, 160
Ross, 311
Royal Botanic Garden (Sydney),
  96
Royal Botanic Gardens
  (Melbourne), 139
Royal Flying Doctor Service
  Tourist Facility, 273
Royal Tasmanian Botanical
  Gardens, 304

S

Safety, 334
  in Alice Springs, 271
  in Brisbane, 163
  crocodiles, 259
  in Great Barrier Reef, 184
  medical needs, 330–331
  in Melbourne, 113
  in Northern Territory, 238
  rip tides, 96
  in Sydney, 59
  Sydney beaches, 93, 94
  when driving, 325–327
  in Whitsunday Islands, 223
  wildlife and, 26–28, 331
  wildlife on roads, 324
Sailing
  in Sydney, 98–99
  in Whitsunday Islands, 221–222
  Whitsunday Islands, 227–228
Salamanca Market, 304
Samson and Delilah, 20
Saving money
  bus passes, 328
  Cairns attractions, 195, 197
  Melbourne events, 108

Saving money *(cont.)*
    Melbourne public
        transportation, 111
    Phillip Island attractions,
        141–142
    rail passes, 327–328
    Sydney accommodations, 62
    Sydney attractions, 89
    Sydney Harbour, 79
    Sydney restaurants, 71
Scenic flights
    in Kakadu National Park, 262
    over Uluru, 288
Scenic World, 103–104
School of the Air, 273
**SEA LIFE Melbourne Aquarium,
    134–135**
SEA LIFE Sydney Aquarium, 87
Senior travel, 334
1770, 230
1770 LARC! Tours, 230
1770 Liquid Adventures, 230
Sharks, 94
Shelly Beach, 95
Shine, 19
Shopping
    in Alice Springs, 275
    in Darwin, 251–252
    in Melbourne, 140–141
    in Sydney, 99–100
Shrine of Remembrance, 134
**Sightseeing buses in Sydney,
    54–55**
**Sir Thomas Brisbane Planetarium
    & Cosmic Skydome, 172**
**Skyrail Rainforest Cableway,
    194–195**
Smoking, 334–335
    in Sydney, 71
Snorkeling
    best of, 11
    Great Barrier Reef, 183
    islands near Cairns, 200–201
    Whitsunday Islands, 227–228
South Bank Parklands, 172–173
South Melbourne, 110
South Yarra/Prahran, 110
Southbank, 109
Southgate, 109
Sovereign Hill, 152–153
Sports Lovers Tours, 138
**St. John's Anglican Cathedral,
    171–172**
St Kilda, 110
    accommodations, 118
    restaurants, 124–126
Stingers, 94
Stolen generations, 16–17
**Story Bridge Adventure Climb,
    173**
The Strand, 215–216
Street art in Melbourne, 129
Street markets
    in Darwin, 246
    in Kuranda, 203
    in Launceston, 318
    in Sydney, 100

Strictly Ballroom, 19
Student travel, 335
Suggested itineraries
    for families, 43–47
    one-week itinerary, 34–40
    two-week itinerary, 40–43
Sun exposure, 331
Sunlover Reef Cruises, 199
Sunrise tours of Uluru, 286–287
Sunset tours of Uluru, 286–287
Surfing, 6
    Melbourne surf park, 107
    in Sydney, 95–96
Susannah Place Museum, 82
Sustainable travel, 28–30
Swimming
    in Darwin, 240
    in Kakadu National Park,
        263–264
    in Sydney, 98
Sydney, 4, 48–104
    accommodations, 59–70
    arrival information, 48–50
    attractions, 78–90
    city layout, 51–52
    day trip to Blue Mountains,
        100–104
    family itinerary, 43–44, 47
    fast facts, 58–59
    neighborhoods in brief, 52–53
    one-week itinerary, 35, 38
    outdoor activities, 93–99
    restaurants, 70–78
    shopping, 99–100
    tours, 91–93
    transportation in, 54–58
    two-week itinerary, 43
    visitor information, 51
    wildlife viewing, 90–91
Sydney Big Ticket passes, 89
Sydney by Sail, 98–99
Sydney Festival, 31
Sydney Film Festival, 32
**Sydney Gay & Lesbian Mardi
    Gras, 32**
Sydney Harbour
    Aboriginal cultural tours, 84
    attractions, 79–86
    beaches, 93–95
    cruises, 91–92
    jet boats, 86
    viewing, 79
Sydney Harbour Bridge, 83–84
**Sydney Hobart Yacht Race, 33,
    302**
Sydney Jewish Museum, 89
Sydney Museums Pass, 89
Sydney Observatory, 84–85
Sydney Opera House, 85–86
Sydney Tours-R-Us, 102
Sydney Tower, 90
Sydney Tower Skywalk, 90

T

Tamar River Cruises, 316
Tamarama, 94
Taronga Zoo, 91

Tasmania, 291–318
    arrival information, 292
    driving in, 292–294
    Hobart, 294–307
    Launceston, 310–318
    visitor information, 292
Tasmanian Devil UnZoo, 306
Tasmanian devils, 306
**Tasmanian Museum and Art
    Gallery, 304–305**
Tasmanian Wool Centre, 311
Taste of Tasmania, 302
Taxes
    customs, 328–329
    GST refund, 335–336
    reef tax, 180, 336
Taxis
    in Brisbane, 162
    in Cairns, 188
    in Darwin, 243
    in Melbourne, 112
    in Sydney, 49, 57
Territory Wildlife Park, 251
Theatre Royal, 305
Three Sisters, 103–104
Tili Wiru Tjuta Nyakutjaku, 286
Tin Shed Arts, 148
Tipping, 336
Tjapukai, 196
**Tjoritja/West MacDonnell National
    Park, 276**
Toilets, 336
Toll roads, 325
Tourist Refund Scheme (TRS), 335
Tours. *See also* Aboriginal cultural
    tours
    of Alice Springs, 274
    of Blue Mountains, 102–103
    of Brisbane, 173–176
    of Darwin, 242
    to Great Barrier Reef. *See*
        Great Barrier Reef day trips
    of Hobart, 306–307
    of Kakadu National Park,
        260–264
    of Macedon Ranges, 146–147
    of Melbourne, 137–139
    Melbourne shopping, 140
    Melbourne street art, 129
    of Northern Territory, 240
    of Sydney, 91–93
    Sydney Opera House, 85
    of Uluru, 286–289
    of Uluru–Kata Tjuta National
        Park, 283
Town Hall, 52
Townsville, 212–219
    accommodations, 214–215
    arrival information, 213
    attractions, 215–217
    day trip to Great Barrier Reef,
        217
    day trip to Magnetic Island,
        217–219
    restaurants, 215
    transportation in, 213
    visitor information, 213

Trains
to Alice Springs, 266
in Australia, 327–328
to Brisbane, 158
in Brisbane, 162
to Bundaberg, 232
to Cairns, 186
to Darwin, 243
to Gladstone, 229
to Kuranda, 202–203
to Melbourne, 107
in Queensland, 179
to Sydney, 50
in Sydney, 56
to Townsville, 213
to Whitsunday Islands, 221
Trams
in Melbourne, 110–111
in Sydney, 56–57
Transportation
in Alice Springs, 267
in Australia, 320–328
in Blue Mountains, 102
in Brisbane, 160–162
in Bundaberg, 232
in Cairns, 187–188
in Darwin, 243
in Gladstone, 229
in Hobart, 296
in Kakadu National Park, 256
in Launceston, 312
in Magnetic Island, 218
in Melbourne, 110–112
in Port Douglas, 206
in Queensland, 179–180
in Sydney, 54–58
in Townsville, 213
in Uluru–Kata Tjuta National Park, 282–283
in Whitsunday Islands, 221–222
Travel insurance, 331
Travel seasons, 30
Travelers with disabilities, 336
Treasury Casino, 173
Trephina Gorge Nature Park, 279
Tribal Warrior Association, 84
Trinity Beach, 193
Tropical illnesses, 331
Tusa Dive, 199–200
Two-week itinerary, 40–43

U

Ubirr Rock, 261
Uluru, 5
accommodations near, 283–286
restaurants near, 283–286
tours, 286–289
two-week itinerary, 41–42
Uluru Camel Tours, 289
Uluru Motorcycle Tours, 288
Uluru–Kata Tjuta National Park, 6, 280–290
accommodations, 283–286
arrival information, 281
entrance fees, 282
Kata Tjuta (the Olgas), exploring, 289–290
restaurants, 283–286

tours, 283
transportation in, 282–283
Uluru, exploring, 286–289
visitor information, 281–282
Unpaved roads, 326

V

Victoria Winery Tours, 146–147
Visitor information
Agnes Water/1770, 230
Alice Springs, 266
Ballarat, 150
Blue Mountains, 102
Brisbane, 158
Bundaberg, 232
Cairns, 187
Darwin, 243
Daylesford, 148
Gladstone, 229
Great Barrier Reef, 178–179
Hobart, 294
Kakadu National Park, 256
Kuranda, 203
Launceston, 312
Macedon Ranges, 146
Magnetic Island, 218
Melbourne, 108
Mornington Peninsula, 145
Northern Territory, 237
Phillip Island, 141
Port Douglas, 206
Sydney, 51
Tasmania, 292
Townsville, 213
Uluru–Kata Tjuta National Park, 281–282
Whitsunday Islands, 221
Vivid, 32
Volunteer opportunities, 29–30

W

***Walkabout*, 18**
Walking tours
of Brisbane, 174–176
of Hobart, 306
reef walking, 201
of Sydney, 92
of Uluru, 287
Warradjan Aboriginal Cultural Centre, 261
Watarrka National Park. *See* Kings Canyon
Water taxis in Sydney, 57
Watsons Bay, 53
***Wavedancer*, 212**
***Wavelength*, 211**
Weather, 25
Werribee Mansion, 136–137
Werribee Open Range Zoo, 137
West End, 160
West MacDonnell Ranges, 276–278
Wet Tropics Rainforest, 4–5
Wetlands cruises, 260
Whale-watching in Brisbane, 175
Wheel of Brisbane, 172–173
Whitehaven Beach, 6, 226

Whitsunday Islands, 219–228
accommodations, 222–224
arrival information, 220–221
attractions, 225–228
diving/snorkeling, 11
restaurants, 225
transportation in, 221–222
visitor information, 221
when to go, 220
Whitsunday Sailing Outrigger, 227
Wi-Fi access, 331
in Brisbane, 163
in Melbourne, 113
in Sydney, 59
Wild Ocean EcoBoat Tours, 142
Wild Ride Australia, 92–93
Wildlife
on roads, 324
safety and, 26–28, 331
threats to, 28
types of, 25–28
Wildlife Habitat, 210
Wildlife Sydney Zoo, 91
Wildlife viewing
best of, 10
in Bundaberg, 233
in Cairns, 197
on Phillip Island, 143–144
in Sydney, 90–91
Williamstown, 110
Willing Workers on Organic Farms (WWOOF), 30
Window on the Wetlands Visitor Centre, 259
Wine, 23–24
in Sydney, 71
Woolloomooloo Wharf, 76
Woolmers Estate, 318
World War II Oil Storage Tunnels, 251

Y

Yachting
on Great Barrier Reef, 189
in Sydney, 98–99
Whitsunday Islands, 227–228
Yellow Water Billabong, 260
Yellow Water Taxis, 92

Accommodations

Adina Apartment Hotel Darwin Waterfront, 244
Adina Apartment Hotel Sydney Central, 64–65
Alice on Todd Apartments, 269
Alice Springs Tourist Park, 268
Alice's Cottages & Spa Hideaways, 314
Arts Hotel, 69
Aurora Alice Springs, 268
Aurora Kakadu, 257
The Australian Hotel, 64
Ayers Rock Campground, 284
Ayers Rock Resort, 268, 283
Bamurru Plains, 257–258

ACCOMMODATIONS INDEX

Beach Club, 224
The Blackman, 9, 116
Cairns Plaza Hotel, 188–189
Cicada Lodge, 255
Cooinda Lodge, 258
Coral Beach Lodge, 208
Coral Sea Resort, 222
Coral Tree Inn, 190
Country Club Tasmania & Villas, 312–313
The Cullen, 9, 116
Customs House Hotel, 298
The Darling, 66–67
Daydream Island Resort, 223
Desert Gardens Hotel, 284
Desert Palms Resort, 269
Elkira Court Motel, 269–270
Ellis Beach Oceanfront Bungalows, 190–191
Emu Walk Apartments, 284
Fraser Suites Sydney, 65
Garnamarr Campground, 257
Georgian Court Guest House, 117
Grand Hotel and Apartments Townsville, 214
Hamilton Island, 223–224
The Henry Jones Art Hotel, 296–297
Heron Island Resort, 231
Hillview House Bed & Breakfast, 315
Hobart Central YHA, 300
Hotel 59, 67–68
Hotel Grand Chancellor Townsville, 214
Hotel Jen, 164
Hotel Lindrum, 113–114
Hotel Ravesis, 69
The Hotel Windsor, 114
The Hughenden, 68
Hyatt Regency Sydney, 65
Ibis Budget Sydney Airport, 70
Ibis Melbourne Hotel and Apartments, 114, 116
Ibis Styles, 164
Ibis Styles Kingsgate Hotel, 117
The Islington, 297
Jasper Hotel, 116
The Johnson, 116
Kirketon Hotel Sydney, 68
Lady Elliot Island Eco Resort, 234–235
The Langham, 62
The Larwill Studio, 9, 116
The Lodge on Elizabeth, 298
Longitude 131°, 9, 284–285
The Lord Nelson Brewery Hotel, 63
The Lost Camel Hotel, 285
Macquarie Manor, 298
Mandalay, 245
Manly Backpackers Beachside, 69
Manly Paradise Beachfront Motel and Apartments, 70
Mantra Boathouse Apartments, 223
Mantra on the Esplanade, 244
Marae, 9, 207
Mercure Alice Springs Resort, 269

Mercure Gladstone, 229
Mercure Kakadu Crocodile Hotel, 258
Mercure Townsville, 214
The MONA Pavilions, 9, 297
More Than a Room Darwin Accommodation, 245
NEXT Hotel Brisbane, 163
Noah's Bondi, 69
Novotel Brisbane, 163–164
Novotel Cairns Oasis Resort, 189
Novotel Melbourne St Kilda, 118
The Nunnery, 117
The Olsen, 9, 116
One Thornbury, 164–165
Outback Pioneer Hotel and Lodge, 285–286
Peppers Seaport Hotel, 313
Peppers Silo, 313
Pier One Sydney Harbour, 62
Port Douglas Accommodation Holiday Rentals, 206
Port Douglas Retreat, 208
Pullman Reef Hotel Casino, 188
QT Resort, 207
qualia, 9, 224
Quality Hotel Colonial Launceston, 314
Quamby Estate, 313–314
Quest Grand Hotel Melbourne, 114
Railway Square YHA, 66
The Reef House, 8
The Reef House Palm Cove – MGallery by Sofitel, 188
The Reef Retreat, 189
Reef View Hotel, 224
The Russell, 9, 64
Rydges Esplanade Cairns Resort, 190
Rydges Gladstone, 229
Rydges South Bank Brisbane, 164
Sails in the Desert, 286
Salamanca Inn, 299
The Schaller, 116
By the Sea, 206
Seagulls Seafront Resort, 214–215
Sir Stamford at Circular Quay, 8, 62–63
Skycity Darwin, 244
Sofitel Sydney Darling Harbour, 8, 67
Spirit of Freedom, 189
Stamford Plaza Sydney Airport, 70
Surfside Backpackers, 69
Sydney Central YHA, 66
Sydney Harbour YHA–The Rocks, 64
The Tank Stream Hotel, 66
Thala Beach Nature Reserve, 207
Tolarno Hotel, 118
Travelodge Hotel Sydney, 66
Travelodge Resort Darwin, 245
Value Inn, 245–246
Vibe Hotel Darwin Waterfront, 245
Vibe Hotel Rushcutters Bay Sydney, 68

Villa La Vue, 245
Waratah on York, 314–315
The Watson, 116
Westin Sydney, 65
Woolbrokers Hotel, 67
Wrest Point, 299
York Mansions, 314
Zen Beach Retreat, 232
Zero Davey, 298

Restaurants

AquaLuna, 194
Aria, 71
Arnguli Grill, 284
Ayers Wok Noodle Bar, 284
Babka Bakery, 124
Babu Ji, 125–126
Bacchus Restaurant, 164
Bamboo House, 120
The Bar, 164
Bar Astor, 164
Barbarella, 121
Barra Bistro and Bar, 258
Barra on Todd, 270
Becco, 119–120
Bennelong, 7, 39, 74
Bills, 77
Bough House Restaurant, 286
Breakfast Creek Hotel, 166–167
Brunetti, 123–124
Brunetti City Square, 123–124
C Bar, 215
Café 1928, 233
Café Hernandez, 77
Café Segovia, 121
Caffiend, 192–193
Candy, 193
Chocolate Buddha, 120–121
Cicciolina, 124–125
City Extra, 75
Conservation Hut Cafe, 104
Curve, 68
Darwin Sailing Club, 248
Darwin Ski Club, 248
Donovans, 7, 125
Drunken Admiral Restaurant, 300
Eat Street Northshore, 165
e'cco bistro, 7, 165–166
Eclectic Tastes, 153
Elephant Bean, 104
Flower Drum, 7, 121
The Four in Hand, 74
Frogs Restaurant, 204
Gecko's Café, 283
Gorge Restaurant, 316
Govinda's, 77, 167
Grossi Florentino, 120
Hanuman, 7, 247, 270
Harts Pub, 74
Harveys, 167
Hemingway's, 225
Hopetoun Tea Rooms Winter Garden, 123
Icebergs Dining Room & Bar, 7, 77–78
Ichi Ni, 126
Il Bacaro, 121

Il Piatto, 246
Il Solito Posto, 122
Ilkari, 286
I'm Angus Steakhouse, 75
Inside Cafe, 315
Jam Corner, 215
Jimmy's on the Mall, 167
Journal Café, 121
Kettle & Tin, 168
Koko, 120
Kulata Academy Cafe, 283
Kuta Café, 166
The Lake House, 150
Lentil as Anything, 125
Love.fish Barangaroo, 39, 75
L'Unico, 191–192
Machine Laundry Cafe, 301
Malmsbury Bakery, 148
Mangrove Jacks Café/Bar, 225
Marios, 124
MCA Café, 82
Me Wah Restaurant, 315
Mindil Beach Sunset Market, 246
Moda, 166

MoVida, 7, 122
MoVida Aqui, 7, 122
MoVida Next Door, 7, 122
Mr Tulk, 121
Mudbar, 315
Nick's Bar & Grill, 75
Nick's Seafood Restaurant, 75
NuNu, 191
Ochre Restaurant, 192
Oscar's, 153
Otto Ristorante, 76
Outback Pioneer Bar, 286
Overlanders Steakhouse, 270
Parap Markets, 246
Peacock & Jones, 300–301
Pee Wee's at The Point, 246–247
Pellegrini's Espresso Bar, 121
Peppermint Bay, 301
Perrotta's at the Gallery, 193
Pizza Verde Woodfire Kitchen, 148
Point Revolving Restaurant, 300
Pompei's, 78
The Portsea Hotel, 146

Red Ochre Grill, 270–271
The Restaurant, 164
The Roma Bar, 247–248
Salsa Bar & Grill, 8, 208–209
Sassi Cucina e Bar, 208
Shakahari, 124
Shakahari Too, 124
Shenannigan's, 247
Sounds of Silence, 42, 285
The Source, 299–300
Stillwater, 316
Summit, 166
Supper Inn, 123
Sydney Cove Oyster Bar, 39, 74
Tali Wiru, 42, 285
Tamarind, 188
The Taphouse, 74
Tetsuya's, 8, 74–75
Tim's Surf 'n' Turf, 247
Vivo Bar and Grill, 192
Whitsunday Sailing Club, 225
Young & Jackson, 123
Zaaffran, 76
Zinc, 209

Map List

Australia   2
Australia in 1 or 2 Weeks   36
Central Sydney Hotels   60
Central Sydney Restaurants   72
Central Sydney Attractions   80
Melbourne Hotels & Restaurants   115
St Kilda Hotels & Restaurants   119
Melbourne Attractions   127
Brisbane Hotels, Restaurants &
Attractions   156

The Great Barrier Reef   181
Cairns   185
The Northern Territory   239
Darwin   241
Alice Springs   265
Tasmania   293
Hobart   295

Photo Credits

p. i: © Mo Wu; p. ii: © ian woolcock; p. iii: © Ingus Kruklitis; p. iv: © ChameleonsEye / Shutterstock.com; p. v, top: © GagliardiImages / Shutterstock.com; p. v, bottom left: © Courtesy of Let's Go Surfing; p. v, bottom right: © alfotokunst / Shutterstock.com; p. vi, top left: © Courtesy of OTTO/ Nikki To; p. vi, top right: © CO Leong / Shutterstock.com; p. vi, bottom: © m. letschert / Shutterstock.com; p. vii, top: © Sean Heatley / Shutterstock.com; p. vii, bottom left: © Neale Cousland / Shutterstock.com; p. vii, bottom right: © patjo / Shutterstock.com; p. viii, top: © matiascausa; p. viii, middle: © Neale Cousland / Shutterstock.com; p. viii, bottom: © Benny Marty; p. ix, top: © Martin Valigursky / Shutterstock.com; p. ix, bottom: © Martin Valigursky / Shutterstock.com; p. x, top left: © Courtesy of Summit Restaurant & Kuta Cafe Pty Ltd; p. x, top right: © Martin Valigursky / Shutterstock.com; p. x, bottom: © Courtesy of Tjapukai; p. xi, top: © Courtesy of Lady Elliot Island Eco Resort; p. xi, bottom: © Martin Valigursky; p. xii, top: © Alberto Loyo; p. xii, middle: © Olga Kashubin / Shutterstock.com; p. xii, bottom: © EpochCatcher; p. xiii, top: © Axel Sandesh / Shutterstock.com; p. xiii, bottom: © pierdest; p. xiv, top: © Robyn Mackenzie / Shutterstock.com; p. xiv, bottom: © ingehogenbijl / Shutterstock.com; p. xv, top: © Prazis / Shutterstock.com; p. xv, bottom: © ingehogenbijl / Shutterstock.com; p. xvi, top: © Cyrus_2000 / Shutterstock.com; p. xvi, middle: © Olga Kashubin / Shutterstock.com; p. xvi, bottom: © Jason Ho / Shutterstock.com; p. 4: © Debra James / Shutterstock.com; p. 5: © Courtesy of Skyrail Rainforest Cableway; p. 6: © dinozzaver / Shutterstock.com; p. 7: © surfing; p. 8: © Courtesy of Donovans; p. 9: © Courtesy of Longitude 131; p. 10: © Michael Zimmer; p. 11: © Meghan Lamb; p. 15: © EcoPrint / Shutterstock.com; p. 18: © Taras Vyshnya / Shutterstock.com; p. 21: © fritz16 / Shutterstock.com; p. 23: © Janelle Lugge; p. 26: © Tourism Australia/Maxime Coquard; p. 32: © Taras Vyshnya; p. 33: © PomInOz / Shutterstock.com; p. 35: © CoolR / Shutterstock.com; p. 38: © Courtesy of Featherdale Wildlife Park; p. 39: © Tjapukai; p. 41: © Maurizio De Mattei / Shutterstock.com; p. 42: © Marc Witte; p. 44: © Johnny Jet; p. 45: © Alan Samuel; p. 46, top: © Vividrange | Dreamstime.com; p. 46, bottom: © Michael Coghlan; p. 50: © Meghan Lamb; p. 51: © Dan Breckwoldt / Shutterstock.com; p. 53: © Dan Breckwoldt | Dreamstime.com; p. 55: © byvalet / Shutterstock.com; p. 56: © PomInOz / Shutterstock.com; p. 63: © tourpics_net; p. 76: © Courtesy of OTTO/ Nikki To; p. 78: © Anthony Ngo | Dreamstime.com; p. 82: © Courtesy of Museum of Contemporary Art, Sydney; p. 83: © Tourism Australia/ Hugh Stewart; p. 95: © CoolR / Shutterstock.com; p. 98: © David May | Dreamstime.com; p. 103: © PomInOz; p. 109: © Tourism Australia; p. 122: © Courtesy of MoVida Bar de Tapas; p. 128: © Courtesy of Eureka Skydeck; p. 131: © Hanafi Latif / Shutterstock.com; p. 132: © MagSpace / Shutterstock.com; p. 133: © Courtesy of Polly Woodside; p. 135: © TK Kurikawa / Shutterstock.com; p. 136: © Courtesy of Puffing Billy Railway; p. 138: © Sunflowerey / Shutterstock.com; p. 144: © www.penguins.org.au; p. 153: © FiledIMAGE / Shutterstock.com; p. 159: © Gordon Bell / Shutterstock.com; p. 161: © ChameleonsEye / Shutterstock. com; p. 171: © Queensland Museum; p. 172: © Martin Valigursky / Shutterstock.com; p. 174: © David Bostock / Shutterstock.com; p. 175: © Courtesy of Brisbane Whale Watching; p. 183: © Tanya Puntti | Dreamstime.com; p. 191: © Courtesy of NuNu, Cairns; p. 194: © Courtesy of Cairns ZOOM & Wildlife Dome; p. 198: © Courtesy of Great Adventure Tours; p. 200: © Courtesy of Delaware North Companies; p. 202: © ChameleonsEye / Shutterstock.com; p. 209: © Courtesy of Adventure North Australia Pty Ltd and the Bama Way Aboriginal Journeys; p. 224: © Tomas Sykora; p. 233: © Amacphoto7 / Shutterstock. com; p. 237: © ronnybas; p. 249: © Daniela Constantinescu / Shutterstock.com; p. 253: © fritz16 / Shutterstock.com; p. 254: © John Carnemolla; p. 261: © GTS Productions; p. 268: © Lauren Cameo / Shutterstock.com; p. 273: © Image courtesy of Araluen Cultural Precinct; p. 274: © Courtesy of Outback Ballooning; p. 279: © mark higgins / Shutterstock.com; p. 281: © Wesley Walker / Shutterstock.com; p. 287: © Marc Witte | Dreamstime.com; p. 289: © wargunner / Shutterstock.com; p. 296: © gnoparus / Shutterstock.com; p. 303: © Courtesy of The Maritime Museum of Tasmania; p. 305: © TK Kurikawa / Shutterstock.com; p. 306: © Kummeleon / Shutterstock.com; p. 308: © Benny Marty / Shutterstock.com; p. 311: © FiledIMAGE; p. 317: © Ikonya.

Frommer's Australia 2019, 19th Edition

Published by
FROMMER MEDIA LLC

ISBN 978-1-62887-412-9 (paper), 978-1-62887-413-6 (e-book)

Editorial Director: Pauline Frommer
Editor: Holly Hughes
Production Editor: Cheryl Lenser
Cartographer: Roberta Stockwell
Photo Editor: Meghan Lamb
Indexer: Cheryl Lenser
Cover Design: David Riedy

For information on our other products or services, see www.frommers.com.

FrommerMedia LLC also publishes its books in a variety of electronic formats. Some content that appears in print may not be available in electronic formats.

Manufactured in the United States of America

5 4 3 2 1

ABOUT THE AUTHOR

Lee Mylne is an award-winning travel journalist, based in Brisbane, Australia. She has specialized in travel writing for more than two decades and has traveled to every corner of Australia, still enthralled by what she sees. She has written several Frommer's guidebooks, and her work appears regularly in a wide range of Australian consumer and trade publications. She is a Life Member and former president of the Australian Society of Travel Writers.

ABOUT THE FROMMER TRAVEL GUIDES

For most of the past 50 years, Frommer's has been the leading series of travel guides in North America, accounting for as many as 24% of all guidebooks sold. I think I know why.

Though we hope our books are entertaining, we nevertheless deal with travel in a serious fashion. Our guidebooks have never looked on such journeys as a mere recreation, but as a far more important human function, a time of learning and introspection, an essential part of a civilized life. We stress the culture, lifestyle, history, and beliefs of the destinations we cover, and urge our readers to seek out people and new ideas as the chief rewards of travel.

We have never shied from controversy. We have, from the beginning, encouraged our authors to be intensely judgmental, critical—both pro and con—in their comments, and wholly independent. Our only clients are our readers, and we have triggered the ire of countless prominent sorts, from a tourist newspaper we called "practically worthless" (it unsuccessfully sued us) to the many rip-offs we've condemned.

And because we believe that travel should be available to everyone regardless of their incomes, we have always been cost-conscious at every level of expenditure. Though we have broadened our recommendations beyond the budget category, we insist that every lodging we include be sensibly priced. We use every form of media to assist our readers, and are particularly proud of our feisty daily website, the award-winning Frommers.com.

I have high hopes for the future of Frommer's. May these guidebooks, in all the years ahead, continue to reflect the joy of travel and the freedom that travel represents. May they always pursue a cost-conscious path, so that people of all incomes can enjoy the rewards of travel. And may they create, for both the traveler and the persons among whom we travel, a community of friends, where all human beings live in harmony and peace.

Arthur Frommer